The American Way

of

EMPIRE

OTHER BOOKS BY JAMES KURTH

Mediterranean Paradoxes: Politics and Social Structure of Southern Europe (with James Petras)

Family and Civilization by Carle C. Zimmerman (Editor)

PRAISE FOR JAMES KURTH'S
THE AMERICAN WAY OF EMPIRE:

"When it comes to deciphering the mysteries and contradictions of American statecraft, no one holds a candle to James Kurth. Let me emphasize that: No one. For nigh on a half-century, he has been a source of insight and wisdom on all matters related to U.S. foreign policy. The appearance of *The American Way of Empire* is, therefore, cause for gratitude and great rejoicing."

–Andrew J. Bacevich, author of *The Age of Illusions:
How America Squandered Its Cold War Victory*

"James Kurth is one of the world's leading scholars of international relations and political economy. With the entire global order rapidly transforming, these concise and splendidly written essays merit everyone's attention."

–Thomas Ferguson, Contributing Editor, *The Nation*

"James Kurth has one of the most incisive and deeply-informed minds in the field of international relations. His new book is a cogent guide to a world undergoing fundamental change."

–Bruce Cumings, University of Chicago

"A comprehensive, masterful analysis of the character of American foreign policy from its 18th century beginnings; to its present superpower status; and, most crucially, to the uncertainty of our mid-21st century future. Professor James Kurth, one of the West's foremost scholars of America's role in the world, has written a tour de force that will exert a powerful influence on those who think seriously about America's future."

–John Fonte, Hudson Institute

"We should be grateful for having a voice like Kurth's that cuts through the ideological reveries of today's elites and forces us to examine the stark and dark possibilities of living in a fallen world."

–Corey Abel, *Academic Questions*

"Kurth may be right or wrong on this or that point, but the message you should take is that the way Americans see the world — Americans of the right, left, and middle — is itself a construction rooted in history, religion, and culture."

–Rod Dreher, *The American Conservative*

General Douglas MacArthur accepting the Japanese Instrument of Surrender aboard the USS Missouri on September 2nd, 1945

The American Way of EMPIRE

How America Won a World —
But Lost Her Way

James Kurth

Washington Books
Washington, DC

Washington Books

Washington, DC

https://washington-books.com

Cover image and frontispiece: MacArthur Memorial, Norfolk, Virginia

Author photo: Swarthmore College, Swarthmore, Pennsylvania

Cover designer: Shelley Savoy

DEDICATION

In memory of Samuel P. Huntington (1927-2008)—the finest political scientist of his generation, a patriot with a deep faith in America, and my mentor and teacher for all of my adult life.

CONTENTS

Part III: Insurgency

Part IV: Political Economy

There is the moral of all human tales;
'Tis but the same rehearsal of the past.
First Freedom and then Glory—when that fails,
Wealth, vice, corruption—barbarism at last.
And History, with all her volumes vast,
Hath but one page.

—Byron, *Childe Harold's Pilgrimage*

PREFACE

THERE IS A GROWING sense, both in America and around the world, that we are now nearing a major inflection point in world history, one comparable in its significance to that at the end of the Cold War in 1989-1991, or even to that at the end of the Second World War in 1945. One era, an era often called the American Century, is coming to an end. Another era, yet unnamed and certainly unknown, is about to begin. But whatever this new era's name and nature will eventually be, it will be the era that will be the mid-21st century.

The American Century was dated roughly from 1945 to 2020. It was defined by America being the leading superpower during the Cold War and the sole superpower during the thirty years thereafter, and it is this kind of superpower which is coming to an end. The next era will most likely be defined by conflicts between this much-diminished superpower and new and renewed great powers—in particular, China and Russia—with China even aspiring to be the next superpower. In other words, the next era will be some kind of multipolar one, and there will be conflicts between these poles, or great powers, that will be greater than anything since the Cold War.

However, a central question about this impending era remains. Will these conflicts be some new kind of peaceful but stressful competition, like the brief periods of Soviet-American détente during the Cold War; some new kind of arms races, dangerous crises, and local hot wars, like most of the Cold War; some new kind of terrible and total destruction, like the Second World War; or some new catastrophe now utterly beyond our experience?

This question is still open, awaiting the answers that will be offered by the leaders of the conflicting powers. But the most consequential answer will come from the leaders of the diminished superpower, the United States. That is, it will be how American leaders manage the transition from the old era, when their predecessors were also leaders of the world, to the new era, where American leaders will merely be the leaders of one great power, albeit the leading one, in a multipolar system. In other words, it will be the heirs of the old era who will preside—for good or ill, for reinvention or destruction—over the birth of the new.

The answers that American leaders give to the central question of our time—of what kind of peace and what kind of war—will not come out of a void, however. They will themselves be shaped and limited by certain continuing features of American foreign policy which fully matured during the American Century but which date back in many aspects to the founding of the United States, or even before. The circumstances in which America has deployed its foreign policy have greatly changed from era to era, but much of the character of American foreign policy has remained the same, at least as variations on a theme. It is this American character that will be tested by the challenges of the next era, and—more immediately and more dangerously—by the challenges of the transition to it.

This book is an exploration into that character of American foreign policy as it was formed into distinctive ideological and strategic traditions, and especially as it was expressed and exercised during the American Century. The different chapters present different aspects of American foreign policy, and more specifically of the rise, apex, decline, and perhaps impending fall of the American empire. This empire began at the end of the 19th century in 1898, with the Spanish-American War and the great leap outward of the United States into the Caribbean and Central America and also into the Pacific and the Philippines. But the American empire was only established on a world scale in 1945, with America's great victory in the Second World War, and it was then that the American Century really began. The empire reached its apex in 1989-1991, with America's great victory in the Cold War and the collapse of the Soviet Union. Its decline noticeably began in 2003, with the U.S. invasion of Iraq and the ensuing Iraq War, and then with the

U.S.-originated global economic crisis that began in 2008. And now, at the end of the 2010s, many seasoned analysts of world affairs are anticipating the empire's fall.

In recent years, there have been many useful books published on aspects of the American empire or the American Century, and most of these are included in the Bibliography which can be found at the back of this book. As that empire and that century near their ends, the number of books on these topics have multiplied, illustrating once again the truth of Hegel's famous observation that "the Owl of Minerva begins its flight at dusk." I will mention several of these which I think are especially illuminating, and I will also mention the ways in which my own book is different and distinct from them.

In many ways, the pathbreaker and premier analyst for these topics has been Andrew Bacevich, beginning with his <u>American Empire: The Realities and Consequences of U.S. Diplomacy</u> (2002) and continuing with his recent <u>Twilight of the American Century</u> (2018). Bacevich's works are essential for understanding the workings of U.S. bureaucratic and ideological elites in operating the American empire and for also understanding their destructive consequences, both abroad—particularly in the Middle East—and at home. My own approach follows him in this, but I place a greater emphasis on the principal importance of particular economic interests and globalist economic elites in the making of U.S. foreign policy. I also place a greater emphasis on America's competition with other great powers, i.e., China and Russia, and on the concept of regional spheres of influence as a basis for some kind of international order.

An essential recent book is Alfred McCoy's <u>In the Shadows of the American Century: The Rise and Decline of US Global Power</u>. Like Bacevich, McCoy focuses on the workings of U. S. bureaucracies—particularly the military and intelligence ones—in operating—and enforcing—the American empire, and he does so with invaluable comprehensiveness and detail. Moreover, he provides a similarly comprehensive, detailed, and systematic analysis of the rapidly growing threat from China. Again, my own approach places a greater emphasis on the principal importance of particular economic interests and globalist economic elites. I also have a more favorable view of the consequences of U.S. foreign policy during the Cold War, particularly within Western Europe and Northeast Asia.

One recent book that does discuss the importance of particular economic interests is A. G. Hopkins' American Empire: A Global History (2018). Hopkins presents a history of globalization by showing the similarities between the globalizing projects of the different Western colonial empires, particularly the British and American ones, and how these imperial projects culminated after the Second World War in American-led globalization. However, his definition of empire is largely limited to territorial ones. Thus, he discusses the territorial empire which the United States acquired after the Spanish-American War but not the distinctive American way of empire, which is exercised through what I call a hegemonic system, rather than through a colonial system, and which uses such methods as informal and indirect rule, spheres of influence, alliances, and international organizations.

Most of the chapters in this book were initially published as articles during the 1990s-2010s, i.e., during the period of the apex and then the decline of the American empire. They have all been revised and updated, however, to address the realities of the current time, on the eve of the 2020s, and perhaps on the eve of the empire's collapse.

The chapters are grouped into five sections, beginning with an Overview, "Hegemony," which discusses the history of the American empire from 1945 to the present. This is followed by four Parts, which focus upon different dimensions of the distinctive American way of empire. Part I, "Ideology," includes four chapters which discuss the ideological character of American foreign policy, or what has long been called its "idealist" tradition. This ideology has often been defined as liberalism, which indeed it is, but Chapter 2 argues that its origins actually lie in American Protestantism. As for the implementation of this liberal ideology in recent American foreign policy, a central issue has been U.S. democratization projects in foreign countries.

Part II, "Strategy," includes five chapters which discuss the strategic dynamics of American foreign policy, or what has long been called its "realist" tradition. A major tension in composing America's strategy in foreign policy has always been in the defining of "the national interest" of the United States. In particular, is this interest best defined as merely national in scope, or global in scope, or somewhere in between, such as regional in scope? As for the implementation of strategic conceptions in recent American foreign policy, a central issue has been what should be America's view of regional "spheres of influence" versus global "rules and norms."

Part III, "Insurgency," includes three chapters which discuss the major challenges to U.S. foreign policy and the American imperial project in the 2000s, i.e., Islamist terrorism and the Iraq War, along with a chapter on the related issue of Muslim immigration. In this regard, a central issue has been the conflict between American aspirations for a global economy and universal values, on the one hand, and Islamist resistance and local realities, on the other.

Part IV, "Political Economy," includes three chapters which discuss the interaction of economics and politics—political economy—in American foreign policy. Here a central issue has been the conflict between the drive by international banks and multinational corporations for a global economy, whose virtues are seen by them to be a self-evident truth, versus the resistance by nationally-focused businesses and populations who are desperately trying to maintain some semblance of a viable national economy.

Part IV, and the book, concludes with a vision of how the 21st century might be, or perhaps might have been, a Second American Century of peace and prosperity, rather than what now seems much more likely—the end of the American empire and the beginning of a new era of great-power conflicts abroad and of great socio-economic conflicts at home.

The grand project of the American empire was to redefine, or even reinvent, the traditional American national interest, which preserved American values, into a new American-led global order, which promoted universal values. During the first fifty years of the American Century, the era of the Cold War, it seemed to the U.S. foreign policy establishment that, with containment and deterrence and with commitment and determination, this project could indeed be achieved. And at the end of the 1980s, it seemed that it had indeed been achieved and that its final and complete realization was merely a matter of time. During the 1990s and early 2000s, during the "unipolar moment," this project became more and more explicitly seen as an impending American empire on a global scale. But the gap between global ideology and imperial visions, on the one hand, and great-power resistance and local realities, on the other, was soon revealed. The return of Russian and Chinese assertiveness, and the "forever" wars of America in the Islamic world, have now demonstrated once again, as has been demonstrated for centuries, that power and realities almost always confound ideology and visions.

The American world-wide empire and the American Century began in 1945, but there was a precise place and time of their birth. That place was on the deck of the battleship *U.S.S. Missouri*, which was then anchored in Tokyo Bay. And that time was the morning of September 2, 1945, when General Douglas MacArthur, at the head of the representatives of the Allied Forces, received the surrender of the representatives of the Empire of Japan. And so, this book begins, on its front cover and frontispiece, with a depiction of the moment when the American empire and the American Century were born.

OVERVIEW

HEGEMONY

CHAPTER ONE

THE AMERICAN WAY OF EMPIRE:
THE SEVENTY-YEAR LIFE OF
THE U.S. ALLIANCE SYSTEM

THE AMERICAN ALLIANCE SYSTEM, the greatest alliance system that the world has ever known, was first constructed in the aftermath in the Second World War and at the beginning of the Cold War. Often calling itself "the Free World," it engaged in an arduous and epic struggle for more than forty years with its great, but smaller, adversary, the alliance system of the Soviet Union. Then, in a remarkably brief period, from 1989 to 1991, the American alliance system achieved total victory over its Soviet counterpart. Its leader, the United States, declaring a "New World Order," then proceeded to try to remake the entire world, and no longer just the "Free World," in its own image, to establish a truly global system, which was to be defined by such distinguishing features as global economy, open society, liberal democracy, human rights, and universal rules and norms.

Now, thirty years after that extraordinary victory of the United States and its allies, the prospects for the future are utterly different. The 1990's were a heady decade of the United States as "the sole super-power," of "standing tall and seeing far," of "the unipolar moment," and even of an "American empire." But with the beginning of the new millennium (nicely symbolized by 9/11), there began a long and trying period of descent and disintegration from these giddy heights. Today, the vast American alliance system is fracturing in all of its directions—i.e., in Europe, in East Asia, in the Middle East, and even in Latin America. It is similarly fracturing in all of its dimensions—i.e., in the military, the economic, and the political and ideological.

Moreover, the fracturing within the macrocosm of the American alliance system is paralleled by the fracturing within the microcosms of many of its component members, particularly within the United States itself and within the major states of Europe. The internal relations within these countries are now marked by economic disparities, political dis-functioning, and ideological and cultural conflicts that are, in many ways, greater than anything in a half-century or more.

How did this extraordinary trajectory of the American alliance system—from slow ascent in the 1940s-1980s, to extraordinary zenith in the 1990s, to rapid decline in the 2000s, and to impending breakdown in the next few years—take place? This is the story that we will tell in this chapter.

I. The American Way of Empire:
The Founding of Three Hegemonic Systems

There have been great empires for at least four millennia, and they have obviously existed in a great variety of forms. But all of them have been ruled by an "imperial" power, i.e., a strong central authority or "core," which governs an ensemble of weaker entities, or "periphery." Empires have varied, however, according to the degree of autonomy which the imperial power allows to these entities. Because of their long observation of the various European empires from the 17th century to the mid-20th century, Americans usually think that a true empire has to be a "colonial" one, i.e., one in which the subordinate entities are governed by "direct rule" and have almost no autonomy at all. But this is a great oversimplification. Even the European empires were characterized by a combination of direct rule over some territories and peoples and "indirect rule" over others, who often were left with great autonomy in domestic affairs and might even be formally-independent monarchies. For example, the famous British empire in India was composed of both British India proper, which was governed by direct or colonial rule, and the Indian Princely States, which were governed by indirect rule, had a great deal of domestic autonomy, and were formally and symbolically ruled by their own monarchs or "princes."

In cases where the degree of real autonomy has been very great, and the degree of formal independence or sovereignty has also been very great, terms like "colony" or "colonial system" are stretched so far that they become misleading. Rather, the imperial power is often referred to as an "hegemonic" power, and its ensemble of weaker powers as a "sphere of influence" or "hegemonic system." To somewhat oversimplify, in a colonial system, the subordinate entities are both formally dependent and really dependent. In a hegemonic system, the subordinate entities are formally independent but really dependent, in any number of important ways. And the United States has almost always chosen to rule over foreign peoples in the hegemonic, rather than in the colonial, way. Hegemonic systems have been the American way of empire.

The Latin-American Prototype

The United States had long maintained a hegemonic system or traditional sphere of influence in most of Latin America, and particularly in Central America and the Caribbean. The security or military basis of this system had, of course, been defined by the Monroe Doctrine and the subsequent Roosevelt Corollary. The economic basis was the classical complementarity between an industrial exporting "core" and an agricultural-product- and raw-material-exporting "periphery." This economic basis for the U.S. hegemonic system in Latin America was similar to the "imperialism of free trade" of the British Empire and the "colonial pact" of the French Empire.

The political and ideological basis of this system was largely rhetorical. The Latin American states were formally liberal-democratic republics like the United States, but in reality, they were usually military dictatorships or, at best, oligarchic regimes. Indeed, they were usually not even real states, and certainly not nation-states, but merely weak government frameworks, which performed few of the functions of a normal European state. For the most part, this system of Potemkin republics suited the elites of both the United States and Latin America perfectly well.

With the end of the Second World War in 1945 and the beginning of the Cold War in 1947, the United States decided to fully regularize and institutionalize its hegemonic system in Latin America. It began with a formal treaty of mutual security, the Rio Pact, in 1947, followed by a formal international institution, the Organization of American States, in 1948. The military, economic, and political bases of the system largely continued on as before. Although during the run-up to and during the Second World War, the United States had, for prudential strategic reasons, briefly tolerated national-populist regimes in such countries as Mexico, Brazil, Uruguay, Bolivia, and Guatemala, it moved decisively against these soon after the war ended, and the national-populist regimes were replaced by the familiar military dictatorships and oligarchic regimes.

This U.S. hegemonic system in Latin America largely continued right down to the 2000s. It was briefly disrupted in the 1960s by the Castro revolution in Cuba, but this threat was soon contained and confined to an isolated Cuba itself. More recently, however, it has been disrupted by the Chavez revolution in Venezuela, accompanied by an ensemble of national-populist regimes in Nicaragua, Bolivia, and Ecuador. Today, the U.S. position in Latin America is itself looking rather like a Potemkin hegemonic system.

The Western European Archetype

The post-1945 U.S. hegemonic system in Latin America grew organically out of a prior, longstanding traditional U.S. hegemonic system or traditional sphere of influence in the region. In contrast, the post-1945 U.S. hegemonic system in Western Europe had no historical precedent whatever. It was created over a very short period, roughly from 1947 to 1951; it represented an extraordinary act of creative imagination; it was immediately multidimensional—military, economic, and political—in its functions; and, once established, it operated effectively for almost seventy years, almost down to the present day. Moreover, along the way, it was crucial in bringing about the extraordinary U.S. victory over the Soviet Union in the Cold War. It is no wonder that U.S. Secretary of State Dean Acheson, one of the chief architects of the system, would famously, and rightly, claim in his splendid memoir that he was "present at the creation." And it is no wonder that many political analysts have concluded that this hegemonic system produced the most successful military alliance in history, formally known as the North Atlantic Treaty Organization (NATO).

The economic basis of the emerging U.S. hegemonic system in Western Europe was the Marshall Plan, which was announced in 1947, and more broadly the U.S.-subsidized export of both industrial and agricultural goods to the war-devastated and impoverished economies of Europe. This was no simple "imperialism of free trade" or "colonial pact" of the traditional sort. Rather, it was a case of an advanced industrial economy, the United States, exporting industrial products to other advanced industrial economies, those of Western Europe. After the First World War, the United States and Western Europe were industrial competitors, and high protectionist tariff barriers against each other were the natural result. During the Second World War, the U.S. Eighth Air Force and the British Bomber Command had bombed much of European industry out of production and into ruins. Thus, for a brief period from 1945 to about 1958, Western Europe provided a great market for American industry, particularly for capital goods. This meant that the Midwestern industry of the United States could, for the first time, join Northeastern finance in supporting international free trade in general, and European economic recovery in particular.

The economic dimension of the emerging U.S. hegemonic system was soon joined by the military or security dimension with the formation of the NATO in 1949, which was soon deepened and further institutionalized with the formation of an integrated military command structure in 1951, headed by a U.S. general. In important ways, NATO took the prototype of the OAS and the Rio Pact in Latin America and expanded and perfected it to fit the needs of a much more challenging region. And, at the very core of the U.S. military alliance with the Western European states was the U.S. nuclear deterrent against the very proximate Soviet conventional military threat.

The political dimension of this emerging U.S. hegemonic system in Western Europe was also quickly established. The preferred political formula was liberal democracy as in the United States. But in Western Europe, liberal democracy had to be real, and not just formal, as was the case in most of Latin America. Moreover, most of the European countries had strong socialist parties, and several (particularly France, Italy, and Belgium) had strong communist parties as well. These parties of the Left were grounded in a well-organized, unionized, industrial working class. The American economic and political elites of the day responded to this challenging Leftist environment with unusual creative imagination. For prudential reasons, they allowed their preferred formula of liberal democracy to be broadened to include social democracy, thereby including socialist parties while totally excluding communist parties from participating in Western European governments by 1948. Naturally, the American elites hoped that this compromise would be merely temporary, and that over time social democracy would steadily become less social and more liberal. And, by the mid-1950s, this largely proved to be the case.

The East Asian Hub-and-Spokes System

The United States faced a remarkably paradoxical situation in East Asia in the aftermath of the Second World War. On the one hand, its total victory over Japan in 1945 and the total weakness of the residual European colonial powers meant that the United States could dominate the region with unprecedented military and economic power. On the other hand, the total victory of the Communists over the Nationalists on the Chinese mainland in 1949 meant that this unprecedented power would be immediately confronted and contained by an adversarial regime that made China more unified and stronger than any time in the previous one hundred years. In short, the United States had undisputed hegemony in the maritime realm of East Asia, and Communist China had undisputed hegemony on the mainland of the region. This geopolitical reality defined the character of the emerging U.S. hegemonic system in East Asia, making it very different than that in Latin America and in Western Europe.

In East Asia (or perhaps more accurately, in the Western Pacific), the United States established a system of bilateral security treaties and economic agreements rather than the multilateral ones that it employed in Latin America and Western Europe. Thus, the U.S. system in East Asia has often been described as a hub-and-spokes system. Its long-standing component members have been Japan, South Korea, the Republic of China on Taiwan, and the Philippines.

The military basis of this U.S. hegemonic system was a series of security treaties made over a period from 1946 (with the Philippines, the former U.S. colony) to 1951 (Japan) to 1953 (South Korea and Taiwan). Because of the extreme poverty of these countries at the time, the military role of the United States in these treaties and the military aid that the U.S. provided were much greater, and even more one-sided, than in Latin America and in Western Europe. In essence, these countries became military colonies of the United States.

The economic basis of this hegemonic system was even more unusual. The obvious export market for Japan, South Korea, and Taiwan would have been China, but this would mean that these countries would soon become dependent upon the America's communist adversary in Asia. Thus, the American economic and political elites, as they had in regard to Western Europe, again came up with an act of remarkable creative imagination. This time, it was to have the vast American market serve as the substitute for the vast Chinese market. The exports of these new East Asian allies, or really dependencies, of the United States were thus given virtually unrestricted access to its market.

This arrangement worked very well, and without much impact on American industry, for about twenty years. By the early 1970s, however, Japanese exports—particularly in the shipbuilding, steel, automobile, and consumer-electronics sectors—were posing a large threat to American producers. Then, by the late 1980s, South Korean and Taiwanese exports were doing the same. The result was that by the end of the Cold War, a large part of American industry had already been hollowed out by East Asian competition. The U.S. hegemonic system in East Asia had succeeded so well in its goal of keeping its component members secure from the communist powers and prosperous in their economic condition that now it was these same U.S. allies that were the greatest practical threat to many American workers.

II. The First General Crisis of the American Empire, 1961-1980

The three new U.S. hegemonic systems functioned more or less as their architects had designed them to do during their first decade or so. By the early 1960s, however, each was facing new challenges. And by the early 1970s, there was a widespread sense among American economic and political elites that they faced a general crisis of the overall U.S. hegemonic order or empire.

First, and most concretely, an opposition nation appeared in each of the three regions. Although the form and degree of these oppositions varied greatly, each opposition nation produced in the American economic and political elites an immense amount of anger and stress, and an intense production of policy responses.

In Latin America, the opposition to U.S. hegemony arose from the Castro Revolution in Cuba in 1958-1960. This, and Cuba's alliance with the Soviet Union, totally shaped U.S. policy toward the region for the entire decade of the 1960s. And, of course, the ensuing Cuban Missile Crisis of October 1962 put much of the world at risk of nuclear annihilation. By the end of the 1960s, however, the various U.S. policy responses—massive economic and military aid, and on occasion covert political intervention or overt military intervention—had largely succeeded in containing and isolating the Cuban Revolution within Cuba itself. The U.S. hegemonic system in Latin America then continued on very much in its traditional way for the next thirty years, until the Chavez Revolution in Venezuela in 1999.

In Western Europe, the opposition to U.S. hegemony was of an entirely different sort, that of French President Charles de Gaulle and his efforts to revive French national independence and identity, and more generally to revive a Europe defined by nation-states. As moderate as this opposition was, it provoked great agitation and outrage in U.S. economic and political elites, especially after de Gaulle in 1967 withdrew

France from NATO's integrated command structure and expelled NATO bases from French territory. But after de Gaulle resigned from office in 1969 and then died in 1970, France gradually reverted to being a NATO member like other NATO members. The U.S. hegemonic system in Western Europe then continued on very much in its traditional way for the next several decades, remaining largely unchanged even after the decisive victory of the United States over the Soviet Union and the end of the Cold War in 1989-1991. Indeed, the system would not face a new major challenge until the beginning of the conflict between Russia and Ukraine in 2013-2014.

The United States did not face an opposition nation among its four allies in East Asia. But of course, on the southern periphery of East Asia, the U.S. certainly faced monumental opposition from communist North Vietnam. The U.S. efforts to extend its hegemonic system into the states of what had been French Indochina were decisively defeated by North Vietnam in 1975. Indeed, this was the most decisive defeat that the United States suffered during the entire Cold-War era. Nevertheless, within a few years, the U.S. had largely succeeded in containing and isolating the North Vietnamese victory to Indochina. Even more, by 1995, communist Vietnam was even on the path to becoming a de facto ally of the United States against communist China.

Thus, from the perspective of U.S. economic and political elites, the overall lesson from their confrontations with the opposition nations of the 1960s was that eventually the massive economic, military, and political strengths of the United States and its hegemonic systems would prevail. Consequently, there was no compelling reason for these elites to change what they were doing, and they could largely continue to run the American empire in the future as they had run it in the past.

The most formidable challenges to the American empire, and the ones that combined to produce its first general crisis, came not from any of its client states, but from within its hegemonic power, the United States itself. And each of the three functional dimensions of the empire—the economic, the military, and the political—issued in a severe challenge and crisis so severe that it would be given its own unique name, one that would become a shorthand term and household word for years to come. The economic challenge became the Great

Stagflation, the military challenge became the Vietnam Syndrome, and the political challenge became Watergate.

The Great Stagflation

The Great Stagflation of the 1970s was the greatest international economic crisis since the Great Depression of the 1930s. It began with the declining competitiveness of American industry vis-à-vis the now fully-recovered industries of Western Europe, particularly West Germany, and of Japan. The resulting trade deficit also produced the financial effect of a weakening dollar. Thus, a central achievement of the U.S. hegemonic systems in Western Europe and East Asia had, after a period of a generation, become a major threat to the economic core of the hegemonic power itself.

Second, the financial effects of the growing U.S. trade deficit were soon amplified by a growing U.S. fiscal deficit. This resulted from the Johnson administration's choice to finance its war in Vietnam with deficit spending in order to minimize any political opposition to the war that might arise if it were to cause higher taxes or reduced social spending. By 1968, these financial effects had resulted in a run on the dollar, and by 1971, they had forced the Nixon administration to abandon the dollar-gold-exchange standard—the foundation of the famous Bretton Woods international financial system and a central pillar of the American empire since 1945—and to replace it with a pure dollar—or fiat-currency—standard. Thus, the efforts of the United States to expand its successful maritime hegemonic system in East Asia to include mainland Southeast Asia had become another major threat to the economic core of the hegemonic power itself.

Third and finally, the oil-producing states of the Middle East—states that had been protected by U.S. military power since the late 1940s—succeeded in the early 1970s to first double and then quadruple oil prices. This produced a massive inflationary shock to the oil-importing client-states of the U.S. hegemonic systems in Western Europe and East Asia, and was also another amplifier of inflation within the hegemonic power itself. At the same time, it greatly diminished the ability of consumers in these oil-importing countries to buy the industrial products which they themselves produced. The result of these three accumulating and combined economic disruptions was the Great Stagflation, which afflicted the United States and its hegemonic systems in Western Europe and East Asia during the entire 1970s.

The Vietnam Syndrome

The United States had achieved its great victories in the Second World War by deploying its vast military forces with an extraordinary, even unique, combination of overwhelming mass and wide-ranging mobility. This became known as the American Way of War. Although elements of this distinctive military method were demonstrated in the American Civil War (U.S. Grant's deployment of overwhelming mass and Robert E. Lee's deployment of wide-ranging mobility), the Spanish-American War (the wide-ranging mobility of the U.S. Navy), and the First World War (the overwhelming mass of the U.S. Army), the apotheosis of this method was the Second World War, when the U.S. military deployed both overwhelming mass and wide-ranging mobility in both the European and the Pacific theaters. It was the American Way of War which decisively defeated both Germany and Japan, and it was thus the American Way of War which cleared the ground for the erection of the U.S. hegemonic systems in both Western Europe and East Asia.

It was, then, not surprising that, in the next U.S. war that came along, the Korean War, the United States first tried to employ some version of its distinctive way of war. By September 1950, this was decisively successful against the original enemy, North Korea, but this very success then provoked the entry into the war of China and the beginning of "a wholly new war." This new war soon became a prolonged, three-year military stalemate conducted within the limited geographical space of the Korean peninsula itself, a war that was the very opposite of overwhelming mass and wide-ranging mobility.

The next U.S. war to come along was, of course, the Vietnam War. The United States initially tried to defeat or at least to contain its North Vietnamese enemy with a variety of military means short of war—military aid, military advisors, and special operating forces. By 1965, however, these means had proven to be inadequate, and the Johnson administration then greatly escalated the U.S, military involvement in Vietnam with the large-scale deployment of conventional land and air forces. Again, it is not surprising that the United States first tried to employ some version of overwhelming mass and wide-ranging mobility, but—in an analogy with the Korean War—with that mobility now limited to the Indochinese peninsula itself. This also soon proved to be inadequate to contain the military forces of North Vietnam, which employed a wholly different strategy of insurgent or "revolutionary" warfare (a sort of East Asian, or at least Maoist, way of war). There then ensued yet another, but even longer, military stalemate—this time one of eight years—conducted within a limited geographical space, an even greater antithesis to overwhelming mass and wide-ranging mobility. It was not long before this antithesis to the American Way of War produced a deep crisis within the American political system, a crisis which by 1972 would metastasize into what became known as Watergate.

On the military dimension, the American frustrations and failures in the Vietnam War produced a determination on the part of both the U.S. military and the American people to have "no more Vietnams," so that nothing like this war would ever happen again. This was the famous Vietnam Syndrome, which completely dominated the military policies of the Ford and Carter administrations. The Soviet Union was quick to take advantage of this period of non-intervention by the United States, and from 1975 to 1979, Soviet-backed communist movements took power in a wide range of Third-World countries, not only in Vietnam, Cambodia, and Laos, but also in Ethiopia, Mozambique, Angola, South Yemen, Nicaragua, Grenada, and finally, Afghanistan. Moreover, several of these new Soviet-backed regimes were ruling countries that were geopolitically important. Several, for example, were athwart or adjacent to vital "sea lines of communication" or SLOCs. Thus, the military power—and certainly the military prestige or credibility—which was a crucial pillar of the American empire was now greatly diminished.

Watergate

During the late 1960s, the U.S. political system demonstrated that it was not able to adequately manage the growing economic and military challenges of the time, i.e., the disruptions caused by declining economic competitiveness and growing inflation, and the frustrations caused by the strategic and operational failures of the Vietnam War. By 1968, the Democratic Party had lost any credibility to resolve these problems, and the Republican Party, which itself had no clear solutions for these same problems, essentially won the 1968 presidential election by default. Moreover, the incoming administration of Richard Nixon, like the Eisenhower administration before it, represented an uneasy compromise between the two long-standing competing elites within the Republican Party, i.e., the "liberal internationalists," centered in the Northeast, and the conservative nationalists, centered in the Midwest.

In his first administration, Nixon was quite successful in managing this compromise. In part, this was because the liberal internationalists gave him a good deal of leeway to solve the economic and military problems which the liberal internationalists in both the Republican Party and the Democratic Party had earlier produced with their policies for international trade and for the Vietnam War. As we have seen, Nixon dramatically, and more or less effectively, resolved the economic problem by taking the United States off the dollar-gold-exchange standard and replacing it with a pure dollar standard. Similarly, he dramatically, and more or less effectively, resolved the military problem by withdrawing U.S. troops from Vietnam and by announcing a "Nixon Doctrine" which put sharp constraints on the future use of U.S. troops in local wars. These impressive policy successes largely explain Nixon's landslide victory in the presidential election of 1972.

But Nixon himself was impressed with his landslide victory. He immediately decided that he didn't need the support of the liberal internationalists as much as before. Rather, in his second administration, he would be more independent in his position, and more conservative-nationalist in his policies, than he had been in his first. At the same time, since Nixon had largely resolved the economic and military problems that he had inherited in 1969 and that the liberal internationalists had earlier caused, these same liberal internationalists in late 1972 no longer needed Nixon as much as they had needed him during his first administration. Thus, when in November and December 1972, Nixon made a series of dramatic moves to establish much greater control by himself and his own appointees over the permanent officials in the executive departments, over the role of Congress in the federal budget, and even in the role of the federal courts, the liberal internationalists—in both the Republican and Democratic parties—came together in their resolve to bring him down.

The ensuing period, from January 1973 to August 1974, represents the prolonged, complex, and relentless implementation of this elite resolve. It saw such unprecedented events as the removal of an elected Vice President (Spiro Agnew) and his replacement by an unelected one (Gerald Ford), which cleared the way for the removal of an elected President (Nixon) and his replacement by an unelected one (Ford), and then, to tidy things up, the selection of another unelected Vice President (Nelson Rockefeller). Thus, by 1975, the liberal internationalists of the Republican Party were in complete control of the executive branch of the U.S. government.

However, all these unprecedented, and quite undemocratic, elite political maneuvers left the Republican Party with little popular credibility heading into the 1976 presidential election. Thus the liberal internationalist elites, who were above both parties, had to ensure that the candidate of the Democratic Party would also be a reliable liberal internationalist (and not like its candidate in 1972, the populist and somewhat nationalist George McGovern). This they did with the nomination of the inexperienced but malleable Jimmy Carter (a protege of David Rockefeller). With Carter's election, a liberal-internationalist Republican administration was replaced with a basically similar liberal-internationalist Democratic administration.

Thus, the general crisis of American empire continued through the 1970s. It would not really be brought to an end until the election of Ronald Reagan as president in 1980 and the advent of his administration in 1981.

III. The Reagan Resolution of the First General Crisis

The new Reagan administration undertook a dramatic and decisive series of measures to address the general crisis afflicting the United States in 1980 on each of the three economic, military, and political dimensions. The Reagan partisans often called the works of the administration "the Reagan Revolution," but this was rhetorical hyperbole. (Indeed, some of these measures had actually been initiated in the last year of the Carter administration, backed as they were by a bipartisan American elite). However, the changes that the Reagan administration instituted in several operating principles and practices of the United States can accurately be termed the Reagan reformation. And the policies that flowed from this reformation and that successively addressed the multidimensional challenges of the general crisis can accurately be termed the Reagan resolution. And, overall, the Reagan administration accomplished a restoration of the American empire.

The Economic Resolution

The most urgent economic problem of the United States in 1980 was inflation. As a result of the "second oil shock" of 1979-1980, this had reached 15 percent annually. The new Chairman of the Federal Reserve Board, Paul Volcker, backed by the Reagan administration and by a bipartisan American economic elite, took the decisive measure of sharply raising interest rates to 18 percent. This quickly broke the back of the inflation (although at the cost of a sudden and sharp recession), thus eliminating the inflation component of the debilitating Great Stagflation.

The Reagan administration then introduced the supposedly new idea of "supply-side economics" as the way to achieve economic growth. In practice, this meant the old and familiar Republican policies of deregulation and tax cuts. The administration did succeed in implementing these policies, however, and impressive economic growth did ensue, bringing an end to the recession and thus eliminating the stagnation component of the Great Stagflation.

Moreover, the economic growth was facilitated by the Reagan administration's large and sustained increase in military spending (although at the cost of a substantial rise in the federal deficit). Together, the three economic measures of (1) using monetary policy to end inflation, (2) using deregulation and tax cuts to stimulate growth, and (3) using military spending to strengthen that growth succeeded by 1984 in resolving the economic challenges posed by the Great Stagflation of the 1970s.

The Military Resolution

In the aftermath of its debacle in the Vietnam War, and in the midst of the Vietnam Syndrome, the U.S. military undertook a radical reinvention of itself to ensure that it would never again have to fight like it did in Vietnam. In actuality, this reinvention was an effort to return to the principles and practices of the American Way of War but now also exploiting the U.S. advantages in the military high technologies of the late twentieth century, particularly in what were called "precision-guided munitions" or PGMs. Each of the military services developed a new doctrine which would guide its weapons procurement, deployment, and employment for the new military era. The most important of these was the new doctrine of the Army, the "Air-Land Battle Doctrine," which envisioned the U.S. Army fighting the Soviet Army in a general but non-nuclear war, with the principal theater being the North European Plain, or NATO's Central Front. The Navy and the Marines developed a parallel plan, which they termed the "Forward Maritime Strategy." At the same time, the Air Force was developing its truly high-tech conception ("doctrine" is hardly the right word for its surreal vision) of the "Strategic Defense Initiative," or SDI, which was supposed to thwart any Soviet ICBM attack upon the United States. All of this was supposed to leverage the U.S. lead in high technology over the Soviet lead in raw numbers, to use U.S. quality to overcome Soviet quantity.

A second effort to leave Vietnam, and particularly the Vietnam Syndrome, behind was the policy of the Reagan administration to gradually acclimate the American public into again accepting military intervention as an effective instrument of U.S. foreign policy. The credible threat by a great power to undertake military intervention is, after all, an essential pillar for any hegemonic system. The administration's idea was to begin with a very small, very weak, very simple country, where a military intervention would be certain of quick and easy success, and then to step-by-step work up U.S. operations to more complex and more challenging interventions. The first move in this process was the invasion of Grenada (which was certainly the perfect place for the first step) in October 1983. This was followed by an air strike on Libya in April 1985, naval operations to protect shipping in the Persian Gulf in 1987-1988, and the invasion of Panama in September 1989. After all this, the U.S. military and the American public were once again acclimated for a truly serious military intervention or even war, as long as it was some kind of conventional operation that fit into the paradigm of the American Way of War. This turned out to be the Gulf War of 1992, which was definitely a conventional war, but also a very high-tech war. Here, the U.S. Army essentially employed its Air-Land Battle Doctrine for the first time, except that its adversary was the Iraqi Army rather than the Soviet Army, and its theater was the Iraq Desert rather than the North European Plain.

Unfortunately, along this step-by-step way to bigger and better U.S. military interventions, the Reagan administration had gotten involved in a military intervention which definitely did not fit the plan. This happened when the administration sent U. S Marines into Lebanon in 1982, which culminated in the disastrous suicide bombing of the Marine barracks in October 1983, at the very time that the U.S. was invading Grenada. Lebanon had turned out to be a kind of miniature Vietnam, and the Reagan administration quietly withdrew its troops in mid-1984. Its dismal experience in Lebanon, however, did cause the administration to undertake a third effort to reinvent the U.S. military along the lines of the American Way of War. This was the Weinberger Doctrine, which was articulated by Secretary of Defense Caspar Weinberger in 1984, and which specified the conditions in which the United States could undertake military operations. These conditions included (1) a clearly defined military objective; (2) the use of overwhelming military force; (3) a plan for early withdrawal of military forces; and (4) the clear approval of the intervention by the American public, expressed through its elected representatives in Congress and by some formal statement such as a declaration of war or a Congressional resolution. These conditions, and thus the Weinberger Doctrine, were very much in conformity with classical American Way of War. The conduct of the Gulf War of 1992 was very much an exemplar of the Weinberger Doctrine.

The Political Resolution

As we have seen, the Republican Party had long been divided between a liberal international wing, centered in Northeastern finance, and a conservative nationalist wing, centered in Midwestern industry. During the 1920s-1930s, the dominant wing was Midwestern industry, but by the 1950s-1970s, the dominant wing had become Northeastern finance. Moreover, insofar as several really large industrial firms had transformed themselves into multinational corporations by the late 1960s, they had become part of the liberal international bloc, reinforcing its dominance in the Republican Party and—since this bloc was largely bipartisan—increasingly within the United States as a whole. It had been this liberal international bloc that had brought down the second Nixon administration. However, during the 1970s, i.e., during the period of the Great Stagflation and the Vietnam Syndrome, these liberal internationalists had not yet been able to establish a strong presidential administration to effectively implement their preferred policies. Both the Ford administration and the Carter administration had been disappointments in this respect, as in so much else.

It was the great achievement of Ronald Reagan to finally bring an end to this party and presidential paralysis. He succeeded in uniting the Republican Party, and more broadly the "conservative movement," to a degree that had not been seen since the time of President Calvin Coolidge. Moreover, he united both the disparate elements among the party's elite, or donor class (the aforementioned liberal internationalists and conservative nationalists), and the different disparate elements among the party's base, or voter class (generally known as economic or fiscal conservatives, national-security or patriotic conservatives, and social or religious conservatives).

The way that Reagan united the Republican elite was, not surprisingly, to give something to both wings. However, there was an asymmetry in what he gave to each. To the liberal internationalists, he gave the top positions in the foreign-policy and national-security bureaucracies and, through these, he gave them their preferred policies. To the conservative nationalists, he gave a great increase in defense spending and a strong military, but not much more.

When it came to uniting the Republican base, a crucial element was Reagan's great talents in soaring rhetoric. To the economic and fiscal conservatives, he did give the decidedly practical policies of deregulation and tax cuts. However, he also embellished these with soaring rhetoric about the free market, even though in practice he turned the actual operation of the economy over to the unelected officials and bankers of the intrusive Federal Reserve System. To the national-security and patriotic conservatives, he gave what he was giving their counterparts in the elite, i.e., increased defense spending and a strong military, but there was a significant difference between the elite and the base. Reagan's liberal-international economic policies were steadily hollowing out parts of Midwestern industry and the jobs therein. They were also steadily bringing in low-paid immigrant workers who were displacing high-paid American workers in many of the remaining jobs. Thus, many workers in the patriotic base ended up with no more than Reagan's soaring patriotic rhetoric. As for the social or religious conservatives, they did get the appointment of a couple of Supreme Court justices. But they received virtually no major positions in the Reagan administration, and they got virtually nothing from its policies. But of course, they too were treated to a continuing flow of inspiring rhetoric, in their case religious. And at the end of the Reagan administration in 1989, social liberalism was even more predominant in American society than it had been at its beginning in 1981.

IV. The Apotheosis of the Reagan Restoration of the American Empire: The Triumph over the Soviet Union

The Reagan administration's resolution of the economic and military problems that the Great Stagflation and the Vietnam Syndrome had posed to the United States itself was certainly an impressive achievement. But the resulting new U.S. economic and military strengths then led directly to a foreign-policy and national-security achievement that was not only impressive but world-historical in its scale and consequences. This was the decisive victory of the United States over the Soviet Union, which climaxed in 1989-1991 after the forty-year struggle that was the Cold War.

The economic reforms of the Reagan administration produced economic growth, including growth in the new high-tech sectors of the American economy. This in turn enabled growth in the U.S. defense budget and military procurement, including the new high-tech weapons that were intrinsic to the new strategic doctrines of the U.S. military services—the Air-Land Battle Doctrine, the Forward Maritime Strategy, and the Strategic Defense Initiative. This great leap forward by the U.S. military had not been expected by the Soviet leadership, and it presented them with serious challenges.

First, the Soviet economy had its own serious problems with stagnation during the 1970s, and these were continuing into the 1980s. Second, the Soviet defense industry was very slow in adopting the new electronic, information, and precision technologies that were rapidly improving U.S. weapons systems in the 1980s. The Soviet military thus was greatly threatened by the new U.S. military developments. The years 1982-1984 were a period of intense disputes within the Soviet Politburo and the Soviet General Staff about what was to be done. The disputes were won by a group of reforming leaders who in 1985 installed a wholly new kind of General Secretary of the Communist Party, Mikhail Gorbachev, to carry out their reforms.

The Soviet reformers believed that the economic stagnation and technological sluggishness resulted from the entrenched inertia and narrow self-interest of the Soviet bureaucrats. The reformers thought that the bureaucrats could be exposed and shaken up by a combination of more energetic direction from above and more lively criticism from below. To enable the latter, the reformers inaugurated a program of "openness," or *glasnost*. When glasnost by itself proved insufficient, the reformers then inaugurated a more radical program of "restructuring" the bureaucracies, or *perestroika*.

Such a reform program was unprecedented in Soviet history. It seemed to make sense in terms of organizational theory, but when these reforms impacted upon Soviet reality, they had massive unintended consequences. Openness soon spread from the Soviet bureaucracies to other sectors of Soviet society. Restructuring of the Soviet bureaucracies soon led to their dis-functioning and then to their deconstructing, and this too soon spread to other sectors of Soviet society. The result was that by 1989 the entire Soviet system was running down and falling apart. The system not only lost its capacity, but it also lost its will. In 1989, the Soviet Union's empire in Eastern Europe quickly collapsed, and in 1991, the Soviet Union itself collapsed and dissolved. Even more extraordinary, this great empire collapsed without firing any final shot at its triumphant adversary, the United States.

V. The New Global Scope of the American Empire

The extraordinary victory of the United States over the Soviet Union meant that what had been a bipolar international system since 1945 suddenly was transformed into a unipolar system. For forty years, the United States had conducted a foreign policy whose basic principle was supposed to be the "containment" of the Soviet Union and its allies. But in actuality, the most important containment going on had been that by the Soviet Union of the United States and its allies. While the United States was containing the Soviets within a Communist World, the Soviets were containing the United States within a "Free World," and particularly within the three American alliances or hegemonic systems of Western Europe, East Asia, and Latin America.

Now, however, the United States was "the sole superpower," and its economic and political elite—flush and confident from the achievements of the Reagan restoration—immediately proceeded to undertake a grand project to construct a "New World Order," which essentially meant to remake the entire world—and no longer just the Free World—in the American image. The economic, military, and political principles of this new American order—really an American empire—were respectively a global economy, a high-tech military, and liberal democracy. These were all integrated and legitimated by an ideology which espoused such ideals as the open society, human rights, and universal rules and norms.

The Economic Dimension: Globalization, Finance, and the Information Age

We have already seen that the American economic and political system had been largely dominated since the end of the Second World War by

23

a bipartisan liberal-international bloc. With the end of the Cold War and the Soviet Union, this bloc immediately sought to transform the old international economy into a new global one. This project, and indeed the whole process that it entailed, was termed "globalization," and the elite often portrayed globalization as a natural, inevitable development rather than a product of their own particular policy choices.

We have also already seen that the liberal-international policies of the 1970s-1980s had already begun to hollow out large parts of Midwestern industry, especially because of competition from Japan. The areas affected became the notorious "Rust Belt." Now, the globalization of the 1990s accentuated and accelerated this hollowing-out process, with South Korea, Taiwan, and Mexico joining Japan as devastating industrial competitors, and with the Rust Belt now spreading from the Midwest to the South.

At the same time that American industry was becoming more multinational and less American, the overall American economy was becoming more financial and less industrial. In the 1990s, finance, still largely centered in the Northeast, became both the largest and the most profitable sector of the American economy. And finance, i.e., the large commercial and investment banks and the new hedge funds and private-equity funds, converted its great economic power into great political power. By the end of the 1990s, financial interests were the principal donors to presidential and senatorial candidates in both the Republican and Democratic Parties. The result was that both the Bill Clinton administration and the George W. Bush administration enacted policies which financial interests had long sought, in particular to largely deregulate the financial sector.

The Military Dimension: High-Tech Weaponry and the Revolution in Military Affairs

As the Soviet Union was disintegrating in 1991, without firing a shot at its American adversary, the U.S. military nevertheless achieved its own dramatic victory, which was its extraordinary performance in the Gulf War against the Iraqi military. The U.S. Army's Air-Land Battle Doctrine, which was based upon the use of high-tech, information-rich, and precision-guided weapon systems, had been designed to fight and defeat the Soviet Army in a conventional war in Europe. Although the doctrine and its weapons never had to be used for its original purpose, the Army now employed them to fight and defeat a Soviet-trained army in a conventional war in the Middle East. The results were spectacular: quick, decisive, and with virtually no U.S. casualties. They were widely seen as heralding the advent of a "Revolution in Military Affairs," which had been much discussed and anticipated by military professionals in the 1980s.

This extraordinary U.S. military performance quickly captured the attention of every other important military in the world, including that of the Russian Federation (which had succeeded the Soviet Union) and also that of China. They concluded that they would also have to adopt some version of this high-tech revolution in military affairs, but it would be many years before they would be fully able to do so. In the meantime, the U.S. military—the sole high-tech military and the one wielded by the sole superpower—would enable the United States to do its will and work its way in carrying out its grand project to remake the world in the American image. It did not take long for the United States to undertake other small wars which could serve as demonstration projects for its proficiency with the Revolution in Military Affairs. This was the case with the Clinton administration's brief wars over Bosnia in 1995 and over Kosovo in 1999, which were also extraordinarily quick, decisive, and with virtually no U.S. casualties.

Moreover, the Kosovo War was not only a demonstration project for the new U.S. capabilities. It was also meant to be a demonstration project for new NATO military objectives. Ever since its founding in 1949, the members of NATO had agreed that its only purpose was to defend its European members against the threat from the Soviet Union in Europe. NATO, as NATO, would undertake no military operations outside of Europe or "out-of-area," for example in the Middle East. But in the 1990s, the threat from the Soviet Union, and even from its successor state, the Russian Federation, had disappeared, and the Clinton administration resolved to enlist NATO for a new purpose, which would be precisely to participate in U.S.-led military operations in the Middle East. These out-of-area operations would be justified as securing "the supply of vital natural resources" (i.e., oil) to Europe. Thus, the administration arranged that at the annual meeting of NATO, which was to convene in April 1999 and would be on the occasion of the fiftieth anniversary of NATO's founding in April 1949, NATO would adopt a "New Strategic Concept." This new strategic concept would now include NATO military operations in the Middle East in order, of course, to secure the supply of vital natural resources. The Clinton administration initiated its war in Kosovo in March 1999, and one of its principal purposes was to demonstrate that a NATO war carrying out the New Strategic Concept and conducted in the nearby Middle East could be quick, decisive, and with virtually no casualties.

Thus, by the end of the 1990s, the demonstrated military supremacy of the United States was a central pillar of the new American empire and its global scope. As the United States entered the new millennium, its economic and political elites were supremely confident that they could continue to advance their grand project of remaking the world in the American image, and that they even might be able to advance some ideals that hitherto would have been considered to be millenarian, such as establishing the global reign of universal human rights and universal rules and norms.

The Political Dimension: Liberal Democracy and Regime Change

With the U.S. victory over the Soviet Union, most of the communist regimes in the Soviet allies in Eastern Europe were quickly replaced with some version of a liberal democracy, much like those that had long characterized the U.S. allies in Western Europe. And even in the successor state to the Soviet Union itself, the Russian Federation, the Yeltsin government of the 1990s gave the outer appearance of being a developing liberal democracy. (In reality, it was a Potemkin liberal democracy, one whose real character was that of a corrupt oligarchy.)

All of this excited the political imaginations of the U.S. elites. They had always preferred liberal democracy as the best political formula, not only for the United States itself, but also for those dependent allies whose economic and cultural development had reached the level that they could support such a complex political system. This had long been the case in Western Europe, and by the early 1990s, it was becoming the case in East Asia, and it even seemed increasingly to be the case in Latin America. If liberal democracy was being established in all of these regions, and it had just been established in Eastern Europe, surely it could be spread to other regions as well, particularly to the Middle East and to the former Soviet republics in Central Asia. Thus began the idea of the "democratization project," by which the United States would promote the spread of liberal democracy throughout the globe.

Up to the early 1990s, however, this recent spread of liberal democracy to new regions had been relatively easy and costless for the United States. In particular, it had not required U.S. military intervention (with the exceptions of Panama in 1989 and Haiti in 1994), and it had not even required covert political intervention by the CIA. But it soon became clear that spreading liberal democracy to the Middle East and Central Asia would require the United States to use these more activist and interventionist methods. The U.S. elites had considerable difficulty in explaining why these regions seemed to pose a greater challenge for the U.S. democratization project. The obvious fact that almost all of the countries in the Middle East and Central Asia were part of the Muslim world yielded an explanation that even then the U.S. elites found to be politically incorrect. In any event, there was little sign that the authoritarian regimes in these regions would be changed by internal forces by themselves; they would only be changed if outside forces (i.e., the CIA or the U.S. military) acted upon the regime. Thus, the United States began to develop a systematic program for implementing "regime change," whose ostensible objective was to establish some kind of liberal democracy. The first country to be the target for this program was a relatively simple and easy case, since it was not actually in the Middle East itself but only on the way to it. This was Serbia, whose defeat in the Kosovo War also made it an unusually vulnerable target. However, at the end of the 1990s, the program was still in its developmental and experimental stage. It would not really be implemented until the 2000s during the George W. Bush administration. Then it would be implemented in a big (although ultimately ineffective) way in a series of "color revolutions" promoted by the CIA and in the U.S. military interventions in Afghanistan and Iraq.

The United States in Western Europe

During the forty-year Cold War, the U.S. hegemonic system in Western Europe had generally operated the way both its original architects and later U.S. economic and political elites had intended. The only significant internal challenge to the system had come from French President Charles de Gaulle during the 1960s, and that proved to be rather superficial and quite brief. Thereafter, the U.S. role in Western Europe operated very much as an archetypal hegemonic system. This was most evident on the military dimension and with NATO.

Underneath the smooth surface created by U.S. military hegemony, however, the dynamics of U.S. economic and political hegemony were gradually but steadily transforming the character of the Western European countries. The most obvious manifestation of this were the step-by-step increases in the integration and power of what had begun in 1958 as the European Economic Community and what had matured by 1992 into the European Union. Ever since 1947, the U.S. economic and political elites had almost always supported more economic and political unification of Western Europe because they thought that this was more likely to produce a stronger economic and political ally of the U.S., not an economic and political rival. In particular, they saw the successive European international organizations as a nice economic and political counterpart and partner to the military organization that was NATO.

Moreover, they also saw these organizations as helping to make the European countries more capitalist and less socialist in their economies, and more liberal and less collectivist in their politics. In other words, European unification, if done in the right—i.e., the liberal capitalist—way, could actually help the United States remake Western Europe in its own image. In addition, the growing presence of American multinational corporations in Western Europe after 1958 obviously worked to open up the European economies, to make them more international and less national.

As we have seen, at the beginning of the U.S. hegemonic system in Western Europe in the late 1940s, the U.S. economic and political elites had to make concessions to the national and social interests that were then strong in these countries in order to create a unified resistance to the Soviet threat. But the U.S. elites really wanted Europe to eventually become less national and less social, i.e., to become more like the United States. And over time, as the dynamics of European international organizations and American multinational corporations worked their way, this is what happened. This process was already far advanced by the end of the Cold War, and it advanced even further and even faster in the 1990s. By the year 2000, many of the most important decisions affecting the lives of Western Europeans were made in Brussels rather than in putatively national capitals. And all of the putatively Socialist or Social Democratic Parties had replaced their socialist economic policies with progressive cultural policies, and thereby with capitalist economic policies.

The total collapse of the Soviet Union and of its allied communist regimes in Eastern Europe meant that suddenly a vast realm, indeed a vast vacuum, opened up to the east of the U.S. hegemonic system in Western Europe, and the United States and its allies were quick to fill it. Convinced that their great victory in the Cold War demonstrated the absolute superiority of their system on all of its dimensions—of a capitalist economy, high-tech military, and liberal democracy—they immediately sought to erect these on the ruins of the communist regimes, i.e., to remake Eastern Europe in their own image. And, within a few years, they had largely succeeded in doing so.

This great leap eastward of the U.S. hegemonic system proceeded on two levels: the international and the internal. The United States had found NATO and the successive European international organizations to be very satisfactory instruments in operating its hegemonic system in Western Europe, so it now used these to expand that system into Eastern Europe. First, East Germany, through German unification in 1991, was incorporated into NATO and the European Union; then Poland, the Czech Republic, Slovakia, and Hungary; and then Romania and Bulgaria. Sometimes a country entered NATO first and then the European Union, and sometimes the sequence was the reverse, but from the point of view of the increasingly worried and annoyed Russians, these two organizations were two sides of the same U.S. hegemonic coin. By the year 2000, all of the above countries were nicely integrated into NATO and the E.U., and the process of soon adding Slovenia, Croatia, and even the former Baltic republics and constituent parts of the Soviet Union itself—Estonia, Latvia, and Lithuania—was already far advanced. It was the admission of former republics of the Soviet Union into NATO and the E.U., i.e., bringing these organizations right up to the borders of the Russian Federation, that especially alarmed and angered the Russians.

Moreover, as we have already seen, the European international organizations had internal consequences for their members, not just international ones. They were powerful engines working to make these countries less national and less social. They soon pushed to have the same effects in Eastern Europe that they had had in Western Europe. This was to steadily replace a national economic and political elite with an international one and to replace social economic and cultural policies with more liberal and capitalist ones. The result, in both Western Europe and Eastern Europe, was to create growing disparities within society in regard to income, wealth, values, and identities.

The United States in East Asia

Like the U.S. hegemonic system in Western Europe, the U.S. hegemonic system in East Asia generally operated throughout the Cold War in the way both its original architects and later U.S. economic and political elites intended. The system not only kept maritime East Asia (Japan, South Korea, Taiwan, and the Philippines) from falling under the sway of any communist power, but it enabled truly spectacular economic growth and prosperity in the first three of these countries.

However, the East Asian system had always been different from the Western European one in important ways. On the military dimension, the U.S. military was even more hegemonic and the local militaries even more dependent in East Asia than in Western Europe. In essence, the U.S. military services served as the real army, navy, and air force of each of these four countries while the putative national militaries functioned more or less like the National Guard does in the United States.

On the economic dimension, the vast U.S. market performed something like the same role. The export-led economies of East Asia were even more dependent on the U.S. market than those of Western Europe. In essence, the U.S. market served as the real export market for each of these four countries because the United States needed it as a substitute for the obvious alternative export market, Communist China. But as time went on and as the export prowess of the East Asian countries greatly increased, an odd symmetry developed. By the end of the Cold War and even more by the end of the 1990s, the industries of Japan, South Korea, and Taiwan were serving as the real industrial producers for much of the U.S. economy, just as the U.S. military services were serving as the real military forces for these countries.

The way that the Cold War ended produced another major difference between the U.S. hegemonic system in East Asia and that in Western Europe. Whereas the Soviet Union completely collapsed, Communist China largely endured. While it is true that the Chinese economic system became much more capitalist than before, the Chinese political system remained an authoritarian communist one. The result was a kind of Market-Leninism which was very successful in producing spectacular Chinese economic growth during the 1990s and beyond. The continuing military threat and the continuing economic temptation that China posed to the U.S. allies in East Asia meant that the United States had to continue both its odd military role and its odd economic role in the region in the years after the end of the Cold War, largely as it had in the years before.

The only new challenge to the East Asian system to develop in the decade after the Cold War came from the Philippines in 1992, and in the benign context of the time, this seemed relatively unimportant and inconsequential. During a period of heightened nationalist consciousness, the Philippines expelled the U.S. Navy from its immense and long-established base at Subic Bay and the U.S. Air Force from its own immense and long-established base at Clark Field. The United States complied with this expulsion but, seeking to minimize the disruptive effects on the U.S. hegemonic system in East Asia, it continued to act as if the Philippines remained a loyal U.S. ally, and the overall system continued to operate in the same reassuring way as it had before.

The United States in Latin America

As we have seen, the U.S. hegemonic system in Latin America had been threatened by the Castro Revolution in Cuba in 1959 and by the resulting communist regime, but during the 1960s the United States succeeded in containing this threat within Cuba itself, and the U.S. system then continued to operate largely as U.S. economic and political elites wanted it to. Similarly, the system was again threatened by the Sandinista Revolution in Nicaragua in 1979 and by the resulting Marxist regime and Cuban ally, but during the 1980s the United States succeeded in containing this threat within Nicaragua itself.

As we have also seen, the U.S. hegemonic system in Latin America had long been characterized by economic, military, and political features which made it more like a traditional colonial system than a true hegemonic one like the U.S. system in Western Europe. The economic dimension was characterized by an unequal exchange (or "colonial pact") between the industrial United States and the agricultural-product- and raw-material-exporting Latin America. The military dimension was characterized by the complete dominance of the U.S. military over the local militaries, which in reality never functioned as militaries at all (in the sense of fighting foreign militaries), but only as local police forces coercing their own citizens. And the political dimension was characterized by what were republics in form but were either military dictatorships or oligarchic regimes in reality. Indeed, even the putative states of Latin America (as in the "Organization of American States") rarely functioned in practice like real states such as those in Europe. Rather, they were merely patrimonial hierarchies exploiting their own citizens while pretending to be states. And of course, hardly anyone ever thought of most of these putative states as being full nation-states like those in Europe. The very words "Guatemalan nation" or "Peruvian nation" sounded like an oxymoron.

By the 1990s, however, the industrial development of several Latin American countries had lifted them closer to the European model. This was especially the case with Mexico, Brazil, and Chile. U.S. economic and political elites recognized this by developing more sophisticated economic formulas, such as the North American Free Trade Agreement (NAFTA), "the Washington consensus," and "neoliberalism," which incorporated Latin American industries into the international supply chains of U.S. multinational corporations. Moreover, in the 1990s, virtually all of the remaining military dictatorships in Latin America were replaced with oligarchic regimes, which was a somewhat more sophisticated political formula than before. All of this made the U.S. elites think that their hegemonic system in Latin America was operating better than ever.

In the year 2000, a decade after the end of the Cold War and the end of the Soviet Union, the view from the top of the sole superpower, the American empire, could not have seemed better. "Standing tall" and "seeing far," the U.S. economic and political elite gazed into "the next American century" with a confidence unknown by any great-power elite within the previous century, or perhaps even within the previous five centuries. On every dimension of the empire—the economic, the military, and the political—and in each of its three hegemonic systems—in the Western Europe that had become all of Europe, in East Asia, and in Latin America, everything was operating very well, and it seemed that everything would operate even better in the future.

But, in a grand trajectory that would have been perfectly understood by the great Greek dramatists and by that great Greek historian, Thucydides, everything would soon turn into its opposite. In 2001, the American empire entered into a long journey through the shadow of decline, and by the U.S. presidential-election year of 2016 and the first Trump administration year of 2017, some observers were reasonably beginning to think that the empire was entering its Valley of Death. There now seemed to be unprecedented and intractable challenges on every dimension of the empire and in each of its three hegemonic systems. How did this happen? And what will happen in the future?

VI. The Second General Crisis of the American Empire, 2008-Present

The Military Crisis: The Wars in Afghanistan and Iraq

The first challenge, or rather shock, to the American empire came in 2001, and that was, of course, the bolt from the blue, the big bang of the Islamist terrorist attack of 9/11. This attack, with the prospect that more like it would soon follow, would in itself have presented an extremely difficult problem to the U.S. economic and political elite.

But the really intractable problems were produced by the George W. Bush administration's military responses to the attack. These were first the invasion and occupation of Afghanistan in late 2001 and then the invasion and occupation of Iraq in 2003.

When the United States undertook these invasions, the U.S. elites understood war almost wholly through the prism of the Revolution in Military Affairs and the commanding superiority of the U.S. military in the high-tech weaponry of the new Information Age. And, indeed, the initial invasions of Afghanistan and Iraq (like the invasion of Iraq in the Gulf War of 1991) went very well, and in accordance with this high-tech plan, with the quick and costless overthrow of the Taliban and Saddam Hussein regimes. However, very soon thereafter, an effective insurgency developed in each country, and the quick and costless invasion became a long occupation and a costly counterinsurgency war. Suddenly, the post-industrial, information-age war was transformed into a pre-industrial, agricultural-age, or even pre-agricultural-age war. After all, empires and their armies have been engaged in varieties of counterinsurgency operations for at least two or three millennia.

As the dreary and costly counterinsurgency wars in Afghanistan and Iraq went on year after year, the image of the U.S. Army as an efficient, effective, and even invincible force for defending, maintaining, and even expanding a great empire has been largely replaced by an image of the U.S. Army as an incompetent, feckless, and even mindless bureaucracy that could do almost nothing right. Since empires have always depended upon the creditable use of the kind of military force that can, when and where necessary, engage in "imperial policing," the current reputation of the U.S. Army is the very opposite of that needed by an empire.

Revisionist Russia: Amputee States and Hybrid Warfare

As we have seen, during the 1990s, the activist and confident U.S. economic and political elites expanded their well-functioning hegemonic system in Western Europe in a great drive eastward, first into East Germany, then into Eastern Europe, and then—with the admission of the three Baltic states of Estonia, Latvia, and Lithuania into NATO and the E.U.—into former constituent parts of the old Soviet Union itself, right up to the borders of its shrunken successor state, the Russian Federation. In fact, the border between Estonia and Russia is only 150 kilometers, or easy artillery range, from St. Petersburg. With each successive move of the U.S. system eastward, the Russians grew increasingly concerned and apprehensive until, with its move into the Baltic states, they became alarmed and angry.

At each stage in this eastward expansion, experienced and seasoned U.S. foreign-policy experts, most notably George Kennan, had warned that now was the time to stop. Russia, under each of its many different regimes, had always seen buffer states on its western borders, ruled by friendly governments, to be a vital national interest. And although there might be a period when Russia was too weak to secure this vital interest, there would eventually again come a time when it would insist upon this interest or even brutally impose it. But the Bill Clinton and George W. Bush administrations, and behind them most of the U.S. economic and political elites, would have none of this. Arrogant in their power and confidence, ignorant in their understanding of Russia, and arrogant in their ignorance, they brushed aside these cautions and recklessly leapt toward the east and into an unknown future.

Even with the admission of the Baltic states into the U.S. hegemonic system, thoughtful and empathetic U.S. statesmen could still have made the case to the Russians that, because of their Roman Catholic and Protestant—i.e., Western—religious traditions and because of their long-standing Western commercial connections, the Baltic countries were exceptional cases, and that the United States would now commit itself to making no further moves into the former republics of the Soviet Union or nearer to the borders of the Russian Federation. But again, the Clinton and Bush administrations, and the U.S. elites behind them, would have none of this. To the contrary, in 2008 the Bush administration proposed that Georgia and Ukraine also be admitted into NATO.

This time, the Russians responded quickly and decisively, and with an innovative and effective political-military strategy. A few months after the Bush administration's provocative proposal, Russia launched a war against Georgia. Given past Russian practice, one might have expected Russia to occupy all of this bordering country and to install a friendly government over every bit of it. However, in the two decades since the breakup of the Soviet Union, the Russians had developed a less ambitious but still effective strategy which would at least neutralize a bordering country. This was to break off—i.e., to amputate—a piece or two of the bordering country and to turn these pieces into statelets with governments friendly to Russia, indeed totally dependent upon it. The now-amputee bordering country might remain unfriendly to Russia, but it would be so crippled that no other state or international organization would be able to absorb it. Russia had used this strategy effectively against Azerbaijan and Moldova in the 1990s, and now, in 2008, it used it effectively against Georgia, breaking off the two statelets of Abkhazia and South Ossetia and thus putting an end to any plans for Georgia itself to join either NATO or the E.U. Today we can see that Russia finds this particular method—irregular and anomalous as it is—to be a very satisfactory solution to a border-state problem.

There should have been no surprise, therefore, when in 2014 Russia resorted to the same method in Ukraine. During 2013-2014, the Obama administration, and the U.S. economic and political elites behind it, were aggressively pushing to have Ukraine join the E.U., which would then be followed by Ukraine joining NATO. This U.S. campaign reached a climax in February 2014 with the overthrow of the relatively pro-Russian president of Ukraine. Russia quickly and decisively implemented its new strategy of amputation by annexing the Russian-speaking Crimean region of Ukraine and setting up a couple of pro-Russian statelets in Eastern Ukraine. This has put an end to any plans for Ukraine itself to join either NATO or the E.U. Today, we can again see that Russia finds this particular method to be a satisfactory solution to a very big and crucial border-state problem.

Amputee states were the political part of Russia's new political-military strategy. The military part was "hybrid warfare." The Russian national-security elite had reviewed the precarious strategic situation in which Russia found itself at the beginning of the 21st century. On the one hand, it was a vital interest of Russia, as it had always been, to reconstruct a belt of friendly buffer states in its "near abroad," and especially on its western borders. This would also be a way of reconstructing some of the functional advantages of the former Soviet Union. On the other hand, the Russian economy was quite brittle and weak, and Russian demography was quite unhealthy and unpromising. Russia's only robust strengths were its highly-developed military industry, its technically-educated workforce, and its immense energy production. This meant that the Russian national-security elite would have to be unusually innovative and diligent in mobilizing and integrating every possible resource—economic, military, and political—of Russia into a comprehensive and coherent national strategy and operational code—i.e., a doctrine—to secure and advance Russia's vital interests. Further, this new doctrine would have to incorporate and exploit the new technologies of the Information Age, and in particular it would seek to establish Russian superiority in the new realm of cyberspace. The result has been what the Russians have called "hybrid warfare."

Russia has effectively deployed hybrid warfare in Ukraine. The most famous example was putting Russian soldiers and special forces who were in uniform but without insignia—the "little green men"— into Eastern Ukraine to engage in military operations to establish and protect the pro-Russian statelets and to produce various disruptions within Ukraine itself. But the Russians have also engaged in effective cyberwar operations there.

However, the most important theater where Russian hybrid warfare now poses a threat to the United States and its European allies is not Ukraine—which has receded into the miasma of an amputee state (which is exactly where Russia wants it). It is the Baltic states—and NATO members—of Estonia, Latvia, and Lithuania. Russia has long included in its strategic culture a theory and practice of tit for tat. That is, if an adversary power made an aggressive move into Russia's strategic realm, Russia would respond by making a comparable aggressive move into the adversary's strategic realm. Thus, when the United States extensively intruded into Ukraine in 2013-2014, this activated a process in which Russia would deploy its new doctrine and capabilities of hybrid warfare into the U.S. strategic realm. From the Russian perspective and for overdetermined reasons, the most attractive and most vulnerable target has been the Baltic states.

When the United States brought the Baltic states into NATO, it assumed a full treaty commitment to protect them against a Russian military attack, but it did so without any accompanying strategy whatever for how to deter such an attack or, if deterrence failed, how to defend these states against it. This was an especially pronounced example of the arrogance and ignorance of the U.S. elites at the time. Now, as Russia has increasingly employed this or that element of hybrid war against or around the Baltic states in the last three years, NATO has taken a number of ad hoc and disparate measures to construct some similitude of deterrence and defense. In essence, however, the Russians are placing a kind of sword of Damocles over the Baltic states, and Baltic security—and, beyond that, NATO credibility—hang by a thread. Perhaps all it would take would be another reckless move by the United States against some Russian vital interest, or perhaps a dramatic U.S. debacle or display of weakness in some other region (for example, in East Asia), and Russia would move against one or more of the Baltic states in a way that would reveal to all the world that the U.S. hegemonic system in Europe was now just a big bluff, a Potemkin alliance, or, as the Chinese would then would surely say, a paper tiger.

Revisionist China: The Three China Seas and Cyber Warfare

The chief architect of China's extraordinary economic growth, Deng Xiaoping, had counseled his colleagues in the Chinese leadership and their successors to steadily but quietly build China's economic and military strengths over a period of two or three decades, adopting during this time an outer appearance of accommodation and cooperation toward foreign powers, and especially toward the greatest and potentially most dangers of these powers, the United States. Then, when China had achieved economic and military superiority in important areas and ways, it could move much more actively and openly to achieve its international ambitions and even to revise the existing international system to better fit its own interests and conceptions. And during the 1990s and 2000s, China did indeed adhere to Deng's counsel, steadily but quietly growing in economic and military power while accommodating and cooperating along the way. Thus, China was welcomed into the World Trade Organization in 2001, with a chief supporter of this being the United States. And during most of the 2000s, there was much discussion of "China's peaceful rise," "China's soft power," and "China's charm offensive in Asia."

At the beginning of the 2010s, several events, particularly a series of maritime incidents in the South China Sea and the East China Sea, demonstrated that Chinese leaders had decided that the era of a more active and open assertion of China's interests and conceptions had at last arrived. And the chief theaters for this new policy have indeed been these two seas, especially with disputes over rights to a motley array of tiny islands, islets, reefs, and shoals within them. In the South China Sea, the disputes have been principally between China and the Philippines, and in the East China Sea, they have been principally between China and Japan. Thus, they involve two of the security-treaty allies of the United States and so represent an ongoing challenge to the U.S. hegemonic system in East Asia.

China has long considered the South China Sea, the East China Sea, and the Yellow Sea (which it sometimes calls the North China Sea) to be "the three China Seas" or "littoral China." In the Chinese conception of the natural shape of China, China will only be properly rounded out when these three seas are definitively part of China, and indeed are really Chinese lakes. Thus, China is not going to give up its claim to these seas and to all the tiny pieces of land within them, and its pressure to achieve its goal of making them part of China will only grow as its military strength to back up this pressure grows also. China's drive toward the three China Seas is thus acquiring the character of something like an irresistible force.

However, the United States for seventy years has seen its hegemonic system in East Asia to be a vital interest and also a central pillar of its broader conception of world order. Thus, the U.S. economic and political elites are not going to give up this system, nor the security guarantees to the Philippines and Japan, which the system entails. Moreover, the military strength to back up these security guarantees comes chiefly from the U.S. Navy and particularly from its great Seventh Fleet in the Western Pacific, whose raison d'etre since 1945 has been the defense of the region. The U.S. position in the Western Pacific, and thus in the three China seas, has therefore acquired the character of something like an immovable object.

China has been steadily developing its military forces, and especially its naval and anti-naval forces, so as to soon be able to demonstrate that it is indeed an irresistible force in regard to the three China Seas. Most obviously, the remarkably-named People's Liberation Army's Navy (PLAN) has procured a large number of conventional naval vessels, of which the most symbolic is an aircraft carrier, but of which the most important is a fleet of high-tech submarines. Even more important, however, is China's development of effective non-nuclear, anti-ship ballistic missiles (ASBMs) which could easily and quickly destroy any U.S. aircraft carriers operating within 500 miles of the three China Seas. The ASBMs are supplemented by a very large arsenal of lower-tech shore-to-ship missiles and aircraft, stationed along the long Chinese coast. Most important of all, however, is the already-demonstrated Chinese proficiency in the high technologies of cyber warfare. These include the capability to destroy U.S. satellites in space which are essential for the command and control of the U.S. Navy's battlefield operations, to intrude into and disrupt the electronic and computer operations of U.S. naval vessels, and to hack into and monitor the flow of U.S. naval information and intelligence.

The advancing Chinese capabilities in cyber warfare are facilitated by a long-standing Chinese policy and practice of "civil-military fusion." This simply means that the Chinese state ensures that innovations and developments in civilian or commercial products and processes, such as cyberspace technologies, are effectively translated into new military innovations and developments, and vice versa.

The U.S. Navy has tried to respond to these growing Chinese threats to its long-established dominance in the Western Pacific, including the three China Seas. One attempt was the "Air-Sea Battle Concept" announced in 2011, which was an obvious effort to replicate the success of the Army's old Air-Land Battle Doctrine of the 1980s, and which envisioned a non-nuclear war against China. And, like the Navy's old Forward Maritime Strategy of the 1980s, the Air-Sea Battle Concept put the Navy's aircraft carriers at the center of the battle. However, the Navy's computer war games soon demonstrated that the carriers would quickly be destroyed and that the war with China would very likely quickly escalate into a nuclear one. The Navy then quietly abandoned the Air-Sea Battle Concept, and thus far it has not found a new battle concept to put in its place.

More recently, the Navy has been conducting Freedom-of-Navigation Operations (FONOPS) in the South China Sea. These are supposed to contest and limit the Chinese claims to the sea and to the pieces of land within it. But these operations are merely at a tactical level and for only a temporary period, giving them a somewhat fitful appearance. In any event, they have not stopped the Chinese from expanding the land on and around the various pieces (thus building a "Great Wall of Sand") or from establishing useful structures and even military capabilities upon them.

The Navy also recognizes the threat posed to it by the Chinese developments in cyber warfare, and it has tried to develop counter-measures to them. But of course the Chinese continue to make even more advances. In effect, there is now a kind of cyber-warfare arms race going on between China and the United States. And thus far, the U.S. Navy, for the most part, remains behind.

In conclusion, then, the Chinese irresistible force is pressing more and more upon the U.S. hegemonic system in East Asia. And the American economic, political, and military elites, who for seventy years have seen that system to be an immovable object, give no indication that they are going to give way. At the present time, then, the prospects are for a great naval collision, and that all this will end badly for all.

The Advent of a Nuclear-Armed North Korea

North Korea's efforts to obtain a nuclear-weapons capability have presented a serious challenge to the United States since at least 1994, i.e., to the Bill Clinton, George W. Bush, Barack Obama, and now Donald Trump administrations. During the first three of these administrations, the United States consistently acted as if it believed that North Korea could be persuaded to give up its nuclear-weapons program by some combination of diplomatic negotiations, economic sanctions, and economic aid. On its part, North Korea sometimes temporarily acted as if this could be the case, but this turned out to be its tactic to gain more time in which to continue its growing and deepening nuclear program relentlessly. Indeed, there has never been any evidence that North Korea would ever abandon its pursuit of an invulnerable nuclear-weapons capability and deterrent. The idea that it would has always been a fantasy, and moreover an obvious fantasy.

Why, then, did all U.S. policymakers act as if they believed in this fantasy? One reason was that the U.S. economic and political elites—capitalist and liberal to their core—have almost always overestimated the power of negotiations, economic sanctions, and economic aid as instruments of U.S. foreign policy. Such actions are what U.S. elites do. But there was another, and more ominous, reason in this particular case. It was because the alternative to believing (or at least pretending to believe) in the fantasy was too horrible to contemplate.

North Korea was indeed in pursuit of an invulnerable deterrent in the ultimate form of nuclear weapons. But from the early 1990s, it already had an invulnerable deterrent of a sort, in the form of a massive, dispersed, and protected arsenal of conventional weapons. This arsenal consisted of more than 50,000 artillery pieces aimed at the South Korean capital city and megapolis of Seoul. A coordinated barrage from this artillery arsenal could destroy Seoul, kill more than ten million South Koreans, and also kill more than 28,000 American soldiers, all in less than 30 minutes. Any U.S. military attack on North Korea's embryonic nuclear deterrent could very likely detonate its already-existing conventional deterrent. And thus, for more than twenty years and through three successive U.S. presidential administrations, this conventional deterrent provided a protective umbrella over the coming, but still vulnerable, nuclear deterrent. And by 2016, this coming deterrent was just about ready to arrive. This was the military reality that the outgoing Obama administration presented to the incoming Trump administration as the most urgent and most grave problem on the new administration's agenda.

The Trump administration, such as it is, has characteristically oscillated between President Trump's bellicose rhetoric threatening U.S. military action and the administration's top national-security officials' predictable preference for yet more and better negotiations and economic sanctions. Neither of these two options provide any solid basis for hope.

There is, however, a third option, and this has been proposed by the Chinese. On the one hand, China would commit itself to use its great economic and political influence on North Korea to get it to first freeze and then, very gradually but steadily, roll back its nuclear and ballistic-missile programs. As compensation to North Korea, China would offer it a firm guarantee to serve as its nuclear deterrent. On the other hand, the United States would commit itself to the following: (1) no movement of U.S. or South Korean military forces into North Korea; (2) no change in the outer form of the North Korean regime (although the Chinese would gradually but steadily work to make its inner substance more moderate, i.e., more like the Chinese regime); (3) no deployment of U.S. nuclear weapons in South Korea; and (4) withdrawal of the U.S. THADD anti-missile system from South Korea (which China sees as directed as much against it as against North Korea).

Whatever the qualities of the current Chinese proposal, it has been rejected out of hand by the Trump administration and by the U.S. elites who are behind its top national-security officials. As they see it, the commitments that the United States would have to make are simply too great a departure from their long-standing U.S. hegemonic system in East Asia. And thus, at the present moment, the most likely path that the United States will follow will be more of the same, i.e., more and hopefully better negotiations and sanctions.

But the likely result of this will be that North Korea will indeed shortly achieve its invulnerable nuclear deterrent, complete with a capacity to strike the continental United States. This will suddenly hollow out the core of the U.S. security-treaty guarantees to Japan and South Korea. The likely result of this will be that Japan and South Korea will then decide to acquire their own independent nuclear deterrents. The impending North Korean nuclear deterrent may not produce a nuclear war, but it seems very likely to produce two new nuclear powers.

And so, the seventy-year life of the U.S. hegemonic system in East Asia does seem to be coming to an end. It may expire by the actions of China, in relatively slow motion in the South China Sea, at the southern reaches of the system. Or it may expire by the actions of North Korea, in relatively quick motion on the Korean Peninsula, at the northern reaches of the system. But, one way or the other, it now seems to be doomed.

The Economic Crisis: The Great Recession and the Responses of the U.S. Elites

During most of the 2000s, the only substantial challenges faced by the American economic and political elites seemed to be the failing wars in Afghanistan and Iraq. The military challenges that would be posed by revisionist Russia and China and a nuclear-armed North Korea then lay several years in the future. The economic systems of the United States and Europe seemed to be functioning very well, with healthy economic growth and low inflation. Their political systems also seemed to be working very well, with every major Western country ruled by those political parties that the elites loved so much, i.e., a long-established center-right party—such as the Republicans in the United States or the Christian Democrats in Germany—or a long-established center-left party—such as Labour in Britain or the Socialists in Spain. This was the benign condition of the United States and its allies all the way up through summer of 2008.

Beginning in early autumn of 2008, however, the U.S. global order suddenly began to change and, within a few years, to change utterly into a full-blown general crisis of the American empire. The changes began with the U.S. financial crisis, which soon metastasized into the U.S. economic crisis or Great Recession, which then produced in 2010 a dysfunctional U.S. political system with a Republican Congress stalemating a Democratic President. Moreover, versions of these phenomena soon migrated to Europe and were reproduced in the economic systems and political systems there, often in an even worse way than in the United States.

The U.S. economy slowly moved out of its crisis mode, but it continued to be marked by stagnation in many sectors and aspects—and in the economic situation of most Americans—right down to the presidential election year of 2016. The European economy continued even longer in a crisis mode, and it was then marked by even deeper stagnation than that in the United States, right down to the tumultuous years of elections and referenda of 2016-2017. In the lives of the majority of Americans and the majority of Europeans, the Great Recession had become the great and prolonged stagnation.

We could discuss this great economic challenge posed by the Great Recession to the U.S. global order in the same detail as we have discussed the various military challenges in the preceding sections of this chapter. However, we will limit our account of the Great Recession and its effects to the responses of the U.S. economic and political elites to this economic challenge.

As we have seen, at the time of the founding of the U.S. hegemonic system in Western Europe in the late 1940s, the U.S. economic and political elites had engaged in an act of creative imagination, or at least of wise and prudent politics. Although they themselves were internationalists and capitalists in their interests and convictions, they knew that they should make some kind of accommodation or compromise with the large number of nationalists and socialists within the Western European countries. Thus, when establishing their system, they provided for the continued existence of strong nation-states and of socialist or social-democratic parties. The nation-states, in turn, protected the interests of the European middle class and also, to a degree, of European industrial workers. And the socialist or social-democratic parties protected the interests of these workers even more.

At the same time, however, when the United States was institutionalizing its hegemonic system in Latin America, the U.S. economic and political elites had made no such accommodation or compromise. The middle class in most Latin American countries was relatively small and weak, as was the industrial working class. This meant that the number of nationalists and socialists within the Latin American countries was small. The U.S. elites could get their way in Latin America without having to permit either strong nation-states or socialist and social-democratic parties. As for the wide-spread populist movements in Latin America, these always sought to nationalize U.S. direct investment or to limit U.S. industrial imports into their countries, so the U.S. elites vigorously and vehemently opposed them.

As we have also seen, at the later time of the first general crisis of the American empire (the Great Stagflation), when that crisis was most acute within the United States itself, the U.S. economic and political elites engaged in a less creative and less demanding kind of accommodation or compromise than had their predecessors. They did this through the distinctive policies and practices of the Reagan administration. In dealing with the American middle class, and particularly with small businessmen, the administration gave them the reality of beneficial economic policies and also rhetoric about the virtues of the free market. However, in dealing with American industrial workers—who were falling behind because of the administration's economic policies— Reagan gave them soaring rhetoric about their patriotic or religious values and virtues. In effect, Reagan diminished their self-interest but enhanced their self-respect.

Still later, at the time of the second general crisis of the American empire (the Great Recession), when that crisis was acute in both the United States and Europe, the U.S. economic and political elites chose to respond to challenges in a very different way than their predecessors, either those thirty years before or those sixty years before. We will look in particular at their responses to the Great Recession and the ensuing great stagnation. But this is very much related to economic changes that had been underway since the Reagan administration. Indeed, these changes were in large measure the result of economic policies which that administration had used to resolve the challenges of the earlier Great Stagflation. For these policies set in train ever-growing disparities within American society in regard to income, wealth, values, and identities. These disparities have reached extreme levels during the second general crisis of the American empire. Indeed, they are themselves a major cause of that crisis.

The real core of the U.S. elites is the economic elites. As we have seen, ever since 1945 and the beginning of the American empire, they have been predominately internationalist and capitalist in their interests and their convictions. This is because they have earned their income and made their wealth much more in the international economy than in the national economy. Consequently, they prefer that there be no barriers, particularly national borders, restraining the intentional movement of economic assets and activities, sometimes called the factors of production. These factors have long been thought of as goods (as in trade), capital (investment), and labor (migration), although technology (knowledge) is now often included. The U.S. economic elite, through their representatives in the political elite, have developed and imposed a policy in regard to each of these factors, especially during the thirty years since the Reagan administration. These policies have worked to the benefit of the economic elite and to the detriment of a majority—probably a majority of at least 70 percent—of Americans, and the economic elite knows this.

Let us examine this elite's policy choices with respect to each of the three traditional factors of production. Perhaps the most agitated and divisive choice involves the free movement of labor, or the issue of immigration. One might have thought that a wise and prudent elite might have insisted upon ample immigration but would have agreed that it should be legal—and not illegal—immigration, i.e., regulated with a framework of law and order. After all, a regime of law and order has always been a vital interest of any economic elite. However, for at least forty years, the U.S. economic elite has refused to make any such accommodation or compromise with the American workers who are harmed by unrestrained, including illegal, immigration, and it has consistently got its way in the actual operation of immigration policy. Moreover, when the Great Recession and the ensuing great stagnation inflicted even more pain upon American workers, the economic elite merely doubled down on its immigration policy. Yet this is the same elite that cannot stop talking about "rules and norms" with respect to other policy issues.

Another divisive policy choice involves the free movement of goods, or the issue of "free trade." One might have thought that a wise and prudent elite might have insisted upon generally unrestrained trade, but that it would have agreed that there could be some exceptions for purposes of national security. After all, an effective military, with a robust and secure defense industrial base to maintain it, has always been a vital interest of any economic elite. However, for at least forty years, the U.S. economic elite has refused to make any such accommodation or compromises with American firms in such vital industries for defense as steel, shipbuilding, and electronics. The result is that these industries have been hollowed out so much in the United States itself that, for them, the U.S. defense industrial base is now in East Asia.

Yet another divisive policy choice involves the free movement of capital. Again, one might have thought that a wise and prudent elite might have insisted upon generally unrestrained capital outflows, but it would have agreed that the U.S. government should not actively promote them, i.e., that it would not actively intervene in foreign environments for capital. After all, this economic elite is always talking about the importance of free markets. Moreover, U.S. capital invested abroad usually does not contribute to the U.S. tax base, and a robust and broad tax base has always been a vital interest of any economic elite. However, for at least seventy years, the U.S. economic elite has successfully pressured agencies of the U.S. government, particularly the State Department and the Treasury Department, to in turn pressure foreign governments to open up their countries to American investors, and to protect those American investments once they are in those countries. And of course, American investments in foreign countries tend to create more jobs for foreign workers, and fewer jobs for American workers. Moreover, when the Great Recession and the ensuing great stagnation demonstrated a need for capital to create new and innovative economic sectors within the United States, the U.S. economic elite instead doubled down on its pressure in support of U.S. capital investments abroad.

A quite different economic policy choice involves the perennial issue of infrastructure. Again, one might have thought that a wise and prudent economic elite would have supported maintaining and improving the vital infrastructure that is all around them, especially highways, bridges, airports, seaports, power plants and grids, high-tech schools, and parks. But the U.S. economic elite is now so rich and powerful, so much above ordinary Americans, that it often does not need public infrastructure because it can buy its own infrastructure in such forms as gated communities, chauffeured limousines, private jets, elite schools, and country clubs. Thus, for at least thirty years, the U.S. economic elite has successfully blocked government spending which would be enough to maintain and improve American infrastructure. Moreover, when the Great Recession and the ensuing great stagnation demonstrated that this was the perfect time for a great increase in government spending on infrastructure (as had famously been done by the Franklin

Roosevelt administration during the Great Depression) in order to lift up the U.S. economy and to put it on a more solid base, the U.S. economic elite doubled down on its blocking of any such spending.

In short, the U.S. economic elite had repeatedly demonstrated during the past thirty years, and especially during the past ten years, that it cares nothing about the economic condition of the majority of Americans and of America itself. Rather, it has come to think about citizens of the United States in a way similar to how it has always thought about residents of Latin American countries. Indeed, as almost any conversation with members of this elite demonstrates, they do not even think of themselves as Americans. They care only about themselves, with their selves defined in the most narrow and exclusive of ways. The most crucial of all the fractures of today is the fractured relationship between the U.S. economic elite and everyone else. And that fracture will not be repaired until that elite is removed.

The Political Crisis: Governmental Dysfunction and the Responses of the U.S. Elites

Like the U.S. economic system, the U.S. political system seemed to be functioning relatively well during most of the 2000s. The Republican Party, and the conventional party elites within it, controlled both the Executive Branch and the Legislative Branch of the U.S. government, and this made for a superficial harmony. Of course, it was a harmony that produced policies that were beneficial for the Republican economic elite but which were detrimental to most Americans, and therefore to America as a whole.

The most obvious of these were the Bush administration's wars in Afghanistan and Iraq. The war in Iraq, in particular, had been promoted by representatives of the global energy corporations (e.g., Vice President Dick Cheney) and the major defense corporations (e.g., Secretary of Defense Donald Rumsfeld) in the administration, and these corporations were normally among the largest donors to the Republican Party. By 2007, the Iraq War had become such a debacle that it seemed very likely that this by itself would cause the Republicans to lose the presidential election of 2008, although not necessarily control of Congress.

However, the Republican economic elite had also used the Bush administration to enact economic policies that were beneficial to this elite but detrimental to most Americans. The reckless deregulation of financial transactions, particularly in the housing sector, had been promoted by representatives of the largest banks (e.g., Secretary of the Treasury Henry Paulson) and real-estate developers in the administration and in Congress, and these too were normally among the largest donors to the Republican Party. The housing bubble burst in early 2008, and this then metastasized into a full financial crisis in September 2008, which then quickly metastasized into a full economic crisis. Republican economic policies had become such a debacle that there was hardly any doubt that now the Republicans would lose control of both the presidency and Congress in the November elections. And this was indeed what happened.

The new Democratic administration of Barack Obama and the new Democratic Congress thus had a mandate in early 2009 to carry out policies that would have benefited most Americans. The most obvious, and the most demanded, example at the time was a massive infrastructure program, which would have been the perfect way to combat the deepening Great Recession. But this was not the choice of the Democratic economic elites, and infrastructure soon disappeared from the Democratic policy agenda. Rather, these elites preferred reform of health care in a way that would benefit the big insurance corporations, and this became Obamacare. And they preferred reform of the financial system in a way that would benefit big financial institutions, and this became the Dodd-Frank Act. Neither of these two Democratic policies did much to help the majority of Americans, particularly the American middle class. One political result was the Tea Party movement, which opposed them both. And the next political result was that the Democrats lost control of Congress in the elections of 2010. And then the next political result was that a Republican Congress would stalemate a Democratic President for the next six years, right down to the elections of 2016. These years of political stalemate became years of governmental dysfunction, so much so that all the liberal-ideological talk in the 1990s-2000s about the superiority of the U.S. political system as a universal model was now revealed to the rest of the world to be hypocritical, nonsensical, and delusional.

Despite the failed wars, economic stagnation, and political dysfunction which their policies had produced, the U.S. economic and political elites in 2015 looked forward to 2016 being an election year like other election years, i.e., with Republican elite candidates contesting Democratic elite candidates, and with the economic elites winning either way. In particular, the Republican elites assumed that Jeb Bush, the perfect establishment representative, would be their presidential nominee, and the Democratic elites assumed that Hillary Clinton, that other perfect establishment representative, would be their nominee. None of the elites had any concern about the deep disparities and divisions that had developed between themselves and the majority of American voters. Rather, they assumed that these voters would simply have no alternative to voting for an elite candidate, as had been the case with every presidential election since 1972. Again, they had come to think of citizens of the United States in a way similar to how they have always thought about residents of Latin American countries.

In reality, the widening in American society between the elites and the majority had now produced a fracture within each party between its elites and its base, between its donor class and its voter class. This was soon revealed during the primary phase of the 2016 election. Large numbers from the Republican base voted for the anti-elite candidate, Donald Trump, against Jeb Bush and any other elite candidate, so much so that Trump eventually, and amazingly, became the Republican nominee. Similarly, large numbers from the Democratic base voted for the anti-elite candidate, Bernie Sanders, so much so that he came amazingly close to being the Democratic nominee.

When Hillary Clinton lost to Donald Trump in the general election, most of the U.S. economic and political elites also lost, and this was the first presidential election in which they had lost in more than a century and a half. It was not surprising, therefore, that they would conclude that elections were symbolic politics for the base, but that the real politics was about government and the policies that it produced. Thus, after Trump's election, both the Democratic and Republican elites determined that there would never be a functioning Trump administration capable of implementing anti-elite policies. Rather, they would conduct an elite-backed insurgency against the anti-elite insurgent candidate who (temporarily) occupied the White House.

Thus, the U.S. political system since 2017 has been characterized by multiple fractures—fractures between the Democratic Party and the Republican Party, fractures within the Republican Party, first between the Republican Congress and the Republican administration, and then merely between the Republican Senate and the Republican administration, fractures within the Republicans in Congress between the establishment leadership and majority and an anti-establishment minority, and even fractures within the Republican administration between officials who represent the establishment or elites, who are a majority of officials, and those who represent Trump's electoral base, and Trump himself, who are a minority. And so, the political events in the United States have now reached the point that much of the world not only sees the U.S. political ideology to be hypocritical, nonsensical, and delusional, but they now see that the U.S. political system itself is fatuous, preposterous, and dangerous.

* * * * *

In the past century and a half, the world has seen the rise, triumph, decline, and death of quite a few empires. The greatest of these empires were distinguished by a great imperial state professing—and sometimes possessed by—a great ideology. One of these was the British Empire, whose fullest development may be dated from Disraeli's proclamation in 1876 of Queen Victoria as Empress of India to the independence of India and Pakistan in 1947. Another was the German empire, which was proclaimed in the Palace of Versailles in 1871 as the Second Reich, which later mutated into the National-Socialist Third Reich, and died a violent death in Berlin in 1945. Yet another was the Russian empire, which actually reached its fullest development under the communist regime of the Soviet Union. This regime began with the Russian Revolution in 1917, and it expired with the collapse and break-up of the Soviet Union in 1991. Finally, there has been, of course, the American empire, which existed in a prototypical form in Latin America before the Second World War, but whose fullest form we have dated from 1945-1947.

As it turns out, and as we have dated them, the British, German, and Russian empires each had a lifespan of a little more than seventy years, rather like the biblical lifespan for a man of three-score-and-ten. It would not be completely surprising, then, if something like this will prove to be true of the American empire as well. Moreover, two of these empires died with something of a whimper—the British and the Soviet—but one of them—the German—certainly died with a bang. We do not yet know which of these will be how the American empire will pass away.

PART I

IDEOLOGY

Chapter Two

The Protestant Deformation:
The Source of the Ideological Tradition

Protestantism as the Unknown Explanation

FOREIGN-POLICY ANALYSTS HAVE DEBATED for decades about the relative influence of different factors in the shaping of American foreign policy. National interests, domestic politics, economic interests, and liberal ideology have each been seen as the major explanation for the peculiarities of the American conduct of foreign affairs. But although numerous scholars have stressed the importance of realism, idealism, capitalism, or liberalism, until recently almost no one has thought that Protestantism—the dominant religion in the United States—was worth consideration. In the 20th century and since, it has seemed abundantly clear that one could (and should) write the history of American foreign policy with no reference to Protestantism whatsoever.[1]

In contrast, we will argue that American foreign policy has been and continues to be shaped by the Protestant origins of the United States, but with a twist. For the Protestantism that has shaped American foreign policy over two centuries has not been the original religion but a series of successive departures from it down the scale of what might be called the Protestant declension. We are now at the end point of this declension, and the Protestantism that has shaped American foreign policy in our time is a distinctive heresy of the original religion, not the Protestant Reformation but the Protestant Deformation. When the United States became the sole superpower after 1991, this Protestant Deformation entered into its greatest, even global influence. But because it is such a peculiar religion, and indeed is correctly seen as a fundamental and fatal threat by all the other religions, its pervasive sway has generated intense resistance and even international conflict. The most intense resistance and conflict has come from Islamism.

The Protestant Reformation versus Hierarchy and Community

Protestantism was a protest, a protest against the form that the Christian religion had taken in the Roman Catholicism of the late Middle Ages and the Renaissance. The Reformation was an effort to reform the Christian religion back to the original faith expressed in the New Covenant or New Testament of the Bible. (The word "testament" means "covenant.") The faith of the New Testament had itself been a protest against the form that the Jewish religion had taken in Pharisaic Judaism at the time of the early Roman Empire. Although the central feature of Christianity, Jesus Christ as the Messiah, was a radical break with traditional Judaism, early Christianity was also in part an effort to reform the Jewish religion back to the original faith expressed in the Old Covenant or Old Testament of the Bible.

The Protestant reformers protested against numerous features of the Roman Catholic Church, including such familiar ones as the authority of the Pope, the role of the Virgin Mary and the meaning of indulgences. But the really central and fundamental issues involved the way that the Christian believer reached a state of salvation and the roles that the priestly hierarchy and the parish community played in the process. The Roman Catholic Church taught that the Christian believer reached salvation through the mediation of the priestly hierarchy and through participation in the parish community. The hierarchy and the community in combination yielded the surest path to salvation, which was participation in communal sacraments and rituals that were administered by the hierarchy.

Similarly, Pharisaic Judaism had taught that the devout Jew reached holiness through observance of the Law and the Commandments, which was aided by the mediation of the Jewish priesthood and through participation in the Jewish community. Here, too, the combination of hierarchy and community yielded the highest degree of holiness, observance which included participation in communal sacrifices and rituals that were administered by the priesthood in the Temple in Jerusalem.

The Protestant reformers protested against the idea that the believer achieves salvation through a hierarchy or a community, or even the two in combination. Although many Protestant reformers accepted hierarchy and community for certain purposes, such as church governance and collective undertakings, they rejected them for the most important of purposes: reaching the state of salvation. Rather, the believer receives salvation through an act of grace by God. This grace produces in its recipient the faith in God and in salvation that converts him or her into a believer.

The believer can achieve greater knowledge of God, however, through reading of the Holy Scriptures. The Protestant reformers placed great emphasis on the Word, as evidenced in the written words of the Bible. But this reading did not necessarily require the interpretations of a hierarchy or a community. Indeed, these might actually impede the right interpretation of the Bible by the individual believer.

All religions are unique, but Protestantism is more unique than all the others. No other religion is so critical of hierarchy and community, or of the traditions and customs that go with them. Indeed, most other religions are based upon hierarchy or community (in addition to Roman Catholicism, also Eastern Orthodoxy, Islam, Hinduism, Confucianism, and even, to a degree, Buddhism). At its doctrinal base, however, Protestantism is anti-hierarchy and anti-community. Thus, Protestantism is a double rejection in a double sense. It is a rejection of both its experience of Roman Catholicism and its image of Pharisaic Judaism, and it is a rejection of both hierarchy and community.

The Protestant reformers sought to remove hierarchy and community so that the individual Christian believer could have a direct relationship with God. More accurately and subtly, so that the individual believer could have a relationship with God directly through the second person of the Holy Trinity, Jesus Christ, and so that he or she could receive salvation from God directly from the third person of the Holy Trinity, the Holy Spirit.

The removal of hierarchy and community, traditions and customs—of any earthly intermediaries between the individual and God—strips away, at least for the most important purposes, any local, parochial, cultural, or national characteristics of the believer. In principle, grace, faith, and salvation can be received by anyone in the world; they are truly universal or catholic in the original sense of the latter term. The Protestant reformers saw the vast variety of cultures and nations through a universal perspective, one that was even more universal than that of the Roman Catholic Church.

The Protestant Churches and Church Governance

Despite their doctrinal rejection of hierarchy and community for the purpose of salvation, many Protestant churches maintained some kind of hierarchy for purposes of church governance. The most hierarchical were those Protestant churches ruled by bishops and archbishops—the Lutherans (Germany and the Scandinavian countries), Anglicans (England), Episcopalians (the United States), and Methodists (England and the United States). (The word "Episcopal" is derived from the Greek word for bishop.) Indeed, the organization of some of the churches in Europe, particularly the Anglican and Lutheran state churches, looked very much like the organization of the Roman Catholic Church, but with the Pope removed and replaced by a "defender of the faith" in the form of the ruler of the state. The secular and political counterpart of this form of church governance, for both Roman Catholicism and this version of Protestantism, was of course monarchy.

Less hierarchical were those Protestant churches ruled by elders—the Calvinists (the Netherlands) and the Presbyterians (Scotland and the United States). (The word "Presbyterian" is derived from the Greek word for elder.) Indeed, this form of organization looked rather like the organization of Pharisaic (and later) Judaism around councils of rabbis.

Here, the secular and political counterpart of this form of church governance was aristocracy or oligarchy.

Least hierarchical were those Protestant churches ruled by the congregation themselves. Many of these were in the United States—the Congregationalists, the Baptists, and a vast variety of American denominational and, especially, non-denominational churches. Here, of course, the secular and political counterpart of this form of church governance was democracy.

Despite their differences in regard to church governance and also in regard to community emphasis, however, all Protestant churches reject hierarchy and community as the means to salvation. At the level of fundamental theology and doctrine, Protestantism denies that hierarchy and community are of fundamental importance. Indeed, Protestants often assert that hierarchy and community, along with the traditions and customs that go with them, are obstacles to what is of fundamental importance—the way that the individual Christian believer reaches the state of salvation.

The Protestant Spread into Secular Life

In the three centuries after the Reformation, this Protestant rejection of hierarchy and community in regard to salvation spread to their rejection in regard to other domains of life as well. First, some Protestant churches came to reject hierarchy and community in regard to church governance and collective undertakings. This was especially the case in the new United States, where the conjunction of the open frontier and the disestablishment of state churches enabled the flourishing of new unstructured and unconstraining denominations.

By the beginning of the 19th century, the Protestant rejection of hierarchy and community had spread to important arenas of temporal or secular life. Again, this was especially the case in the new United States. In the economic arena, the elimination of hierarchy (monopoly or oligopoly) and community (guilds or trade restrictions) meant the establishment of the free market. In the political arena, the elimination of hierarchy (monarchy or aristocracy) and community (traditions and customs) meant the establishment of liberal democracy.

However, the free market could not be so free, nor the liberal democracy so liberal, that they became anarchy. Although they could no longer be ordered by hierarchy and community, by tradition and custom, they had to be ordered by something. That something reflected the Protestant emphasis on written words and was a version of the written covenant between individual Protestant believers. In the economic arena, this was the written contract; in the political arena, it was the written constitution.

The Protestant Reformation was giving birth to what by the early 20th century would become the American Creed. The fundamental elements of that secular creed—liberal democracy, free markets, constitutionalism, and the rule of law—were already fully in place in the United States of the early 19th century.

This outer spread of the Protestant rejection of hierarchy and community from the arena of salvation to the arenas of economics and politics was driven by a particular inner dynamic, or rather decline, within the Protestant faith itself. Today, half a millennium after the beginning of the Protestant Reformation in 1517, we can discern six stages of what might be called the Protestant declension.

The Six Stages of the Protestant Declension

1. <u>Salvation by grace.</u> At the personal level the original Protestant (and the original Christian) experience is that of a direct, loving, and saving relationship between the believer and God. This direct relationship and state of salvation is brought about by God through his sovereign love or <u>grace</u>, and not by the person through his own efforts or <u>works</u>. This is the experience of being "born again" into a new life.

Obviously, anything that could stand in the way of this direct relationship, e.g., any intermediaries, traditions, or customs, must be swept aside. The original Protestant and born-again Christian experiences this new life as an open field, a blank slate, a <u>tabula rasa</u>. This enables him or her to also experience a release of previously-constrained energies and an intense focus of them upon new undertakings. This in part explains the great energy and efficacy of some newly-Christian persons. When the number of such persons is greatly multiplied, as it was at the time of the Reformation, it also in part explains the great energy and efficacy of some newly-Protestant nations (e.g., the Netherlands, England, and Sweden in the 16th and 17th centuries).

2. Grace evidenced through work. However, a serious problem soon arises, within a generation and indeed with the next generation. The children of the original born-again Protestants are born into a Protestant family and church, but they themselves may not be born-again Protestants, i.e., they may not have personally experienced grace, and the direct relationship with God and the state of salvation that it brings. As Max Weber famously discussed in his The Protestant Ethic and the Spirit of Capitalism, this can give rise to great anxiety about just what kind of state that the second-generation Protestants are in.

For persons in some Protestant churches, especially the Anglican and Lutheran state churches of Europe but even the Episcopal and Lutheran churches in America, there was something of a solution close at hand. These churches had remained hierarchical (but with the Pope removed and replaced with the state monarch) and even somewhat communal. Perhaps, in some way that was not theologically clear but was psychologically reassuring, the state of salvation could be reached by participation in the rituals and works of the church. In these churches, therefore, the focus upon grace gradually shifted in practice to a focus upon works, as had been the case in the Roman Catholic Church before the Protestant Reformation.

However, for persons in other Protestant churches, especially those known as the Reformed churches—the Calvinist churches of Europe and the Presbyterian and Congregational churches in America—the solution to the dilemma of the Protestants who were born-in but not born-again had to be a different one. The stricter Reformed theology of these churches did not easily permit the fading-away of the necessity for grace. Further, their relative absence of hierarchical and communal features meant that they had a less-developed structure for the exercise of rituals and works. And yet, without the personal experience of grace, what evidence was there that the second-generation or birth-right Protestants had received it?

As Weber discussed, the evidence for grace became a particular and peculiar kind of work, not the performance of works in the church, but the success of work in the world. This was how the Protestant ethic became the capitalist spirit. Because the Reformed churches had reformed away the legitimacy of hierarchy, community, tradition, and custom, this work in the world could be unconstrained by these obstacles. Thus, this second-generation and later-generation version of Reformed Protestants also could experience worldly life and worldly work as an open field, a blank slate, a tabula rasa. This enabled them also to experience a release of previously-constrained energies and an intense focus of those energies upon new undertakings. Indeed, this version of Protestantism in its worldly work was so focused that it became methodical and systematic in ways that had never been seen previously. This also in part explains the great energy and efficacy of some second-generation and later-generation Reformed Protestants. Again, when the number of such persons was greatly multiplied, it also in part explains the great energy and efficacy of established Protestant nations, not just for the second generation, but for several generations thereafter (e.g., the Netherlands and Sweden until the 18th century; England, Scotland, and America until the late 19th century).

3. Salvation by works. After several generations of this kind of Reformed Protestantism, a certain Protestant culture, even traditions and customs, developed. The number of Protestants who had experienced the culture but who had not experienced the grace greatly increased. Finally, even in the Reformed churches (Calvinist, Presbyterian, Congregational), the idea of the necessity of grace began to fade. Work in the world was no longer seen as a sign of grace but as a good in itself. Works as a good became a new version of good works.

4. The unitarian transformation. As the focus on grace faded, so too there was among some a fading of the focus upon the agencies of grace, Jesus Christ and the Holy Spirit, the second and the third persons of the Holy Trinity. Thus Reformed Protestantism, with its highly-articulated trinitarian doctrine, turned into unitarianism, with its abstract concept of a Supreme Being or Divine Providence. Unitarianism was an actual denomination, complete with its own churches, but it was also a more widely-held theology and philosophy. This was the stage in the Protestant declension that some of the American political elite, including some of the Founding Fathers, had reached by the beginning of the

19th century. At least the public documents of that time frequently made reference to the Supreme Being or Divine Providence and rarely to Jesus Christ or the Holy Spirit.

5. The American Creed. The fifth stage in the Protestant declension was reached when the abstract and remote God, the Supreme Being or Divine Providence, disappeared altogether. Now the various Protestant creeds were replaced by the American Creed, which reached its fullest articulation in the first half of the 20th century. The elements of the American Creed were free markets and equal opportunity, free elections and liberal democracy, and constitutionalism and the role of the law. The American Creed definitely did not include as elements hierarchy, community, tradition, and custom. Although the American Creed was not itself Protestant, it was clearly the product of a Protestant culture and was a sort of secularized version of Protestantism.

6. Universal human rights. The sixth and final stage in the Protestant declension was reached only in the 1970s. Now the American Creed was replaced by the universal conception of human rights or, more accurately, the elements of the American Creed were generalized into universal goods. Finally, in the 1990s, with the collapse of the Soviet Union and communist ideology, along with the stagnation of what had been the German social market and Japanese organized capitalism, all of the familiar alternatives to American economic and political conceptions seemed to have been discredited. America had seemingly brought the world to "the end of history."

Protestant Pluralism and the American Creed

At its birth at the end of the 18th century, the United States was populated by a wide variety of Protestants. They were found in a wide variety of churches ranging through Episcopalians, Methodists, Presbyterians, Congregationalists, Baptists, and Unitarians. And they were found on a wide spectrum of the Protestant declension ranging through its first four stages from born-again Christians to unitarians. No one church and no one stage represented a majority of the American population (or even a majority of that part of the white male population which comprised the only persons with the right to vote).

This condition of Protestant pluralism meant that public pronouncements on religious themes that honored citizens situated in one church or stage were just as likely to offend those situated in another. This drove public officials to a religious rhetoric of the least-common, and least-offensive, denominator. This was the rhetoric of Unitarianism, which was the fourth stage of the Protestant declension. Not all American Protestants could believe in the full implications of each of the three persons of the Holy Trinity, but all of them could believe that God was a supreme being and that providence was divine. The adoption of this unitarian rhetoric was facilitated by the fact that some of the political elite already believed it.

In the early 19th century, there were periodic religious revivals among portions of the American population. These moved some Protestants back up the scale to higher stages of belief. (The religious revival in America during the 1970s-1980s did the same.) However, this did not change the religious rhetoric in public pronouncements. The logic of religious pluralism, reinforced by the substantial numbers of Roman Catholics and even Jews immigrating to the United States in the 1840s and after, continued to drive public officials even further toward the rhetoric of the least-common and least-offensive denominator. This would be a public rhetoric that, while it would use conceptions that were congruent and congenial to the Protestant ones, would make almost no references to religion at all. In regard to economic matters, the central conception was the free market; in regard to political matters, it was liberal democracy. By the early 19th century, most Americans had come to believe that the only legitimate form of economics was the free market, ordered by written contracts, and that the only legitimate form of politics was liberal democracy, ordered by a written constitution. This was the mentality, really ideology, that was described so brilliantly and so beautifully by that young Frenchman who was both an aristocrat and a liberal, Alexis de Tocqueville, in his <u>Democracy in America</u> (1834). The full development of these ideas would eventually lead to the fifth stage of the Protestant declension, the American Creed.

The Protestant Declension and American Foreign Policy

During the 19th century, these transformations down the scale of Protestant declension did not have much impact upon American foreign policy, even though they had tremendous impact upon American domestic politics (including the origins of the Civil War). As long as the United States was focused upon the great task of westward expansion across the North American continent and as long as it was on the western margins of the international competition between the European great powers, the American ideology of the free market and liberal democracy could have little effect upon international affairs. Its chief foreign impact was upon the native American tribes (which, however, were sometimes called "nations") and upon the Mexican population annexed by the United States after the Mexican War.

With the beginning of the 20th century, this all changed. The grand project of continental expansion was completed and was replaced within a decade by a new project of overseas expansion, at first into the Caribbean, Central America, and the Pacific. The era of the United States being on the margins of the great-power competition was followed, after the U.S. victory in the Spanish-American War and its construction of the Great White Fleet, by an era where the United States was clearly one of the great powers.

In the 19th century the United States had few opportunities to bring this particular ideology into its foreign policy. But when, at the beginning of the 20th century, it suddenly became a great power, it had many opportunities to do so. And for some Americans, most obviously President Woodrow Wilson but also most U.S. presidents from Franklin Roosevelt to Barack Obama, opportunity has been redefined as necessity.

The Fourth Stage of the Protestant Declension: Wilsonianism as a Protestant Heresy

Woodrow Wilson was a Presbyterian and the son of a Presbyterian clergyman. His pronouncements on public policy, however, seem to have more in common with Unitarianism than with Presbyterianism. He seems to have believed that he was carrying out God's will, but he does not seem to have given much thought to the other persons of the Trinity, Jesus Christ and the Holy Spirit. As we have already discussed, this is not surprising from someone who was president of a vast nation which was characterized by a wide range of religious diversity and by now even by a substantial amount of secularization.

Wilson's political identity was as a Progressive and his political program was known as "the New Freedom." These were congruent and isomorphic with his religious identity as a Presbyterian and his religious actuality as a unitarian. Wilson believed deeply in free markets, ordered by written contracts, and in liberal democracy, ordered by a written constitution. He also seems to have believed that God meant for him to advance these ideals both at home and abroad, e.g., "to make the world safe for democracy." Conversely, Wilson had almost no sensitivity or sympathy toward those non-Protestant conceptions of hierarchy, community, tradition, and custom.

These political and economic conceptions of Wilson were repeatedly expressed in his foreign policies: (1) his notion that the problems of Latin American countries could be solved by formal elections, written constitutions, and the enforcement of contracts; (2) his focus upon freedom of the seas, international law, and democratic ideology as he led the United States into the First World War; (3) his relentless opposition to the Habsburg Monarchy, the very embodiment of hierarchy and community, tradition, and custom (and the only Roman Catholic great power), in the name of self-determination, which was an individualist or even Protestant conception inappropriately applied to a communal or even Catholic condition; and (4) his insistence upon the abstraction of collective security, as written down in the Covenant of the League of Nations, as the solution to the perennial problem of international conflict.

Each of these notions seemed normal and obvious to Wilson and to millions of other Americans. Indeed, in their updated versions, they seem normal and obvious to millions of Americans today. They only seem normal and obvious, however, to a people growing up in a culture shaped at its origins by Protestantism, rather than by some other religion. It is difficult to imagine a statesman who was Eastern Orthodox, Muslim, Hindu, Confucian, Buddhist, or even Roman Catholic coming up with these notions so consistently and continuously as did Wilson and his fellow Americans. It is even difficult to imagine a statesman of secular convictions but growing up in a culture that was shaped by one of these other religions developing this particular ideology. The ideologies of such democratic figures as Jawaharlal Nehru, Sun Yat-sen, and Konrad Adenauer were quite different.

The Fifth Stage of the Protestant Declension: The American Creed in 20th-Century American Foreign Policy

The last and grandest of Wilson's projects, the League of Nations, was of course a failure, being rejected in 1920 by the U.S. Senate and by millions of other Americans as well. But most of Wilson's Protestant-like notions became permanent features of American foreign policy.

It is a cliché of American diplomatic history that the United States "retreated into isolationism" after the First World War. In fact, this U.S. retreat or withdrawal really only applied to Europe (and there only in regard to security and military matters). In other regions of the world, particularly Latin America and East Asia, the United States continued and even expanded its presence in the 1920s under Republican administrations in much the same way as it had under the Wilson administration. Then, under the impact of the Great Depression of the 1930's, the administration of Franklin Roosevelt adopted new approaches toward Latin America (the Good Neighbor Policy and an end to U.S. military interventions) and East Asia (a renewed focus upon the Open Door Policy and China). But throughout the interwar period, American foreign policy in these two developing regions was dominated by the promotion of the central elements of what was by now the fully-developed American Creed: free markets and equal opportunity, free elections and liberal democracy, and constitutionalism and the rule of law.

A central reason why the United States withdrew from European security matters after 1920 was because Americans had come to believe that they could not make over the European nations—economically developed, militarily strong, and politically independent—in America's image, i.e., they could not convert the European nations to the American Creed. In Latin America and East Asia—economically underdeveloped, militarily weak (except Japan), and politically dependent—it was a different story. Because of the weakness and therefore openness of these countries, it seemed plausible that they might actually be converted to

American ways. Of course, this could only seem plausible if the cultural and social features, the traditions and customs, of these countries could be dismissed or ignored. But these features were formed around such religions as Catholicism and Confucianism, which, to the Protestant mind of Americans, seemed obviously retrograde and irrational. With just a little persuasive effort on the part of Americans, this would become obvious to Latin Americans and East Asians as well. Then they too would adopt some version of the American Creed.

Thus, a characteristic pattern had developed in the conduct of American foreign policy in peacetime. When a country was strong in relation to the United States, particularly if it was a great power, American foreign policy tended to be marked by either prudence or distance, by either "realism" or "isolationism." The United States acted toward that country in ways similar to those of the other great powers. In contrast, however, when a country was weak in relation to the United States, American foreign policy was marked by the drive to convert that country to free markets and liberal democracy, by "idealism" (really secularized Protestantism). The United States sought to remake that country in the image of the American Creed.

A problem would arise, however, if the United States, while seeking to convert a particular weak region, came into conflict with a particular great power. Then the idealism and the insistence would come into conflict with the realism and the prudence. This of course is what happened from 1931 to 1941 when the American vision for China came into conflict with the expansion of Japan. The result was the U.S. entry into the Second World War.

In the course of that war, Franklin Roosevelt mobilized and deployed many of the same notions that Woodrow Wilson had promoted during the First World War. Formally, Roosevelt was an Episcopalian, whereas Wilson had been a Presbyterian, and his foreign policies were rather more realistic and pragmatic than those of Wilson. In their actual religious beliefs, however, they both seem to have been some kind of unitarian, and in their wartime policies they both vigorously advanced free trade and liberal democracy. And, of course, Roosevelt brought about at the end of the war the resurrection of Wilson's League of Nations in the form of the United Nations Organization.

After the Second World War, the characteristic pattern of American foreign policy—"realism" toward the strong and "idealism" toward the weak—developed further. When the United States was dealing with weak nations (and in the post-war era this was the condition of the European states and Japan), American foreign policy sought to remake them into an image resembling the American Creed. When the United States was dealing with great powers (in the Cold-War era this was first the Soviet Union and later also China), however, American foreign policy was different. An interim period of conflict with these communist powers over their weaker neighbors (Central and Eastern Europe for the Soviet Union; Korea, Taiwan, and Southeast Asia for China) was followed by the establishment of a rough division of the contested region into spheres of influence, and the ensuing U.S. policy tended to be marked by realism, be it prudence (toward the Soviet Union) or distance (toward China until 1973).

During the Cold War, another characteristic of American foreign policy also reached its fullest development. This was the peculiarly American focus upon international organizations as the solution to international problems, a feature that we have already noted in Wilson's League of Nations and Roosevelt's United Nations Organization. This characteristic also seems to have roots in Protestantism.

International Organizations and Protestant Conceptions

When great powers have become great enough to create a sphere of influence composed of themselves and several smaller states (usually neighbors in their own region), they have normally established some kind of international association which has served to legitimize and institutionalize their hegemony. These associations have usually been termed "confederations" or "leagues." Thus, Napoleon's France established the Confederation of the Rhine, Metternich's Austria the German Confederation and the Italian League, Bismarck's Prussia the North German Federation, and twentieth-century Britain the Commonwealth of Nations. This variety of examples demonstrates that great-power status and interest in themselves are a sufficient explanation for a great power establishing an international association.

In the history of international associations, however, the United States has a unique place. It has established more of them than any other great power, and indeed it has established more than all of the other great powers of the modern era combined. It has established them with a greater range of functions—economic as well as security—than the other great powers. It has established them with a greater degree of complexity, resulting not just in associations but in organizations or even institutions. And it has sought to establish not just organizations with a regional scope but also those with a global or universal scope as well. International organizations are clearly a central part of the American way, the American Creed, in foreign policy.

Much of the U.S. focus upon international organizations can be explained by a realist theory of U.S. foreign policy. As the greatest of the great powers, it is to be expected that the United States would establish international organizations wherever its power or hegemony has extended. At first, this was only Latin America (the Pan-American Union, followed by the Organization of American States). After the First World War and then again after the Second World War, it briefly seemed to be the world itself (the League of Nations, followed by the United Nations, the International Monetary Fund, and the World Bank). Then, during the Cold War, U.S. power extended into several regions—Western Europe (the North Atlantic Treaty Organization), the Middle East (the short-lived Middle East Treaty Organization), and Southeast Asia (the Southeast Asian Treaty Organization).

With the end of the Cold War and with the end of any other great-power competitor, the United States returned to the construction of international organizations with a global or universal scope (a new economic institution, the World Trade Organization, and an expanded role for the United Nations). But it also continued to develop regional organizations (the creation of the North American Free Trade Area and the expansion of NATO). And it articulated an elaborate ideology about the moral superiority of "international institutions" and "rules and norms."

The establishment of these myriad international organizations in particular places and at particular times can be explained by the particular opportunities for and limitations on American power. Still, the consistency and continuity of the American practice with international organizations does seem extraordinary. Americans clearly have both a drive and a gift for international organizations that goes beyond that found in other nations that have been great powers. For these other nations, the most natural way of organizing international relations between a great power and smaller ones is through some sort of explicit hierarchy, ordered by customary deference. For Americans, the most natural way is through some sort of formal equality ordered by a formal treaty. This American way is the only way that is congruent and iso-morphic with the Protestant conceptions of ordering relations between individuals.

The American focus upon international organizations represents a bridge between the fifth stage of the Protestant declension, the Ameri-can Creed, and the sixth stage, universal human rights. In the moment from one stage to the next, it almost seems that international organiza-tions are transformed from being a means by which U.S. policymakers advance American foreign policy to being a means by which they advance abstract universal values.

The Sixth Stage of the Protestant Declension: Universal Human Rights as the Protestant Deformation

In the 1970s, American political and intellectual elites began to pro-mote the notion of universal human rights as a fundamental goal of American foreign policy. This conception took the central elements of the American Creed and carried them to a logical conclusion and to a universal extent.

It was a conjunction of factors that caused American elites to embrace universal human rights at that time. First, those elites who had condemned the U.S. intervention in the Vietnam War needed to develop a new doctrine for American foreign policy to replace the doctrine of containment, which in their eyes was now discredited. Sec-ondly, the surge in U.S. trade and investment in newly-industrializing countries beyond Europe and Japan caused some elites to see a need to develop a new doctrine for American foreign policy that could be applied to a wide variety of different (and often difficult) countries and cultures. Most importantly, however, were changes within the American people themselves. America was changing from an industrial to a post-industrial economy and thus from a producer to a consumer mentality. It was also changing from a modern to a post-modern society and thus from an ideology of "possessive individualism" to an ideology of "expressive individualism." The new post-industrial, consumer, post-modern, expressive-individualist America was embodied in the baby-boomer generation and the "me generation." For them, the rights (and definitely not the responsibilities) of the individual (and definitely not of the community) were the highest, indeed the only good.

In the new ideology, human rights are thus seen as the rights of individuals. The individual's rights are independent of any hierarchy or community, traditions or customs, in which that individual might be situated. This means that human rights are applicable to any individual anywhere in the world, i.e., they are universal, and not merely communal or national. There is thus a close logical connection between the rights of the individual and the universality of those rights. Individual rights are universal rights, and universal rights are individual rights.

The ideology of individualism thus reaches into all aspects of society; it is a total philosophy. The result appears to be totally opposite from the totalitarianism of the state, but it is a sort of totalitarianism of the self. Both totalitarianisms are relentless in breaking down intermediate bodies and mediating institutions that stand between the individual and the highest powers or the widest forces. With the totalitarianism of the state, the highest powers are the authorities of the nation state; with the totalitarianism of the self, the widest forces are the agencies of the global economy.

Individualism—with its contempt for and protest against all hierarchies, communities, traditions, and customs—represents the logical conclusion and the ultimate extreme of the secularization of the Protestant religion. The Holy Trinity of original Protestantism, the Supreme Being of unitarianism, even the American nation of the American Creed have all been dethroned and replaced by the imperial self. The long declension of the Protestant Reformation has reached its end point in the Protestant Deformation. The Protestant Deformation is a Protestantism without God, a reformation against all forms.

The foreign policy of the Protestant Deformation is universal human rights. But during the Cold War, there were constraints on the full pursuit of this project. As long as the United States was engaged in its great bipolar struggle with the Soviet Union and communist ideology, it had to show some respect for and make some concessions to the particularities of hierarchy, community, traditions, and customs in the countries that it needed as allies. These concessions were often departures from the normal U.S. promotion of free markets and liberal democracy. In Western Europe and Japan, the United States accepted restrictions on free markets while continuing to promote liberal democracy. In Latin America and Southeast Asia, in contrast, the United States accepted violations of liberal democracy while continuing to promote free markets. Some of these concessions were beneficial to the people of the countries concerned, as when the United States accepted the policies of the Christian Democratic (usually Roman Catholic) parties and Socialist parties in Western Europe and supported the activities of the Roman Catholic Church in Eastern Europe. Some of these concessions were detrimental, as when the United States supported brutal dictatorships in Central America and the Caribbean.

However, the collapse of the Soviet Union in 1991 and the discrediting of communist ideology removed much of the necessity for such compromises and concessions. At the same time, the spread of the global economy and the competition among national governments to liberalize their economies in order to attract foreign capital legitimated the idea of free markets. Now the United States could be unrestrained and uncontained in pursuing its grand project of universal human rights.

As was discussed by Samuel Huntington and others, this universalist and individualist project of the United States generated resentment and resistance in societies whose religious traditions are different from the Christianity of the West. Huntington called this "the clash of civilizations," a struggle between "the West and the rest."[2] There was almost no resistance in those nations with a Protestant tradition, there was some resistance in those with a Roman Catholic tradition, and there has been the greatest resistance in those with an Islamic or a Confucian tradition.

Virtually all nations whose religious tradition is Protestant have by now adopted some version of the human-rights ideology, if not the full extent of expressive individualism (Canada, Australia, New Zealand, the Netherlands, the Scandinavian countries, and even Britain and Germany). More resistant but eventually driven into at least free markets and liberal democracy were those nations whose religious tradition is Roman Catholic (France, Italy, the former corporatist countries of Spain and Portugal, the former communist countries of Eastern Europe, and the former authoritarian and protectionist countries of Latin America). However, the Roman Catholic Popes—John Paul II, Benedict XVI, and Francis—have consistently and comprehensively criticized particular elements of the American project (i.e. liberal ideology and the market economy) in several papal encyclicals. The Popes clearly recognize that the liberal program, the Protestant deformation, represents the idolatry of the self.

As Huntington observed, the contemporary, modernized versions of Islam and Confucianism represent a counterpart to the most secularized version of Protestantism, a sort of Counter-Deformation to the Protestant Deformation.

The Human-Rights Projects of the Clinton and Bush Administrations

The election of Bill Clinton in 1992 marked the arrival to political power of that generation of Americans who were true believers in expressive individualism—the baby boomers. The Clinton administration promoted universal human rights more than any previous administration. It saw human rights, free markets, liberal democracy, and individual freedom as the solutions to virtually every human problem. When in turn the George W. Bush administration came to power, it made a big show of rejecting much of the foreign policy of its predecessor. Moreover, its individualism was more the possessive than the expressive kind. However, with respect to the promotion of American values abroad—free markets, liberal democracy, individual freedom, and even human rights (such as women's rights in Afghanistan and Iraq)—the Bush administration was largely a continuation and even an amplification of the Clinton administration. In its public rhetoric, the Bush administration's preferred term was democratization, whereas the Clinton administration's preferred term was globalization, but both administrations vigorously promoted both.

The circumstances of the 1990s (the challenges posed by failed communist states) caused the Clinton administration to focus upon the Balkans (a region once known as the Near East) as the arena for its democratization project; the circumstances of the 2000s (the challenges posed by Islamist terrorist networks) caused the Bush administration to focus upon the Middle East and more broadly upon the Muslim world. The Clinton administration waged two wars (Bosnia and Kosovo) while carrying out its project, and so did the Bush administration (Afghanistan and Iraq). Of course, the Clinton administration was rather more successful in its wars than the Bush administration was; it did bring a decisive end to the violence in Bosnia and Kosovo, while the violence in Afghanistan and Iraq persisted and even worsened. However, the Clinton administration was not really successful in establishing democracy in Bosnia and Kosovo; each remains under the rule of an international protectorate even today. The Bush administration was not able to achieve even this in its two target countries, much less a genuine democratization.

There were also significant differences between the two administrations with respect to the politics of their democratization projects. The Clinton administration was directly and actively pressured to undertake its project and the associated military interventions by the human-rights lobby. It was also supported in this by the globalization lobby, i.e., by business firms with global economic interests. In contrast, the Bush administration was directly and actively pressured to undertake its project and the associated military interventions (particularly the Iraq War) by the neo-conservative lobby. The neo-conservatives also took the lead in building a political coalition in favor of democratization and intervention by recruiting some members of the human-rights lobby and the globalization lobby to provide support. They similarly recruited some members of the evangelical-Protestant lobby. However, these evangelicals only provided support; they did not take the initiative or apply the pressure.

Of course, President Bush himself often spoke of his evangelical faith and convictions. He also often spoke of freedom as God's gift to America and to mankind and of America's calling to be the light of the world and to bring freedom to everyone. His strongest electoral base came from evangelical Protestants.

However, the evangelicals supported the Bush democratization project because it was a <u>Bush</u> project; i.e., they supported Bush on his foreign policy because they were already committed to because of his policy (more accurately his rhetoric) on cultural and social issues. Conversely, the human-rights proponents supported the Bush democratization project because it was a <u>democratization</u> project; they opposed Bush on just about every other policy, especially those involving cultural and social issues. (Indeed, human-rights proponents normally have despised evangelical Christians.)

Evangelical Protestants and American Foreign Policy

If we were to ask who are the closest representatives of the original Reformed Protestants to be found in the United States today, it would of course be evangelical Protestants. For the most part, however, evangelical Protestants have not considered American foreign policy to be one of their priority political issues. They were utterly indifferent to U.S. democratization efforts when these were a project of the Clinton administration. If democratization should come about in a foreign country, evangelicals will be pleased, all the more so because it might open up the country to missionary activity. But evangelicals think that this opening will come about through God's work and not through their own political actions. Certainly, evangelical Protestants who take their Bible seriously know that Jesus Christ is the light of the world and that to hold that America is this light is a form of idolatry and heresy (i.e., what we have called the Protestant Deformation).

Many evangelical Protestants believe in U.S. support for Israel. This is because they believe that Christians are a people who have been grafted onto the vine of the original Israel, the first people chosen by God. But once again, evangelicals <u>support</u> the U.S. policy; they do not normally take the initiative or apply the pressure but instead follow the lead of others. Overall, then, the foreign policy perspective of the last remnants of the Protestant Reformation is very different from that of the Protestant Deformation.

The Protestant Reformation and the Protestant Deformation

The Protestant Reformation was a prime movement in the making of the modern era. Five hundred years later, the Protestant deformation is a prime movement in the making of the post-modern era. The Protestant Reformation was the most unique of all religions. The Protestant deformation seeks the end of all religions, or rather it seeks to replace the worship of God with the expression of the self.

The Protestant Reformation brought into being the first nation states and the first great powers of the modern era such as the Netherlands, Sweden, Prussia, and Britain. The most Reformed Protestant of all nations was the United States, and it became the greatest of all great powers as well. Much of the power of the United States can be traced to the energy, efficacy, and organization that was a legacy of its Reformed Protestantism. However, the Protestant deformation, because of its universalist and individualist creed, seeks the end of all nation states and to replace loyalty to America with gratification of oneself. In doing so, it relentlessly undermines the authority of the United States itself, the very superpower which promotes that creed throughout the world.

In his The Decline and Fall of the Roman Empire, Edward Gibbon wrote that the Roman Empire spread the Christian religion throughout the ancient world, but that the Christian religion then undermined the Roman Empire. In our time, when the American empire has sought to spread the Protestant deformation throughout the modern world, the Protestant deformation has undermined the American empire.

One day, on the open and hostile terrain that has become the global economy and amid the empty formalisms of what was once liberal democracy, there will be found an individual. Once so intoxicated with his boisterous self-expression but now so exhausted from stress and strain, he at last recognizes how lonely and isolated he has become. Then he will turn and seek his refuge and his safety in the protection of a hierarchy, the support of a community, and the comfort of traditions and customs. We should not be surprised if he also seeks his salvation by turning to a God.

CHAPTER THREE

WAR, PEACE, AND THE IDEOLOGIES
OF THE 20TH CENTURY

IT IS NOW TWENTY years, a generation, after the end of the 20th century. It is an appropriate time and distance for looking backward and asking what was the distinctive nature of that era. In this essay, I will suggest that the 20th century was both a century of world wars and a century of global ideologies, and that its distinctive character was shaped by the interaction between the two.

Many historians have viewed the period from the French Revolution to the First World War (1789-1914) as "the long 19th century." The 19th century was really the era of the French Revolution and Napoleonic Wars and their long aftermath. Similarly, some historians (most notably, Eric Hobsbawm) came to view the period from the First World War to the end of the Cold War (1914-1989) as "the short 20th century." The 20th century was really the era of the two World Wars and their long aftermath. (As it happens, the long century and the short one, each beginning with a period of great war and great revolution, together add up to a total of exactly 200 years.)

At the mid-point of the 20th century, Raymond Aron termed it "the century of total war." At its end, Samuel Huntington referred to it as the century of ideological conflict. These two characterizations, total war and ideological conflict, were integrally connected. Historians in the 21st century will likely look back in amazement at these two phenomena and their conjunction, for in the history of the world there has rarely been anything like them. Perhaps the closest comparison is with "the crisis of the 17th century," when during the Thirty Years' War and its long, unsettled aftermath (from 1648 to about 1689—the year of the Glorious Revolution in Britain), the peoples of Europe were totally disrupted by religious or theological conflicts.

International Peace and the Tripartite System of Ideologies

At the beginning of the 20th century, there were in Europe five great powers—Britain, France, Germany, Austria-Hungary, and Russia. To the far west and to the far east of Europe were two other rising powers, respectively the United States and Japan. The international system was a multipolar one.

At the beginning of the century, there were also several great ideologies or "isms." Their identities were not as clearly defined as those of the great powers, but most were products of the Industrial Revolution of the 19th century as it had developed within the aftermath and legacy of the French Revolution of the 18th century. The ideological system was also a multipolar one.

The central ideology at the beginning of the 20th century was liberalism. In the economic arena, this meant free-market capitalism; in the political one it meant liberal democracy. The great powers that most represented liberalism and its capitalist and democratic affiliates were the United States, Britain, and France, the western great powers of the international system. Contending with liberalism on the right was conservatism. In the economic arena, this meant some state-imposed constraints on free-market capitalism; in the political arena, it meant some state-imposed constraints on democratic parties. The great powers that most represented conservatism and its authoritarian affiliates were Germany, Austria-Hungary, Russia, and Japan, the eastern great powers of the international system. Contending with liberalism on the left was socialism. In the economic arena, this meant state ownership of major industries and utilities; in the political arena it meant what was termed "social democracy." Of course, at the beginning of the 20th century, there were no great powers that represented socialism and its affiliates.

Thus, at the beginning of the 20th century, there was a plurality of powers and of ideologies. Of course, as we shall see, by the mid-point of the century there was a duality of powers and of ideologies, and by the end of the century there was a hegemony of one power and of one ideology.

Different nations, because of their particular historical legacies from the French and Industrial Revolutions, were distinguished by particular variations and combinations of these three themes of liberalism, conservatism, and socialism. The tripartite pattern was most clear in the leading power of the day, Britain, where it was embodied in the Liberal, Conservative, and Labour (socialist) parties. In France, the Revolution had left a permanent division of the nation between Catholicism (conservatism) and anti-clericalism, often termed "Radicalism" or "Republicanism" (which were really forms of liberalism). The 19th century had also left a division among the anti-clericals between socialists, syndicalists, and anarchists. In the United States, as had been famously observed by analysts from Alexis de Tocqueville (<u>Democracy in America</u>) to Werner Sombart (<u>Why There Is No Socialism in America</u>), there were neither conservatism nor socialism in the European sense. In America, there were really only varieties of liberals, be they called Democrats or Republicans.

The three ideologies of liberalism, conservatism, and socialism had developed during the 19th century as responses first to the French Revolution and then to the Industrial Revolution. Each had its main base within an industrializing economy. The base of liberalism (and capitalism) was in industry and finance. That of conservatism was in agriculture, most obviously landlords but also on occasion (e.g., in regions of France, Germany, and Austria) independent farmers. That of socialism was in industrial workers. This tripartite division was not wholly a stable equilibrium, and the relationship between the three parts was shifting. The progress of industrialization meant that the power of industry and finance was increasing and that of agriculture was declining. At the same time, however, the growth of industry meant the growth in the numbers and power of industrial workers, and this steadily increased the natural base for socialism. Together, this led to some rather odd conjunctions and coalitions such as the Lib-Lab coalition (Liberal and Labour) in Britain, the Radical-Socialist party in France, and conservative-initiated social welfare programs in Germany and Austria-Hungary.

With an international context of peace and progress, the natural and logical development of this ideological system might have led in the mature industrial society to a pattern defined by one ideology and political party based upon pro-capital positions and another ideology and political party based upon pro-labor ones. But since labor had more voters than capitalists, the pro-capital party had to add some other ideological element to attract other voters. This element could be variously pro-religion (e.g., Catholicism in France), pro-nation (e.g., nationalism in Germany), pro-empire (e.g., imperialism in Britain), or against some particular group (e.g., anti-Semitism in Austria).

The First World War and the Radicalization of Ideologies

The First World War was not caused by any of these ideologies (although some simplistic analyses have blamed the ideologies of nationalism or imperialism), but rather by the peculiar form that the balance of power and the balance of trade had taken by the beginning of the 20th century. The real cause of the First World War was the inability of the old power and trade balances to absorb the great and rapid rise in the military and economic power of Germany after its unification in 1871. Bismarck had tried to use conservative ideology (in the form of the Three Emperors League between Germany, Austria-Hungary, and Russia) to finesse this rise in German power, but this effort quickly fell apart under his successors after Kaiser Wilhelm II dismissed him in 1890.

Once the First World War started, however, it had profound consequences for the existing ideologies. In the course of the long bloodletting, each ideology became a starker, harsher, more extreme version of itself. Conservatism became nationalism (especially in Germany and France), liberalism became Democracy (especially in the United States with Woodrow Wilson's portrayal of the Great War as a great struggle between Democracy and Autocracy), and part of social-ism became communism (especially in Russia, with Lenin portraying the war as a great struggle between competing imperialisms).

Had the Great War remained a European war, it would have ended in a German victory. The German defeat of Russia in the East in 1917 and the German offensive in the West in the Spring of 1918 would have led to this. The natural development of European history would have issued in German hegemony over the European continent. It was only because of the U.S. entry into the war and the millions of fresh American troops arriving on the Western front in 1918 that the Ger-man offensive in the Spring was turned back and then reversed with the Allied offensive in the Fall. A German hegemony would have had distinct ideological consequences and problems. The dominant ideol-ogy in Germany was conservatism in the form of nationalism. German nationalism would have been a rather awkward ideology with which to legitimate and justify German hegemony over a Europe of other nations with their own nationalisms, even if each nation was less pow-erful than the German one. Some other ideological element would have had to have been added to the German ideology to make it justify a privileged position for the German nation among the other more numerous European nations.

As it happened, this ideological element had already been devel-oped within the Habsburg Empire. The Germans, although a minority in the demographic sense, could be seen as an elite in the cultural (and also economic and political) sense. This ideology of cultural superiority could easily, given the Social-Darwinist fashions of the time, become an ideology of biological superiority, i.e., racism. A German victory in the First World War might have led to a German hegemony over Europe justified by a German ideology of racial superiority. Of course, this is what did happen twenty years later when Germany briefly achieved hegemony over Europe in the early years of the Second World War.

The victory of the Western Allies appeared to validate their ideology of liberalism, including democracy and capitalism. This was the case not only in nations of the West but initially also those in the East, where dis-credited monarchies were at first replaced by apparent democracies. But although defeated by the allies, Germany and Austria-Hungary were not conquered by them. And although convulsed for a few months in 1918-1919 by leftist revolutions, the peoples of Central Europe were not transformed by them. The absence of either conquest or revolution meant that the pillars of the old social order and the old conservative ideology—particularly the landlords—were, after being shaken up a bit, restored to their old place. Military defeat and the fall of the monarchies may have brought liberals and democrats to formal power, but the deeper social realities were not liberal or democratic. These were now societies traumatized by the vast and now wasted sacrifices of the Great War and by the grave threats from the communist upsurge, a Red Scare or Great Fear that was especially compelling in the neighbors of Soviet Russia. The Great War and the Great Fear served as the great ideological simplifiers in Central Europe: liberals became more democratic and some even became radical; socialists became more Marxist and some even became communist; and conservatives became more nationalist and some even became fascist.

The Fascist Appeal and the Second World War

By the end of the 20th century, the ideology of fascism certainly seemed to be unintelligent and unintelligible. This was especially the case with its most extreme version, national socialism. How could these ideologies appeal to large numbers of ordinary people in such advanced societies as Germany and Italy? This phenomenon seems bizarre and surreal.

Eighty or ninety years ago, however, the perception was rather different. During the 1920s, in the aftermath of the First World War and the Bolshevik Revolution, and especially during the 1930s in the midst of the Great Depression, fascism and national socialism appeared to many to offer the best solutions to critical social problems. In particular, they appeared to be better solutions than those offered by liberalism or democracy or by socialism or communism. The appeals of fascism and national socialism derived from three major sources: (1) their relevance to the traumatic experience of front-line soldiers during the Great War; (2) their relevance to the traumatic experience of ordinary citizens during the Great Fear; and (3) their creative combination of popular elements found within the earlier ideologies of conservatism, including nationalism, and socialism (but definitely not liberalism).

First, the experience of front-line soldiers in the First World War was virtually unique in its unrelieved horror. The uselessness and meaninglessness of the vast sacrifices in blood and treasure were especially traumatic in the defeated countries, Germany and Austria-Hungary, and in Italy, which, although formally a victor, actually gained very little in the peace settlement. For years, front-line veterans would be haunted by these sacrifices by themselves and their comrades, and they would seek recognition and redemption for them. The liberal, democratic, and socialist political parties—born decades before in an era of international peace and led by older men who had come of age long before the Great War—could not truly understand this yearning. But the new fascist parties—with their glorification of the nation, their rhetoric of combat, and their military uniforms (e.g., blackshirts, brownshirts) and marching—were perfectly in tune with it.

Second, the experience of ordinary citizens during the brief but intense post-war period of communist upsurge had left a widespread fear of revolution. This fear was especially intense, again, in the defeated countries, Germany and Austria-Hungary (communist parties had actually seized power for several months during 1919 in Bavaria, Thuringia, and Hungary), and in Italy where for several years both industrial and agricultural workers engaged in numerous disruptive strikes and occupations of factories and farms. For years, ordinary citizens would be haunted by the humiliations of themselves and their neighbors, and they would seek recognition and redemption for them, or at least assurance that the communists would never again come to power.

Third, fascism combined popular elements of the two pre-war non-liberal ideologies—conservatism (especially its nationalism) and socialism. Obviously, this was most explicit with the National Socialist (Nazi) party in Germany. From conservatism and nationalism the new ideologies drew the idea that the state was right in controlling the society. From socialism they drew the idea that the society was right in supporting the state. From both they drew the doctrine and practice that the state could and should impose constraints upon free-market capitalism and upon particular political parties and, if conditions should necessitate, even impose direction upon them.

The conservatives and nationalists had emphasized conditions of war-like economic struggle; the socialists had emphasized conditions of depression-induced economic stagnation. By the 1930s, both conditions were clearly present and had created the necessities. Operating within the legacy of the Great War and within the reality of the Great Depression, the fascists and national socialists could convincingly emphasize both conditions. The Great War had demonstrated the necessity for organization, planning, discipline, and energy in running the war-time economy. The Great Depression and its attendant international economic struggles, it was natural to think, demonstrated the necessity for all of these once again.

Within a few years after coming to power in 1933, national socialism eliminated unemployment in Germany and appeared to have solved the problem of the Great Depression better than any other ideology, certainly better than the liberal governments of the United States, Britain, and France, where unemployment remained close to 20 percent or above. We now know that this astonishing success of national socialism came at great costs: first military rearmament and then military aggression. However, this was not obvious in, say, 1936, the year of the Berlin Olympics, which provided another apparent demonstration of the peacetime achievements of national socialism.

The coming of the Second World War brought a new demonstration of the superiority of national socialism, with the extraordinary victory of the German army over the French army in May-June 1940. This brought Germany to where it would have been in May-June 1918 if the United States had not intervened in the First World War. At long last, after tremendous sacrifices but with ultimate redemption, the natural development of European history—German hegemony over the European continent—had been realized. The New Order of national socialism appeared to be the final solution to the European question. In the Summer of 1940, this was the reasonable conclusion to be drawn from the torturous and tortured path that European history had taken since 1914. Communism was of limited appeal everywhere, discredited by its twenty-year history of brutality and terror. But liberalism was also of limited appeal on the continent, discredited by its failure to solve the Great Depression and by its dramatic defeats in the new Second World War. It was national socialism that seemed the path to the future.

Of course, history very soon took the opposite path. Embedded within national socialism was its fatal flaw of German racism. As we have seen, that racism derived more from the experience of the German minority within the Habsburg Empire than from that of the overwhelming German majority within Germany itself. In any event, it was that racist component which drove Hitler (who had grown up in Austria) to invade the Soviet Union and which largely shaped Germany's occupation policies in the conquered territories in the East, including of course the Holocaust. More than anything else, it was the war with the Soviet Union that brought about national socialism's destruction.

The Cold War and the Bipolar System of Ideologies

Before the Second World War, there had been three main ideological families in contention: (1) liberalism and democracy; (2) fascism and national socialism; and (3) socialism and communism. At the beginning of the war, national socialism seemed to have won the contest. At the end of the war, however, the decisive defeat and conquest of Nazi Germany and Fascist Italy served as a great simplifier, removing fascism and national socialism from contention and leaving the remaining two ideologies to confront each other in a long duel, which became the Cold War. But this ideological duality took place within an odd linguistic unity.

The Grand Alliance of the United States, Britain, and the Soviet Union had fought the Second World War in the name of democracy, and after the war virtually every new political formation had to include the word democratic in its name. This was most evident in the defeated nations of Germany, Italy, and Japan, whose recreated conservative parties called themselves Christian Democratic (West Germany, Italy) or Liberal Democratic (Japan). Some socialist groups renamed themselves Social Democratic parties. And even communist parties called their new regimes People's Democracies.

After several years, this promiscuous use of "democracy" generated a reaction within the power most committed to the liberal ideology, the United States, and especially within the Republican Party. The 1950s saw a great emphasis among Americans on the words "liberty" and "freedom"—as in free enterprise, the Free World, Radio Free Europe, and Radio Liberty. This helped to clarify the ideological duel between liberalism and communism.

We have already noted that the experiences of front-line soldiers during the First World War in Europe later led some of them to become fascists or national socialists. Similarly, the experiences of partisan guerrillas during the Second World War in Asia led many of them to become communists (e.g., in China, Korea, Vietnam, and Malaya). These wartime experiences from the Second World War would continue to shape (and distort) the domestic policies of the communist regimes in China, North Korea, and North Vietnam for decades thereafter, and also the ways in which they would fight the United States in two hot wars in Asia, within what was the Cold War more generally.

The defeats of Germany and Austria-Hungary in the First World War and the punitive peace treaties that followed had created a question of national independence, a question for which fascist and national socialist parties could plausibly claim that they had the clearest solution. Similarly, the defeats of the colonial regimes in Asia in the Second World War created the potential for national independence, a potential for which the communist-led guerrilla movements plausibly could claim that they had the clearest solution.

Among their other appeals, fascism and national socialism had claimed that they were best able to protect and promote heavy industry and capital goods (steel, chemicals, machinery, and of course armaments), especially with the collapse of international trade during the Great Depression. Communism made the same claim, but it made heavy industry even more central to its ideology (Joseph Stalin's own name was a pseudonym which meant "steel," and he seems to have considered steel to be the solution for most problems). In this respect, communism equaled national socialism minus the capitalist organization of industry. In the first two decades after the Second World War, communism proved to be very good at rapid development of heavy industry and capital goods ("forced-draft industrialization"). These happened to be the industries that had been so crucial to the Allied victories in the First and Second World Wars, and communists expected them to be crucial in winning the Cold War. This conjunction of war communism and steel communism seemed to produce spectacular achievements for national independence and national industrialization.

By the 1970s, however, it became apparent that this kind of communism was incapable of moving from a wartime environment to a peacetime one, from capital goods to consumer ones, and from heavy industry to high technology. Communism had brought great achievements for national independence and industrialization at one stage of development, but at the next stage, it brought only national autarchy and stagnation. To some communist reformers, it became clear that Marxist-Leninism would have to be replaced with something like market-Leninism, i.e., a market economy within authoritarian politics. This was the project that Mikhail Gorbachev tried and failed to effect in the Soviet Union, and that Deng Xiaoping tried and succeeded in effecting in China.

The Liberal Triumph and the New International Peace

After its victories over fascism and national socialism in the Second World War and its victories over Marxism and communism in the Cold War, liberalism stood triumphant and alone.

Over the second half of the 20th century, it succeeded in undermining both the social bases and the problem-solving appeals of all of its ideological adversaries. Advanced by the United States as the sole superpower and the leader of the global economy, liberalism promised to make the coming 21st century one of ideological consensus, indeed the end of ideology, and of international peace.

Conservatism. The main base of conservatism was agriculture, most obviously landlords but also independent farmers. Unlike the defeats of Germany and Austria-Hungary in the First World War, the defeats and occupations of Germany and Japan after the Second World War resulted in major land-reform programs imposed by the United States (and in eastern Germany by the Soviet Union), which eliminated the German and Japanese landlord classes. However, a social base for conservatism still remained in the large number of independent farmers who in the 1950s comprised 20-25 percent of the populations of such major nations as France, West Germany, Italy and Japan. Over the next three decades, however, the American-constructed liberal order of international trade and economic growth resulted in the steady growth of the industrial sector and the steady decline of the agricultural one within liberal-capitalist economies. This brought about a profound undermining of the social base for conservatism.

Fascism. One of the major appeals of fascism and national socialism was its protection and promotion of capitalist industry. Had there been a new Great Depression a few years after the Second World War, the collapse of international trade would have presented a renewed crisis for capitalist industry, and this might have driven it to some kind of nationalist, even neo-fascist or neo-national-socialist solution despite the debacle of these ideologies in the Second World War. However, the American-constructed liberal order worked effectively to prevent a new Great Depression and provided capitalist industry with international integration as an alternative to national separation. Any new version of fascism or national socialism became unnecessary.

Socialism. The main base of socialism was industrial workers. At first, the liberal order, with its economic growth, was conducive to the expansion of this base. But the process of economic development moved on: from capital goods to consumer goods, from heavy industry to high technology, and even from the industrial economy to the post-industrial or information economy. Like the agricultural section and the independent farmer class earlier, the industrial sector and the industrial working class have shrunk in the past several decades within the liberal-capitalist economies. This has brought about a profound undermining of the social base for socialism.

Communism. One of the major appeals of communism was its protection and promotion of national industry. Had the most advanced capitalist economies remained stuck at the level of heavy industry, communism might have seemed a reasonable and effective way of reaching this stage. But as the capitalist economies moved up and beyond this level while the communist ones did not, it became clear that communism no longer produced national independence, but rather a new form of international dependence.

It was surely an extraordinary historical irony—and tragedy—that the Vietnamese communists led by Ho Chi Minh fought for thirty years, at a cost of two million lives, to achieve national independence and a communist society for Vietnam while twenty years after their victory over the United States, the Vietnamese communists led by Ho's successors were energetically promoting Vietnam's integration into the American-constructed liberal international economy.

The fatal flaw of national socialism had been its element of German racism. This meant that it could never serve as a stable ideology with which to govern Europe, a continent composed of many nations which together were far more numerous than the Germans. Communism had an analogous fatal flaw. At its core was the idea of the dictatorship of the proletariat, which might be seen as a sort of proletarian classism. This meant that it could never serve as a stable ideology with which to govern an economy which was moving beyond heavy industry and a society composed of many classes which together were more numerous than the industrial workers. Of course, the national socialist and communist regimes compensated for their limiting and unstable ideologies by developing brutal and ruthless repression. This is what Hitler and Stalin both did. But what would national socialism have looked like forty years after Hitler? We know what communism looked like forty years after Stalin.

The Islamic and Confucian Resistance to Liberalism

Does liberalism confront any serious adversary that can thwart its grand project of global economy and international peace? Samuel Huntington famously argued that the central conflicts of the 21st century would not be between ideologies but between cultures or civilizations. Already the major resistance to the American-led liberal project has been mounted by countries with either an Islamic or a Confucian tradition and culture. They see liberalism as merely the distinctive product of a particular civilization, i.e., the Western one. The contemporary, modernized versions of Islam and Confucianism could be seen as successors to the anti-liberal ideologies of the past, especially some kinds of conservatism (and perhaps fascism?).

Some Americans have focused upon the resistance of revivalist or political Islam, i.e., Islamism. For political analysts who stress alien ideologies and terrorist actions as the main source of foreign threats, Islamism has clear analogies with the previous enemies of national socialism and communism. However, this analogy does not impress other political analysts who see hostile great powers as the main source of foreign threats (the "realist" position). They note that there is no Islamic great power, certainly not in the center of the Eurasian landmass and certainly not on the scale of Nazi Germany or the Soviet Union. The closest candidate is Iran and its Shi'ite version of Islam. In any event, for great power realists the problem of Islamism could be readily handled by a policy of playing off the Sunni and the Shi'ite versions of Islamism against each other.

Other Americans have focused upon the resistance of China as the leading country with a Confucian tradition, the leader of "Sinic civilization." For political analysts who stress hostile great powers and military forces as the main threat, China has clear analogies with the pre-1989 Soviet Union and with pre-1945 Germany. There is a strong view among some Americans that China will become the central threat to the United States and that containment of it should be the organizing principle of U.S. foreign policy.

Does liberalism have a fatal flaw, as did national socialism and communism? At the turn of the 21st century, it was difficult to discern any such flaw. Now, twenty years into the new century, it is increasingly easy to discern. Liberalism was the product of the international peace and economic growth of the long 19th century. It then, astonishingly, turned out to be the ultimate victor in the world wars—two hot and one cold—and the economic depression of the short 20th century. But war and depression produced formidable enemies of liberalism, which could only be vanquished at the cost of millions of lives and trillions of dollars. As long as liberalism could seem to make the 21st century one of peace and prosperity, it was able to maintain its ideological hegemony. But it now seems that liberalism is no longer able to provide this prosperity, or perhaps even this peace. But if the liberal 21st century should become a short one, then a new and different 21st century will ensue, and in its own way, it is likely to be a century of total war and ideological conflict.

CHAPTER FOUR

DEMOCRATIZATION:

SUCCESSES AND FAILURES

FOR A FULL CENTURY, the United States has been engaged in a succession of democratization projects abroad. President Woodrow Wilson in particular was an enthusiast in promoting democracy, first in the Caribbean basin and Central America ("I will teach the South Americans to elect good men") and then in Europe and beyond (the U.S. entry into the First World War was supposed "to make the world safe for democracy").

Even earlier, during the 19th century, the United States had given rhetorical encouragement to democratic movements abroad, but it was not in a position to give them substantive support until it became a great power, a status that it achieved with its victory in the Spanish-American War of 1898. The Republican administrations of Theodore Roosevelt and William Howard Taft were quick to employ America's new power to promote regime change in the Caribbean basin, but their objective was merely to establish new governments which would make their countries safe for American security and business interests, i.e., regimes which certainly were liberal, but were not really democratic. With the Democratic administration of Woodrow Wilson, however, the United

States embarked upon the promotion of democracy abroad in the full sense and in a big way. In the course of the 20th century, there ensued a great parade of U.S. democratization projects that marched around the world.

The Success Stories

Some of these democratization projects were great successes. The most famous cases, of course, were Germany and Japan after their defeat in the Second World War, but these two examples (and exemplars) were joined by similar successes in Austria and Italy. In these four cases, of course, U.S.-style democratization was imposed by U.S.-led military occupation.

Also famous are the cases of Eastern Europe after the transformation—really, the defeat—of the Soviet Union in the Cold War. Here, of course, the United States did not impose a military occupation (but crucially the Soviets did withdraw theirs). Nevertheless, the result has been a wide swath of successful transitions to established liberal-democratic systems, stretching from the Baltic to the Balkans, or about a dozen countries in all. This has been a major achievement for U.S. foreign policy indeed.

Rather less sudden and dramatic, but still substantial and impressive, has been the U.S.-supported democratization of South Korea and Taiwan since the early 1990s. Along with the earlier U.S.-imposed democratization of Japan, these two East Asian cases demonstrate that democratization projects can succeed not only in Europe (which, being part of Western civilization, might be expected to be receptive to liberal and democratic values), but also in at least one region beyond, one which has a very different cultural inheritance.

The Failure Stories

Unfortunately, our long parade of U.S. democratization projects includes some rather substantial failures as well. Not surprisingly, given the normal American tendency to be optimistic and to look upon the good side of some new project, these past failures are not nearly as famous as the past successes. They have been important, however, and they may be more relevant to the notorious project of the George W. Bush administration to democratize the Middle East and the Muslim world more generally. These earlier failures also raise cautions about any future U.S. effort to promote democracy in other regions as well.

The original Wilsonian failures. Ironically, given the common and contemporary identification of democratization with "Wilsonianism," the original democratization projects of Woodrow Wilson himself *all* ended in failure. By the late 1920s, every country in Latin America where Wilson had employed U.S. military forces or another kind of intervention to teach the local citizens to elect good men had ended up with a military dictator or some other form of authoritarian regime. The same outcome occurred in Europe, where the consequences of failure would be much greater and much graver. Again, by 1930, almost every country in Central and Eastern Europe where Wilson had employed U.S. pressure to bring about democratization—usually in the form of "self-determination"—had ended up with some form of authoritarian regime. Democratic systems still remained in Germany, Austria, Czechoslovakia, and Finland, however, and it still could be said that Wilsonianism's achievements remained impressive. But then, with the onset and impact of the Great Depression, the democratic systems in Germany and Austria collapsed, and the consequences of these failures were more momentous and terrible than anything that could have been imagined.

What explains the failures of the original Wilsonian democratization projects? The most common factor—one characteristic of both the Latin-American and the Eastern European failures in the 1920s—was the absence of a substantial middle class and, therefore, the presence of a large gap between a small upper class, largely composed of landlords and merchants, and a large lower class, most of whom were peasants. In contrast, in the Central European cases of Germany, Austria, and Czechoslovakia there was a very substantial middle class and a very substantial industrial working class as well, and these two classes continued to provide strong support for large democratic parties. However, the Great Depression, which had a disastrous impact upon industrial production around the world, knocked the props out from this support, at least in Germany and Austria where democratic practices were relatively new. (We will have more to say about the supporting factors for democracy—and the differences between successes and failures—below.)

The later Cold War failures. During the Cold War, the United States undertook a major democratization project in Southeast Asia, particularly in the Philippines in the 1950s-1960s and in South Vietnam in the 1960s. The epic U.S. military and political failure in South Vietnam (and in Cambodia and Laos as well) has cast this particular project into the darkest recesses of the American memory and has caused it to be largely forgotten. It would have been better to have remembered it, however, because some of the failed democratic initiatives tried in South Vietnam were repeated and failed in Iraq (e.g., expecting formal elections to solve fundamental conflicts). It should also be remembered that the U.S. project in the Philippines ended in the dictatorship of Ferdinand Marcos, which lasted from 1972 to 1986, when a democratic system of sorts was restored. Even today, however, Philippine democracy is afflicted by a large gap between a few rich and many poor, and the system remains fragile and fitful. In some ways, the Philippines can be seen as a kind of Latin Asia, bearing similarities to much of Latin America.

The Bush Administration's Failed Project in the Middle East

Beginning with the declaration of the Bush Doctrine in 2002 and with the invasion of Iraq in 2003, the Bush administration drove the United States into yet another democratization project in yet another foreign region, this time the Middle East and the Muslim world more generally. The rhetorical apotheosis of this particular project was President Bush's Second Inaugural Address in January 2005, and the highpoints of its apparent progress were the "Cedar Revolution" in Lebanon in 2005 and a series of hyped elections in Iraq in 2005 and 2006. Today, this project lies in ruins, destroyed by the Israel-Hezbollah war in Lebanon in 2006 and the de facto civil war in Iraq from 2004 to 2017 (to say nothing of such results of democratic elections as the surges of votes for radical Islamists whenever they appear on the ballot, such as Hamas in Palestine and the Muslim Brotherhood in Egypt).

Is it possible that democratic elections in the Middle East and the Muslim world will actually have as their consequence the rise to power of "Islamo-fascism," the very totalitarian enemy which the Bush administration sought to defeat with its democratization project? If so, one should not be totally surprised. After all, it was successive free elections in the very democratic Weimar Republic after 1930 which brought the Nazis—the most extreme case of the original fascists—to power in 1933.

What lessons can be drawn from this record of successes and failures? Are there particular conditions which make a U.S. democratization project more likely to succeed (and also more likely to be worth its cost in the blood of American soldiers and the treasure of American citizens)? We will begin with an account of the legendary successes in Germany and Japan, along with the similar successes in Austria and Italy.

The Exceptional Cases from the Second World War

For America, the biggest event of the 20th century was the Second World War. It is not surprising that the war's epic narrative has continued to shape the American public mentality (and political mythology), along with U.S. foreign policy, ever since. Munich and appeasement; Pearl Harbor and surprise attack; early 1942 and national desperation; later 1942 to 1945, resurgence and total victory; and, finally, the successful post-war democratization of our defeated enemies—each of these dramatic episodes in the Second World War narrative has had a powerful hold on the American imagination. This largely explains why the successes of democratization in Germany and Japan have remained so salient and why Americans have easily been led into the temptation to think that those successes can be replicated elsewhere. However, the conditions which were common to those two cases (and also to the similar cases of Austria and Italy) have rarely been found in other times and in other regions. In particular, they are almost totally absent in the contemporary Middle East and most of the Muslim world.

Five conditions were important facilitators for the U.S. democratization projects in Germany, Japan, Austria, and Italy after the Second World War:

(1) <u>An industrial economy and a modern society</u>. Economic development in these four countries had reached the point that there was, as we discussed above, a substantial middle class and industrial working class; in normal times, these had achieved their political representation in democratic political parties (liberal democratic in the case of the middle class, social democratic in the case of the working class).

Turning to the contemporary Middle East, we might think that several countries now have a substantial middle class (although clearly not an industrial working class). However, the economic wealth of Middle Eastern countries is almost wholly the result of oil exports, and the middle class is largely found among the employees in the state sector. It is a dependent and unproductive middle class rather than the independent and productive one which characterized Central Europe and Japan; the former provides a weak and unstable basis for liberal democracy.

(2) <u>A prior liberal-democratic experience</u>. Our second condition flows out of the first. Democratic parties had already existed in these four countries in the 1920s or, in some cases, even earlier decades, i.e., before the Great Depression (Germany, Austria, and Japan) or other social conflicts (Italy) brought about the collapse of the liberal-democratic system and the advent of an authoritarian regime. This meant that the United States in the late 1940s could reach back and build upon democratic memories, practices, and even particular leaders from the earlier democratic era. The four countries actually had considerable experience with some version of liberal democracy between the First World War and the Great Depression. The Weimar Republic, with is grand drama of blighted hopes and dark tragedy, is especially well-known, but Japan also experienced liberalization and even democratization in the 1920s, Austria had a political system similar to the Weimar Republic, and Italy had a functioning liberal democracy for more than two decades before Mussolini put an end to it in 1922. During their liberal-democratic period, each of these countries had developed liberal, democratic, and even social-democratic parties. Although these parties were repressed by the later totalitarian or authoritarian regimes, in the late 1940s the experience was still there in the memories of substantial portions of the population. Indeed some of

the prominent leaders of the liberal-democratic period were still there, and the U.S. occupation authorities soon drew upon them to assume leadership in the new (really renewed) liberal-democratic systems (e.g., Konrad Adenauer in Germany, Karl Renner in Austria, Alcide de Gasperi in Italy, and Shigeru Yoshida in Japan).

In this respect, the contrast of our four post-war cases with the contemporary Middle East could hardly be greater. Hardly any Middle Eastern country has ever been a liberal democracy (Turkey and perhaps Lebanon are arguable exceptions); in one country after another, there is no historical base or precedent whatsoever for the U.S. democratization project.

To get some sense of how successful externally-imposed democratization would be in the absence of internally-developed historical experience, one would have to look instead at the U.S. efforts to impose democracy upon such countries as Cuba, the Dominican Republic, Haiti, Nicaragua, and Panama. Here, the only cases that can be said to be successful were the slow establishment of a liberal-democratic system in the Dominican Republic during the decade or so after the U.S. military intervention and occupation in 1965-1966 and the quick establishment of such a system in Panama after the U.S. intervention and occupation of 1989-1990. In contrast, each of the U.S. democratization projects of the 1900s-1930s ended in failure, with the liberal-democratic system overthrown and replaced by some kind of dictatorial regime.

(3) <u>Total military defeat</u>. In 1945, the old authoritarian regimes in the four enemy countries had been totally defeated militarily by the United States and its allies. As a consequence, they had been totally discredited ideologically. This opened up a great political space which could be filled by the liberal-democratic ideology of the victorious United States.

One might argue that Saddam Hussein's regime experienced a similar military defeat and ideological discrediting in 2003. However, the Sunni population of Iraq, which was tied so closely to the Baath regime, obviously did not agree. Military defeat is not the term that comes to mind when we are describing the Sunni insurgency in Iraq. Moreover, since the U.S. military is now so tied down and stretched so thin around the world, there is no prospect whatever that it will be able to totally defeat and occupy another Middle Eastern country as it did with the enemy countries in the Second World War.

(4) A greater foreign threat. Probably more important, West Germany and Japan in the late 1940s each perceived a foreign threat that was even greater than the one posed by the U.S. occupation. As oppressive as the military forces of the United States were to the West Germans and Japanese, there was the fear of something that would be even worse, and that was the military forces of the Soviet Union. The threat was especially obvious to the West Germans, who had ample evidence of the reign of pillage, rape, and murder which the Red Army had inflicted upon Germans in the East and could be expected to inflict upon Germans in the West if they ever got the chance. But even the Japanese feared a possible conquest by the Soviet military and revolution by the Japanese communists, particularly after they saw what the Soviets did to the Japanese colonists and soldiers captured in Manchuria. As bad as the reality of the American occupation was for both nations, the specter of a Soviet occupation was a good deal worse. And it soon became clear to many West Germans and Japanese that only the American military stood in the way of that specter being realized.

Some semblance of this condition has also been present in Iraq. The Kurds fear a threat posed by Turkey, but they fear the Sunnis of Iraq even more. This is why they have been such close and cooperative allies of the United States. The Sunnis themselves view the Shi'ites of Iraq as their greatest enemy, but many of them continue to loathe U.S. military forces as well. As for the Shi'ites, it is possible that one day they might come to fear a threat posed by Sunni Saudi Arabia or even by Shi'ite Iran. For now, however, they fear the Iraqi Sunnis most of all, but their militias also loathe the U.S. military. All in all, the complex array of foreign threats in Iraq does not wonderfully concentrate Iraqi minds in the way the Soviet threat did in our four cases after the Second World War.

Again, to get some sense of how acceptable a U.S. military occupation would be in the absence of a still-greater foreign military threat, one would have to look not at West Germany and Japan but instead, and again, at the U.S. occupations in Cuba, the Dominican Republic,

Haiti, Nicaragua, and Panama. In the cases where the occupation was prolonged beyond a couple of years, there developed substantial local resentment and even resistance. And in the two most successful cases (the Dominican Republic in 1965-1966 and Panama in 1989-1990), the United States withdrew its military forces and ended its occupation in less than a year.

(5) <u>An ethnically homogeneous population</u>. This fifth condition may be the most relevant to the contrast between the four post-war successes and the contemporary Middle East. Although these four countries were certainly divided by class conflicts, they were, in ethnic terms, among the most homogenous societies in the world. There was very little prospect that one ethnic group, especially one located in a distinct territory, would try to secede from the rest of the country.

The contrast with the contemporary Middle East, and particularly with Iraq, again could not be greater. As is now well-known (and was always well-known to scholars of Middle Eastern politics and society), Iraq has never been ethnically homogeneous. From its creation in 1920, it has always been divided into three ethnic parts: the Sunni Arabs, the Shi'ite Arabs, and the Kurds (who are Sunni but non-Arab), with the Sunni minority until 2003 imposing an authoritarian and usually brutal regime upon the Shi'ite majority and the Kurdish minority. Moreover, the three ethnic parts have roughly corresponded to three territorial parts, with the Sunni Arabs in the center, the Shi'ite Arabs in the South, and the Kurds in the North (with mixed populations in major cities). Iraq was always an unstable equilibrium, a partition waiting to happen, artificially held together by the iron bonds of an authoritarian and brutal regime. In such circumstances, "regime change" would inevitably result in state change or even country change; in particular democratization would mean that one or more of the three ethnic and territorial parts of Iraq would vote to separate itself from the others. One could have an Iraq, but without democracy. Alternatively, one could have democracy, but without an Iraq. But one could not have both.

To get some sense of what democratization could produce in a country with such pronounced ethnic heterogeneity, one would have had to look not at West Germany and Japan in the late 1940s but instead at the recent (and very extensive) experience of democratization in the former communist countries. Certainly, one would have to especially look at the experience of democratization in the Balkans, which were once collectively called the Near East and which are not that far geographically and sociologically from the contemporary Middle East. Here, the evidence is unambiguous. In virtually every country in the communist world where there was ethnic heterogeneity, democratization (which included free elections) was followed immediately by secession and partition. This was largely peaceful in the case of the Slavic and the Baltic republics of the Soviet Union and in the case of the "velvet divorce" between the Czech Republic and the Slovak Republic. It was violent and even genocidal in the case of the Caucasian republics of the Soviet Union and in the case of several of the republics of Yugoslavia. But be the process peaceful or violent, the democratization of multiethnic societies almost always issued in secession and partition. Given these results of democratization in multiethnic countries of the communist world in the 1990s—especially the violent results in the Caucasus and the Balkans which are so proximate to Iraq both geographically and historically—it is incredible that anyone could seriously argue that the most relevant comparisons to Iraq were the homogeneous nations of West Germany and Japan in the 1940s. When the neo-conservative writers who promoted the U.S. war in Iraq did so, they were therefore either frauds or fools.

The Pervasiveness of Ethnic Divisions in the Muslim World

Ethnic divisions and conflicts are especially evident in Iraq, but they are seen throughout the Muslim world. This has important implications for any democratization project there. In appearance, a common faith in Islam unites Muslim countries; the ideal of Islam is that the Muslim world forms one great Islamic community or nation, known as the umma. In reality, however, this appearance of Islamic unity lies atop a myriad of ethnic and tribal divisions that existed before Islam (especially in Muhammad's own Arabia) and that have never been eliminated by Islam. Indeed, one might interpret the Muslim world's intense proclamation of unity as rhetorical compensation for persistent conflict among a multitude of ethnic communities or tribes.

Almost all Muslim countries are really multiethnic or multitribal societies, usually composed of one large ethnic community plus several smaller ones. Often, each ethnic community is concentrated in a particular region of the country. The actual basis for most political behavior in Muslim countries is these ethnic or tribal communities; most people act to preserve or promote the interests of their own ethnic community or tribe against the interests of other ones. Very little sense of the public interest or the common good exists; left alone, these communities or tribes would war with each other despite the purported unity of Islam.

In most cases, one ethnic community or tribe imposes a peace of sorts on the others and then becomes strong enough to form a state. Given the condition of persistent and pervasive ethnic and tribal conflict, this state will be authoritarian—a Hobbesian Leviathan. As we have seen, this pattern of a uniethnic state ruling over a multiethnic or multitribal society clearly characterized Saddam Hussein's Iraq. Similarly, before being ousted by the United States in 2001, the Taliban regime in Afghanistan represented the domination of the Pashtuns—a plurality but not a majority—over several other ethnic groups. This pattern also exists in contemporary Iran, Syria, and Sudan, and some version of it exists in Pakistan, Indonesia, Saudi Arabia, Yemen, Algeria, and many other Muslim countries as well. When the ruling community is especially small, it compensates for weakness in its numbers by extreme brutality in its repressive measures (e.g., Baathist Iraq and Syria). In any case, the multiethnic society is held together and held down by a uniethnic state, particularly by its security apparatus.

These Muslim political systems are really small multinational empires. Indeed, they are governed in ways similar to those that the Ottomans used to govern their empire. The Ottoman Turks provided the state or "ruling institution" that kept a wide variety of ethnic communities or "millets" (some Muslim and some non-Muslim) operating within one imperial system. A millet often served a distinct economic or social function; the function of the Ottoman Turks was to rule the rest. The Ottoman Empire ended almost a century ago, but its basic pattern lives on in most contemporary Muslim countries, which remain miniature and stunted versions of the old Ottoman imperial system, with the contemporary state security apparatus playing the ruling-institution role. The members of the different ethnic communities under the ruling state do not see themselves as citizens who enjoy equal rights within one homogenous nation. Instead, they see themselves as distinct tribes or ethnic groups, at most a collection of nations within a nation but not of it, or a nation within an empire. This is hardly a promising basis for a viable liberal democracy.

Such multiethnic society/uniethnic state contraptions are inherently unstable. They are accidents, secessions, and partitions waiting to happen. Whenever the state is suddenly and sharply weakened (as with Iran during the Revolution of 1979 and with Iraq during the Gulf War of 1991 and during the Iraq War after 2003), the subordinate ethnic communities try to break away from what they see to be a brutal but now-failed empire. Since these communities are concentrated in particular regions, their efforts amount to secession. The multiethnic empire survives when a new or renewed brutal state security apparatus is constructed, which then puts down the secession. Of course, in contemporary Iraq, the United States, because of the very nature of its democratization project, prevented the construction of any such security apparatus. The result was an Iraq that was neither a multiethnic empire nor a liberal democracy, but merely an ongoing anarchy amounting to a civil war.

Idealists versus Realists

The perennial U.S. efforts at democratization abroad have given rise to a perennial debate over U.S. foreign policy—the famous and long-standing debate between "idealists" and "realists." As it happens, each of these two camps can make a useful contribution to our examination into the successes and failures of U.S. democratization projects. Unfortunately, it is also the case that each camp can lead us into serious errors as well.

The idealist error. In their pure form, idealists neglect the historical record of the failed projects, and they therefore ignore the lessons that might be drawn from these failures. This kind of behavior has certainly been true of the promoters of the recent U.S. project in the Middle East. The idealists also neglect the historical record in another sense: they normally ignore the cultural and social particularities—and therefore the realities—of the countries which they seek to democratize. This too has been a characteristic of the promoters of the recent project in the Middle East. The most pronounced examples of this willful ignorance of cultural, social, and historical particularities have been the neo-conservatives, especially (and most consequentially) in their writings on Iraq. One can read the entire published works of Paul Wolfowitz, Norman Podhoretz, William Kristol, Richard Perle, Robert Kagan, and Charles Krauthammer, in which they promoted the invasion of Iraq, and learn nothing about those cultural and social features of Iraq which have caused the debacle of the U.S. democratization project—and indeed of the U.S. war effort itself—in that torn and tormented country (most obviously, nothing about the Sunnis, the Shi'ites, and the sectarian strife between them).

Indeed, the idealists normally ignore the cultural and social particularities of America itself. The neo-conservatives are always talking about America being a "propositional nation" (i.e., one based upon universal ideals and with no distinctive, inherited ethnic or even national identity), as if Americans were all intellectuals engaged in discourse and debates about propositions like the neo-conservatives themselves. But, of course, most Americans have their own very real, immediate, and particular ethnic identities and economic interests, and they normally do not see these identities and interests advanced by abstract (and bloody and costly) democratization projects abroad. This is why the Bush administration's (and the neo-conservatives') project in Iraq was left with virtually no support within the American public.

The realist error. Conversely, in their pure form, realists neglect the historical record of the successful democratization projects, and they therefore overlook countries where conditions have developed which could facilitate democratization in the future. This kind of failure of imagination led realists in the 1980s to be skeptical of the real potential for successful democratization in most of Eastern Europe. Their focus on past cultural, social, and historical particularities led them to assume that the dismal political history of the region could only be repeated. However, by the 1980s, the economic development of much of Eastern Europe had created social and economic conditions comparable to those reached in Central Europe several decades before, i.e., by the 1920s. In addition, the growing connections between communist Eastern Europe and liberal-democratic Western Europe made the liberal-democratic alternative seem both very attractive and very feasible.

Moreover, and ironically, the realists normally neglect a cultural and social particularity of America itself, and that is the fact that virtually any major U.S. foreign policy has to be legitimated with some kind of democratic rhetoric. This is a necessary part of bringing certain groups (especially liberal professionals and professional liberals) into a grand coalition to support the policy. Finally, a fundamental reality about America's position in the world is that in general U.S. national interests are indeed best served and advanced when other states become established liberal democracies.

A Different Kind of Democratization: Illiberal Democracy

Democratization in the Middle East is now obviously a failed project. Is it possible, however, there are other regions where democratization might still have a promising future? As it happens, there is one such region, and that is Latin America. However, the form democratization is most likely to take there will not be similar to the American one, i.e., *liberal* democracy, complete with some kind of separation of powers, constitutionalism, rule of law, and minority rights. It is more likely to be what Fareed Zakaria has called "illiberal democracy," particularly *populist* democracy, marked perhaps by generally free elections but also by presidential dominance, pervasive executive discretion, and majority rule.

Populist, or illiberal, democracy seems to be a natural political tendency, and a perennial political system, in much of Latin America. It certainly returned in a big way in that region in the 2000s, replacing the more liberal-democratic regimes of the 1990s (which were often derided as imposing "neo-liberalism" and "the Washington Consensus" on their citizens and on behalf of U.S. interests). The most extreme versions of populism now rule in Venezuela and Bolivia, but some version of populist democracy now prevails in Mexico, Brazil and Uruguay. Populist movements also were recently in power in Argentina, Chile, and Ecuador. All in all, Latin America has been swept by a major wave of populist democracy since the 2000s. Populism in Latin America is also anti-"imperialism," which means that it is usually anti-Americanism. As with Islamism in the Middle East, free elections in Latin America often put into power governments which resent or even loathe the United States. If America were not now bogged down in its forever wars in the Greater Middle East, U.S. policymakers and the American media would forever be talking about the populist threat in Latin America.

In the fullness of time, the recurring economic and social failures of populist democracy will probably discredit it, just as the failures of liberal democracy have lately discredited that political alternative. Some new (or renewed) system will then arise in Latin America, perhaps yet another variation on an authoritarian theme. But it will probably be at least a generation before we see a revival of the distinctively-U.S. project of liberal democracy in Latin America.

A Different Kind of Liberalism: Liberal Undemocracy

If democracy without liberalism is the likely future for Latin America, is there a place where we might hope for the obverse, i.e., liberalism without democracy, or liberal undemocracy, so to speak? After all, most Western European countries passed through this stage in the 19th century on their path from authoritarian monarchy to liberal democracy. As it happens, there was indeed one very large country where, until recently, a phase of liberal undemocracy seemed to be a reasonable prospect—China.

The extremely rapid economic development of China since the early 1980s has produced a new and extremely numerous middle class, and, like the classical European and American middle classes, the Chinese middle class is largely independent and certainly productive. For many practical purposes, the Chinese Communist Party devolved economic decision-making to a new and dynamic elite of entrepreneurs. Moreover, there developed a very well-educated but also very sensible professional sector. But entrepreneurs and professionals normally seek the legal and political stability and predictability that come with the expansion of the rule of law and constitutionalism. Historically, these two sectors have formed a strong constituency for liberal institutions, even if these institutions are not yet really democratic, and in the 2000s they seemed to have done so in China. It thus seemed that China would follow along a path taken in earlier decades by other East Asian countries, in particular Japan, Taiwan, and South Korea.

However, because of the vast size and diversity of China, full democracy itself would probably unleash a variety of centrifugal tendencies and secessionist movements. At least, this is what the Chinese Communist Party firmly believes. Any road to democracy in China will be far more rocky and risky than it was in the much smaller and more homogenous countries of Japan, Taiwan, and South Korea. Consequently, we are not going to get democratic institutions in China anytime soon, even though we might see some liberal institutions there—in short, liberal undemocracy.

Is There Any Future for Liberal Democratization?

Finally, despite the somber analysis, the dismal science, that we have offered in this chapter, is there any place where there can be progress in the future in the direction of good old, American-style liberal democracy? Perhaps the place to look is near where there has been such dramatic progress in that direction in the recent past. Certainly, the grand narrative of post-communist Eastern Europe represents one of the most striking successes of democratization, although not yet consistently liberal democratization. Is it possible that the region immediately to the south and the east of Eastern Europe (which is once again better thought of as Central Europe) might provide another chapter in the success story of liberal democratization? This region is the Balkans.

At the moment, this region does not seem very promising. Illiberal, particularly populist, democracy seems to be the most prevalent political tendency in much of the contemporary Balkans, specifically in Romania, Bulgaria, Serbia, and Macedonia. These countries are democratic in the sense of free elections, but they are hardly characterized by stable and effective political institutions or by the rule of law. However, much of the populations of these countries wanted to become members of the European Union, and Romania and Bulgaria became so in 2007.

The E.U. has exerted great pressure upon these countries to strengthen the rule of law, constitutionalism, and liberal institutions generally, as a condition for membership. Thus, the struggle between populist democracy and liberal democracy is now the main story in this region.

It is a story, however, whose major author is the European Union, not the United States. The E.U., closer to this region in almost every sense—geographical, economic, and cultural, is both necessary and sufficient to make this one more success story for liberal-democratization projects. The United States has very little that it can add (although with its perennial, crude oversimplifications, it can subtract). And so, it seems that, as we look around the world and peer into the future, we can discern a variety of ongoing democratic and liberal projects—populist democracy, liberal undemocracy, and even liberal democracy. But in regard to any traditional U.S. democratization project, we can now discern nothing in the future at all.

CHAPTER FIVE

THE ADOLESCENT EMPIRE:

AMERICA AND THE IMPERIAL IDEA

THE PRINCIPAL FOREIGN-POLICY INITIATIVE of the second Clinton administration was the enlargement of the North Atlantic Treaty Organization to include the Czech Republic, Poland, and Hungary. These old and much-abused nations, having been historically a part of Mitteleuropa or Central Europe and having passed through a forty-year confinement within Soviet-dominated Eastern Europe, eagerly sought to become part of Western Europe or even of the North Atlantic. In support of this undertaking, there was formed a group of foreign-policy leaders and specialists from different NATO countries whose name was, appropriately, the New Atlantic Initiative. They gathered for a conference, the "Congress of Prague," in that most ancient and beautiful of Central European capitals in May 1996.

I had attended and enjoyed the Congress of Prague, both the Congress part and the Prague part, but I was now sitting in the late afternoon of a beautiful spring day on a bench in the main square of another ancient and beautiful Bohemian town, Kutna Hora, some 50 kilometers east of the Czech capital.

Kutna Hora was now small, but it still had within it a splendid ensemble of Renaissance and Baroque buildings, monuments to the time when its vast silver mines provided the financial basis not only for magnificent churches, monasteries, and palaces, as well as the town square in which I was now sitting, but for an entire empire, that of the Habsburgs. The Habsburgs were the first to believe that the master of Bohemia was the master of Europe, and the silver mines of Kutna Hora were a big part of the reason. The Habsburg empire had fought and won many battles to keep the town and its mines in its domain, and it had succeeded in doing so right down until 1918.

But in the 20th century, Kutna Hora had experienced the rule of two other empires, that of Nazi Germany, when the town found itself in the Reich Protectorate of Bohemia-Moravia, and that of the Soviet Union, when it found itself in the Czechoslovak Socialist Republic. Needless to say, these empires left no architectural legacy comparable to that of the Habsburgs.

Now, it seemed, a fourth empire, that of America, was about to extend its protection over Kutna Hora and over the Czech Republic in which it found itself. Indeed, in a sense, the American empire had already extended its "soft power" there with its popular culture. For as the sun dipped beneath the lofty spines and gabled roofs above the old square, I heard the sound of rap music coming from the boom boxes carried by the adolescent boys—wearing their baseball caps and baggy pants—of the town.

A Tale of Two Tales

Thus, in the 20th century, three great empires had been the master of Bohemia—the Habsburg Monarchy, Nazi Germany, and the Soviet Union. Now a fourth great power, also an empire in its own way, was preparing to extend its power and promising to extend its peace and prosperity over Bohemia and the other ancient lands of Central Europe. But unlike the earlier empires, the United States was extending its realm with the full concurrence and even urging of the Central European peoples themselves, of whom the most welcoming were the people of Bohemia. From the perspective of the Central Europeans at this historical moment and from the perspective of the Americans themselves, American power had nothing in common with empire. There is much to be said for this view, and Americans never cease to say it.

From the perspective of other Europeans on other occasions, however, American power has been the last in a grand parade of empires that have marched through the past half-millennium or the modern age. This age could be said to have begun with Columbus's discovery of the New World. But this in turn was quickly followed by the rapid ascent of Habsburg power, so that it held sway over both the New World and much of the Old, extending from Bohemia to Spain to the Americas and even to the Philippines. As we will see, there is much to be said for this view too.

The story of American power in international affairs, then, is really a tale of two tales—an American tale, the story of a democratic republic and the steady spread of its universal values, and a European tale, the story of an American empire and the steady spread of its imperial idea.

The American Tale: The Democratic Republic

Americans, of course, have rarely been comfortable with the notion that their role in international affairs might be an imperial one. The United States was born in a war of independence by the American colonies against the British empire, the greatest empire of the time. It fought a second war of independence, the War of 1812, against that empire, and throughout the 19th century it thought of itself as the American republic standing up to the European empires, with the British one continuing as the principal threat.

Americans saw their successive expansions during the 19th century as territorial annexations, which were clearly natural, even "manifest destiny," rather than imperial acquisitions which made subjects of foreign peoples in far-flung lands. The acquisition of the Philippines and other territories in the Pacific and of Puerto Rico and other territories in the Caribbean in the 1890s were in fact very similar to the overseas acquisitions of the European empires at the time. The Americans were so uncomfortable with this reality, however, that they soon began to call it something else (e.g., the Commonwealth of the Philippines, later followed by the Commonwealth of Puerto Rico; the quick granting of formal independence to Cuba and to Panama).

The rhetoric and even policies of President Woodrow Wilson in the First World War and President Franklin Roosevelt in the Second World War were explicitly anti-colonial in their visions of what should be the shape of the post-war world. This led to ongoing tensions with the allies, Britain and France, who possessed the two largest overseas empires in the world. And although the United States itself acquired more overseas territories in the course of these wars—the Danish West Indies, which became the U.S. Virgin Islands, in the First World War; Micronesia and other Pacific Islands in the Second World War—Americans never thought of these acquisitions as part of an empire. Indeed, since they cannot fit into any American concept of themselves, they have almost never thought about them at all.

Finally, in the aftermath of the Second World War and with the advent of the Cold War, American power and presence extended throughout the Free World (especially Western Europe, Northeast Asia, and Latin America), if not the globe. That power and presence extended farther in the aftermath of the Cold War. Yet at no time during the past seven decades have either the public officials or the common public in the United States ever referred to themselves as an empire or to their role as an imperial one. Even terms which are softer (and more precise), such as "hegemony" and "sphere of influence," have been applied to the United States only by academic specialists in international affairs. The American terms for the American international role have been "collective security," "treaty organizations" or alliances, "international institutions," "trade associations," and "the advancement of human rights." If America is an empire, it has to be the least explicit one in history.

A European Tale: The American Empire

It is simple, however, to compose an account of the U.S. role in international affairs that shows its similarity with various European empires. In the past, Europeans, along with Latin Americans and East Asians, have often done so.

In the 1990s, however, many Europeans wanted the United States to extend its military and economic role into Central and Eastern Europe (the enlargement of NATO and the investment of capital), and discussion about an American empire was impolitic and subdued. Similarly, many Latin American elites wanted the United States to expand its economic role in their region in particular ways (the enlargement of NAFTA and again the investment of capital). Here, too, it was impolitic to indulge in all that discussion of "American imperialism," which was so widespread in so many generations of Latin Americans.

In the present, however, there are disappointments with this or that aspect of the expanded American role in Europe and in Latin America, and there are bound to be further disappointments in the future. This has generated among some Europeans and Latin Americans a revival of discussions about an American empire. In any event, the Chinese are developing their own analyses of the United States in imperial perspective. We shall refer to accounts of the similarities between the United States and the European empires simply as "the European tale."

In the European tale, the American experience is not just compared with the overseas and formal empires of Britain, France, and Spain, which are relatively well-known in the United States and which seem clearly unlike the American practice, with the exception of such obvious anomalies as the Philippines and Puerto Rico (and irrelevancies such as the Virgin Islands and the Pacific islands). Comparisons are also made with the informal versions of these overseas empires and with the overland empires of Prussia and Russia. Distinctions and differences that are important in the American tale are far less prominent in the European one. This is the case with the difference between overseas and overland expansion and with the difference between formal and informal rule.

In the European tale, the 19th-century overland annexations of the United States (especially the Louisiana Purchase and the Southwestern annexations after the Mexican War) were reminiscent of the 18th-century overland annexations of Prussia (especially Poland) and the several-century overland annexations of Russia (again Poland, but also the Caucasus, Central Asia, and Siberia). On this view, the major difference between the American "Westward Movement" and the

German "Drive to the East" is merely one of direction. (Germans and Russians sometimes added that while they may have exploited people that they conquered, the Americans largely exterminated them.)

More relevant in our time, however, is what the European tale says about the 20th century. Here, the important idea is that empire can be "informal" as well as "formal," that there are different kinds and degrees of imperial rule, but they are all variations on an imperial theme. With the European empires, formal rule over colonial peoples was the norm. But some of these empires, most notably the British one but also the French and the Russian, included an "informal empire," i.e., less formal rule over a variety of protectorates, client states, and dependencies. These countries were formally independent or autonomous, but really dependent and constrained. One ideal-typical and colorful example was the "princely states" of India, with their maharajahs, which existed side-by-side with British India proper, with formal direct administration by British officials.

While with the European empires, formal rule was the norm and informal rule the exception, with the American empire, informal rule has been the norm and formal rule the exception. But both Europeans and Americans have engaged in both formal and informal varieties of imperial rule. From a European perspective, there was not much difference in the first half of the 20th century between British rule over the Federated Malay States, French rule over the monarchies of Indochina (Annam, Cambodia, and Laos), and American rule over the Commonwealth of the Philippines. Nor was there much difference between British rule over its mandates and clients in the Middle East (Iraq, Jordan, and Egypt), French rule over its mandates in the region (Syria and Lebanon), and American rule over its sphere of influence in the Caribbean and Central America (not only during the first half of the 20th century but also during the second).

The most important similarities between the European and the American empires, however, do not lie in the realm and at the scale of specific dependent territories, even ones as large as a sub-continent (India) or a continent (Latin America). The most important feature of an empire is how it seeks to order not just its own territories but an entire world, to set the standard for a way of life and for the spirit of an age. This is exemplified in the empire's particular vision of politics, economics, culture, and ultimately of such fundamentals as human nature and the meaning of life itself. These compose its imperial idea. We will consider the imperial ideas of six great empires, from the Habsburg to the American.

The Habsburg Empire and the Roman Catholic Faith

It was the Roman empire that first taught Europeans what an empire could and should be. It set the standard and haunted the imagination of Europeans for more than a millennium after its fall. The Roman imperial idea was expressed in the Roman law and the Latin language and embodied in classical architecture and the Roman family. Long after the power of empire had disappeared, these four features remained as a venerable legacy of the empire's achievements as an empire of the mind. But the Roman empire also lived on in a concrete, institutional way as well, in the form of the Roman Catholic Church, whose structure and offices (including the highest one, the master bridge-builder between the temporal and the spiritual realms or Pontifex Maximus) mirrored those of the empire. The Roman Catholic Church was a far more real heir to the Roman empire than its more temporal and sometime rival, the medieval Holy Roman Empire.

It was wholly natural then, for the first empire of the modern era, that of the Habsburgs of Austria and Spain, to believe that it was bringing about a long-awaited restoration of the Roman empire. Indeed, this restored empire would be more complete and more fulfilled than the original, for it would include not just the Old World but also the New, and not just the temporal world but also the spiritual one. The Habsburg empire was a renaissance empire in a double sense, not only in its particular era but also in its imperial idea.

At the center of the Habsburg imperial idea was the Roman Catholic faith. Every major feature of the empire was an expression of the Roman Catholic conception of the human condition. This can be seen in such disparate areas as government, law, economics, city planning, public architecture and, in the Spanish realm, even the design of the private home. Human nature was understood to be a complex product of both divine grace and human sin, with human beings capable of both great good and great evil. The good would be nurtured and the evil subdued within a strong governing authority and a strong spiritual authority that worked closely together. These authorities, however, allowed local energies to flourish within the universal (catholic as well as Catholic) order. Real local autonomy was contained within formal centralized authority.

In the Habsburg and Catholic vision, the ideal human type was the saint. But as was shown most clearly in the Spanish version, saints might be as varied as the soldier in the perpetual service of the faith (Saint Ignatius of Loyola, the founder of the Jesuits or Soldiers of Christ) or the mystic in perpetual communion with the divine (Saint John of the Cross, Saint Theresa of Avila). More commonly, however, the human ideal was the mature person who had experienced enough of life's challenges, trials, and sorrows to have acquired strength, wisdom and judgment, and who could now govern and guide others for the common good. Such a person was needed to find the poised balance that was energy within order. And such a degree of maturity could only be reached after many decades of adulthood, probably not until one's 50s, if then.

The British Empire and the Benevolent Monarchy

The British empire is not normally regarded as having anything like a vision of the sort that we have described for the Habsburgs. There definitely was some kind of British imperial ideal, however, even though its vision was less cohesive, less centralized, so to speak, than that of the Habsburgs. In fact, there were several ideas at the center of the British conception of empire.

One idea, parallel to the Roman Catholicism of the Habsburg empire, was Protestant Christianity. This idea had a remarkably long run, from the time of Elizabeth I (as the "Virgin Queen," a Protestant counterpart to the Catholics' Virgin Mary) to the time of Victoria and its numerous and active missionary societies. But the Protestant faith in the British empire was less pervasive and comprehensive than the Roman Catholic faith was in the Habsburg one. Another idea was that of the British (or English) nation (or, for a while, race), which was parallel to the central idea of the French empire, which is discussed below. But the British nation really consisted of a complicated mixture of English, Scottish, and even Welsh nations, gathered together in a United Kingdom rather than in an unambiguous nation-state like that of the French. This idea, too, could not be truly pervasive and comprehensive, especially for an empire whose peoples were so disparate and (even the British people themselves) so far-flung.

Probably the most central of the ideas of the British conception of empire was the British monarchy. The soul of the British empire was loyal service to King (or Queen) and Country. Much of the empire's legitimacy derived from the legitimacy of its monarchy, which was seen as a benevolent one, and from the loyalty of the civil and military officers who served it. The American war of independence, which replaced a monarchy with a republic, helped make the remaining loyal parts of the empire even more attached to the monarchy—the more loyalist, the more royalist. The clearest example was English-speaking Canada, largely founded by refugees or émigrés from the American revolution, who called themselves the United Empire Loyalists.

For the British empire, the ideal human type was the soldier, later joined by the civil administrator, in the service of the King (or Queen). The virtues upheld in this ideal were loyalty, duty, honesty (from honor), integrity, common sense, and good judgement. These were qualities normally found only in mature men. But this British ideal of maturity could be reached at an earlier age than that of the Habsburgs, probably in one's 40s.

The French Empire and the Rational Nation-State

The French empire was not as far-flung or as long-lasting as the Habsburg and the British ones. For more than a century (1830s-1950s), however, it was the second largest empire in the world. The center of the French imperial idea was the French nation-state, organized according to the principles of reason (or Reason). By its nature, this idea would seem to be less universal than that of the Habsburgs (less catholic, more national) or even than that of the British (less global, more national). However,

Reason was usually seen as being even more universal than Catholicism. The French had to deal continually with the tension between the national claims of France and the universal claims of Reason.

The French imperial idea was even more constrained by the fact that France was so clearly the ideal-typical nation-state. In addition, the French empire, more than the Habsburg and the British, was characterized by formal rule and by formal distinctions between who was in and who was out. The French claims to universalism rested upon the remarkable notion that, because French national culture was the most classical, logical and rational of cultures, its distinctive feature was that it was really the most universal (certainly the most superior) culture of all. As the highest culture, the high culture of France was supposed to have the widest appeal. In theory human nature was perfectible, and in practice the human nature of an elite few was perfectible through the reason expressed and the education organized by the French state.

For the French empire, the ideal human type was the man of action (or of affairs) in the service of reason. The human ideal was a mature man who had lived and reasoned long enough to become an effective and efficient administrator of others for the public good. But this French ideal of maturity could be reached at an earlier age than that of the Habsburgs or even the British, probably as early as one's 30s.

The Nazi Empire and Racial Identity

The brief rule of Nazi Germany over other peoples was so brief, so extreme, and so perverse that it hardly deserves to be called an empire—which connotes at least some degree of order and durability—at all. However, Germany's central place in Central Europe and its special role in Bohemia (the Reich Protectorate of Bohemia-Moravia) makes this case an interesting story in its own right.

As is well-recognized, Germany's national unification in 1871 was peculiar: it not only came late, but it also remained incomplete. At that time virtually all of the British people were in Britain or, when elsewhere (e.g., Canada, Australia), under British rule. Similarly, virtually all of the French people were in France (the exceptions being Belgium, some Swiss cantons, and Quebec).

The situation of the German people was quite different. The political circumstances of German unification had meant that the Germans in the Habsburg Monarchy, who were the dominant or imperial people in its Austrian half, could not be included in the new German state. This would not have been a problem to the Germans in Austria if they could have continued to rule. By the end of the 19th century, however, this was becoming problematic. The German proportion of the empire's population was declining while the democratic suffrage was increasing. The conjunction of the demographic trend with the democratic one made it clear that the Germans could become merely one of several minorities in what had been their own empire. This sense of a steady and relentless decline in their proportion of the population and in their political and social position gave rise in the German communities of the Habsburg Monarchy to a "politics of cultural despair." The consequence was an acute sense of cultural identity which, given the reigning intellectual ideas of the time, became an acute sense of racial identity. The consciousness of German cultural and racial identity was much more intense in Austria-Hungary—i.e., outside of Germany—than it was in Germany itself. Unfortunately, this was the atmosphere in which Adolf Hitler came of age.

In later decades, other imperial peoples underwent their own demographic and democratic transitions and declines, issuing in their own politics of cultural despair. The one million French in Algeria and the one million British in Northern Ireland are the most well-known examples. But the twelve million Germans in the Habsburg Monarchy presented a problem of vastly greater magnitude. With the collapse of the Monarchy in 1918, the problem became a disaster.

The peace settlement after the First World War created a fatal dynamic toward a murderous empire. Given Germany's central place in Europe's geography and its leading place in Europe's economy, it was inevitable that German power would eventually revive. Given the parcelling-up of the non-European world between the victorious empires of Britain and France, if a powerful Germany sought to create its own empire, it would have to create it within Europe itself. Given the new but weak states between Germany and Russia (now the Soviet Union), it was inevitable that Germany would create this empire in the East. Finally, given the fact that two of these new states (Czechoslovakia and Poland) together ruled five million Germans, who would always be exposed and vulnerable minorities in their states, it was inevitable that any German empire would have as a central project, a fixed idea, the protection and preservation of these German minorities. The majority of these Germans, more than three million, were concentrated in Bohemia alone.

The protection and preservation of a once-dominant and now-subordinate minority is a hard task, and the methods used will normally be hard as well, at minimum institutionalized discrimination and repression (as the white population in the American South—actually a demographic majority—believed for a century after the Civil War). But from 1939 to 1945, the German empire in East-Central Europe combined the power of the revived German state with the ideology of racial identity, which had sprung from the politics of cultural despair of Austria-Hungary. This ideology of racial identity was the imperial idea of Nazi Germany.

For the Nazi Empire, the ideal human type was the S.S. officer in the service of the German *Volk* and the Aryan race. The virtues upheld in this ideal were courage, strength, endurance, heroism, and loyalty (the S.S. motto was "loyalty is my honor"). These are not the distinguishing qualities found in a mature man. Indeed, they are most likely to be found in a young man in his physical prime, i.e., in his 20s.

The Soviet Empire and Industrial Growth

The Soviet or Russian empire shared some important qualities with the Nazi or German one. They both sought to rule the same territory, East-Central Europe. They both sought to legitimize their rule with a secular ideology.

The fundamental dynamics of the German and the Russian empires were different, however. There were no significant Russian minorities in East-Central Europe (although there were such further east in Estonia, Latvia, and Ukraine). It was not the peoples of East-Central Europe that represented a threat to the Russians; it was the geography. Poland in particular had been the springboard for repeated invasions of Russia from the West (e.g., Napoleonic France, Wilhelminic Germany, Nazi Germany, and even Poland itself in 1919). From the Russian perspective, the real Polish corridor went from West to East and was Poland itself. Other countries in East-Central Europe (e.g., Hungary and Romania) also had served as a base for invasions. At the end of the Second World War, Stalin insisted upon converting East-Central Europe into a vast buffer zone between the Soviet Union and the West, one which would be ruled (in the words of the Yalta agreement) by "governments friendly to the Soviet Union." For the next four decades, the central project of the Soviet empire was the protection and preservation of this buffer zone. No other European empire had at its core quite this kind of problem and project.

The Soviet empire was unique in another way. In almost every empire, and in the other five that we are discussing, the imperial people has been economically and, yes, culturally more advanced than the subordinate ones. The Russian empire was one of those rare and perverse cases (the Ottoman empire was another) where the imperial people was less advanced than those that were subordinate. The Russians combined superior power with inferior culture. This made their empire particularly loathsome to East-Central Europeans.

The Russians therefore had an especially difficult task in legitimizing their empire with a higher idea. Of course, they initially made a big effort to have that imperial idea be Marxist ideology, but this was soon replaced in practice with the claim that Soviet communism and the Soviet development model were superior in providing for economic growth. By the early 1980s, however, this particular imperial idea clearly had proven false, and it now actually delegitimated the empire and helped to bring about its sudden fall.

What was the ideal human type of the Soviet imperial idea? In the Stalinist era, it was of course "the new Soviet man," the industrial worker whose virtues were strength, endurance, loyalty, and, in time of war, heroism. Like those of the S.S. man, these were the virtues of a young man in his 20s. But in the later decades of the Soviet empire this young Soviet man grew older without acquiring any new virtues or growing any more mature. Indeed, it soon became clear that in the Soviet imperial idea there was no place for an ideal human type, but just different kinds of utterly prosaic, mundane, and boring human beings.

The Young Empire and the Mature Americans

During and after the Second World War, American power and presence, the American empire, underwent a great leap outward from the western hemisphere to the world itself, or at least to Western Europe and Northeast Asia. "Present at the creation" of this new, world-spanning empire was that extraordinary generation of "wise men"—especially George Marshall, Dean Acheson, and George Kennan—and three successive presidents—Franklin Roosevelt, Harry Truman, and Dwight Eisenhower.

Of course at the time, not everyone acknowledged that these leaders were "wise men." Indeed, even among themselves, they occasionally belittled each other. The two who were generally held in the widest and highest regard, George Marshall and Dwight Eisenhower, had the advantage of having been the leading American soldiers of the Second World War, respectively "the architect of victory" and "the liberator of Europe." Seen from the perspective of later decades, however, these men do seem to be not only wise, but extraordinarily so. They exemplify a maturity of experience, understanding, character, and judgment that has been achieved only rarely in American history (George Washington, along with several of the other Founding Fathers, and Abraham Lincoln come to mind), and indeed only rarely in the history of the world.

Some other things were also at work, however. The wise men of the post-war decade had not just been leaders during the challenges of the Second World War. They and their generation had experienced directly three successive periods of crisis and challenge that together had filled most of their adult years—the First World War and the Great Depression along with Second World War. Some had experienced personal affliction or tragedy as well, most obviously Roosevelt but also Marshall and Eisenhower. In addition, most of these American leaders had extensive, even intimate, experience with Europe. In this, they had experienced vicariously some of the triumphs and tragedies of several generations of old nations, not just those of their own generation of Americans. This kind of understanding was perfectly expressed in the writings of George Kennan. No American in public affairs (indeed, probably no American in academic life) has ever demonstrated a more

European sensibility or wiser and more mature understanding than Kennan did in his memoirs and diaries.

The wise men at the center of the new American empire were joined by comparable men in the old nation-states that had become the new American allies. During the post-war decade, unusually mature and seasoned men served as the leaders of West Germany (Konrad Adenauer), Italy (Alcide de Gasperi) and Japan (Shigeru Yoshida). Reaching their country's highest office a decade after the Second World War, these leaders actually had been born a generation before Hitler, Mussolini, and Tojo, the men who had led their countries into disaster during the war. The wartime leaders had been radicals, albeit radicals of the right; their successors, who were a generation older in age as well as a decade later in leadership, were true conservatives. The political leadership in Britain and in France, during the post-war era, was more varied. However, that seasoned British conservative, Winston Churchill, returned to power during 1951-1955, and his French counterpart, Charles de Gaulle, returned to power during 1958-1969.

In its first generation, then, an extraordinary group of wise men presided over the center of the American empire, designed its structures, composed its policies, and governed its energies. A similarly extraordinary group of wise men presided over the major dominions of the empire and adapted and applied the imperial policies to the local realities of their own nations.

The American Empire: Peace and Prosperity

During the next two generations, the American empire brought peace and prosperity to its major dominions, the industrial nations of Western Europe and Northeast Asia (first Japan and later South Korea and Taiwan). The peace and prosperity were less evident in other regions of the empire, particularly Latin America. But even here the benefits of peace and prosperity were enjoyed by the local elites.

Peace and protectorates. The long peace in Western Europe was due in part to the Cold War in Central Europe. The potential for Soviet aggression made manifest the need for American protection. The United States provided this with the security guarantees of NATO which can be seen as an unusually sophisticated system of military protectorates (which President de Gaulle not only saw but also said).

Many empires have included a form of military dependency which has been called a protectorate. The British empire was especially rich in these (e.g., the princely states of India, the Malay States, and a whole array of dependencies in Africa) but the French empire included such protectorates too (formally Annam, Cambodia, Laos, Morocco, and Tunisia). In most empires, the protectorates were more like protection rackets, with the imperial power really providing protection against itself. In the American empire, however, the protectorates of Western Europe and Northeast Asia were protected from a threat of foreign aggression, be it from the Soviet Union or from Communist China, that both the protectorates and the imperial power perceived and about which they largely agreed. Where the threat of foreign aggression was less obvious, as in Latin America and in the Middle East, American military protection was less meaningful. The U.S. security pacts (the Rio Pact in Latin America, the short-lived Baghdad Pact in the Middle East) were perceived by substantial parts of the local populations as being protectorates or even protection rackets in the conventional imperial (or imperialist) sense. The end, or at least radical decline, of the foreign (i.e., Russian) threat to Europe eroded a major basis for the legitimacy and stability of the American system.

The long peace in Western Europe was also due to the fact that the American empire seemed to have provided the final solution to the German question. From 1871 to 1945, unified Germany, which normally was both the greatest economic power and the greatest military power on the Continent, presented an intractable problem for its neighbors. After 1945, however, Germany was no longer the central military power in Europe but was divided down the middle of Central Europe by the two superpowers on either side of Europe. (As Soviet Marshal Georgi Zhukov said to President Eisenhower in 1955, "You have your Germany, and we have ours. It is better that way.") Further, Germany was no longer the leading economic power in Europe; that was now America. Finally, German minorities were no longer in a prominent but vulnerable position scattered around East-Central Europe. Rather, as a result of the great and terrible refugee flights of 1945, they were now crammed into Germany itself (mostly West Germany, where they were safely bottled up within a stable democratic state tightly integrated into the American alliance system).

Prosperity and preferences. The long prosperity in Western Europe was largely due to the open international economy organized by the United States. The memory of the Great Depression made manifest the need for American economic leadership. The United States provided this with the economic aid of the European Recovery Program (Marshall Plan), the International Monetary Fund, and the World Bank. Together, these institutions can be seen as an unusually sophisticated system of economic organization from an imperial center.

All empires have included some form of economic dependency. The British called theirs imperial preference, while the French termed theirs the colonial pact. In most cases, imperial preference and colonial pacts were really the preference of the imperial power for itself, at the expense of the colonial peoples; most familiar are the arrangements for the imperial powers to be the manufacturer of industrial goods while the colonial peoples remained the providers of agricultural ones. In the American empire, however, the preference of the imperial power was for its economic dependencies to rapidly reconstruct their old industries and even to construct new ones. As it turned out, for four decades the chief beneficiaries of the American system of open economies were the industries of the major dominions of the American empire, the nations of Western Europe and Northeast Asia.

This was no longer the case by the 1990s, however. The very prosperity of these major dominions lifted them onto the levels of high-wage, even post-industrial economies, and their industries became less competitive in the world market. With their unemployment rates from 10 to 15 percent, the Western European nations in particular were no longer confident that they benefitted from the open global economy.

The Future Bases for Imperial Legitimacy

What will be the bases for the American empire's legitimacy in the future? We shall consider three elements that have often been central to an imperial idea—peace, prosperity, and a pervasive, even popular culture.

For a long time, the Roman empire provided all three of these elements, and this was the reason for its enduring legitimacy. The Habsburg empire was stronger in prosperity than in peace and stronger still in its pervasive culture. The British empire, like the Roman, provided all three elements during "the long peace" of "the long nineteenth century." The French empire, like the Habsburg, was stronger in prosperity than in peace and stronger still in its cultural prestige. In contrast, the Nazi empire provided almost nothing of these three elements, and the Soviet empire provided little more. The Nazis sought their legitimacy in a battle for racial superiority, which they lost. The Soviets sought their legitimacy in a battle for economic growth, which they also lost.

As we have seen, the American empire has been largely successful in providing peace and prosperity. These, accordingly, have been the real and central components of the American imperial idea.

The peace component could continue to have a great deal of strength. The contemporary Russian threat is obviously a reduced version of the old Soviet one. But just as obviously, it loomed large enough in the strategic mind of virtually every country in Central and Eastern Europe so that it wanted to become a member of NATO. The specter of Russia will continue to haunt at least the eastern half of Europe.

Although there could be a greater potential for a Chinese threat to neighbors than a Russian one, the Chinese threat does not loom large in the strategic mind of the countries of East and Southeast Asia in the same way that the Russian threat looms in the strategic mind of those of Central and Eastern Europe. The reasons for the difference are many and complex, but a principal one is that the Soviets actually occupied their neighbors while the Chinese have not. Nevertheless, the potential for a Chinese threat is there, and thus the basis for a new U.S. containment policy and a new system of American security guarantees and military protectorates.

A policy of containment toward Russia and another policy of containment toward China are the likely result. Such policies may not be the best ones for the United States to follow toward these two difficult nations. They are certainly not the most discerning and subtle. Together, however, the two containment policies would provide a strong basis for the legitimization and continuation of an American system of military protectorates in Europe and in Asia, which are for America the most important regions in the world other than North America itself.

The prosperity component is more problematic. As we have noted, the very prosperity of major dominions of the American empire, particularly in Western Europe, lifted them onto the levels of high-wage, even post-industrial economies. Now, the most competitive economies in low-tech and mid-tech industries are the recently-industrial nations of East Asia, especially China but also Vietnam, Indonesia, and Malaysia. These are now the chief beneficiaries of the American system of open economies. Yet none of these nations has been a formal member of an American system of military protectorates. China, of course, has actually been a target of that system. Similarly, few of these nations have embraced the full principles and practices of the American system of open economies. Again, China has been most direct in rejecting them. In short, several of the major current beneficiaries of the American empire have not been socialized into its institutions and norms. Indeed, the largest beneficiary, China, has been socialized into—as well as socialist in—confronting them.

It is the cultural component of the American imperial idea that is now coming to the fore. While the peace component based upon military protection is becoming more ambiguous and the prosperity component based upon open economies is becoming more dubious, the "soft power" of popular entertainment based upon global media is becoming more pervasive.

It is a cliché that American popular culture is something different from the pervasive cultures of many of the empires of the past. The cultures that these earlier empires put forward to legitimize and embellish their rule were both pervasive and elevating. Spanish painting, Austrian music, Baroque architecture, British literature, and French elegance were all the expressions of a high culture, as were the public buildings and urban design in the Habsburg, British, and French empires. More fundamentally, as we have seen, the ideal human type of these empires was an elevated and elevating model, a mature person of admirable virtues.

It is no accident that high culture has never been a major component of the American imperial idea. Insofar as an American high culture even existed, it was lower than its European counterpart in every cultural genre. What might be called the "American empire style" of art (especially that of the late 1940s-early 1960s) was the always-ugly and now-discarded abstract expressionism. Its counterpart in architecture was the always-banal and now-tiresome international style or modernism. The real culture of the American empire, of course, has been what we call popular culture (although it is often forgotten that the high cultures of the earlier empires were rather popular too).

At the beginning of the American empire, however, at least its ideal human type was still a mature person of admirable virtues as exemplified by its "wise men." Two generations later, the ideal human type of the American empire had become the popular entertainer or sports star. These receive its highest public renown and its highest monetary rewards. The qualities (virtues don't even come to mind) needed to be an entertainer or sports star are inherent talent, self-centeredness, energy, and aggressiveness. As with the S.S. officer and the new Soviet man, these are not the distinguishing qualities of a mature person. Indeed, those who have them didn't even have to wait until their 20s to acquire them; they were already there in their teens.

In short, the ideal human type of the American imperial idea is an adolescent. It is no accident that adults in America are more and more adopting the qualities of adolescents—particularly self-centeredness and aggressiveness—in such professions as business, politics, law, and academia. It is also no accident that the most pervasive rule of American styles, fads, and fashions is found among the adolescents of the world.

It has always been the nature of adolescents to reject adults and to reject authorities. What is new is for adults in authoritative positions in American institutions (academic, media, and politics) to teach adolescents to reject all adults and authorities (family, church, and law) other than themselves. It is also new for adults in authoritative positions in the American empire to teach the adolescents of the world to reject them. Five decades after the wise men of the American empire, its leaders had come to act as if they were five decades younger.

The peace of the American empire has rested upon its military, and its prosperity has rested upon its productivity. An effective military and a productive economy both require a minimum of deference to authority and of discipline of one's self. These qualities have been relentlessly attacked and undermined by the soft power of the American empire. Daniel Bell once wrote of "the cultural contradictions of capitalism"—that the very success of capitalist production produces an excess of popular consumption, which in turn undermines capitalist production. This is paralleled in the cultural contradictions of the American imperial idea, where the peace and prosperity of the empire produces a self-centeredness and self-indulgence which in turn undermines the empire. The American empire is becoming an empire of adolescents, by adolescents, and for adolescents. But in the end—in its erratics, its entertainments, and its emptiness—an adolescent empire will be no empire at all.

PART II

STRATEGY

Chapter Six

Grand Strategy:

The Source of the Realist Tradition

In the past two decades, people in the American foreign-policy community have made many proposals about what should be the future direction of American foreign policy. Among them have been the promotion of democracy or the market, the containment of Islamist radicalism or Chinese expansionism, and the protection of human rights or the global ecology. Each of these foreign-policy directions would imply a particular grand strategy to carry it out.

This chapter will make some such proposals of its own. It will argue, however, that the best course for American foreign policy in the future has already been largely set by its legacy from the past. In most respects, the most appropriate foreign policy and accompanying grand strategy of the United States have already been composed by their historical tradition and trajectory and by the peculiar strengths and weaknesses of the American nation.

Three Cycles of American Foreign Policy

The United States has experienced three great cycles in its foreign policy. The first two cycles were each about eighty years in length, and we now are more than seventy years into what appears to be the third.

Each cycle commenced with a decisive victory by the United States in its epic war of the century—the Revolutionary War in the 18th century, the Civil War in the 19th, and the Second World War in the 20th. From that war and that victory, America drew lessons that would define and drive U.S. foreign policy for the next several decades. In the course of these decades, the United States at times interpreted these lessons with wisdom and discernment to expand and consolidate the legacy from the great victory. The results were major successes and even great and lasting achievements.

At other times, the United States was driven by a misreading, even an idolatry, of the past achievements to go beyond what Clausewitz called "the culminating point of victory" and to engage in what Paul Kennedy termed "imperial overstretch." The results were major failures and even great and damaging disasters. From these failures, the United States then drew new lessons, which became the basis for a more discerning and more focused version of the national project of expansion and consolidation. And from the disasters, it drew new and even deeper lessons which then became the basis for the next great victory and the beginning of the next great cycle.

We are now in the 2010s and near the end of the third cycle. At the equivalent phase in the previous two cycles, the United States had recently experienced a major success in its foreign policy (i.e., the Mexican War, the First World War), but it had then entered into a time of division and disorientation which in the end issued in disaster (the Civil War, the Great Depression and the Second World War). The challenge for U.S. foreign policy, after its great success in the Cold War and its division and disorientation since the Iraq War, is to rise above this fatal pattern from the past.

The First Cycle and Territorial Annexation:
From the Revolutionary War to the Civil War

After the achievement of its independence in the Revolutionary War, the new American nation focused its foreign policy upon the goal of expansion across the North American continent. The grand strategy to carry it out—territorial annexation—was the most obvious and simple one of all, but the American tactics were often extremely subtle, even by the standards of the long-experienced powers of Europe.

There were great achievements in this national project of continental expansion, especially the Louisiana Purchase, which was accomplished through the extraordinary diplomatic virtuosity of the Jefferson administration, but also the southwestern annexations, which were achieved through the U.S. military victory in the Mexican War. In the former case, the United States took advantage of the fact that the greatest European powers, Britain and France, were then engaged in their own epic war against each other. In the latter, the United States similarly took advantage of the fact that Britain and France were disrupted by serious internal turmoil (the Chartist Movement in Britain, the Revolution of 1848 in France). But it was also crucial that the arenas of expansion did not contain modern and organized societies equivalent to the United States (they were the Indian nations in the Louisiana Purchase, and the Mexican frontier in the southwestern annexations), nor did the U.S. expansion directly threaten the vital interests of any great power.

The situation was different in regard to the U.S. effort to carry its project of continental expansion into Canada, and this resulted in one of the two major failures of the first cycle, the War of 1812. In 1812, the United States thought that it was continuing its great national enterprise by its invasion of Canada. As British North America, this was a major pillar and vital interest of the empire which the British had reconstructed after the loss of their thirteen American colonies, but the United States thought that Britain would be distracted by its continuing war with France. This was a grave miscalculation, however. Canada was an organized society comparable to the United States and capable of offering stout resistance, and with Napoleon's defeat in Russia the British were fully able to deploy enough military forces to put the American experiment in grave danger (and in 1814 to put Washington, D.C. to the torch).

But the gravest failure of the first cycle occurred in the aftermath of the Mexican War, when the national project of continental expansion mutated into two competing sectional projects—Northern and Southern—of the expansion of liberty and the expansion of slavery. In the late 1850s the United States was torn, like Britain and France in the late 1840s, by grave internal division, which in the American case even went to the fundamental question of national identity. In this context, the preceding territorial annexations became vital stakes in an escalating conflict between two sections, even two nations. This was one of the fundamental causes of the greatest disaster in American history, the Civil War.

The Second Cycle and the Regional Sphere: From the Civil War to the Second World War

After the achievement of reunion in the Civil War, the renewed American nation again focused its foreign policy upon the goal of expansion—now really consolidation—across the North American continent. In fulfilling this great national project, the United States experienced almost unalloyed success. But this focus and this success were based upon some lessons learned from the previous failures. Now the United States drove straight westward, turning away from annexations of territories to the south and to the north, which were either populated by peoples of a different culture (the Dominican Republic, Haiti) or protected by a great power (Canada).

When in the 1890s the United States neared the completion of its national project of continental expansion ("the closing of the frontier" then observed by Frederick Jackson Turner), the obvious question was what kind of national project would come next. The simple answer was more territorial annexations beyond the continent, even further to the west (e.g., Hawaii, the Philippines, and beyond) and even to the south (e.g., Cuba, Puerto Rico, and beyond). The subtle and ultimately sounder answer was to create a new and different mode of expansion that better suited these new and different arenas of expansion, i.e., to replace the grand strategy of territorial annexation with the grand strategy of a regional sphere of influence.

The new arenas to the west and to the south of the continental United States had much larger and denser populations than had the territories gained through the Louisiana Purchase and the Mexican War. But unlike Canada, their societies were less modern and organized than that of the United States. It would be difficult to annex such peoples, but it would be easy to influence them. A regional sphere of influence was accordingly the suitable strategy. Further, a good number of the territories in these new arenas were not part of the empire of a European great power, but merely remnants of the empire of decrepit Spain or, as nominally independent countries, part of no empire at all. This meant that the European great powers had no vital interest in these territories. But because of their proximity to the United States as an emerging great power, the U.S. could easily persuade the European powers that it had a vital interest in them. This asymmetry between a U.S. vital interest and no European one in most of the Caribbean and Central America meant that the U.S. could easily establish a sphere of interest in that region and have it accepted as legitimate by the European great powers.

After its victory in the Spanish-American War, the United States thus established a secure sphere of influence and interest in the Caribbean and Central America. This was the second major success of U.S. foreign policy in the second cycle. It went beyond the first success of continental consolidation, not only geographically but conceptually by creating a new grand strategy of expansion.

At the same time, however, the United States made major errors which resulted in problems that would only be fully revealed decades later. The annexation of the Philippines immediately gave rise to the costly Philippine Insurrection and eventually set up a long-term conflict with Japan. The quasi-annexation of Cuba eventually resulted in Castro's revolution and Cuba's alliance with the Soviet Union.

In short, the grand national project of expansion and consolidation could continue in the second cycle, but certain distinctions now became important for the national strategy. Expansion through annexation had reached its natural limit with the end of expansion westward across the continent and the closing of the traditional frontier. The further annexations westward and southward were at best somewhat anomalous (Hawaii, Puerto Rico, and the Panama Canal Zone) or at worst exceptions that proved the rule (the Philippines and the quasi-annexation of Cuba). As for annexations northward, these were out of the question, put there by the consistent opposition of the Canadians and by the vital interests of the British Empire.

Instead, expansion would now take place through the projection of influence and interests, specifically with the construction of a regional sphere of influence (and also a sphere of concrete interests). This became the American grand strategy in the Caribbean and Central America in the 1900s-1910s and in Latin America more generally in the 1920s-1930s. But in this cycle the United States only cast its sphere of influence over societies that were culturally different from itself and much less economically developed. And it only cast it over one region which was an immediate neighbor.

The United States was now a great power, and when there broke out a great war between the European great powers, the U.S. also became involved. The U.S. participation in the First World War was crucial in breaking the stalemate on the Western Front and tipping the balance in favor of beleaguered France and Britain. The results were the decisive defeat of Germany and Austria-Hungary and the apparent triumph of the American ideals of democracy and self-determination. However, in terms of the pattern of U.S. foreign policy that we have discussed, there was very little connection between the U.S. victory in Europe in 1918 and the national projects of the previous 130 years. There was no way for the United States to engage in territorial annexations on the European continent as it had on the American continent. And there was even no way for the U.S. to construct a regional sphere of influence in Europe as it had in the Caribbean and Central America. The U.S. strategy for Europe would have to be a new invention, not a familiar tradition.

President Woodrow Wilson of course had a conception of such an invention with his proposals for the League of Nations and for a security guarantee to France and Britain. Later, some American business leaders had another conception of such an invention—the Dawes Plan of 1924 to finance the recovery of the German economy. These were embryonic versions of a new mode of expansion and consolidation, one based upon American leadership in international organizations or in the international economy, rather than upon regional spheres of influence or territorial annexations. But for most Americans in the 1920s, this new grand strategy—with its international scope and its innovative methods—required too great a stretch beyond the old strategies. The connections with American traditions were not clear enough, and with American interests, not broad enough to sustain it. The collapse of the new grand strategy and the return to the earlier strategies on a continental or regional scale were, as is well known, basic causes of the Great Depression, of German and Japanese aggression, and finally of the Second World War. The division and disorientation in U.S. foreign policy that followed upon the U.S. victory in the First World War, like the earlier division and disorientation that followed upon the U.S. victory in the Mexican War, brought about a new great disaster.

The Third Cycle and the International Order: From the Second World War to the Present

After the achievement of its great victory over Germany and Japan in the Second World War, the United States was once again ready to focus its foreign policy upon the goal of expansion, this time on a truly international scale. It had learned fundamental lessons from the great disasters of the recent past. From the Great Depression, it learned that the massive American economy—the leading industrial economy in the world—could also prosper in an open international economy, one that included its recent enemies Germany and Japan. From the Second World War, it learned that its own American continent and regional sphere could only be secure if no single great power dominated the European continent, or more broadly, the Eurasian landmass. The grand strategy to achieve these goals would now be the most sophisticated of all—American design and leadership of new international organizations, which in turn would institutionalize the opening of the international economy and the containing of any potential European or Eurasian hegemon.

There were grand achievements indeed in this national project of international expansion. It was not the United Nations, where American leadership was often checked by Soviet vetoes, that best represented these achievements, but the international organizations that helped to restore and open the international economy, especially the International Monetary Fund, the World Bank, and the General Agreement on Tariffs and Trade (the "Bretton Woods system"). Further, when the

United States had to solve the problem of European security, it created the North Atlantic Treaty Organization (NATO) to help contain the Soviet threat, and it added to this the Organization for European Economic Cooperation (OEEC) to help implement its economic aid program (the Marshall Plan). In NATO and the OEEC, the United States combined its concept of international organizations with its earlier concept of the regional sphere of influence. Indeed, in its leadership of Western Europe, the U.S. perfected the regional sphere of influence to the point of including nations that were modern and organized, and not merely underdeveloped, and that were located at a remote distance, and not merely in the immediate neighborhood. These achievements made this time "the heroic age of American foreign policy." For the rest of their lives, the men who participated in them would be proud to have been "present at the creation."

But, of course, there would soon be major failures in this third cycle as well. As it happened, each of them would involve a violation of the central norm of a regional sphere of influence, the very strategy at which the United States had been so successful in the second cycle.

The first major failure of the third cycle occurred early in the Korean War. The error in Korea was not entering the war to defend South Korea; this was necessary for the defense of Japan, which was a central pillar and vital interest of the emerging American international order. Nor was it crossing the 38th Parallel to punish North Korea; this may have been necessary to deter aggression in the future. Nor was it refusing to extend the war into China itself after the Chinese intervened in Korea. The error was carrying the war with North Korea to the point of eliminating it as a political entity and bringing U.S. troops to the border of China itself. By eliminating China's own Korean buffer state, the American advance to the Yalu River violated the central norm of any neighboring regional sphere of influence, be it the traditional Chinese order in East Asia or the modern American sphere in the Caribbean. The cost of this violation was a dramatic American defeat inflicted by the Chinese armies in the winter of 1950-1951 and two years of military stalemate until the armistice agreement of 1953 provided China and America each with their own Korean buffer state.

The second major failure in this cycle involved Cuba and was a violation of a sphere-of-influence norm in the opposite direction. The causes of Fidel Castro's revolution in Cuba are still a matter of debate. (My own view is that it largely resulted from years of intrusive American involvement that went beyond that appropriate for a sphere of influence.) The consequences, however, were extremely dangerous. When Cuba defected from the American sphere of influence into a Soviet alliance and when the United States allowed Cuba to get away with it (e.g., at the Bay of Pigs), this also violated the central norm of a neighboring sphere of influence. This violation of international expectations led the Soviets into grave miscalculations and into the Cuban Missile Crisis, which had the potential (President Kennedy himself put the chances as between one in three and one in two) to issue in a nuclear war and the greatest disaster in world history.

The third major failure of this cycle was the Vietnam War. From the Korean War the United States had correctly learned the lesson to not threaten the existence of a Chinese buffer state, which in this new war was North Vietnam. But this of course imposed major limitations on the ways that the U.S. military traditionally carried out its military operations. Given the geographical, political, and military circumstances of South Vietnam, these limitations in effect made the Vietnam War unwinnable. In this sense, the most important battle of the Vietnam War had actually been fought and lost at the Yalu more than fifteen years before. Under such conditions, the U.S. error in Vietnam was to undertake military intervention in the first place. The far better course would have been to use the different Asian communist states, especially China and Vietnam, to contain each other (as indeed happened as early as 1979). In short, the great failure, even disaster, of the Vietnam War would never have occurred if the United States had better understood and integrated the concepts of the regional sphere of influence and the regional balance of power. Indeed, less than twenty years after the U.S. political defeat in Vietnam, communist Vietnam was doing everything it could to enter into the American-led open international economy. In some ways, the war that the United States had once lost by an aberrant military strategy had now been won by its global economic strategy.

Indeed, in this sense the really decisive battle of the Vietnam War had actually been fought and won at Bretton Woods in 1944.

The causes of the ultimate victory of the United States over the Soviet Union in the Cold War were many. It is clear, however, that among the central causes were the dynamism of the open international economy, the inability of the Soviet system to cope with this, and the pressures that this put upon the Soviet leadership to change—and ultimately to abandon—that system.

The U.S. victory in the Cold War certainly brought an era to an end. But it did not bring our third cycle to an end. Rather, it seems to have initiated that cycle's most dangerous phase. In the 1990s, it seemed possible that after its Cold War victory, the United States could now look forward to successes and achievements comparable to those after the Revolutionary War, the Civil War, and the Second World War. But in the 2000s, with its clumsy response to Islamist terrorism and its ordeal in the Iraq War, the prospect arose that the United States might experience failures that would be comparable to those after the Mexican War and the First World War. To grasp the promise of the first prospect and to avoid the perils of the second, the United States will have to construct a foreign policy and grand strategy that draw upon certain enduring features of past U.S. grand strategies while transcending other equally enduring features. These two kinds of features come into sharpest relief when the American strategic tradition is contrasted with that of two other great powers.

The British and German Traditions of Grand Strategy

The American tradition of grand strategy as it developed in the 20th century can be usefully compared with the equivalent traditions of the European great powers. In particular, Britain and Germany represent two great and opposing national traditions of grand strategy.

The British strategic tradition was based upon Britain's position as an island off the European continent and its identity as a maritime power. As is well known, Britain sought to prevent a single land power from gaining hegemony over the continent. It did this by maintaining a balance of power in Europe and, when an expanding power threatened to gain hegemony, by organizing a coalition of other powers against it. Britain's chief instruments in implementing its balance-of-power strategy were the proficient diplomacy that organized its allies, the Royal Navy that protected them, and the financial subsidies that rewarded them.

Since Britain had a comparative disadvantage in land power, its use of its army was relatively modest. It was chiefly deployed to tip the balance or to provide a missing ingredient for the coalition of allied armies. Britain also preferred to deploy its army in peripheral theaters rather than on central fronts. This "indirect approach" was articulated by Basil Liddell Hart between the two world wars and was put into practice by Winston Churchill in the midst of those two wars (e.g., Gallipoli in 1915, Italy in 1943, and his proposal to invade the Balkans in 1944). But as Wellington's Peninsula Campaign against Napoleon exemplifies, it was established long before then.

The German strategic tradition was based upon Germany's position in the middle of the European continent (and in the middle of threatening great powers) and its identity as a land power. As is well known, Germany was peculiarly open to invasion from both east (usually from Russia) and west (usually from France). This threat wonderfully concentrated the minds of first Prussian and then German military leaders. They sought to prevent a single large power, or worse a coalition of them, from quickly invading and occupying vital and vulnerable German territories. Germany did this by maintaining a large standing army that could be rapidly deployed in either direction. This direct approach culminated in the Schlieffen Plan of the First World War and the blitzkrieg strategy of the Second.

It is obvious that the British condition led naturally to a major emphasis on diplomatic solutions, backed by a sophisticated array of naval and financial instruments, while the German condition led naturally to a major emphasis on military solutions, with much less proficiency in diplomacy and finance. Both powers had a tradition of grand strategy, but the British tradition was wider in its geographic scope, more varied in its use of instruments, and more patient in its sense of time. The British tradition often seemed subtle and sophisticated, while the German tradition often seemed simple and crude.

In short, of the two traditions of grand strategy, the British was the grander and the more successful.

The Grand Combination and the American Way of War

When it became a great power in the 20th century, the United States created a third national tradition of grand strategy, which was based upon America's position as its own continent separated by great oceans from both Europe and Asia. In many respects, the American strategy has been the grandest of all.

Since the beginning of the century, the United States has been both a maritime and a land power, and with the Second World War, it became an air power as well. As a maritime and a land power, the United States has combined central elements of the British and the German grand strategies. Like the British, the Americans have been proficient in the use of diplomacy to organize its allies, naval powers to protect them, and economic aid to reward them. The great achievements of the third cycle of American foreign policy were in many ways variations (and improvements) on a British theme, "America in Britain's place." However, like the Germans, the Americans have also been proficient in the rapid deployment of large armies, in excelling in both the mass and the mobility of their land forces. Indeed, some military analysts have seen this to be the distinctive feature of "the American way of war," with the origins of the American use of mass in the Civil War campaigns of Ulysses S. Grant and of mobility in those of Robert E. Lee.

The United States demonstrated this proficiency on several occasions in the 20th century, particularly in France in the last months of the First World War, in both the European and Pacific theaters in the Second World War, at Inchon during the Korean War, and in Iraq during the Gulf War of 1991. The strategies and successes of the American army on these occasions were equal or superior to those of the great campaigns of the German army. Conversely, there was almost no campaign of the British army in the 20th century that came close. In contrast, however, the United States was not able to use the mass and the mobility of its land forces against the Chinese in the Korean War or against the North Vietnamese in the Vietnam War. The fact that the

U.S. land forces could not deploy the strengths of "the American way of war" in these two land wars in Asia is a prime explanation for the American failures there. As we have seen, this fact grew out of the realities of the Chinese regional sphere of influence.

Finally, whereas both Britain and Germany were proficient in various high-technology weapons, only the United States has excelled in the mass production of them. This has been especially significant as the basis of the United States becoming the supreme air power.

However, the greatest strength of American grand strategy derives from its distinctive combination of elements from British and German strategies. The United States deployed this distinctive American strategic combination in the Second World War against both Germany (especially coalition diplomacy, economic assistance, army mass and mobility, and high-technology weaponry) and Japan (especially economic warfare, naval mass and mobility, and high-technology weaponry). It deployed a version of it again in 1991 in the Gulf War against Iraq (especially coalition diplomacy, economic sanctions, army mass and mobility, and high-technology weaponry). The fact that the United States since 1947 has had—in the Navy, Army, and Air Force—three co-equal military services has often been bemoaned as resulting in inter-service rivalry, excessive competition, and wasteful duplication. This trinity of co-equal services also means, however, that each of the three strengths of the American geographical position is represented and institutionalized in a powerful and permanent bureaucracy.

Threats and the Concentrated Mind

In clarifying a grand strategy and in composing a political consensus to support it, it is extremely helpful for the political leadership to be able to identify one particular power as the principal adversary, to be able to wonderfully concentrate the national mind upon a visible foreign threat. As it happens, this has been a common feature of American foreign policy and grand strategy throughout its history.

For most of the period from the Revolutionary War until near the end of the 19th century, the United States viewed Britain as the principal foreign threat to its security and its interests. After the War of 1812, this sense of threat diminished, but it would occasionally be revived in this or that diplomatic crisis. The last major dispute raising the specter of armed conflict between the United States and Britain was probably the Venezuelan Crisis of 1895 (in which Britain substantially yielded to the United States). Then, for most of the first half of the 20th century, from the Spanish-American War until the end of the Second World War, the United States viewed Germany as its principal threat in Europe, the Atlantic, and Latin America; and Japan as its principal threat in Asia and the Pacific.

After the Second World War, the foreign threat to the United States seemed unusually clear. The Soviet Union had so many similarities to Nazi Germany (alien ideology, totalitarian dictatorship, closed economy, ambition to dominate the Eurasian landmass, and a massive army) that it was easy to translate the comprehensible and familiar German threat into an equivalent Soviet one.

In contrast, the foreign threat to the United States was not clearly defined after the Mexican War (it was variously seen as Britain, France, or, most often, no one) or after the First World War (Japan, Germany, Britain, or for a while, no one). It is no surprise that these periods with no clearly-identified foreign threat were also periods of division and disorientation in U.S. foreign policy. And it is also perhaps no accident that these periods ended in the great disasters.

A version of this problem arose even during the Cold War era. It was much easier to develop a political consensus about the threat if it could be seen as analogous to a previous one, as the Soviet Union was seen as analogous to Nazi Germany. It was not so obvious, however, that Communist China was analogous to Imperial Japan (or even to the Soviet Union). The groups and organizations that had seen Japan as the principal enemy in the 1930s and early 1940s (e.g., much of the Republican Party, the U.S. Navy) did see China as the new and analogous enemy in the late 1940s and 1950s. But other groups and organizations (e.g., much of the Democratic Party, the U.S. Army) never adopted this view with clarity and conviction. This meant that during the Cold War there was never as much consensus around U.S. policy toward China as there was around the policy toward the Soviet Union. This partly explains why the consensus in the Korean War ("the wrong war at the wrong place at the wrong time") was so weak and a consensus in the Vietnam War, the most divisive foreign war in U.S. history, hardly existed at all.

The American way of grand strategy, then, has included a focus upon a particular foreign power, which has wonderfully concentrated the mind and the energies of the American nation. In this respect, the American way has been somewhat different from either the British way or the German way. The British way of grand strategy was to focus upon a particular nation only insofar as it represented the current threat to the European balance of power. In Palmerston's words, Britain had neither permanent friends nor permanent enemies, but only permanent interests. Conversely, the German way of grand strategy was to focus not on one particular country but on two (or more), usually France and Russia. In Bismarck's words, Germany was haunted by the nightmare of encirclement.

This feature of the American way of grand strategy has important and disturbing implications for the international challenges of our own time. Taken by itself, it would indicate that American strategy in the future will only be effective if it can once again focus upon a particular foreign threat, especially one that can be seen as analogous to the old Soviet one. As it happens, two current nominees for chief threat can appear to have this feature.

One analogue to past threats is Islamist radicalism. For those that stress alien ideologies as the main source of threats to the United States, Islamist radicalism has clear analogies with Communism and Nazism (thus the use of the term "Islamo-fascism"). However, this does not impress those that see hostile great powers as the main source of threats (the "Realist" position). They note that there is no Islamist great power, certainly not in the center of the Eurasian landmass and certainly not on the scale of Germany or the Soviet Union (or China). The closest candidate is Iran. For great-power Realists the problem of Islamist radicalism can best be handled by a strategy of balance of power, e.g., the United States acting as an "offshore balancer." Some Realists would go beyond this and also use a strategy of divide-and-rule, e.g., pitting Sunni Islamists and Shi'ite Islamists against each other. These considerations help to explain why, after the Islamist terrorist attacks of 9/11, there did not develop a political consensus that Islamist radicalism is the central threat to the United States and that opposition to it should be the organizing principle of U.S. grand strategy, analogous to opposition to communism during the Cold War.

The other analogue to past threats is China. For those that stress hostile great powers as the main threat to the United States, China has clear analogies with the Soviet Union and with Germany earlier. However, there is no political consensus about the kind of ideological threat that might be posed by China. It is no longer a coherent Communism, as exemplified by Mao (having become more Market-Leninism than Marxist-Leninism). Conversely, it is not a coherent Confucianism as was exemplified by Singapore's Lee Kuan Yew (the current Chinese version being pseudo-Confucianism, rather than neo-Confucianism). There is a strong view among some American groups that China will become the central threat to the United States and that containment of it should be the organizing principle of U.S. grand strategy. But the analogies with previous threats have been incomplete, and the political consensus behind this view is not yet broad or robust.

In short, it seems that the United States is now in a period similar to the periods after the First World War and after the Mexican War, when for some Americans there seems to be not a single foreign threat but several. Indeed, for some Americans (particularly in academia and the left wing of the Democratic Party) there seems to be no real foreign threat at all.

From Germany to China

During the second half of the 20th century, the Soviet Union posed a strong military threat to the United States, but it only briefly (in the 1950s) appeared to pose an economic one. Conversely, Japan posed a strong economic threat, but of course not a military one. During this era, the United States did not really have to confront a great power that could simultaneously pose both a military and an economic threat.

During the first half of the 20th century, however, Germany did pose both a strong military threat and a strong economic threat to the United States, and to the international security and economic order more generally. The rapid rise after 1871 of German military and economic power first disrupted and eventually destroyed both the European balance of power and the European balance of trade. In doing so, it drew the United States into the European war, for by 1917 it was necessary to call in the New World to redress the new imbalance within the Old.

The great success of British grand strategy in the first half of the 20th century was to recognize that Germany was the central, indeed the only potentially fatal threat to Britain at that time. A related success was its guiding the equally rapid rise of American naval and economic power into the path of supporting international order and stability. The greater failure of British strategy, however, was to not similarly guide the rise of German power into this path. The results of that failure were the two greatest wars in history. However, it is not easy to see, even now with the benefit of decades of hindsight, how Britain might better have better addressed this problem. This is especially so since its attempt in the 1930s to do exactly this was the policy of appeasement. Still, it sometimes has been argued that the British error lay not so much in the idea of appeasement, but in its timing. The problem was that Britain used appeasement when it should have used containment (the 1930s), and it used containment when it should have used appeasement (the 1900s and perhaps the 1920s).

During the first half of the 21st century, China will pose both a strong military and a strong economic threat to the United States and to the global security and economic order more generally. The rapid rise after 1976 of Chinese economic power and the accompanying modernization of Chinese military power together have disrupted both the global balance of trade and the Asian balance of power. The great problem for American grand strategy in the first half of the 21st century will not be to recognize that China is the central threat to the United States. Given the natural analogies between the Soviet Union of the past and the China of the future, this will be all too easy—even facile—to do. The great challenge is instead to somehow channel the rise of Chinese power into the path of supporting global order and stability. This will require a supple synthesis of elements taken from strategies that have been successful in the past, such as the balance of power, the international economy, and the regional sphere of influence.

As we have seen, misunderstandings of regional spheres of influence were a factor in the greatest failures of American foreign policy during the Cold War, i.e., the Korean War, the Cuban confrontations, and the Vietnam War. Moreover, the once-familiar concept of the regional sphere of influence now conflicts with the currently dominant concept among U.S. elites of global rules and norms. This conflict of concepts has already led to confrontations between the United States and Russia, especially over Ukraine, and between the United States and China, especially over the South China Sea, and it is likely to be the source of major great-power crises in the future. Consequently, we will discuss regional spheres of influence in some detail.

Spheres of Influence

A central principle of wise grand strategy is that a great power will seek a sphere of influence over neighboring small states, those that are in its "own backyard" or "near abroad." This has been especially true of emerging great powers which are newly-industrializing economies and newly-modernizing societies. This was the case with the United States, Germany, Russia, and Japan a century ago, and it is the case with China today. But declining great powers may also be defensive about what sphere of influence still remains to them. This is true of Russia today. In diplomatic content, this will be a sphere of influence; in economic content, a sphere of interest; and in military content, a sphere of insulation.

The United States created such a sphere in the Caribbean and Central American at the beginning of the 20th century. It did this so readily and with so little opposition from other great powers that Americans came to take their sphere almost for granted. However, U.S. policymakers worked hard at maintaining it, as evidenced by the occasional military interventions in the Dominican Republic, Haiti, Nicaragua, and Panama; by the U.S. purchase of the Danish West Indies in 1917 as insurance against their becoming a base for Germany; and by the monumental conflicts and risks that resulted when Castro's Cuba escaped from the American sphere into a Soviet alliance.

Other great powers have sought their own spheres of influence too, but for them the circumstances normally have been less favorable and their achievement less secure. In the 20th century, Britain established such a sphere in parts of the Middle East from the 1920s to the 1950s; Germany sought to create one in Southeast Europe in the 1930s; Japan similarly sought to do so in Southeast Asia in the 1940s; and the Soviet Union established its huge sphere in Eastern Europe after the Second World War.

A great power will define the limits of its sphere according to its shifting perception of its diplomatic, economic, and military interests. This might seem to result in inconsistency, confusion, and misunderstandings. In practice, however, the definition is usually rather obvious. Most experienced diplomats, area specialists, and scholarly experts have a quite clear and consistent sense of what a particular great power considers to be its necessary and legitimate sphere of influence. It is grounded in historical and cultural traditions which persist throughout the ups and downs of power and the zigs and zags of interest.

Two great powers are now intent upon restoring some version of their traditional spheres of influence, and, even though their situations are very different, each will continue in this intent for the foreseeable future. These are, of course, Russia and China.

For Russia, its most important traditional sphere was based upon cultural affinity, i.e., Eastern Orthodoxy. This included the Slavic countries of Ukraine ("Little Russia"), Belarus ("White Russia"), Bulgaria, and Serbia, but also most non-Slavic Orthodox countries, i.e., Armenia, Georgia, Moldavia, and Romania. Even in the absence of a cultural affinity between a great power and the countries in its sphere, a pronounced geopolitical interest can provide a historical tradition (as the U.S. sphere in the Caribbean and Central America illustrates). For Russia, there has long been a geopolitical interest and thus historical basis in its "near abroad" or soft underbelly to the south, i.e., Transcaucasia and Central Asia. Russia systematically annexed these territories in the 19th century.

For China, its traditional sphere was "the Chinese world order" or Confucian tributary system. For imperial China, this meant Korea, Taiwan, northern Vietnam, and more vaguely the East China Sea and the South China Sea. It is evident that something like this realm is the concept of contemporary China as well. How the United

States deals with the Chinese drive to re-establish this traditional sphere is probably the most portentous question facing American foreign policy today.

The normal pattern in spheres of influence is for the central power to be more advanced than the small countries in its sphere (e.g., the United States in Latin America, Russia in Central Asia). Indeed, it is this difference in development that gives a sometimes-effortless strength to the great power's influence. However, the Soviet Union was less advanced than its East European satellites (as Czarist Russia had been less advanced than its Baltic and Polish territories). Similarly, China in general is still less advanced than South Korea, Taiwan, and Singapore. However, much of coastal China has largely caught up.

Russia and China: A Different Kind of Containment

Despite all its varied foreign involvements in the 20th century, the central concerns and conflicts of the United States were with a limited number—really a "big four"—of great power adversaries. During the first half of the century, Germany and Japan were the two adversaries, but, with its great victories in the Second World War and its great achievements in the third cycle, the United States transformed and tamed these aggressive military powers into productive "trading states." During the second half of the century, Russia (as the Soviet Union) and China (as the PRC) were, in different ways and at different times, the two adversaries. Each of them is still torn between a military and an economic vocation, although again in very different ways. (The Chinese show every evidence of having superb entrepreneurial abilities; the Russians show almost no evidence at all.)

For the first half of the 21st century, Russia and China will continue to be the central concerns because they could again generate the central conflicts facing American foreign policy. Russia is the only potential great-power threat to Europe. To address this potential threat, the United States does need a potential policy of containment. However, it would have been best if, after the Cold War, that policy had remained only potential or latent, ready to become effective if the necessity arose. Unless or until that happened, the actual or manifest U.S. policy toward

Russia should have remained a policy of engagement. Most importantly, the U.S. definition of the area of containment should have taken into account Russia's definition of its regional spheres. It has been a case of containment overstretch to seek to deny Russia a sphere of influence in the Eastern Orthodox countries of the former Soviet Union (Belarus, Ukraine, and Moldova) and in the "near abroad" of Transcaucasia and Central Asia. We will be discussing the Russian spheres of influence in more detail in chapters seven and nine.

An analogous analysis can be applied to China and its potential threat to East and Southeast Asia. Here, too, the United States needs a potential policy of containment, ready to become effective if the necessity should arise. However, the actual or manifest U.S. policy toward China should continue to be a policy of engagement in regard to matters which do not impinge on the military security and economic vitality of the United States. Further, the U.S. definition of the area of containment should take into account China's definition of its regional sphere, which is more complicated than that of the Russians. As we have seen, this sphere includes such contested areas as Taiwan, Korea, the South China Sea, and the East China Sea. Unlike the spheres of Russia, which have land borders with Russia itself, these areas of the Chinese sphere are all maritime, i.e., either an island, a peninsula, or seas. This should make it easier for the United States to accept the vital security interests of China while maintaining open access for other nations with respect to economic and social matters and independence of the sphere's countries with respect to domestic political matters (we will be discussing the Chinese sphere of influence in more detail in chapters 7 and 10).

American Interests—Economic, Ethnic, and Ideal

Any effective national grand strategy must be grounded in the long-term, concrete interests of organized groups. This is necessary to sustain the strategy through the ebbs and flows, the fads and fashions of media attention in foreign affairs. In the United States, these interests have been economic, ethnic, and (a peculiarly American characteristic) ideological or "idealist."

In this current era of the global economy, it has been frequently argued that the United States has economic interests in every part of the globe. While this is true in some abstract sense, there are enormous differences in the importance and weight of these interests in different regions. U.S. trade and investment are concentrated today, as they have been since the end of the Second World War, in four great regions: Europe, East and Southeast Asia, the Middle East, and Latin America. There is much less trade and investment with Africa, South Asia, and Central Asia. Given the "failed states" and social violence in much of these latter regions, this low level of economic interests will continue for the next decade and more.

Similarly, in this era of the multicultural society, it has been frequently argued that the United States or at least particular Americans have ethnic interests throughout the world ("America as the world-nation"). This also is true in some abstract sense, but there are substantial differences in the emotive importance and political organization of these interests in different regions. There has been a decline in the ethnic identities of European Americans. Jewish Americans, however, maintain an identity with Israel and an interest in U.S. policies toward the Middle East. There has also been an increase in the foreign-affairs interests of some African Americans and Latino Americans. The Congressional Black Caucus is a major influence shaping U.S. policy toward Africa and toward Haiti, and Cuban Americans are the major influence shaping U.S. policy toward Cuba. But these groups have not really constructed a broad national consensus to support their particular foreign policies. In any event, for most African Americans and Latino Americans, foreign policy is not a salient arena for advancing their group interests. This low level of ethnic interests will continue for the next decade or more, and will not be pronounced enough to alter the prevailing regional pattern of U.S. economic interests. Together, these considerations mean that only American economic or ethnic interests will provide a solid basis for U.S. foreign policy only in respect to the traditional and familiar regions of Europe, East and Southeast Asia, the Middle East, and Latin America.

It is also often argued that the real national interests of the United States are its national ideals or ideology. Compared with most European nations, America in many respects is an artificial nation, not a natural one. Its national interests accordingly will often appear to be artificial, even "socially constructed." And its national ideals will often appear to be ideological, as with "the American Creed" or "universal human rights." For much of the 20th century, the national ideal of democracy served as the least common denominator that bridged disparate definitions of the national interests. In justifying U.S. involvement abroad, the ideal of democracy has almost always been necessary, but in itself it has never been sufficient. Democratic ideology provided the moral energy, while practical interests provided the specific direction for U.S. military interventions.

During most of the 20th century, the American democratic ideal was seen more in terms of majority rule than of minority rights. It thus tended more toward the older idea of self-determination rather than toward the more recent idea of universal human rights. It is important to observe that this idea of universal human rights, which in America is a creation largely since the 1970s, does not yet serve as a least common denominator for disparate interests. Rather, it is merely the ideal of particular groups whose agendas are really rather parochial. Most commonly, these are the liberal professionals and the professional liberals of the media and academia.

Building upon the Three Legacies

Each of the three cycles of American foreign policy offers a particular contribution to the history and the legacy of U.S. grand strategy—successively, territorial annexation and consolidation, regional sphere of influence, and international order. Each strategy resulted in great and lasting national achievements. As it moved from one cycle and one set of challenges to the next, the United States managed to transcend the limitations of its earlier strategy and achievement and to undertake a major innovation. It is crucial to appreciate, however, that the United States never abandoned the earlier achievements but rather built upon them. The American strategic process was characterized by innovation of the new coupled with its integration with the old. Thus, the foundation of the new great-power status and regional sphere of influence of the 20th century was the continental, consolidated nation-state inherited from the late 19th century. Similarly, the foundation of the new superpower status and American-led international order of the mid-20th century was both the regional and now hemispheric sphere of influence and the continental nation-state, a double inheritance. The future grand strategy of the United States will achieve its greatest success if it builds upon each of these three legacies and upon their associated lessons. However, these legacies and lessons are progressively harder to understand the further that their origins lie in the past.

International Order. The legacy and lessons of international order are the easiest to grasp; these are the most recent in time and the most regarded in the current foreign policy discourse. Until the arrival of Donald Trump, virtually all political leaders, Democratic and Republican, agreed on the proposition that the United States must be the leader in maintaining a stable international order, especially an open global economy. These same leaders, however, neglected the reality that strong American leadership in the global economy requires a strong American economy within the United States itself. The foundation for American leadership in the Bretton Woods system, for the heroic age of American foreign policy, was the most productive and competitive industrial economy in the world, and the high employment, economic prosperity, and social cohesion that were the result. Without these, there would not have been the political consensus necessary to sustain American leadership.

Today the American economy is centered upon information and services—e.g., computers, telecommunications, internets, finance—rather than upon industry. The United States no longer has the most productive and competitive industrial economy in the world. That role has been assumed by one or more of the newly-industrial economies with their "advantages of backwardness," i.e., the peculiar combination of high technology and high skills with low wages and low regulation (most obviously, China and Vietnam).

The United States will rather have to be the most productive and competitive information economy in the world. Further, this information economy will have to provide enough high employment, economic prosperity, and social cohesion within the United States itself to form the base for a political consensus to sustain American leadership. This is not the direction of the American information economy or the wider global economy today, which are instead accentuating and accelerating economic, social, and political divisions among the American people.

Sphere of Influence. The legacy and lessons of the regional sphere of influence are harder to grasp. Because the United States was so successful in maintaining its original sphere in the Caribbean and Central America and its sophisticated sphere in Western Europe, it often still takes its own regional spheres and their realities for granted and forgets about how other powers think about spheres of influence. This can be dangerous, for the same three great powers that dominated the second half of the 20th century will also dominate the first half of the 21st (the United States, Russia and China), and their conceptions of spheres of influence are quite different. As we have seen, Russia and China again seek a full sphere of influence in those regions where they have had one historically. At the same time, only one power, the United States, can lead a global international order and influence Russia and China to support it. For this to happen, the United States must understand and accept the vital interests of these powers.

Although only the United States is a credible leader of the global international order, the other great powers have their own neighboring regions, and they can be credible leaders of their respective spheres. The temptation for the United States is to presume that the goal of international order means the prevention of regional spheres (except for our own). A version of this notion in regard to China led to disaster in Korea in 1950 and, in a different way, in Vietnam in 1965. If the United States pursues this overstretched notion with China or Russia in the future, it will lead to disaster again.

Rather, the task for the United States is to negotiate with China and Russia with the objective of having them shape their spheres in ways similar to those that the United States followed in its own spheres. The American spheres were closed to the military presence of other great powers but open to the commercial transactions of the international economy. Although the Americans were in a position of economic advantage, the economies of the spheres were open to the process of competition and change. This should be the U.S. objective in regard to the Chinese and the Russian spheres.

Territorial consolidation. The legacy and lessons of territorial annexation and consolidation are the hardest of all to grasp. Because this happened so long ago and because the United States was successful for so long in maintaining its continental consolidation and national unity, it has taken these achievements for granted. As we have noted, however, America is an artificial nation, not a natural one, a nation that has been "socially constructed," not organically grown. America must also be socially reconstructed periodically. Otherwise, it will cease to be a nation.

The generations of Americans from the 1770s to the 1840s achieved great successes in territorial expansion, but the generation of the 1850s threw these away when it divided over slavery and sectionalism. These divisions were only overcome with the Civil War. The generation of Americans from the 1860s to the 1890s achieved great successes in territorial consolidation, but the generation of the 1900s-1910s undermined these with policies that promoted class polarization, massive immigration, and conflicts among "hyphenated Americans." These divisions were overcome eventually with the economic policies of the New Deal, cultural programs of Americanization, and the unity that came out of the Second World War. The generation of the 1940s-1960s achieved great successes in further consolidation of the American nation. But the generation of the 1990s-2010s (whose leaders have largely been baby boomers) has undermined these gains with its own reckless economic and cultural policies.

Economically, national consolidation is being undermined by an unbalanced pursuit of the global economy, putting at risk "the promise of American life" for a majority of Americans. Culturally, it is being undermined by uncontrolled immigration (especially from neighbors in the original regional sphere) and by the ideologies of multicultural-ism, diversity, and intersectionality, putting at risk the *e pluribus unum* of the American nation as a whole. These divisions will have to be healed with a new New Deal and a new Americanization project, suited to the specific conditions of our time. Otherwise, we could eventually degen-erate into a new civil war, this time not a "War between the States" but more a war of all against all.

Over the course of two centuries, the United States developed its own distinctive grand strategy, and over the course of three historical cycles this strategy became progressively grander. Indeed, by the end of the Cold War, it had become the grandest strategy of any power of the 20th century and probably of the modern era. American strategy could continue on this upward trajectory through the 21st century, but there are multiplying signs that it may not do so. At its deepest foundations, the grand strategy of the United States has always required that the United States itself be united.

CHAPTER SEVEN

GRAND STRATEGY IN THE GLOBAL ERA

A NATIONAL STRATEGY, TO be robust and effective, must take into account the economic and social realities of the nation that it is meant to serve. The national strategy of the United States during the Cold War era—whose core elements consisted of the foreign policy of containment and the military strategy of nuclear deterrence—was based upon the particular economic and social conditions. The economic realities were American industrial power and American leadership in the international economy. The social realities were the ordering of Americans into numerous large and hierarchical organizations, a distinctive feature of what has been termed "modern society," and the existence of a basic national consensus around a particular set of ideas or ideology, what was often termed "the American Creed."

Within ten years after the end of the Cold War, however, there was no longer an American national strategy that consisted of a containment policy and a nuclear strategy. Indeed, there sometimes seemed to be no American national strategy at all. There was no longer an American economic reality of industrial power within an international economy or an American social reality of a modern society adhering to the American Creed. Instead, a series of economic and social trends which were global in their scope had brought about a whole new era—which, for the sake of simplification, can best be called the global era. These global trends produced the necessity for a new American grand strategy, but even now, in the late 2010s, this necessity has not yet become a reality. What then, should be America's grand strategy in the global era?

Four Global Trends and the New International Relations

Four fundamental and interrelated global trends have shaped the new era, and they now provide the context for any American grand strategy, all the more so since these trends were led, promoted, and even driven by the United States. These trends developed during the last two decades of the Cold War, but they really matured only in the 1990s. Indeed, it was the end of the Cold War—and of the Soviet threat and U.S. containment policy—that brought about the dismantling of some of the ideas and institutions (e.g., national unity against the foreign adversary, government intervention in the market economy) which had helped to hold these trends in check. The U.S. containment policy had not only contained the Soviet Union; it had also contained forces operating within that part of the world which was led by the United States.

These four global trends are (1) the development of the post-industrial economy, particularly the information economy, replacing what had been the industrial economy; (2) the development of the global economy, replacing what had been merely an international economy; (3) the development of the post-modern society, replacing what had been the modern society; and (4) the decline of the nation-state and its replacement in some countries (particularly the United States, Canada, and Western Europe) with something that is more a multicultural society and ideology, or even a multicultural regime. Two of these trends, therefore, are principally economic, and two are principally social.

The contemporary era in international relations has been given different names. Three of the more common ones—the information era, the globalization era, and the post-modern era—testify to the prominence and the defining power of the first three of the trends. And the conflicts over multiculturalism and identity politics in American society testify to the prominence of the fourth.

These four trends have been global in their consequences, but they have developed more in some countries than in others. Among the major powers, they have advanced most within the United States and Britain, less so in Germany and Japan, and still less so in Russia and China. Indeed, it is the uneven development of these global trends, combined with the U.S. leadership in driving them, that probably has produced even greater international misunderstandings and conflicts than have the general trends themselves. And within the United States itself, these four trends have issued in a series of transformations which have made it a very different country than it was during the Cold War and made it different in new ways from the other major powers. In addition to these economic and social effects, these transformations have had major consequences for American ideas, ideals, and even identity. And, as we shall see, they have also had major consequences for American grand strategy, and for the foreign policy and military strategy accompanying it.

The Great Transformations within the United States

As early as the end of the 1990s, the first decade after the end of the Cold War, the maturing of these four trends had resulted in great transformations in American economy and society.

The transformation from an industrial to an information economy. First, there had been the transformation of the United States (along with Canada, Australia, and some of the most advanced European countries) from an industrial economy to a post-industrial, particularly information, one. At the most obvious level, this meant the replacement of industrial production with service processes, particularly those based upon the rapid communication of vast amounts of information. These changes had been noted and discussed for more than a generation, at least since Daniel Bell published his seminal The Coming of Post-Industrial Society (1973). But their maturity only came in the 1990s, as discussed in the work of Peter Drucker, including his Landmarks of Tomorrow: A Report on the New "Post-Modern" World.[1] This "information revolution" was seen by many observers to be the equivalent of those three global economic revolutions of the past—the agricultural, the commercial, and the industrial.

Moreover, many social analysts observed that the development of the information economy and the displacement of the industrial economy had increased individual choice and devalued conventional hierarchies. The information economy thus reinforced the traditional American idea of liberal democracy. But it also promoted a newer and broader idea, that of the open society.

The information revolution, like the earlier economic revolutions, also had important military consequences. Numerous military analysts discussed how the technologies of the information economy brought about a "revolution in military affairs" (RMA), C4I (command, control, communication, computers, and intelligence), and "info warfare" or "cyberwarfare." To its advocates, the revolution in military affairs provided the opportunity, indeed the necessity, for the U.S. military services to implement a revolution in military strategy.

Each of the past economic revolutions had generated a corresponding military revolution and new forms of military power. Thus, the agricultural revolution gave rise to land power, the commercial revolution to sea power, the industrial revolution to air power, and, by analogy, the information revolution gave rise to info or cyber power. However, the earlier economic revolutions and new forms of military power did not eliminate the need for the old kinds of military power. Rather, some states developed revolutionary means for deploying the old military power in new ways. For example, although the industrial revolution eventually enabled the introduction of air power, it also brought about revolutionary means for deploying land power (e.g., the machine gun, followed by the tank) and for deploying sea power (e.g., the battleship, followed by the aircraft carrier). Perhaps the main military consequence of the information revolution has been to generate new means for deploying land, sea, and air power.

However, some advocates of cyber warfare argue that the military consequences of the information revolution will be even more radical than this. Military power in large measure resides in the capacity to combine mobility and mass; in the oft-quoted words of Confederate General Nathan Bedford Forrest, it is the capacity "to be the firstest with the mostest." As different as they were, the old land, sea, and air power all moved bodies through space. The new cyber power, however, moves minds, not bodies, and by doing so instantaneously, it eliminates space altogether. The old kinds of power included the capacity to use space (land, sea, and air) for oneself and to deny the use of space to others. The new info power will have the capacity to use and deny the *absence* of space (military operations whose every dimension—intelligence, analysis, decision, execution, destruction, assessment—would be conducted in "real time").

The transformation from an international to a global economy. Under U.S. leadership, and for U.S. corporations and banks (along with those of other advanced countries), there had also been the transformation of the international economy into a truly global one. At the most obvious level, this meant the replacement of national production that had been engaged in international trade with global production that was now engaged in a worldwide market in trade, investment, and technology. These changes have been noted and discussed for a generation, ever since Raymond Vernon published his seminal Sovereignty at Bay (1971). But their maturity only came in the 1990s, as Vernon discussed in his Defense and Dependence in a Global Economy.[2]

We will note here a couple of political consequences of this global economy, which in turn have consequences for U.S. foreign policy. The globalization of production meant the relocation of industrial production from high-wage and high-skill advanced-industrial countries to low-wage but high-skill newly-industrial countries (NICS). This meant the deindustrialization of the United States and other advanced countries, the dark half of the post-industrial transformation that we discussed above. The two transformations—from industrial to post-industrial and from international to global—were intimately connected.

Although the United States became post-industrial, the world did not. The world continued to have industrial countries existing alongside the post-industrial ones. When in the 19th century countries like Britain became industrial (and "post-agricultural") economies, this did not mean that the world became post-agricultural. Indeed, there was an even greater demand for agricultural commodities than before (fibers for industrial products, food for industrial workers), except that now these were supplied by the most efficient producers in international trade (e.g., the United States).

Similarly, when countries like the United States became information (and post-industrial) economies, there was an even greater demand for industrial products than before, and these too were supplied by the most efficient producers in international trade, now a global market. The countries where efficient industrial production took place were well-known. Many were found in East Asia, where Japan took the lead, South Korea and the other "little tigers" followed, and the rapid growth and massive scale of the Chinese economy soon became a dominant reality in the global economy.

What was overlooked by contemporary U.S. economic and political elites was that strong U.S. leadership in the global economy had required a strong economy within the United States itself. As we saw in Chapter 6, the foundation for U.S. leadership in the Bretton Woods system during 1945-1971, and for what has been called the heroic age of U.S. foreign policy during the Cold War, was the most productive and competitive industrial economy in the world, and the high employment, economic prosperity, and social cohesion that were the result. Without these, there would not have been the political consensus necessary to sustain U.S. leadership in international affairs. However, since the 1990s, the two economic trends of post-industrialization and globalization have greatly accentuated economic, social, and political divisions among the American people. This has hollowed out the base for U.S. global leadership.

Related to this is the fact that the development of the global economy has increased the freedom and mobility of business enterprises and weakened the constraints of governments. The global economy has thus reinforced the traditional American idea of free markets. But it too has promoted the newer and broader idea of the open society. The information economy and the global economy are therefore two powerful forces whose natural ideology is that of the open society. But the ideology of the open society implies, indeed advocates, the limitation of state sovereignty and the weakening of the nation-state. This ideology of the open society, which is now held by most American political, economic, and intellectual elites, represents a fundamental challenge to traditional conceptions of international relations.

These two economic trends, which had matured in the 1990s, had also contributed mightily to a third trend, one which was even more fundamental in that it had transformed the very character of modern society.

The transformation from a modern to a post-modern society. The United States (along with Canada, Australia, and some of the most advanced European countries) had also been transformed from a modern society into a post-modern one.

Modern society, especially as it existed in Europe, Japan, and the United States for much of the 20th century, was distinguished by its high degree of mass organization. The cultural, economic, and security dimensions of social life were organized into the social sectors of education, industry, and the military. These sectors were institutionalized in the school, the factory, and the army, which were engaged in mass education, mass production, and mass conscription (and mass destruction), respectively. These mass activities gave rise to mass political parties, mass labor unions, and even mass professional associations as well.

By the late 1990s, however, this modern era had come to an end within the United States. Each of the three social dimensions—cultural, economic, and military—had undergone a profound change in the previous two decades. The United States was no longer a modern society, but a post-modern one.

Post-modern society, especially American society, is not characterized by standardized schools engaged in mass education in a national, often high culture. Rather, post-modern society is characterized by organized media engaged in mass entertainment in an international, usually pop or low culture. There are still entities called public schools, but it is doubtful that much education occurs in them. Post-modern schools result in less literacy and less numeracy than their modern predecessors.

This cultural transformation in part derived from the economic one. In the industrial economy, useful information became available through mass education conducted in the schools. In this information economy, useful information becomes available through a multitude of resources. Indeed, the problem now is not that information is too dear,

173

but that it is too cheap, not that there is too little information but that there is too much.

The very plethora of information is so stressful or tiresome that it drives many to flee into some kind of entertainment. Since information technology can provide mass entertainment as easily as it can mass education, the information economy naturally is characterized by the former rather than the latter.

Post-modern society, as we have seen, is not characterized by efficient industries engaged in mass production, principally for a national market. Rather, it is characterized by financial enterprises and corporate management engaged in information processing within a global market. This might be called the high economy. It is also characterized by a mass of service workers engaged in low-skill tasks for a local market. This is the low economy. Those services that can be exported, such as financial ones, are part of the high economy. Most services, however, must be consumed at the point they are performed (as in restaurants) and are part of the low economy. (In contrast, almost all industrial products can be exported as long as they are competitive.) Thus, post-modern society is characterized by a very large gap between the high-skilled and the low-skilled parts of its population. This further diminishes the social cohesion of post-modern society compared with that of modern society.

The shift out of mass production into different kinds of work is joined by the shift into mass consumption, which has been reinforced by the shift from an international to a global economy. In the international economy, goods became available through mass production conducted in factories, which for the most part were located in one's own country. In the global economy, goods become available from a multitude of places around the globe. For residents of the most advanced economies (i.e., those that are information or post-industrial) the global economy is characterized not by mass production but by mass consumption.

The moves from mass education in schools to mass entertainment and from mass production in factories to mass consumption result in another move. This is the move from disciplined membership in hierarchical organizations, which promotes self-denial, to fluid participation in egalitarian networks, which promotes individual gratification.

The development of the post-modern society has meant the erosion of the great pillars of modern society, bureaucracies and organizations, and of the attitudes of deference, duty, and loyalty that often went with them. In their place, the post-modern society has promoted the two interrelated ideas of expressive individualism and universal human rights. Together, they form a new ideology in which individual rights are universal, universal rights are individual, and such rights are fundamental, even absolute.

These post-modern features have also had important military consequences. There is an obvious gap between the expressive-individualist nature of contemporary society and the group-loyalty needs of the conventional military. More and more, it may be said that the military is in society but not of it.

Post-modern society is not characterized by large conventional armies, based on mass conscription and providing for defense of the national territory. Rather, post-modern society was initially characterized by nuclear weapons providing extended deterrence for permanent international alliances (as with NATO). Then, in the 1990s, it was characterized by high technology, precision-guided, and stealth weapons providing military power for temporary coalitions (as in the Gulf War of 1991), or for peace-making operations (as in Bosnia and Kosovo). Post-modern society not only rejected mass conscription, it abhorred any military casualties (as in Somalia in 1993), and military operations were carefully designed to minimize casualties by maximizing technology. Post-modern society, in short, had produced what was called "post-heroic" or "post-Clausewitzian" military strategies.[3]

Moreover, the transformations wrought by both the new post-industrial economy and the new post-modern society have impacted upon what has been called "the American war of war." Two of its distinguishing characteristics have been the wide-ranging mobility and the overwhelming mass which have been deployed by U.S. military forces. The transformations enhanced the use of mobility in particular ways but have greatly diminished the use of mass. The traditional American mass production of weapons systems is no longer feasible in post-industrial America. Indeed, since the early 1980s, many of the mass-produced electronic components of U.S. weapons systems have been imported from the industrial countries of East Asia. Likewise, the traditional American mass deployment of land forces is no longer feasible in post-modern America with its volunteer military composed in large part of specialized and precious individuals. Indeed, the mass deployment of the Gulf War of 1991 (with the Seventh Corps being transported from its bases in Germany) can now be seen, from a logistical perspective, as the final act of the Cold War, using large land forces that had been built up to fight the Soviet army but that later disappeared almost as much as the Soviets had. The American way of war is not the American way in post-industrial and post-modern America.

The transformation from a nation-state to a multicultural regime. Finally, by the end of the 1990s, the United States (again along with Canada, Australia, and a few European countries) had been transformed from something approximating a nation-state to something more like a multicultural regime.

Much of international politics from the French Revolution to the Second World War consisted of the relations (and wars) between great powers which were also nation-states. The nation-state was the most highly organized form of human society in history. The increasing organization of the nation-state was closely connected to the increasing modernization of society. These two interrelated developments reached their peak in the first half of the twentieth century, when the modern nation-state was exemplified by Britain, France, Germany, Japan, and—in a complex, federal form—the United States. The nation-state had brought into being an ensemble of mass organizations, which in turn made the nation-state even more of a super-organization, the organization of organizations, than it had been before. The nation-state was a powerful engine modernizing its society, and the modern society had a functional need for the nation-state. In short, the two had an "elective affinity" for each other.[4]

The organization of the nation-states was further heightened by the two world wars among them and by the continuing prospects and preparations for war, which drove them into even more intense modes of organization in order to be able to deploy every material and human resource in the great contests.

The United States was never a homogeneous nation-state in the European sense. But it was organized very much and acted very much like one during much of the 20th century, "the century of total war," particularly from the First World War through the first part of the cold War. During the 1980s-1990s, however, the United States underwent a reverse development, a sort of denationalization. It became instead post-national or multicultural.

This transformation derived from changes which most American judged to be positive developments. In part, it resulted from the change in the immigration law in 1965 and the subsequent increase in the Latino-American and the Asian-American populations of the United States. It also built upon the civil rights movements of the 1960s and the subsequent increase in the status of African-Americans. Even more important, however, was the increase in the status of women, which is closely connected with the shift from an industrial to a post-industrial economy.

These major social changes, however, together generated a revolution in the ideas and identities of much of the U.S. intellectual and political elite. This revolution was centered upon the academic theories of deconstructionism and post-modernism and the ideologies of multiculturalism and feminism. What was once "the American Creed" was displaced by the creed of multiculturalism.[5]

The development of a multiracial or multicultural society promoted the idea of cultural diversity. Like the development of a post-modern society, the development of a multicultural society also promoted the idea of human rights. Although it might seem that a multiplicity of cultural groups might lead logically to an emphasis on the rights of the community, in practice it led instead to an emphasis on the rights of the individual. And, like the ideology of the open society, the ideology of human rights advocated the limitation of state sovereignty and the decline of the nation-state.

This ideological transformation also had important consequences for the role of the military. Although African-Americans, Latino-Americans, and Asian-Americans have achieved great success by serving in the U.S. military, the actual ideologies of multiculturalism and feminism, and the liberal elites who hold them, despised military values and institutions as well as the traditional American national identity which the military has seen itself defending. Like the ascendancy of expressive individualism, the ascendancy of multiculturalism opened a gap between the American intellectual and political elite and the U.S. military. Here again, it may be said that the military was in society but not of it.

Together, these four global trends came together in the 1990s to produce the most characteristic U.S. foreign policy and military operations of that decade. This was humanitarian intervention.

Liberal Globalism and Humanitarian Intervention

The traditional American ideology has advocated liberal democracy and free markets. In foreign affairs, this ideology has been known as liberal internationalism, and its most prominent proponents have been Presidents Woodrow Wilson and Franklin Roosevelt. In the 1990s, this familiar ideology was revived and revised into a new American ideology which promoted human rights and the open society. This too is a version of liberal internationalism, one that is more accurately termed liberal globalism; its most prominent proponents have been President Bill Clinton and his Secretary of State, Madeleine Albright, followed by President Barack Obama and his two Secretaries of State, Hillary Clinton and John Kerry.

The new American ideology of human rights and the open society—liberal globalism—in turn provided the justification, even the compulsion, for a new kind of U.S. military operation. This was humanitarian intervention, as in Somalia, Haiti, and Bosnia; the culmination of this development was the U.S.-led NATO war against Serbia over Kosovo in 1999.[6]

The idea that there should be a new purpose for U.S. military operations, and that it should be humanitarian intervention, or more broadly, intervention in support of human rights was not held equally by all parts of the American public. It was an idea held primarily by political and intellectual elites, especially those in the media and in academia (i.e., liberal professionals and professional liberals).

Humanitarian intervention was the natural consequence of liberal internationalism and particularly liberal globalism when carried to its logical conclusion and in the unconstraining conditions of the post-Cold-War era in which the United States faced no superpower adversary or even a peer competitor. Humanitarian intervention thus represented a rejection of realist internationalism, whose ideas were so prominent in U.S. foreign policy during the constraining conditions of the Cold War era, during which the United States confronted a formidable nuclear superpower that had many military and ideological allies. Humanitarian intervention subordinated the criterion of vital national interests to the criterion of universal human rights; however, since in the conditions of the 1990s-2000 there were no obvious threats to the vital interests of the United States, American political and intellectual elites thought that they could get away with this clear violation of realist tenets.

Humanitarian intervention also represented a rejection of the "Weinberger-Powell Doctrine" for U.S. military operations, which, for the U.S. military, summed up the "lessons learned" from the failures of the Vietnam War and which seemed to be confirmed by the successes of the Persian Gulf War of 1991. The doctrine had been originated by Caspar Weinberger, Secretary of Defense in the Reagan administration, and refined by General Colin Powell, Chairman of the Joint Chiefs of Staff in the administration of George H.W. Bush. One of its core principles was that when the United States goes to war, it should do so as a *nation* defending its vital *national* interests against another nation, and that when the U.S. Army goes to war, it should do so as an army fighting another army. Only this kind of war would receive the sustained support, through thick and thin, of the American people. In practice, the Weinberger-Powell Doctrine totally contradicted the humanitarian intervention ideology, and that is why the political and intellectual elites had to reject it.

In truth, most of the American people, and virtually all of the U.S. military, did not want to expend American military casualties for human rights alone. This political reality had important consequences for military operations. First, it drove the liberal elite to avoid seeking Congressional approval for military operations from the more conservative Congress and to justify this avoidance by saying that Congress was isolationist and irrational. Since this avoidance of Congress, which is composed of the elected representatives of the American people, was an evasion of a principal element of the Weinberger-Powell Doctrine (the necessity for public support of military operations), the liberal elite was driven to denigrate the doctrine itself. Second, this political reality drove the liberal elite to avoid the use of ground forces in combat operations, and therefore to avoid the use of overwhelming force, because unacceptable casualties would likely result. Since this avoidance of overwhelming force was an evasion of another principal element of the Weinberger-Powell Doctrine, the liberal elite was again driven to denigrate it.

The military consequences were not without irony. The liberal ideology of humanitarian intervention necessitated military operations, but the political reality negated ground operations. This left only air operations, in particular punitive bombing, as in Bosnia in 1995, Iraq after the Gulf War and especially in 1999, and Serbia in 1999. But the Serbian campaign suggested that, by themselves, these air operations might only achieve their political objectives when they expanded to the point of hurting civilians, either by killing them in "collateral damage" or by deliberately targeting their economic necessities such as electric-power grids and water-supply systems. These kinds of actions against civilians hardly seemed to fit the normal definition of "humanitarian."

Four Sources of Opposition: Losers and Winners

The great transformation in international relations in the 1990s generated opposition from a significant number of countries. The major sources of opposition were soon found in four large countries or areas.

First and most obviously, there was the opposition from the losers in the global economy of the 1990s. These included:

1. <u>Russia</u> and, more generally, most countries with an Eastern Orthodox religious tradition. For a variety of reasons, countries with an Orthodox tradition were unsuccessful in making the transition from communist regimes to liberal democracies and market economies which were then able to adapt well to an open society and a global economy (e.g., Russia, Belarus, Ukraine, Moldova, Romania, Bulgaria, and Serbia). Conversely, most countries with a Roman Catholic tradition have been successful in making this transition (e.g., Poland,

Lithuania, the Czech Republic, Slovakia, Hungary, Slovenia, and Croatia). (Countries with a Protestant tradition also have been successful, e.g., Estonia and Latvia.) This contrast among ex-communist countries, between the more western and more eastern, between the Roman Catholic or Protestant and the Eastern Orthodox, means that the political and economic developments on the globalizing 1990s revived and reinforced an historic divide, one that corresponds to the great schism between Western Christianity and Eastern Christianity and even to the ancient division between the Latin and Greek halves of the Roman Empire.

In their resulting condition of political and economic weakness, the governments of Russia and the other Orthodox countries could not immediately mount an effective and sustained opposition to the United States and its various projects of global economy, open society, and humanitarian intervention. But among the populations of these countries, there was substantial resentment and resistance directed at the United States. And with the establishment of the regime of Vladimir Putin in Russia in the early 2000s, that resistance began to take on an effective form.

2. The Middle East and, more generally, most countries with an Islamic religious tradition. Most countries with an Islamic tradition have also been unsuccessful in establishing a viable liberal democracy and a market economy able to adapt well to an open society and global economy. For those that experienced the heady years from 1973 to 1985, when OPEC seemed to be a world power, the decline in oil prices deepened their sense of failure and their alienation from globalization. Here, too, the governments have not been willing and able to mount opposition that is effective and sustained. But among their populations there has been widespread resentment and resistance, whose most obvious representatives have been radical and militant Islamist organizations such as Al Qaeda and Islamic State.

Conversely, there has been growing opposition even from some of the winners in the global economy. These include:

3. China and, more generally, most countries with a Confucian tradition. Most Chinese, both in China itself and among the "overseas Chinese," see their economic success as resulting from their own

culture or "Asian values," i.e., from engaging in the global economy in their own way.

4. <u>India</u>. The entry of India into the global economy has been recent, and its benefits have been unevenly distributed. It has occurred, however, at the same time as the growth of Hindu nationalism, the development of Indian nuclear weapons, and an increased confidence in rejecting certain Western ways.

The sources of opposition to the United States and its globalization project are thus very disparate. Some are politically and economically weak and divided (the Orthodox and Islamic countries). Some are economically strong but still divided amongst themselves (the Confucian countries). But together these sources of opposition comprise a vast region, really all of Eurasia and more, which stretches from Russia and Eastern Europe, through the Middle East, through South Asia, to China and East Asia. In this vast region are found the four great civilizations that Samuel Huntington identified as most likely to oppose the West in "the clash of civilizations"[7] These are, in his terms, "Slavic-Orthodox," Islamic, Hindu, and "Sinic-Confucian" civilizations. In this region, too, are four established nuclear powers—Russia, Pakistan, India, and China, each of them seeing themselves as the center of their civilization.

Uneven Developments and Opposite Directions

Thus, the trends that we have discussed have been global in their consequences, but they have been very uneven in their development. As a result of these trends, much of the West has become post-industrial, post-modern, and post-national (and therefore less industrial, less modern, and less national). At the same time, however, much of the East (especially China but also much of East and Southeast Asia) has become more industrial, more modern, and more national. Indeed, it is these very qualities of contemporary China and other Asian countries that account for their great successes in the U.S.-led global economy.

This different, even opposite, movement by the West and the East (and especially by the United States and China) in respect to such fundamentals as economy, society, and nationality gives rise to very different perspectives on international affairs and indeed on human nature.

This difference in perspectives toward the modern era as it culminated in the twentieth century—a difference between those that are eagerly leaving the modern era behind (the United States) and those that are eagerly entering into it (China)—is generating misunderstandings and conflicts. The clash of civilizations depicted by Samuel Huntington is greatly amplified by the clash of centuries.

One such difference in perspective is over strategic concepts. At the beginning of the twentieth century, two of the major strategic concepts used by Western powers were balance of power and sphere of influence. At the mid-point of the twentieth century, two of the major strategic concepts were containment and deterrence. From the perspective of post-modern and post-national American elites, who conceive of international affairs as largely the global economy and the open society, these four strategic concepts are now hopelessly old-fashioned and irrelevant. From the perspective of newly-modern and newly-national Chinese elites, however, these concepts are the essence of international affairs. They are now breathing new life into these old concepts. As with other kinds of self-fulfilling prophecies, if the Chinese think that these concepts are real, they will make them so. It will be a strategic reality that American elites would be wise to take into account, despite their revulsion against their own strategic past, which they so earnestly wish to leave behind.

Russia is another country that is of strategic importance to the United States and that has experienced uneven or even opposite development. Russia represents a failed industry, a failed modernity, perhaps even a failed nationality. But it also has been incapable of moving into a post-industrial, post-modern, and post-national condition. A country perennially torn between a Eurasian identity and a European identity, Russia is now experiencing a new version of its old story. What path has this torn and tormented people sought out of their new "time of troubles"? They or at least the supporters of the Putin regime are trying to succeed at least where they have failed so terribly, i.e., to become industrial, modern, and national in some sense that brings social order and self-respect. And so Russia, like China but attended with a darker self-conception, has been moving in the opposite direction and with the opposite perspective as the United States.

The Islamic Middle East is another area that is of strategic importance to the United States and that has experienced uneven or opposite development. The Middle East also represents a failed industry, a failed modernity, and a failed nationality. And it also obviously has been incapable of moving into post-industrial, post-modern, and post-national conditions. In contrast with the ideological confusion of Russia (to which the Orthodox religion provides a partial exception), however, Islam provides a highly coherent rationale for rejecting both the modern and the post-modern worlds. Indeed, Islam provides for the most coherent reconstruction of the pre-modern world that exists today. Thus, the Islamic Middle East is also moving in an opposite direction and with an opposite perspective to that of the United States. At the same time, however, it is also moving in a different direction and with a different perspective than China or Russia.

The contemporary international arena thus presents a quite extraordinary scene. The dynamics of uneven development have reached the point of simultaneous movements into three different eras. The United States is leading the West into the post-modern era. China is leading the East (and perhaps eventually Russia) into the modern era. And Islam is leading the Middle East into the pre-modern era.

Global Transformations versus Strategic Traditions

In the 1990s, therefore, U.S. foreign policy and military strategy were being shaped by the four global trends and transformations. But they also had been shaped previously by certain American strategic traditions such as those that we have discussed in Chapter 6. Consequently, there was an interaction—and in some respects a contradiction—between the trends and the traditions, between the exogenous and the indigenous factors, which were then working to produce U.S. foreign policy and military strategy.

Important elements of the American strategic tradition did not fit well with the new, transformed America which had recently been brought into being. This was especially the case with the contradiction between the new global economy and open society and the old sphere of influence. As we saw in Chapter 6, the sphere of influence is a central issue in composing any grand strategy. We will therefore discuss this issue in detail. There was also a contradiction between, on the one hand, the use of U.S. military forces, particularly the U.S. Army, to achieve global objectives, particularly humanitarian intervention, and on the other hand, the traditional American way of war. As we have seen above, the American way of war is a central issue in composing any military strategy. We will therefore also discuss this in detail. Finally, we will conclude this chapter with a comment on the even broader and deeper contradiction between the four new transformations and the old American leadership of the international order—and now of the global order.

Spheres of Influence versus Liberal Globalism

In our discussion of spheres of influence, we will focus particularly upon Russia and China, respectively the main Cold War adversary of the U.S. and the main potential adversary of the U.S., as the most important powers to be considered in any sound and realistic American grand strategy. Spheres of influence, in particular, remain important to Russia and China, but they are definitely alien to the new American ideology of liberal globalism.

As we discussed in Chapter 6, it has always been a central reality of international politics that a great power will seek a sphere of influence over neighboring small states. There is a clear contradiction, however, between the contemporary American conception of the global economy, which has become so central to U.S. foreign policy, and the Chinese and the Russian conceptions of their regional spheres of influence. In the past, spheres of influence usually have served as areas of economic advantage for their dominant power, and they often have excluded or restricted the economic interests of other powers. This notion is now rejected by the globally-minded United States. Of course, it was not rejected by the United States when it, too, was only a rising regional power. The United States created a sphere of influence in the Caribbean and Central America at the beginning of the 20th century.

Today, both Russia and China are intent upon restoring some version of their traditional regional spheres of influence. Although Russia is much weaker than China, each will likely continue in this intent in the future. This is a regionalist reality that the globalist United States has to take into account.

The Russian Spheres of Influence

Since the time of its czars, Russia has relied upon either a cultural basis or a geopolitical basis for its traditional spheres of influence. The cultural basis for the Russian sphere of influence has been Eastern Orthodoxy, or what Huntington has termed "Slavic-Orthodox" civilization. Among contemporary countries, this includes most clearly Belarus, Ukraine, Bulgaria, and Serbia. Less clearly, the Russian sphere includes most non-Slavic Orthodox countries, i.e., Armenia, Georgia, Moldova, and Romania. (The exception is Greece).

Historically, Russia has permitted and even encouraged Orthodox nations to be nominally-independent states. But apart from Greece during the Cold War and since, there has been no case of Russia accepting an Orthodox nation becoming an ally of a great-power adversary. There is nothing in the cultural or intellectual tradition of Russia that can interpret such a development as being stable or legitimate.

This of course was a large part of the explanation for Russia's behavior during the Kosovo War in 1999. The U.S.-led NATO war against Serbia was a direct challenge to this Russian conception of its traditional cultural sphere. The surprise occupation of the Pristina airport by 250 Russian troops—an action that was seen in the West as reckless, annoying, or just silly—was a desperate attempt by Russia to retain the symbol of its presence in its historical sphere while the substance was being extinguished by NATO's occupation of Kosovo.

In the absence of cultural affinity, a pronounced geopolitical interest can provide a basis for a traditional sphere of influence. For Russia, there has long been a geopolitical interest in its near abroad or soft underbelly to the south, i.e., the countries of Transcaucasia (of which Armenia and Georgia also provide the cultural connection of Orthodoxy) and Central Asia. Russia systematically annexed territories of Transcaucasia and Central Asia in the 19th century. In itself, this might suggest that it will strive to annex them again at a favorable time. It is just as likely, however, that Russia would continue to permit these countries to remain independent states as long as they continue to abide by the norms of a Russian sphere of influence.

Similarly, and more ominously for its relations with the West, Russia has long had a geopolitical interest in its near abroad immediately to the west, i.e., Finland and the Baltic countries of Estonia, Latvia, and Lithuania. Russia systematically annexed these territories in the 18th century, and the Soviet Union annexed the latter three again in the 1940s. How these countries can retain their character as Western societies and independent states while being a pronounced geopolitical interest of Russia is one of the major dilemmas of international politics in contemporary Europe.[8]

What should be the American grand strategy toward the traditional Russia spheres of influence? A related question is: what should be the role of NATO (which is, in some ways, an American sphere of influence) in relation to the Russia spheres?

The first round of NATO expansion in 1999 added Poland, the Czech Republic, and Hungary, but there seems to have been almost no attention given to any military strategy which might be used to defend these new members. Perhaps this was because Russia was then so weak that no military strategy seemed necessary and because, for all practical purposes, the new members did not directly border on Russia itself. (An exception is Poland's border with that odd geographical anomaly, the Kaliningrad region of Russia.)

The second round of NATO enlargement in 2004 was a different matter, however. It included the Baltic countries, which do directly border on Russia (with Estonia being only 150 kilometers from St. Petersburg). What is the NATO and U.S. military strategy to defend them? If it were conventional defense, how would this be practical? If it were nuclear deterrence, how would this be credible? Similar puzzles would be posed for any U.S. military strategy in the other, less Western Russian spheres.

If it is difficult to envision the efficacious use of U.S. military forces in general in the Russian spheres of influence, it is even more difficult to envision such use of U.S. naval forces there. The U.S. Navy has never considered the seas adjoining these spheres (principally the Baltic Sea and the Black Sea) to be suitable theaters for naval operations.

(The closest suitable seas would be the North Sea and the Eastern Mediterranean.)

Overall, then, the traditional Russian spheres of influence cannot be included, realistically and practically, as objectives of American military strategy. Although the United States can use a variety of incentives and threats, principally non-military ones, to encourage Russia to engage in liberal and enlightened policies toward its spheres, the U.S. should not seek to convert the Russian spheres into its own.

The Chinese Spheres of Influence

Since the time of its emperors, China has relied upon either a cultural basis or a geopolitical basis for its traditional spheres of influence. The cultural basis for the Chinese sphere of influence has been "the Chinese world order" or Confucian tributary system,[9] what Huntington has termed "Sinic-Confucian" civilization. For imperial China, this meant Korea, Taiwan, northern Vietnam, and more vaguely the East China Sea and the South China Sea. This realm is also the goal of contemporary Chinese nationalism. These areas are obviously ones in which China has a pronounced geopolitical interest as well.

Also of geopolitical interest but with much less cultural affinity, are Tibet and Sinkiang. They are the equivalent for China of what Central Asia was for the Russian Empire and the Soviet Union. Under imperial China, these territories were ruled more or less as a sphere of influence. Under Communist China, as is well known, they have been directly and severely ruled as annexed provinces.

What should be the American grand strategy toward the traditional Chinese spheres of influence? Of the countries in the culturally-defined sphere, two were the focus of military confrontations between China and the United States in the 1950s and are particularly likely to be the focus of serious conflicts in the future: these are Taiwan and Korea. As for Tibet and Sinkiang, they have at times been objects of dispute. However, hardly any U.S. foreign-policy maker believes that the United States can do very much about Chinese rule there.

The Chinese conception of Taiwan is that it is formally a part of China and that, in the fullness of time, this formality will become an actuality. The change in the status of Hong Kong in 1997 is seen as a prototype for a change in the status of Taiwan in the future. In the Chinese perspective, Taiwan in the meantime should not do anything to put formal obstacles in the way of this "natural development;" the most obvious obstacle is for Taiwan to gain international recognition as an independent state. The Chinese have been willing to accept a Taiwan that formally is a part of China but really is an independent economy. This Chinese conception has also been congruent with the interests of many Taiwanese businessmen, who have found their most promising business ventures to be on the mainland and who have invested $100 billion there.

Consequently, although the United States has been right to use the U.S. Navy to prevent China from using military force to threaten Taiwan (as in 1996), the U.S. would be prudent to deter Taiwan from making further moves toward formal independence. However, the commitment of Americans to their ideology—to liberal democracy, free markets, and human rights—makes such prudence unlikely or at least episodic and inconsistent.

In sharp contrast to the situation in the Russian sphere of influence, U.S. naval forces can be efficacious in the Chinese sphere of influence. The East China Sea and the South China Sea, along with the island of Taiwan and the peninsula of Korea, have long been suitable theaters for naval operations. However, this very efficacy and familiarity has tempted U.S. policymakers into believing that it is not necessary to work out mutually-beneficial understandings in regard to the traditional Chinese sphere.

We have already indicated that such understandings could be feasible in regard to Taiwan. More generally, the United States and China have compatible interests in maintaining an open trading system in East and southeast Asia and, as part of this, open access to the sea lanes or SLOCs in the East and South China Seas. Although China does not have an interest in maintaining a balance of power in the region as does the United States (China wants an imbalance of power in its favor), it does have an interest in avoiding a potential Sino-Japanese arms race. Continued U.S. military power in the region could make Japanese military rearmament unnecessary and unlikely.

There is much to be said in favor of an American grand strategy for the global era that would accept some version of spheres of influence for Russia and China. However, such a strategy would contradict the traditional American ideology of liberal democracy, free markets, and liberal internationalism. It would contradict even more the new American ideology of open society, global economy, and liberal globalism. It would be a strategy, however, that would be consistent with the sometime American practice of realist internationalism, as during much of the Cold War. And it would be a truly grand strategy calculated to take America off its current movement down the road to a new great war.

The American Way of War versus Liberal Globalism

Military strategists and historians have discerned in some nations a distinctive strategic culture or way of war. In the last third of the 20th century, there was a widespread understanding among these professionals that there was a distinctive American way of war and that it was characterized by a reliance upon such advantages as (1) overwhelming mass (i.e., a pronounced advantage in men and materials), (2) wide-ranging mobility (i.e., a pronounced advantage in transportation and communication, (3) high-technology weapons systems, and, underlying and sustaining them all, (4) high public support of the war effort.[10] The purest expression of this American way of war was of course the Second World War. Another excellent example was the Persian Gulf War of 1991. However, the origins of the American way of war lay in the greatest American war of all, the Civil War. The use of overwhelming mass was crucial to the final victory of the North; it was exemplified by the strategy of Ulysses S. Grant. Conversely, the use of wide-ranging mobility was crucial to the initial victories of the South; it was exemplified by the strategy of Robert E. Lee.

The classical American way of war was a product of the distinctive geographical and economic features of the United States. The U.S. possessed a vast continental territory which was endowed with ample natural resources and with a population larger than that of most European powers. This meant that the United States almost always had a pronounced advantage in men and material, i.e., mass. Only the Soviet

Union could surpass the U.S. in this respect. In turn, the vast continental area and widespread population created a need for a correspondingly extensive transportation and communication network, and the large industry and advanced technology of the U.S. economy provided the means with which to build it. Furthermore, the United States was bordered by two vast oceans; it was not only a continent but also a continental island. This also created demand for a transportation and communication network that extended to other continents. This meant that the United States always had a pronounced advantage in the rapid movement of people and products in peace and of men and material in war, i.e., mobility. No power has ever surpassed the U.S. in this respect. The conjunction of a pronounced advantage in both mass and mobility made the United States the most successful military power of the 20th century and thereby made the 20th century the American century.

On the rare but important occasions when the United States could not deploy its advantages in both mass and mobility, the U.S. military faced serious problems. Both the Korean War and the Vietnam War degenerated into wars of attrition in which the U.S. military had the advantage in mass firepower but no obvious advantage in the mobility of its ground combat forces. In the last two years of the Korean War, both the U.S. Army and the communist armies were trapped in a static war of position near the 38th Parallel, and the end result was a stalemate. In the Vietnam War, the communist guerrilla forces had the advantage in mobility, and this contributed greatly to the U.S. defeat. Indeed, it is the nature of any guerrilla war that the insurgent forces have the advantage of mobility, and the counterinsurgency forces have the advantage of mass. It seems that the classical American way of war has no obvious answer if the military challenge comes from guerrillas and insurgents.

In the aftermath of its Vietnam debacle, the U.S. Army painfully examined the lessons of that war, and it largely concluded that the classical American way of war was really the only right way of war for the Army.[11] The lessons learned were institutionalized in the curriculum of the Army War College, as well as several other military schools, and in the strategic doctrine, bureaucratic organization, and weapons procurement of the Army itself. Many of the lessons learned were crystallized in the Weinberger-Powell Doctrine. As we discussed above, central to the classical American way of war and its recapitulation in the Weinberger-Powell Doctrine is the idea that when the United States goes to war, it should do so as a nation defending its vital national interests against another nation, and that when the U.S. Army goes to war, it should do so as an army fighting another army. Since the interests being defended were vital national ones, they would be recognized as such by the American people, and they would support the war. Conversely, wars to advance peripheral imperial interests and wars against insurgent forces were violations of the American way of war. They would be unlikely to receive the sustained support of the American people.

The Rumsfeld Transformation Project

From the very beginning of the administration of George W. Bush, Secretary of Defense Donald Rumsfeld worked vigorously and systematically to overthrow the classical American way of war and the Weinberger-Powell Doctrine and to replace them with a new program of military "transformation."[12] He moved to reduce the role of heavy weapons systems (armor and artillery) and large combat divisions in the U.S. Army and to increase the role of lighter and smaller forces (airborne and special operations); in effect, he sought to reduce the role of mass and to accentuate the role of mobility. To implement his transformation project, he canceled the Crusader heavy artillery system, and he appointed a retired Special Forces general as the new Army Chief of Staff. Most importantly, however, Rumsfeld saw the upcoming Iraq War as the pilot plan and exemplary case of his grand project. If the U.S. could win a war in Iraq with a transformed military and a transformed doctrine, it would also be a decisive bureaucratic victory in Washington for a thoroughly new American way of war. More fundamentally, the Rumsfeld project sought to transform the U.S. Army into an instrument which would fight for peripheral global interests, and not just for vital national ones.

The Rumsfeld transformation project gained credibility because there were indeed some serious problems with the classical American way of war—particularly with the idea that the U.S. Army should only fight another army. The most obvious difficulty was that there no longer seemed to be any other real army to fight. Indeed, in the early 2000s, neither the Army, the Navy, or the Air Force of the United States had any equivalent force or "peer competitor."

The United States did have and still has enemies, however, most obviously in transnational networks of Islamist terrorists but also in particular "rogue states" which oppose globalization and the American empire, such as North Korea and Iran. These enemies seek to attack the United States not with conventional military forces or an American-style way of war but with "asymmetrical warfare." At the upper end of the war spectrum, this could be weapons of mass destruction (WMD), particularly nuclear ones (e.g., North Korea). At the lower end of the spectrum will be terrorist operations (e.g., Al Qaeda and Islamic State) and guerrilla warfare. Of course, the most ominous threat comes from a diabolical synthesis of the upper end and the lower end— weapons of mass destruction in the hands of transnational terrorist networks. For all of these unconventional or asymmetrical threats, the classical American way of war has no credible strategy or solution.

However, neither did the transformation project of Rumsfeld. The transformation project did not really address the challenge of North Korea, i.e., of rogue states which have already acquired nuclear weapons. Hypothetically, some combination of highly-accurate intelligence and highly-effective weapons (e.g., nuclear "bunker bombs") could destroy an enemy's stock of WMD. However, the failure to find any such weapons in Iraq certainly cast doubt on the accuracy of U.S. intelligence. And even highly-effective weapons systems would have a hard time destroying widely-dispersed stocks of biological weapons. The only way that the transformation project could deal with the WMD threat would be when a rogue state has not yet acquired such weapons, and a U.S. military operation can destroy the rogue regime before it does so. But this would really be a preventive war, not a pre-emptive one. This was the case with Iraq. Some advocates of the Bush administration's innovations, particularly neo-conservatives, also thought that it could next become the case with Iran.

The transformation project also did not really address the challenge of transnational terrorist networks such as Al Qaeda or Islamic State.

This threat is better dealt with by a multidimensional array of agencies and instruments (intelligence, security, and financial) working with their counterparts in other countries which face similar threats, particularly those in Europe.

The Rumsfeld Army and Imperial Wars

Other than dealing with non-nuclear rogue states, the only task which the new Rumsfeld army—with its lighter, more mobile configuration—could arguably have performed better than the old classical army—with its heavy armor and artillery configuration—was operations against an enemy that was even more light and mobile, i.e., guerrillas and insurgents. It appears that the new Rumsfeld army was really designed to engage in colonial kinds of war, with the U.S. Army putting down rogue states and insurgent movements who were resisting the American globalization project, rather than in a national kind of war, with the U.S. Army fighting another nation's army. The Rumsfeld project can be seen as providing the military dimension of the globalization project, the stick that must go along with the carrot. As such, the proposed new American way of war was indeed the "neo" way of war, since it was the way of war that was promoted by the advocates of global perspectives, especially the neo-liberals and neo-conservatives. These groups knew that the old American way of war, with its large numbers of troops, required the sustained support of the American people, and they knew that the American people were unlikely to give that support to wars for their global purposes. These purposes could only be achieved with a new American way of war and with an American military that was so light and mobile that it didn't need the support of the American people at all.

There were, however, several ironies attending the Rumsfeld transformation project. First, the origins of the Weinberger-Powell Doctrine lay in the lessons learned from the Vietnam War, and its basic impetus was "no more Vietnams." Among other things, this meant that the regular units of the U.S. Army would fight no more counterinsurgency wars. The Rumsfeld transformation project amounted to a radical overthrow of the Weinberger-Powell Doctrine, and it sought to return the Army to the period at the beginning of the Vietnam War—the era when Secretary of Defense Robert McNamara was engaged in his own radical program of military transformation, and when other political appointees of the Kennedy and Johnson administrations were enthusiastic advocates of some major combination of high-technology and counter-insurgency as the new way that the United States would fight its future wars.

Second, even before Rumsfeld began his construction of his new army and his deconstruction of the old one, the United States already had a long-established, lighter, and more mobile ground force, which was the U.S. Marines (the Navy's Army). During the first half of the 20th century, the Marines had far more experience and success with light and mobile operations than did the Army. This included operations against insurgents in the Caribbean Basin and in Central America. With only minor modifications and some modest expansion, the Marines by themselves could perform many of the colonial tasks that Rumsfeld's lighter, more mobile, transformed Army was supposed to perform (although not an invasion and conquest of large rogue states such as Iraq and Iran). But his new Army would not have been able to perform some of the tasks that the old Army could perform so well, e.g., quickly overwhelming another "peer competitor" army, if one should ever come into being and pose a threat to the vital national interests of the United States.

In the end, as we shall discuss in detail in Chapter 12, the Rumsfeld transformation project ran aground, and ran into a dead end, in the Iraq War. The very war that was supposed to be the exemplary demonstration of the project proved to be its undoing. It was not even able to put down the Iraqi insurgents that sprang up soon after the U.S. invasion, and these had to be put down by a completely different way of counterinsurgency war. As it turned out, this would be a new version of an older American way of counterinsurgency war, one that was far more sophisticated about local realities than anything conceived of in Rumsfeld's global strategy.

Global Order versus the Global Transformations

Only the United States can be a credible leader of the global order. This is due not only to such traditional measures as the superiority of its military forces and the size of its economy, but also because the U.S. has been the leader in the global trends and great transformations of our time—the development of the information economy, the global economy, the post-modern society, and the multicultural society.

This grand strategic task of global leadership requires a high degree of social cohesion and political consensus within the United States itself, along with a careful and proficient use of the U.S. military to support the purposes of the strategy. However, as we have seen, the same global transformations that have called the U.S. to its grand strategic task have also made it less capable of carrying it out. Each of the four transformations has contributed to the erosion of American social cohesion and political consensus. Moreover, at least two of them—post-modern society and multicultural regime—have opened up a gap between the U.S. military and much of American society. And at least two of them—post-industrial economy and post-modern society—have also opened up a gap between the strategic traditions of the U.S. military and its strategic capabilities in the future. The strategic challenges that confronted the United States and its military during the long Cold War were great indeed. Those that now confront them, as they try to carry out the role of the leading global power, may prove to be greater still.

CHAPTER EIGHT

THE AMERICAN WAY OF VICTORY

THE 20TH CENTURY, THE first American century, was also the century of the three world wars. The United States was not only victorious in the First World War, the Second World War, and the Cold War, but it was more victorious than any other country, enabling American strategies to shape three post-war worlds. These post-war strategies also did much to prepare the ground for the subsequent world wars—the Second World War and the Cold War. Now, a generation after American victory in the third of these world wars, it is time to evaluate the U.S. victor strategies of the 1990s-2010s to consider whether they would make the 21st century a second American century of world peace and prosperity, or alternatively lead, sometime in the next few decades, to a fourth world war.

The First and Second British Centuries

Like America at the beginning of the 21st century, Britain in the early 19th century had passed through a century of three wars that were really worldwide in scope—the War of the Spanish Succession (1702-1713), the Seven Years' War (1756-1763), and the successive Wars of the French Revolution and Napoleonic Wars (1792-1815). Britain had been victorious in each of these wars, making the 18th century something of a British one. The victor strategy that Britain pursued after the Napoleonic Wars laid the foundations for what has been called "the Hundred Years' Peace" (1815-1914), making the second British century as peaceful as the first one was warlike.[1]

The central elements of the British victor strategy were four: two involved international security and two involved the international economy.[2] The security elements were established immediately after the victory over Napoleon. They were (1) a British-managed balance-of-power system on the European continent and (2) British naval supremacy in the rest of the world. The economic elements were established about a generation later. They were (3) British industrial supremacy operating in an open international economy (Britain serving as "the workshop of the world") and (4) British financial supremacy, also operating in an open international economy (the City of London serving as "the world's central bank").

By the beginning of the 20th century, however, British naval and industrial supremacy were threatened by the rise of Germany and the spectacular growth of German military and economic power. When in August 1914 it appeared that Germany was also about to destroy the continental balance-of-power system with its invasion of Belgium and France, Britain went to war to stop it. The Hundred Years' Peace and the second British century came to a crashing and catastrophic end with the First World War.

Victory therefore presents a profound challenge to a victor power, especially to a pre-eminent one: it must create a victor strategy to order the post-war world in a way that does not lead to a new major war. The British victor strategy after the Napoleonic Wars was successful in meeting this challenge for almost a century. But even this sophisticated strategy, which addressed and integrated four different dimensions of international security and economy, failed to manage the rise of German military and economic power, and the Hundred Years' Peace ended with a world war even worse than the one after which it began.

As shall be discussed below, the American victor strategies after the First and Second World Wars were similar to the earlier British one in their efforts to combine several different dimensions of international security and economy; indeed, the American strategies relied upon some of the same elements, particularly naval, industrial, and financial supremacy. They did not, however, succeed in preventing the Second World War and the Cold War. The fundamental question for our time is whether the American victor strategy after the Cold War will succeed in preventing some kind of a new world war in our current century.

Living with Victory after the First World War

It took four years of war and the massive engagement of the United States, but in November 1918 the Western Allies succeeded in defeating Germany. But even in defeat, the nation whose rise to military and economic power Britain had failed to manage still retained most of its inherent strengths. The German problem, which had been at the center of international relations before the war, was redefined by the Allied victory, but it was still there, and it was still central. Western victory still had to focus upon German reality.

The renewed German problem. Germany remained the central nation on the European continent. Demographically, it had the largest and best-educated population in Europe. (Russia, which had a larger population, was convulsed by revolution and civil war.) Economically, it had the largest and most advanced industry in Europe. Strategically, it faced formidable powers to the West (France and Britain). But to the East, it faced only new and small states (Poland and Czechoslovakia). In this sense, Germany's strategic position was actually better after its defeat in the First World War than it had been before the war began, when to the East it had faced Russia as a great power. It would only be a matter of time until Germany recovered its political unity, gathered up its inherent strengths, and once again converted these into military and economic power. This was the long-term reality that the victorious Allies had to consider in the midst of their short-term victory and as they composed their victor strategies.

There were four basic strategies that different allies employed at different times: (1) territorial dismemberment, (2) military containment, (3) security cooperation, and (4) economic engagement. These strategies were not new inventions; they derived from the strategies employed by victor powers after earlier wars. The first two derived from territorial annexations and frontier fortifications, strategies that the continental powers had used against each other in the 18th and 19th centuries. The last two derived from the "concert of Europe" or balance-of-power system and the open international economy that Britain had managed in the 19th century. But these strategies also were not obsolescent conceptions; the latter three prefigured the victor strategies that the United States would employ after the Second World War and after the Cold War.

Territorial dismemberment and military containment. One apparent solution to the German problem was territorial dismemberment. This was the strategy preferred by France. The dismemberment of a defeated enemy can sometimes be carried out by victorious powers, and the Allies did so with that other Central Power in the First World War, the Austro-Hungarian Monarchy. But while this division destroyed a former adversary, it unleashed a sort of international anarchy in Southeastern Europe, which still reverberated down to the 2000s (as in the former Yugoslavia). Dismemberment is also what happened to the Soviet Union after the Cold War. Here too, while this division greatly diminished a former adversary, it has unleashed international and internal anarchy in the Caucasus and Central Asia (as in Chechnya and Georgia) and in Ukraine.

Whatever might be the advantages of dismemberment as a victor strategy, they were not applicable to Germany in 1919. By that time, the German nation had become a solid reality, and it had a solid identity; it could not be permanently undone by artificial territorial divisions unless these were enforced by military occupation (which is how the division of Germany was enforced after the Second World War). There are today a few international analysts who argue that the United States should encourage the territorial division of troublesome powers, particularly Russia and China. There are, however, hardly any specialists on China or even Russia who believe that a permanent division of these nations is possible.

An alternative but closely-related solution to the German problem was military containment. This was the objective of the Treaty of Versailles, which set up what was known as the Versailles system to carry it out. Military containment was another victor strategy chosen by France. In the early 1920s, the French were quite active at implementing this strategy, as in their military occupation of the Ruhr in 1923.

The Democratic administration of President Woodrow Wilson advanced a kinder, gentler version of the Versailles system in its proposals for a League of Nations and a U.S. security guarantee to France and Britain. The military containment of Germany embodied in the security guarantee would be institutionalized and legitimated in a collective-security system embodied in the League. But of course, the Republican-controlled U.S. Senate rejected these proposals, and the United States never again considered the strategy of military containment as a solution to the German problem.

Economic engagement and security cooperation. Instead, a few years later, the United States addressed the German problem (now accentuated by the unstable French occupation of the Ruhr) with a strategy of economic engagement. This took the form of the Dawes Plan, an ingenious project for financial recycling, in which American banks loaned capital to Germany, Germany paid war reparations to France and Britain, and France and Britain repaid war debts to the American banks. The Dawes Plan thus encouraged an open international economy among the most advanced economies, and it sought to integrate Germany into this mutually-beneficial international economic system.[3] The Dawes Plan succeeded very well from 1924 to 1929. It formed the basis for Germany's reintegration not only into the international economic system but into the international security system as well. It encouraged France and Britain to develop a new strategy of security cooperation toward Germany. In 1925 they signed the Locarno security treaty with Germany, and in 1926 Germany entered the League of Nations. The new American strategy of economic engagement seemed to be working far better than the earlier French strategy of military containment.

But as Charles Kindleberger famously demonstrated, an open international economic system requires an "economic hegemon" to keep it running, in bad times as well as good.[4] The economic hegemon performs three essential functions: (1) providing long-term loans and investments (as in the Dawes Plan); (2) providing short-term credits and foreign exchange in times of currency crises; and (3) opening its markets to receive the exports of economies which are passing through recession. Britain had performed these functions before the First World War; they had provided the economic foundations for the Hundred Years' Peace. After the war, however, Britain no longer had the economic strength to play the hegemon role, even though it still had the will. Conversely, the United States now had the economic strength to play this role, but it had not yet developed the will to do so. The Dawes Plan was only one step in the right direction, and it was a step in only one dimension. Still, for a few years in the prosperous 1920s, the international economy seemed to be operating well enough without an economic hegemon.

The prosperous and open international economic system of the 1920s allowed the victor powers to engage in a strategy of security cooperation (or even appeasement, in the then-innocuous term). Given the success of the strategies of economic engagement and security cooperation, the strategy of military containment appeared unnecessary or even counterproductive, and it was largely abandoned even by France. But, with the exception of the Dawes Plan, neither Britain or the United States stepped forward to take leadership in managing either the German problem or the international economy, in either good times or bad.

With the beginning of the Great Depression (which Kindleberger ascribed to the failure of the United States to act as an economic hegemon), the prosperous and open economic system of the 1920s collapsed and was replaced with the impoverished and closed economic system of the 1930s. Whereas the prosperity system had permitted a strategy of appeasement, the poverty system required a strategy of containment. But because of political reasons (polarization between the Left and the Right), France in the 1930s no longer had the political will to provide leadership for this strategy. Leadership in managing the German problem fell by default to Britain, which had never been a strong believer in the strategy of military containment. It chose instead a modest version of the strategy of economic engagement when the conditions of the Depression made this no longer adequate and attractive for Germany. Further, the strategy of economic engagement seemed to imply a strategy also of security appeasement, which was now even less appropriate for Germany. As for the United States, with the collapse of the Dawes Plan it gave up on any effort to manage the German problem at all. Thus, by the early 1930s, none of the three victor powers from the First World War—France, Britain, and the United States—were pursuing a coherent and consistent strategy to preserve their victory. With the coming to power of the National Socialist regime, Germany decided to manage the German problem in its own way. The Second World War was the result.

The new Japanese problem. On the other side of the world in East Asia, the United States pursued a quite different strategy. Here it faced the rising power of Japan, which had been an ally of Britain since 1902 and which was one of the victor powers in the First World War. Japan's growing military and economic strengths and its ambitions in China presented a serious challenge to the dominant powers in East Asia in the early 1920s, the United States and Britain.

The Republican administration of President Warren G. Harding, particularly his Secretary of State Charles Evans Hughes, took the lead in designing an innovative strategy of security cooperation to deal with Japan.[5] It convened a conference in Washington in 1921-1922, out of which came the Washington Naval Treaty, an agreement between the United States, Britain, and Japan to limit the numbers of their battleships; the Four-Power Treaty, which provided for consultations on security issues among these three powers plus France; and the Nine-Power Treaty, which provided for common principles and cooperation in regard to China. These arrangements, which were later called "the Washington system," were an elaboration of the U.S. strategy of security cooperation. However, the United States did not develop a comparable strategy of economic engagement for Japan to serve as the basis for this security strategy. Instead, it largely relied on conventional international trade between the two nations, which seemed sufficient in the prosperous and open international economy of the 1920s. But with the beginning of the Great Depression, this international trade largely collapsed, and the collapse of the Washington system of security cooperation soon followed.

Thus by the mid-1920s, the United States had conceived of some important elements for a victor strategy. In Europe, the Dawes Plan echoed the 19th-century British use of financial power in an open international economy. In East Asia, the Washington system echoed the 19th-century British use of naval power and balance-of-power management. But there was not much of a U.S. security strategy in Europe or a U.S. economic strategy in East Asia. The U.S. victor strategies after the First World War had not added up to a grand design. They failed to prevent the Great Depression and the ensuing Second World War.

Why did the United States fail to adopt a coherent and consistent victor strategy after the First World War? The traditional explanation blames American immaturity and "idealism" and the resulting "isolationism." A related explanation blames the isolationism and protectionism of the Republican party. However, the Dawes Plan and the Washington system were quite sophisticated projects (even by British standards), and they can hardly be described as isolationist; further, these were projects advanced by Republican administrations.

The main reason why the United States did not have a coherent and consistent victor strategy after the First World War was that its victory was too complete. In the 1920s, the U.S. faced no obvious great-power adversary or "peer competitor" which could wonderfully concentrate the American mind into a coherent and consistent strategy. Conversely, in the 1930s, the Great Depression produced a real American isolationism. It also produced real great-power adversaries (Germany and Japan), but these posed quite different strategic threats in quite different regions. This too made it difficult for the United States to compose a coherent and consistent strategy.

Living with Victory after the Second World War

The United States learned profound lessons from the failure of the Versailles and Washington systems to manage the German and Japanese problems and to prevent the Second World War. As it turned out, these lessons were largely expanded versions of the lessons that the Wilson administration, the Harding administration, and the American bankers had already learned from the First World War. As the second war was drawing to a close, the U.S. took the leadership in establishing a number of international institutions that would complete the first but abortive steps taken after the first war.

Security cooperation and economic engagement. On the security dimension, the United Nations was to succeed and perfect the League of Nations. On the economic dimension, three organizations were to help the United States perform the role of economic hegemon, one for each of the three functions identified by Kindleberger. The task of long-term lending would be promoted by the International Bank for Reconstruction and Development (the World Bank); the task of short-term currency support would be promoted by the International Monetary Fund (IMF), and the task of opening trade would be promoted by an International Trade Organization (ITO). Together, the three organizations were known as the Bretton Woods system. As it happened, the Republican-controlled U.S. Senate rejected the ITO treaty in 1947, but a less institutionalized arrangement, the General Agreement on Tariffs and Trade (GATT), took its place. (Almost fifty years later, the World Trade Organization was established, and this at last completed the original grand design.) The overall victor strategy of the United States was one of security cooperation based upon economic engagement.

This strategy and its elaborate systems—consisting of the United Nations system for security management and the Bretton Woods system for economic management—might have been perfect for dealing with the German and Japanese problems that existed after the First World War. But the problems that now existed after the second war were altogether different. Whereas after the first war, Germany was not defeated enough, after the second it was defeated too much. The victorious allies, including the United States, could easily, and almost automatically, impose the alternative and simpler victor strategy of territorial division and military occupation, and at first they did so.

Conversely, whereas after the first war, Russia was in a sense doubly defeated (first by the German army and then by the chaos of the Russian Revolution and Civil War), after the second it was doubly victorious (first by defeating Germany and then by occupying or annexing—along with its allies of Poland and Czechoslovakia—the eastern half of it). The German problem suddenly ceased to be the central problem of international security and instead became a subordinate part of the new central problem, which was the Russian one.

The United States initially tried to apply its overall strategy of security cooperation and economic engagement to this new Russian problem. But it was crucial to this strategy that it be implemented through international institutions led by the United States, i.e., the United Nations system and the Bretton Woods system. Both the strategy and its systems were incompatible with the interests of the Soviet Union as they were defined by Stalin. Security cooperation and economic engagement required some degree of an open society and a free market, and these contradicted the closed society and the command economy that characterized the Soviet Union.

Instead, the worldwide reach of the American system was aborted by the Cold War and the establishment of the Soviet bloc.

The United States therefore was only able to apply its strategy and system to the Free World, especially the First World. In Europe, the United Nations was replaced by NATO, and the Bretton Woods system was reinforced by the Marshall Plan. NATO represented a sort of second coming of Wilson's abortive security guarantee to France and Britain, and the Marshall Plan represented the same for the Dawes Plan. In East Asia, the United States concluded a series of bilateral security treaties and bilateral economic aid programs (including the Dodge Plan for Japan). The ensemble of security treaties echoed the earlier Washington system, and since it was based upon U.S. naval supremacy in the Pacific, it also echoed earlier British strategies based upon naval supremacy.

This American strategy and system, whose prototype had been aborted after the First World War and whose application was confined to only half the world after the Second World War, was extraordinarily successful where it did operate. It certainly helped to solve a good part of the old German and Japanese problems. However, it could not solve the new Russian problem (some historians think that it even accentuated it). The result was the Cold War.

Military containment. The Russian problem was addressed by a version of the alternative victor strategy, military containment—containment not of the defeated recent enemy but of the victorious recent ally. The rapidity of the transformation from enemy to ally and from ally to enemy, from Second World War to Cold War, was quite breathtaking, but it was readily accepted by the American public. In his famous novel, <u>1984</u> (written in 1948 as this transformation was being completed and with 84 being the reverse of 48), George Orwell portrayed the sudden reversal of the alliance between Oceania and Eastasia against Eurasia into an alliance between Oceania and Eurasia against Eastasia. By 1948 there had already been the sudden reversal of the alliance between the Western Allies (Britain and the United States) and the Soviet Union against Germany into an emerging alliance between the Western Allies and Germany against the Soviet Union.

When the communists came to power on the Chinese mainland in 1949, they presented a new security problem. For a brief time, the Truman Administration was inclined to hope that some version of the strategy of security cooperation (perhaps based upon traditional Chinese suspicions of Russia) and economic engagement would solve this new Chinese problem, but this strategy was aborted by Mao's alliance with Stalin in January 1950, the Chinese entry into the Korean War in November 1950, and the closed society and command economy that characterized Communist China. The United States therefore turned to the classic alternative strategy—military containment.

Although containment of the Soviet Union and Communist China was necessary, it did present problems of its own. Military containment once led to defeat for the U.S. (the Vietnam War) and once led to near-disaster for the world (the Cuban Missile Crisis). And military containment by itself was not sufficient to defeat the Soviet Union, reform Communist China, and to bring about a U.S. victory in the Cold War. The successful and sustained operation of the free-market and open international economy in the First or Free World, in contrast with the gradual but steady exhaustion of the command and closed economic systems in the Second or Communist World, exerted a magnetic force upon the Soviet Union and China and drove them by the 1980s, each in their own way, to reform their economies and to engage in the American-led international economic system. But of course this did not happen quickly or easily. Forty years of Cold War and military containment were the price.

Why did the United States succeed in adopting a generally coherent and consistent victor strategy after the Second World War? The main reason was that its victory was in some sense a Pyrrhic one. The German enemy was replaced almost immediately by the Russian one, and the Japanese enemy was soon replaced by the Chinese one. Even more, since both enemies were communist and initially were in alliance, they could easily be seen as one enormous enemy. This wonderfully concentrated the American mind into a generally coherent and consistent strategy in the late 1940s and 1950s.

Living with Victory after the Cold War

The international situation of victory and defeat after the Cold War had more in common with that after the First World War than that after the Second.

The redefined Russian problem. Russia was more defeated after the Cold War than Germany after the First World War (but less defeated than Germany after the Second). As the Soviet Union was reinvented as the Russian Federation, it lost a quarter of its territory and half of its population. The Russian economy in the 1990s was beset by both deep depression and high inflation, and the Russian military was beset by weakness and incompetence, with only an arsenal of nuclear weapons remaining as the legacy from the era of Soviet power. The strategic position of Russia was removed from the center to the periphery of the European continent, and it remained the central nation only in the emptiness of Central Asia. The Russian problem was redefined from being one of organized power into one of organized crime. Only in 2000, with a new President, Vladimir Putin, with modest economic recovery, and with ambiguous military success in the Chechnya war came signs that Russia had begun a revival to the degree that Germany did in the mid-1920s.

At first the U.S. victor strategy toward this "Weimar Russia" was a variation on victor strategies toward Weimar Germany of security cooperation and economic engagement. Russia's generally positive role in the United Nations echoed Germany's role in the League. However, the expansion of NATO into Eastern Europe (really a form of military containment of Russia) echoed Wilson's abortive security guarantee to Western Europe (really a form of military containment of Germany). The extensive U.S. and international economic aid to Russia echoed the Dawes Plan. But just as the U.S. victor strategy toward Germany in the 1920s depended upon integrating that nation into an international economy that remained open and prosperous, so too did the U.S. victor strategy toward Russia in the 1990s. It would fail if either the international economy collapsed into one that was closed and depressed (like the 1930s) or the Russian economy reverted into one that was closed and command (like the 1940s-1970s). As it happened, these two extreme outcomes did not occur, but in the 2000s-2010s, more mild versions did. These were the global economic crisis and Great Recession that began in 2008, and the establishment of a bureaucratic-oligarchic economic system by the Putin regime in the 2000s. Together, these two economic developments did much to bring about the failure of the U.S. victory strategy toward Russia.

The new Chinese problem. In East Asia, the United States faced the rising power of China, a situation not unlike that it faced with Japan after the First World War. China's growing economic and military strengths and its goals regarding Taiwan and the South China Sea presented a serious challenge. Indeed, the Chinese problem after the Cold War was an even greater challenge for the United States (although it was not nearly as threatening as the Russian problem was after the Second).

The U.S. strategy toward China in the 1990s was in some senses an inversion of the U.S. strategy toward Japan in the 1920s (and an expansion of the U.S. strategy toward Weimar Germany). Whereas the strategy toward Japan provided for an elaborate system of security cooperation (the Washington system) but only for relatively simple economic engagement (conventional international trade), the strategy toward China provided for an elaborate system of economic engagement ("the Washington consensus," including the admission of China into the World Trade Organization), but for relatively simple security cooperation (conventional military visits). In a more important sense, however, the U.S. strategy was an innovative combination of economic engagement and military containment (particularly in respect to

Taiwan and the South China Sea). But since China thought of Taiwan and the South China Sea as being properly part of China, what the United States perceived as its strategy of military containment, China perceived as a U.S. strategy of territorial dismemberment.

We have seen that the U.S. strategies toward Germany and Japan in the 1920s depended upon integrating those nations into an international economy that remained open and prosperous, and that the U.S. strategy toward Russia in the 1990s depended upon the same. The U.S. strategy toward China even more had as its foundation the integration of that giant nation—one with more and more of a nationalist mentality—into a global economy that remained open and prosperous. If the global economy were to exclude China from its benefits, or if it were to become a closed and depressed economy, the entire complex U.S. strategy toward China would collapse. The United States would be driven down at best to the classic alternative, a simple strategy of military containment, or at worse, as was the case in the 1930s in regard to both Germany and Japan, to no strategy at all. As it happened, these two extreme outcomes did not occur. However, the global economic crisis and Great Recession convinced the Chinese leadership that the United States and its liberal internationalism were no longer capable of maintaining an open and prosperous global economy. Rather, China's national interests, and also those of the Chinese Communist Party, would be best served by a state-guided economy and neo-mercantilist policies operating within the global economy. These economic developments did much to bring about the failure of the U.S. victory strategy toward China.

The Culminating Point of Victory

Even when a victor power conceives a victor strategy that is sound and appropriate to the military and economic realities of the time, there will be challenges that arise from how it is implemented. The first of these challenges is to determine what is, in Clausewitz's phrase, "the culminating point of victory" and to not go beyond it. Victor powers are prone to succumb to "the victory disease;" they continue to pursue the strategies that brought them victory in the utterly new and inappropriate circumstances which the victory created. Concentration in war becomes compulsion in victory. The most famous example of the 20th century was Hitler following his successful blitzkriegs of Poland and France with his disastrous invasion of the Soviet Union in 1941. The most familiar American example was General Douglas MacArthur following his successful landing at Inchon and recovery of South Korea with his disastrous drive to the Yalu River and the Chinese border in 1950. This threatened China and brought it into the Korean War.

A contemporary American example of going beyond the culminating point of victory was the expansion of NATO. Although the admission of Poland, the Czech Republic, and Hungary may not have passed that point, the "second round of enlargement," which included the Baltic states and which reached the most sensitive borders of Russia, may have done so. We will discuss this NATO expansion in detail in Chapter 9.

This kind of victory disorder also developed with the U.S. promotion of human rights over national sovereignty and especially with the U.S. use of military force for the purpose of humanitarian intervention. The U.S.-led humanitarian intervention in Bosnia (1995) was accepted by all of the other major powers. The U.S.-led humanitarian intervention in Kosovo (1999) was greatly resented and in some measure rejected by Russia and China. The U.S.-led military invasion of Iraq in 2003, whose official justifications included humanitarian ones, was also rejected by Russia and China, and even by several of America's traditional European allies. The Iraq War clearly took the United States beyond the culminating point of victory. Along the way, humanitarian intervention had become humanitarian compulsion, even a humanitarian disease.

The Realistic Range of Opportunities

The second challenge for the victor power is in some sense the opposite of the first. It is to determine what is the realistic range of opportunities resulting from victory. The victor power is suddenly in a position where all things seem possible. It may erratically pursue this objective, then that, and then another. Versatility in war becomes diffusion, even dissipation, in victory. This is an error to which pluralist democracies, with their different interest groups, are prone.

It has often been argued that Britain succumbed to this victory disorder in the 19th century. The British continued to expand their colonial empire, one of the opportunities that came with their victory in the Napoleonic Wars, until they entered into the condition of "imperial overstretch." One result was that Britain had to undertake numerous and continuous military operations on "the turbulent frontier." Another result, more serious in its long-run consequences, was that the ample British investment capital was diffused across a wide range of colonies and foreign countries rather than concentrated upon the development of new technologies and industries within Britain itself. Such new technologies and industries would have better suited Britain for its competition with Germany.

A contemporary American example of the error of diffusion or dissipation seems to be developing with the U.S. promotion of every aspect of the American way of life in every part of the world. The U.S. promotion of economic globalization may be inherent in the U.S. performance as economic hegemon, but it does weaken the economic conditions and social bonds of many Americans. Even more, the U.S. promotion of social and cultural globalization—of the American way of expressive individualism, popular culture, and the dysfunctional family—has generated resentment and resistance in a wide arc of countries in the Middle East, South Asia, and East Asia. This, it seems, is the American way of producing a turbulent frontier.

The Balancing Effect

The third challenge is the most familiar and the most fundamental, although Americans are inclined to think that they are exempt from it. It is derived from the well-known balancing effect. Victory brings the pre-eminent victor power hegemony, which in turn can initiate a realignment of the lesser victor powers against it (perhaps joined by the defeated one).

The United States has served as an offshore or rather overseas balancer for Europe and also for East Asia. Even more than for Britain, its overseas and remote position permitted it to exercise an overseas hegemony over the nations of Western Europe (while balancing against the Soviet Union) and East Asia (while balancing against China). Indeed, the United States has continued to exercise this overseas hegemony, now over all of Europe, even with the collapse of the Soviet Union and with only the much weaker Russian Federation to balance. By historical comparison with the European past, this hegemonic security system has been an extraordinary achievement on the part of the United States. Were America located on the continent where France is or even thirty miles offshore where Britain is, it probably would not have occurred; it can exist because the United States is located an ocean away and in another hemisphere.

The United States also continues to exercise something of an overseas hegemony in East Asia while balancing against China. The U.S. hegemonic security system there continues to include Japan, South Korea, the Philippines, and the problematic Taiwan; it provides the basis for any strategy of military containment of China.

The overseas location of the United States thus enables it to avoid the balancing effect and instead to perform the role of security hegemon in Europe and in parts of East Asia. Of course, the United States also acts as the security hegemon in Latin America where there is no prospect of a balancing effect against "the colossus of the North" (a case of an opposite phenomenon, which international relations specialists call the "bandwagoning effect").

Hegemony versus Hyper-Victory

The U.S. role as the security hegemon in several regions complements the U.S. role as the economic hegemon in the global economy. The U.S. security hegemony is acceptable because of its unique overseas location and the sustained peace that it has provided. The U.S. economic hegemony is acceptable because of the unique economic functions that it performs and the sustained prosperity that it produced, at least until the global economic crisis of 2008. The United States has operated the security and economic dimensions of hegemony together to consolidate and preserve its great victory after the Cold War. It has done so in ways reminiscent of Britain appending the security and economic dimensions of its supremacy together to consolidate and preserve its great victory after the Napoleonic Wars.

This splendid achievement of the United States has been under-mined, however, by actions coming from the U.S. itself. The most obvious example was the Iraq War, but the George W. Bush and Barack Obama administrations engaged in others, particularly by their pro-vocative initiatives in countries bordering Russia. The victory disorders of compulsion and dissipation are now overcoming even the powerful U.S. advantages of overseas position and economic performance and are driving some major powers—particularly China and Russia—-into the balancing effect and even into a sort of containment policy directed at the United States. This outcome would become even more likely if the prosperous and open global economy should turn into a poor and closed one.

Whatever form a balancing effect or containment coalition might take, however, at its core will be China. It will be the new Central Power on the Eurasian landmass, just as it was once the Middle Kingdom. The arrival of this coalition on the international scene would mean that the U.S. victory after the first cold war would have been followed by a sec-ond cold war (or worse) and that this would be another war on a world scale. This alone makes living with China the single most important challenge facing a United States which is still living with victory, and which, with dangerous over-confidence, is still expecting to do so for decades to come.

CHAPTER NINE

EUROPE:

NATO EXPANSION VERSUS
THE RUSSIAN SPHERE

IN 1951, WASHINGTON, D.C. was the scene of what was then called the Great Debate. The issue was the conversion of the rather spare North Atlantic Treaty of 1949 into something that would be much more of an American military commitment: an integrated military organization under an American supreme commander and the permanent stationing of U.S. troops in Europe. Thirty years before that, Washington was the scene of an even more famous great debate. In 1920, the issue was U.S. membership in the League of Nations and a permanent U.S. security guarantee to Britain and France.

In June 2001, President George W. Bush proposed in a major address in Warsaw that "Europe's new democracies, from the Baltic to the Black Sea and all that lie between" be admitted into NATO, with invitations for some to be issued at the forthcoming NATO summit soon to be held in Prague. Although Bush did not mention specific countries, it was taken for granted that he had the three Baltic states of Estonia, Latvia, and Lithuania in mind. Other nations that had applied to become members of NATO and that were being given positive consideration were Slovakia, Slovenia, Romania, and Bulgaria.

Although the admission of these countries into NATO would entail an extension and transformation of U.S. military commitments as serious as those at issue in 1951 and in 1920, there was little sign of any Great Debate, just as there was no great debate during the late 1990s over the admission of Poland, the Czech Republic, and Hungary. This lack of interest was all the more curious, given that great powers traditionally have considered their alliance obligations and military commitments to be at the heart of their foreign policies and that both the First World War and the Second World War began because particular great powers were honoring such commitments. NATO was supposed to be a military alliance, but there was almost no public discussion about the implications of NATO enlargement for its military strategy. And although there was much talk about not drawing a new line which would divide Europe like the old Yalta agreement did, the whole point of a military alliance is to create an alignment, to draw a line.

It seemed clear enough that the line that would be drawn by NATO expansion would be one between Europe and Russia. Russia had consistently argued that it should be defined as part of Europe, and it had frequently proposed that it be admitted into NATO. Conversely, the United States had referred to almost every other country in Europe as a prospective member of NATO, but it had consistently refused to include Russia among them. This refusal, however, had not been based upon a Russian military threat to NATO's prospective new members.

In the minds of the U.S. foreign policy leadership, NATO expansion was not really about the expansion of a military alliance but about something else. Its real purpose is to consolidate Europe into a coherent and integral part of the American vision and version of global order; it was to make of Europe not a *Festung Europa* but a kind of American fortress in the global struggle that was now developing over the grand American project of globalization. But because NATO itself still remained a military alliance, its expansion had, and will have, serious military and strategic consequences.

Globalization and Its Limits

During the 1990s, the grand project of the United States in world affairs had been globalization. Indeed, globalization had been so central to the United States, and the U.S. had been so central to world affairs, that it had given its name to the new era that has succeeded the Cold War; the contemporary period was being defined as the era of globalization. Globalization itself had been defined by American leaders as the spread of free markets, open borders, liberal democracy, and the rule of law, of a world governed by what Thomas Friedman called the "electronic herd" and the "golden straitjacket."[1] Most accounts of globalization had assumed that the phenomenon was indeed global in its scope or that it would soon become so. In fact, this assumption was mistaken, and the awareness that globalization is not global and that it probably never will be would itself later become widespread.

After three decades of experience with globalization, we can see a greatly variegated map of the globe, and the reality that it presents is not a linear and smooth progression, but a lumpy and jagged construction. It is a pattern of uneven development, uneven acceptance, and uneven resistance. When even the U.S. State Department—one of the most enthusiastic promoters of globalization—identifies several dozen countries (including such major ones as Indonesia, Pakistan, Iran, Nigeria, and Venezuela) that Americans should avoid entirely because of war, crime, anti-American hostility, or simply chaos, it is clear that globalization still has a great distance to travel.

Indeed, vast areas of the globe are less integrated into the global economy and a world order than they were fifty years ago. This is the case with most of Africa, most of Southwest Asia, and parts of the Andean region of South America. These three regions add up to a vast realm where globalization has already failed. In fact, no one has offered a credible plan or even hope for turning these regions into stable parts of the global economy and global order. On the contrary, they have created their own perverse and underworld version of the global economy, consisting of a global traffic in narcotics, diamonds, weapons, and human beings, and run by global criminal or terrorist organizations.

Furthermore, major powers, in particular China and Russia, have declared that they oppose the American version of globalization. China is probably the biggest single winner from globalization, and Russia may well be the biggest single loser, but they can agree on one thing: they are not going to be globalized in the American way. There are also those "rogue states," especially Iran and North Korea, which persist in trying to thwart the American project.

The regions where the American way of globalization has succeeded are actually rather few, and together they add up to much less than half the area of the globe and much less than half its population. These regions include almost all of Europe, much of Latin America, some of the peripheral countries of East Asia, and of course Australia and New Zealand. As it happens, these four regions largely correspond to the U.S. system of alliances as it already existed by the early 1950s (NATO, the OAS, a series of bilateral treaties with Asian countries, and ANZUS). The extent of "globalization" today is not that different from the extent of the "Free World" back then.

There is one major exception, of course, and that involves what was then Eastern Europe, the communist Europe, and is now once again Central Europe, a liberal-democratic and free-market Europe. This is also the region where the first round of NATO expansion occurred in 1999 and where the second round of expansion was proposed in 2001. It is in this difference that the link can be found between the American way of globalization and the American project for NATO enlargement.

Globalization and America's Europe

The United States of course wanted to expand and secure its new trade and investment relations with Central Europe. More fundamentally, however, it sought to consolidate all of Europe—Western, Central, and Eastern—into a secure core of the American way of globalization. It was crucial that this European core be integrally joined with the American one (which had recently been defined by NAFTA) and that Europe accept American leadership on matters of major importance.

It might seem odd to imagine that Europe would accept American leadership at a time when much of the European media was criticizing Americans on issues ranging from the death penalty to the global-warming treaty and many young Europeans were demonstrating against globalization. But in fact there was now a vast realm of Europe that was willingly recreating itself in the American image. This was especially the case with people engaged in the new information economy and the technical professions. It was also especially the case with the peoples of Central Europe and of the Baltic states. It is true that many of the peoples there were not enthusiastic about NATO, especially after the recent experience with Kosovo in 1999, but they did want to be part of an American alliance, even of something that would be akin to an American commonwealth. They loathed the Russians, were suspicious of other Europeans, and were attracted to the Americans, and these features have largely continued to be the case down to the present day. For these Central and Eastern Europeans, it has been true since the 1990s what was true for many Western Europeans in the 1950s-1980s: the purpose of NATO is to keep the Russians out, the Americans in, and the Germans down.

With its project of NATO expansion, the United States sought to influence the economic and diplomatic policies of European states and to balance the weight of the European Union, which was dominated by Western European countries, within the wider European continent. The countries of Central and Eastern Europe were less critical and more accepting of America than those of Western Europe, and the U.S. objectives would best be met by bringing in the former as a balance to the latter. This would be furthered by the expansion of the European Union; it would be furthered with even more assurance by the expansion of NATO. The result of NATO expansion would be the consolidation of Europe under American leadership and its transformation into an embodiment and expression of the American way of globalization. The inclusion of the Baltic states would consolidate this American-led European core up to the frontier where the American project of globalization met one of its principle opponents—Russia. The inclusion of the Balkan states would consolidate this core up to the frontier where the American project meets another set of opponents—the rogue states of the Middle East.

NATO Expansion: A Default Position

What might be the ideal form of organization for this American-led Europe which would be characterized by all the goals of American-style globalization—free markets, open borders, liberal democracy, and the rule of law, all within a security community or zone of peace? It would actually be some sort of American Commonwealth of Nations. It would be rather like the British Commonwealth of Nations of the first half of the 20th century (composed of Britain and the "dominions" of Canada, Australia, New Zealand, and South Africa). But, of course, this ideal form was not a practical possibility. The idea of an American Commonwealth would seem too close to the idea of an American Empire, and it would be unacceptable to both most Europeans and most Americans. Since the beginning of the 20th century, it has always been a distinctive feature of the United States to actually be an empire while always denying that it is one.

There was only one American-led organization for Europe that could have legitimacy among the major states of Europe: NATO. The fact that NATO was supposed to be primarily a military alliance made it a poor form for organizing all of the complex relations between Europe and America, which added up to something that was actually as dense as an American commonwealth. On the other hand, it was because NATO is supposed to be a military alliance and provides useful military benefits to the Europeans that it could remain legitimate while actually furthering other purposes and performing other functions. But of course the military character of NATO, which makes it more legitimate with the Europeans, makes it at the same time illegitimate with the Russians.

The expansion of NATO to include the Baltic states, however, brought this American military organization right up to the Russian border. Of course, this was not the first time that an American military alliance had immediately abutted a Russian border. NATO with Poland had bordered the Kaliningrad region of Russia since 1999; NATO with Norway had bordered the Kola Peninsula of Russia since 1949; and the United States itself has bordered eastern Siberia at the Bering Sea since it purchased Alaska in 1867. From the Russian perspective, however, the admission of the Baltic states into NATO produced a quantum leap in the strategic significance of their vulnerable border regions, with Estonia being only 150 kilometers from St. Petersburg and with the three Baltic countries together located astride the military approaches to all of Russia lying between St. Petersburg and Moscow.

In the early 2000s, some international-affairs analysts argued that there were better ways to provide for collective security in the Baltic region than by NATO expansion. One alternative was to follow the example of Finland, actually a Baltic state, and one that was a member of the European Union but not a member of NATO. Finland was clearly in the Western sphere in regard to politics, economics, and culture even though it was practically in the Russian sphere, at least as a buffer state, in regard to security. Another alternative, plausible at the time, was to admit Russia itself into NATO. This would have redefined NATO from an American military alliance into a European collective security system. It would have dissolved the line dividing Russia from Europe.

There was something to be said in favor of each of these two (very different) alternatives to NATO expansion.[2] Clearly the Russians preferred them, but many Western Europeans did so as well. However, just as clearly, the Baltic states themselves much preferred NATO expansion, as did the United States. From the perspective of the Baltic states, only NATO membership would consolidate their hard-won national independence. From the perspective of the United States, only NATO expansion would consolidate Europe into a secure core of the American way of globalization. This is why the United States pressed forward with an expansion of NATO that focused upon the Baltic nations, which had progressed so far and so successfully along the American way.

A Tale of Three NATOs

Almost all discussions of NATO speak of it as a homogenous alliance with its different members integrated into the organization in similar ways. In fact, however, NATO has always included a wide variety of forms and degrees of integration. It might be helpful, particularly if there should ever be any future negotiations with the Russians, to distinguish between three quite different NATOs, to be found respectively on the Central Front, the Northern Flank, and the Southern Flank.

The Central Front: High NATO. During the Cold War, the highest, fullest degree of integration of NATO was reached on the Central Front, especially in regard to West Germany but also at times with the Netherlands, Belgium, and Britain. High NATO was distinguished by three major features: (1) U.S. troops were permanently stationed on the member's territory; (2) U.S. nuclear weapons were positioned on the member's territory; and (3) the member possessed serious and substantial military forces which were integrated with U.S. military forces in regard to strategy, planning, and command. The ideal type or model for NATO was West Germany. Given the central importance of West Germany and the Central Front during the Cold War, it was natural to think of this model when thinking of NATO. But even in regard to the Central Front, France provided an exception after 1967, when President de Gaulle had France, including French forces in West Germany, withdraw from NATO as an organization while remaining within the North Atlantic Treaty as an alliance.

The Northern Flank: Low NATO. A very different NATO existed on the Northern Flank, particularly in regard to Denmark and Norway. Here, none of the three features of high NATO was present: (1) U.S. troops were never permanently stationed on Danish or Norwegian territory (although they did engage in periodic exercises there); (2) U.S. nuclear weapons were never positioned in these countries, and U.S. naval ships carrying nuclear weapons normally did not visit their ports; and (3) the military forces of Denmark and Norway were hardly serious and substantial—in reality they were more like a national guard—and they were not integrated with U.S. forces in any operationally important way even though symbolic joint exercises were held at times. For all practical purposes, the NATO of the Northern Flank was neither an integrated organization nor even an alliance of equivalent powers; it was essentially a unilateral military guarantee given by the United States. Yet Norway actually borders upon Soviet territory (for about a distance of 80 kilometers along the Kola Peninsula).

The Southern Flank: Pseudo NATO. Yet another very different NATO existed on the Southern Flank, particularly in regard to Greece and Turkey. Here, each of the three features of high NATO was present but in a greatly reduced form: (1) U.S. air forces were permanently stationed on Greek and Turkish territory, but U.S. ground forces were not; (2) U.S. nuclear weapons were occasionally positioned in these countries, but they were rather peripheral to U.S. nuclear strategy (and even expendable, as was the case with the Jupiter missiles in Turkey on the occasion of the Cuban missile crisis of 1962); (3) the military forces of Greece and Turkey were large but not modern, and have always been more of a threat to each other than to the Russians; they could not be integrated with U.S. forces in any substantive way. For all practical purposes, the NATO of the Southern Flank was neither an integrated organization nor an alliance of equivalent powers; it was essentially a loose military coalition grouped around a leading power, the United States.

These three fronts or versions of NATO during the Cold War can help us in thinking about NATO expansion in the contemporary era, even though no one today thinks in terms of the old Central, Northern, and Southern fronts.

If there were a successor to the old Central Front in today's NATO, it would seem to be Central Europe, especially those three members admitted in 1999—Poland, the Czech Republic, and Hungary. But these countries have been integrated into NATO not like the high NATO of the old Central Front but instead like the low NATO of the Northern Flank: (1) no U.S. troops are permanently stationed upon the territory of these three countries (or even on the territory of the old East Germany—the six eastern states of united Germany); (2) no U.S. nuclear weapons are positioned in these countries; and (3) despite (or because of) their Warsaw Pact past, the military forces of these three countries are not serious modern forces and have not been integrated with U.S. forces in any substantive way. Of course, the United States could conceivably decide to transform one or more of these three features of low NATO into a feature of high NATO. To do so, however, would entail breaking yet another agreement between the United States and the old Soviet Union (in this case, the agreement that led to the reunification of Germany). It was a transformation in the Soviet threat (evidenced by the outbreak of the Korean War) that led to the transformation of the original NATO of 1949 (merely a military alliance) into the NATO of 1951 (with all the features of high NATO on the Central Front). On the other hand, despite the ups and downs of the Soviet threat over the forty years from 1949 to 1989, the United States never seriously attempted to transform the Northern Flank from low NATO to high NATO.

It was a serious change, therefore, when the United States installed U.S.-manned Patriot anti-missile batteries in Poland (and also in Romania) in the late 2000s. The Russians interpreted this initiative as a major degradation of the earlier U.S.-Russian agreement on the military status of Central Europe. This has contributed greatly to the downward spiral in U.S.-Russian relations in the 2010s.

The Baltic States as Low NATO

When NATO was expanded in 2004 to include the Baltic states, this could have been interpreted as an expansion of NATO's new central front, i.e., an extension of Central Europe. The historical connections between Poland and Lithuania lent themselves to such an interpretation. Alternatively, the inclusion of the Baltic states could have been interpreted as an expansion of NATO's old Northern Flank, i.e., an extension of Northern Europe. The historical connections between Estonia and Latvia, on the one hand, and Finland and Sweden, on the other, lent themselves to such an interpretation. In either event, however, the expansion to the Baltic states could have been merely the expansion of low NATO. By itself, a version of low NATO could be made more acceptable to the Russians than the notion of NATO in general. They had already accepted a version of it on their Norwegian border for many years. And until the mid-2010s, i.e., until the Ukrainian conflict began in 2013, Russia more or less accepted the Baltic states being members of NATO.

Before 1945, what is now the Kaliningrad oblast or province of Russia was the northern half of East Prussia, a province of Germany. East Prussia was rich in its history (it had been a center first of the Teutonic knights and then of the Junker class), but poor in its economy (the Junkers' grain-producing estates could not compete in an unprotected market). The city of Kaliningrad itself was then Königsberg, known as the home of Immanuel Kant and also for its beautiful buildings and promenades. But between the two world wars, East Prussia was best known for being a strategic anomaly, separated from the rest of Germany by the famous Polish corridor. As such, it was a perpetual irritant in Polish-German relations; along with the city of Danzig, the Polish Corridor provided the occasion for the beginning of the Second World War.

The Soviet Union conquered East Prussia in 1945, annexing the northern half while giving the southern half to Poland. Virtually every German living in the Soviet portion was either expelled or killed, and virtually every building in Königsberg was either destroyed or demolished. The Soviets renamed the city after Mikhail Kalinin, who served as the titular president of the Soviet Union for Stalin, and they rebuilt it as an especially ugly and dreary example of the typical Soviet style. They also made of the Kaliningrad region a vast military complex, which included the headquarters for the Soviet, now the Russian Baltic Fleet. Today, the province (whose population is about 900,000 and whose area is less than that of Connecticut) represents a miniature version of the worst aspects of contemporary Russia; its rates of narcotic abuse, infectious diseases (particularly AIDS), environmental pollution, and criminal activity are among the highest in the Russian Federation. Its condition and its contrast with the three Baltic states and with the old East Prussia are a vivid reminder of what a mess Russians can make of a part of Europe when they are utterly free to be themselves.

Since the dissolution of the Soviet Union, the Kaliningrad province has been separated from the rest of Russia by the territory of independent Lithuania, as a sort of Lithuanian Corridor. Across this corridor there runs a military railroad line which supplies the Russian military forces in the province. The strategic anomaly and dismal slum of Kaliningrad is a black hole located right at the center of NATO's military commitment to the Baltic states.

During the Cold War era, West Berlin was a Western island and strategic anomaly which was surrounded by a Soviet sea. For many years, it was a crisis in waiting, and indeed it became an actual crisis in 1948-1949 and again in 1958-1961. When the Baltic states were admitted into NATO, Kaliningrad became a Russian island and strategic anomaly surrounded by a NATO sea (along with the Baltic Sea itself). In its earlier incarnation during the interwar era as East Prussia, it was similarly a German island and strategic anomaly; it was also a crisis in waiting, and it became an actual crisis in 1939. Given these historical and geographical antecedents, it should not be surprising if, in what is supposed to be the new era of globalization, this obscure and backward place should also become a crisis in waiting, a blast from the past.

Of course, the very vulnerability of Kaliningrad might make it into a hostage for Russian good behavior in international affairs, particularly their behavior in Baltic region (rather like the vulnerability of West Berlin was a factor in restraining U.S. behavior on occasion). On the other hand, the Russians already have in place a nuclear tripwire in Kaliningrad (dozens of nuclear weapons), which makes the territory more like a landmine than a hostage.

Since the time of Peter the Great, no European power had ever made a commitment to defend the Baltic countries from Russia. As different as they were from each other, Sweden, Prussia, France, Germany, and Britain all concluded that the risks and costs of guaranteeing the independence of the Baltics from their massive Russian neighbor were beyond their interests and their capabilities. When the United States in 2001 made such a commitment to the Baltics, it was therefore doing something that was not only unprecedented in American history (the closest prototype had been the U.S. commitment to defend Norway and Denmark), but it was unprecedented in European history as well. This historical leap by the United States rested upon the then-current American conviction that, for decades to come, America would remain as strong and as committed, and Russia would remain as weak and as feckless as it was then. In the minds of the globalizing U.S. elites of 2001, the current balance (or imbalance) of American and Russian military power in the Baltic region was inconceivable, or at least they did not want to conceive of it. As such, they demonstrated that it was they, and not the Russians, who were weak and feckless.

Slovakia and Slovenia as Strategic Consolidation

The admission of Slovakia into NATO in 2004 actually removed a strategic anomaly, one that was created by invitations to Poland, the Czech

Republic and Hungary in 1997. This left Slovakia as a geographical wedge inserted between the other three states. When Slovakia joined, this wedge was transformed into an integral component of a neat and compact bloc of four.

The admission of Slovenia removed yet another strategic anomaly. Of course, many Americans confuse Slovenia with Slovakia (the two countries not only have similar names but nearly identical flags), and many others think that Slovenia is in the Balkans (it is actually geographically closer to the Alps and culturally closer to Austria). However, Slovenia had made more progress in establishing a liberal democracy, free market, and the rule of law than any other country then being considered for membership. Its admission also provided a direct geographical connection and transit route between Italy (and NATO's southern region) and Hungary, making NATO's central region even more coherent. (Of course, it also meant that Switzerland and Austria, two non-NATO states, were now completely surrounded by NATO members).

The Balkan States as Pseudo NATO

The expansion of NATO to include the Balkan states brought with it another set of anomalies. The hope of U.S. foreign policy elites was that the Balkan region would become an American sphere of influence. For most of the period since the middle of the 19th century, however, the majority of the Balkan countries had been in a Russian sphere of influence. This had been especially true of peoples that were both Orthodox in their religion and Slavic in their ethnicity, i.e., Bulgaria, Serbia, Macedonia, and Montenegro. However, Romania (Orthodox but not Slavic) had often been in the Russian sphere. Of course, NATO has had an Orthodox member, Greece, since 1952, but Russia could always interpret Greece as an anomaly, more of a Mediterranean country than a Balkan one. Similarly, they could interpret Croatia (which was Roman Catholic in its religion and which was admitted into NATO in 2009) as being more of a Central European country than a Balkan one. (The Croatians certainly think of themselves in this way.) However, the admission into NATO of Bulgaria and Romania in 2004 and then

Montenegro in 2017 demonstrably put an end to any semblance of a Russian sphere in the Balkans.

The Balkan states have never achieved political stability in the same way as the other members of NATO, be they in Western Europe or in Central Europe. Indeed they are hardly states in the European scene at all. They are the heirs to very different religious traditions (Orthodox or Islamic rather than Roman Catholic or Protestant) and to a very different imperial history (Ottoman rather than Habsburg), and their political cultures reflect this. If Greece and Turkey have been difficult and troublesome members of NATO, the Balkan states could prove to be so as well.

America in the Baltic States: Interests, Ideals, and Identity

The issue of the second round of NATO expansion and of concomitant American military commitments did not produce a new Great Debate in Washington, but it did represent a new chapter in an old and ongoing debate over American foreign policy. This is the perennial great debate which is variously defined as being between interests and ideals, between realism and idealism, or between conservatism and liberalism (recently joined by neo-conservatism as well). A conflict between these two perspectives can now arise over any of the countries which were admitted into NATO in the second round of expansion, but it will be especially intense and serious in regard to the Baltic states.

From the realist (and conservative) perspective, there are no U.S. national interests at stake in the Baltic states. These three small countries together add up to an area that is only 50 percent of Finland's (whose admission to NATO has never been seen as a U.S. national interest) and a population that is only 50 percent more. The United States has no significant strategic or economic interests in these countries, and certainly none that are anywhere near as weighty as the very substantial strategic risks and costs that come with a U.S. military commitment to them. When the Baltic states are weighed in regard to U.S. interests and when NATO is defined as a military alliance, their admission into NATO simply seems to have been reckless and irresponsible.

Conversely, from the idealist (and both the liberal and neo-conservative) perspective, there are fundamental American values at stake in the Baltic states. Over a period of more than seven centuries and in at least four successive incarnations, these countries have represented the easternmost extension of Western civilization; they have long seen themselves, and have been seen by other Europeans, as the East of the West.[3] (Just as, ever since they were acquired by Peter the Great, they have been seen by the Russians as their "window on the West," the West of the East.) Today, thirty years after their heroic restoration of their national independence, the Baltics have been extraordinarily successful in establishing and embodying the American values of liberal democracy, the free market, and the rule of law. If any countries ever deserved to become members of NATO by virtue of their achievements by American standards, these did. It was fitting indeed that, after one decade of national independence, they were welcomed into many decades of American protection. When the Baltic states weighed in with regard to American values and when NATO is defined as a liberal-democratic and free-market community, their admission into NATO seems to be one of those truths that we hold to be self-evident.

In reality, what is at stake in the Baltic states is not just American interests or American ideals. It is American identity, in particular the reinvention of American identity by American political, business, and cultural elites to make it fit their new era of globalization. When America is by far the strongest power and the largest economy on the globe, these elites think that it is no longer enough for America to be located only on the American continent and to be composed only of American citizens; that definition of America is now obsolete. However, when America was far from being the only strong power and the only large economy, it was not yet possible for America to be located equally on every continent and to be composed equally of every people on the globe; that definition of America was then premature. From the perspective of American elites, the definition of America that best fits the contemporary era—the era of globalization as an ongoing project, rather than the merely international era of the past or the fully global era of the envisioned future—is one that includes Europe, the continent that it most advanced along the American way, as part of the new and expanded American identity. When American elites have come to define America as the free market, the open society, liberal democracy, and the rule of law, they have come to define Europe as being, in all important respects, America. And this American Europe extends to the Baltic states.

In the twentieth century, America met and won three great challenges presented by the old international era—the First World War, the Second World War, and the Cold War. It did so because of its great military power and economic strength, to be sure, but more important were the sophistication and the determination with which these assets were deployed by successive generations of American statesmen. When either the sophistication or the determination lapsed, as with the Korean War and the Vietnam War, all of America's military and economic assets could not prevent a debacle or a defeat.

The extension of an American military commitment to the Baltic states, up to the very border of a sullen and resentful Russia that was armed with a sense of historical entitlement and 5500 nuclear weapons, presented to the United States a strategic and diplomatic challenge with particular complexities which were unprecedented. At the same time, the integration of the Baltic states into America's Europe represented the culmination of an American calling, of a 225-year project of spreading American values and re-creating Western civilization in the American image until it has at last reached its easternmost frontier, the East of the West. To bring both the challenge and the calling into a stable synthesis, to create a Baltic order distinguished by both peace and justice, will require of the American statesmen of the 21st century a level of sophistication and determination that would have amazed those of the 20th.

Chapter Ten

The Pacific:

The U.S. Alliance System Versus the Chinese Seas

During the past several years, there have been numerous and somber reflections, rather like those during a traditional period of mourning, about the great and tragic events that occurred a century ago—the First World War. And in the course of these melancholy reflections about the past, there naturally have arisen anxious concerns about the future. Is it possible that we may once again be entering into an era of great conflicts, or even of a great war between the great powers of the time? Are there important and ominous similarities between the international situation before the First World War and the international situation of today?

Today, there are at least two theaters or regions where the great powers now seem to be heading toward greater conflict. In Europe, the most immediate theater of concern is of course that involving Russia and Ukraine, and more broadly Russia's "near abroad," where acute confrontation between Russia and the West has been occurring since 2014. But the theater that has been the scene of dangerous confrontations for an even longer period, especially since 2010, has been that involving China and its three littoral seas—the South China Sea, the

East China Sea, and the Yellow Sea (or as the Chinese often call it, the North China Sea).

There are certainly important features common to international politics leading up to the First World War and the increasing Sino-American confrontation of our own time. These are to be found at the level of some perennial, even classical, themes in the long history of international politics. In particular, we will consider two such themes: (1) the dynamics of hegemonic transitions; and (2) the dynamics of alliance systems.[1]

The Dynamics of Hegemonic Transitions

The first of our themes is that of the recurring drama of a rising and revisionist power confronting a dominant but declining status-quo power. Scholars of international relations refer to this phenomenon as "the hegemonic transition." It is of course a phenomenon well-known and long-remembered in European history, one evoked by such examples as the Spain of Phillip II, the France of Louis XIV and Napoleon, and the Germany of Wilhelm II and Hitler. In 1914, the most obvious rising power was Germany, and the most obvious status-quo power was Britain, and more broadly the British Empire. Today, of course, the most obvious rising power is China, and the most obvious status-quo power is the United States, and more broadly the American alliance system in the Western Pacific, including its Northeast Asian treaty allies of Japan and South Korea. This analogy between Germany versus Britain, on the one hand, and China versus America, on the other hand, has been a topic of concerned and continuing discussion for almost two decades, and this has been true both in China and in the United States. The analogy is a critical concern of Henry Kissinger in both of his two most recent books, On China and World Order.[2]

In the long history, the great parade, of rising powers versus status-quo ones, the final act of the drama has almost always been a great war. This of course was the case with the famous, and notorious, European examples which we have mentioned above. In one variation on this theme, the rising power becomes so confident in its newly-acquired power that it engages in a series of revisionist and aggressive actions which then provokes the status-quo power into a military reaction and resistance. Conversely, the status-quo power, observing and fearing the growing strength of the rising power, launches a preventive and pre-emptive military action against its challenger.

The alternative of containment. This dismal history gives us good cause to be concerned about the growing conflicts between China and America. However, there have been a few exceptions to this story of the hegemonic transition leading either to expansion, aggression, and war or to prevention, aggression, and war. One of these involves two powers who were in effect rising at the same time, i.e., the United States and the Soviet Union after 1945. In this case, there was no longer a truly great status-quo power, Britain having exhausted itself during the Second World War. The long, forty-five-year history of the Soviet-American conflict showed that there could be an alternative variation on the theme of the hegemonic transition, one defined by a policy of containment coupled with a strategy of nuclear deterrence, with the result being the long Cold War, rather than a great hot war. Although we normally think of containment as being the policy which the United States deployed against the Soviet Union (which is true), it was also a policy which the Soviet Union deployed against the United States, most obviously in Eastern Europe but also, in some respects, in regard to several countries of the Middle East (e.g., Egypt, Syria, and Iraq in the 1950s-1970s).

Containment is now seen as a great success, but it entailed two very destructive, if local, hot wars in the course of the long and general Cold War—the Korean War and the Vietnamese War (and one might add the Soviet war in Afghanistan as well). It also produced two extremely dangerous nuclear crises—the very well-known Cuban Missile Crisis of October 1962 and also the largely unknown but close to catastrophic "Able Archer" (the name of a U.S. nuclear exercise) crisis of November 1983.[3] As it eventually turned out at the end, deploying the policy of containment during the long Soviet-American conflict did succeed in displacing a hot world war with a cold one, but the international system was often perched unsteadily on the brink of the nuclear abyss.

Moreover, it will not be very easy for the United States to simply re-deploy the policy of containment from the Soviet Union of the

20th century to the China of the 21st century. Containing the Soviet Union was usually a matter of containing it within clearly-demarked land boundaries, and these red lines of containment also served as trip wires for deterrence. In contrast, containing China, at least with respect to its three littoral seas, entails ambiguous and disputed maritime zones and uninhabited islands and islets. It is difficult to draw a red line in blue water. In any event, the Chinese have thoroughly studied the U.S. containment of the Soviet Union, and they have determined that they are not going to let something like that succeed against them.

The other notable exception to the normal course of hegemonic transitions involves another case of two powers who were rising at the same time, i.e., the United States and Germany in the early 20th century. At that time, there was indeed a status-quo power, and it was Britain and its empire. Confronted by a kind of dual challenge posed by these two quite different rising powers, Britain responded in two very different ways.

Toward Germany, Britain essentially pursued a policy of containment. As the Germans rapidly built a large and advanced navy and deployed it in their two adjacent seas—the Baltic Sea and the North Sea—the British responded by building up their own navy so that it was even larger and more advanced than it had been before. The tensions and alarms produced by this naval arms race spilt over into other arenas where there were disputes—diplomatic (e.g., alliances), colonial (e.g., the Boer War), and economic (e.g., trade competition). Britain's actions in all of these arenas were shaped by its containment policy toward Germany, and Germany's actions in all of these arenas were shaped by its determination to break out of this containment. In the end (1914), Germany did break out, Britain did try once more to contain it, but this time with military force, and the First World War was the result.

The alternative of appeasement. In contrast, toward the United States, Britain essentially pursued a policy of appeasement. As the Americans rapidly built up a large and advanced navy and deployed it in two of their adjacent seas—the Gulf of Mexico and the Caribbean Sea—a number of incidents and disputes occurred between Britain and the United States with respect to this region, culminating in the

Venezuelan Crisis of 1895. In this case, however, Britain backed down, and over the course of the next decade, it steadily withdrew its military forces and ceded its leading role in the region to the United States. The mentality of accommodation provided by this military appeasement spilt over into other arenas where there had been disputes—diplomatic (e.g., new treaties), colonial (e.g., the new Panama Canal project), and economic (e.g., a new preponderant role for American trade and finance in the region). In the end (1917), the United States had come to such a mutuality of interests with Britain that it came to its aid not only in the First World War, but in the Second World War also.

Of course, the British only adopted appeasement toward the United States because they saw it as a more remote and less threatening adversary than Germany, and they had to concentrate their forces against the greater enemy. Thus, a policy of appeasement, which avoided one possible war, only came into being because there was simultaneously a companion policy of containment in the opposite direction, which resulted in another war. It seems, then, that the exceptions to the general pattern that hegemonic transitions end in a great war may really only be exceptions that prove the rule.

Given this generally dismal history of hegemonic transitions, there is ample reason based upon this theme alone to be concerned about the growing confrontations between China and the United States. And this concern is deepened when we observe another theme which is amplifying and aggravating these confrontations.

The Dynamics of Alliance Systems

Our second theme is that of the potentially destructive dynamics of alliance systems, and particularly of the commitments that great powers make to their allies. In the aftermath of the First World War, a vast literature grew up which focused upon the dual-alliance system, that is the alliance between the Entente Powers of France, Russia, and Britain, on the one hand, and the Central Powers of Germany and Austria-Hungary on the other. This was seen as the principal cause of turning a local crisis in the Balkans into a European, and ultimately a world, war. (The sequence or domino effect is well-known: the Austrian attack on

Serbia over a Balkan quarrel activated the Russian commitment to Serbia, which activated the Russian attack on Austria, which activated the German alliance with Austria, which activated the French alliance with Russia, which activated the German attack on France through Belgium, which activated the British alliance with France).

Today, we hardly have a dual-alliance system—China having only one ally, which is North Korea—but we certainly have a very elaborate and established one-alliance system, with the United States having security treaties with Japan, South Korea, and the Philippines, and having other security commitments to Taiwan. In the past decade, China has repeatedly challenged Japanese claims in the East China Sea and Philippine claims in the South China Sea, and therefore it has begun to challenge the U.S. security commitments and alliance system as well.[4]

The U.S. response to the Chinese challenge. The United States has responded to these challenges by reinforcing and even extending its security commitments in the region. In the Fall of 2012, following several incidents involving abrasive confrontations between Chinese and Japanese naval vessels near the Senkaku (Diaoyu) Islands in the East China Sea, the Obama administration publicly announced that the U.S. security treaty with Japan applied to these disputed islands. In actuality, this was the first time that the United States had officially extended its security commitment to these territories. At the time that the Nixon administration returned the Ryukyu Islands to Japan in 1971, it extended the U.S. security treaty with Japan to that chain of islands. That extension, and therefore revision, of the treaty was duly ratified by the U.S. Senate. However, the Nixon administration officially acknowledged that Japan had never administered the Senkakus as part of the Ryukyus, that the international status of the islands was in dispute between Japan, China, and Taiwan, that the final status of the islands should be the subject of future negotiation between the disputing parties, and that the U.S. security commitment therefore did not apply to the Senkakus themselves. This remained the official U.S. position until the Fall of 2012. The extension of the U.S. commitment at that time therefore represented a substantial enlargement of the U.S. guarantee to Japan and a risky escalation in the Sino-American confrontation in that region. A year earlier, in November 2011, following several incidents involving confrontations between Chinese and Philippine vessels near the Spratly (Nansha) Islands and other islets in the South China Sea, the Obama administration publicly announced that the U.S. security treaty with the Philippines applied to these territories. This also represented a substantial extension of prior official U.S. security commitments to the Philippines. It was also characterized by potentially dangerous ambiguity, particularly since the actual definition of what is an islet—and therefore an included territory—and what is merely an often-water-covered reef or part of a disputed maritime zone is much less clear than in the case of the Senkakus.

The U.S. security commitment to Japan with respect to the Senkakus and to the Philippines with respect to the Spratlys, in the context of ongoing confrontations between China and the United States in the region, have created the risk that the U.S. could be dragged into a military conflict with China simply by military initiatives undertaken by allies who have their own distinct political interests and practices (as well as their own operational dysfunctions and incompetencies). Each issue is a potential flash point that, in the midst of a crisis confrontation, could easily escalate into a military explosion. They are accidents waiting to happen. Indeed, their combination of official commitment with ambiguous delineation and uncertain resolve make these flash points as unstable as any seen in the long history of great-power security commitments to the small and obscure interests of allies. They are, for example, potentially more unstable even than the famous and dangerous case of West Berlin during the Cold War, which at least had the stabilizing elements of a clear territorial definition and a permanent presence of U.S. combat troops which served as a clear tripwire for U.S. military deterrence. And these two East Asian maritime flash points are certainly more imprecise, ambiguous, and unstable than any particular territorial issue that arose during the international crisis of July 1914.

The risks and dangers which usually come with alliance systems are accentuated and aggravated by two dynamics which are often associated with them. One is the phenomenon of arms races. When two powers confront each other, it is natural that each will try to enhance its security against the other by increasing its own armaments. But the increase in the security of the first produces an increase in the insecurity of the second—the infamous "security dilemma." The second power then responds in kind, and an arms race is on. Since allies either can add their own arms to those of the protecting power, or they have to be secured with additional arms from the protecting power, or both, an alliance system can amplify a security dilemma.

This dynamic of an arms race involving alliance systems was clearly operating in the years before the outbreak of the First World War. And we can now see the signs of a naval or, more broadly, a maritime race between China, on the one hand, and the United States and its ally Japan, on the other.

Another dynamic arises from the phenomenon of successive crises. When two powers confront each other and a crisis results, it is certainly possible that this particular crisis will be managed in a way that averts a war. However, if the powers continue to engage in successive confrontations, there will also be successive crises. At some point, and with some unfortunate conjunction of events, a crisis may be mismanaged and escalate into a war. Since each ally and its particular interests may become the occasion and cause of a crisis, an alliance system can multiply the number and quicken the pace of successive crises.[5]

Again, this dynamic of successive crises involving alliance systems was clearly operating in the years before the First World War. In particular, there was a series of crises involving both Britain and Germany for more than a decade before 1914. And during the past decade, we have seen those successive confrontations between China and U.S. allies, although none has yet really become a full-blown crisis involving the United States.

It seems, then, that the history of the dynamics of alliance systems is largely pointing in the same dismal direction as the history of hegemonic transitions, i.e., toward an eventual outbreak of a great war. However, following our earlier practice, perhaps we should look for exceptions to the general pattern and see if we can learn something from them.

The alternative of withdrawing a commitment. The history of alliances actually includes very few cases where a great power withdrew from its formal military commitment to an ally. The most famous, and notorious, case was of course the Munich agreement of 1938, when

France abandoned its security guarantee to Czechoslovakia. (Britain, which also signed the agreement, did not actually have a formal security commitment to the Czechs.) But since the abandonment of Czechoslovakia at Munich led, within a year, to the outbreak of the greatest war in history, this particular case hardly provides a useful guide to how to avoid a war.

The Munich agreement was about the only case in the first half of the 20th century when a great power backed down from a military commitment to an ally. Perhaps this is one of the reasons why that era produced not just one but two truly great wars. However, the second half of the 20th century, the era of the Cold War, does provide one notable example of a great power withdrawing from an alliance commitment, and therefore provides an exception to the general pattern of alliance dynamics. Intriguingly, this case involves China and a couple of islands in the East China Sea.

The Soviet Union concluded something of a security treaty with the People's Republic of China (PRC) (officially a "Treaty of Peace and Friendship") in January 1950, and this provided a degree of Soviet protection for China against the United States during the Korean War (1950-1953). Then, beginning in 1954 and continuing until 1958, China engaged in a series of military threats and actions to gain control over several islands in the Taiwan Straits which were still held by the Chinese Nationalist regime on Taiwan (officially "The Republic of China"). The United States had concluded a security treaty with the Republic of China in 1954, and although it had persuaded the ROC to withdraw from some of these islands in 1955, the ROC still retained two very exposed islands—named Quemoy and Matsu—just off the coast of China's Fujian province, and it was intent on keeping them. In 1958, China initiated a confrontation over the islands, which soon advanced to a full military crisis, with the United States committed to defend the ROC and the Soviet Union committed to defend the PRC. There was much alarm at the time that this crisis over two extremely small islands would lead to a Sino-American war and perhaps even to a Soviet-American war. Then, with tensions at their highest, the Soviet leader, Nikita Khrushchev, let the Chinese leader, Mao Zedong, know that the Soviets would not protect China against the United States with a threat or use of Soviet nuclear weapons. This forced Mao to back down and brought an end to the crisis. Indeed, Quemoy and Matsu remain occupied by Taiwan even today. (One of the most intriguing contemporary questions in international politics is about a non-event rather than an event: why, given all the loud and dramatic current confrontations over islands in the East China Sea and the South China Sea, has nothing been heard or done involving Quemoy and Matsu?)

At any rate, the Taiwan Straits crisis of 1958 immediately had important consequences for international politics. It was a major factor in bringing about the full and public split between China and the Soviet Union a few years later, and it was also a major factor in Mao's determination that China must have its own nuclear weapons, a goal which China achieved in 1964.

Our review of two perennial themes in the history of international politics has led to a disturbing and ominous conclusion. When we look at the contemporary Sino-American confrontations through the prism of each of these themes, the result is the same: it seems probable that these confrontations will eventually end in a great war between the United States and China. And with each of these themes leading to the same result, the combination of the two of them would seem to indicate that the probability of such a war is actually quite high. It may require heroic efforts—or rather unprecedented wisdom—on the part of both American and Chinese leaders to avoid it.

Western Theories versus Eastern Realities

But of course, our review of the history of international politics has actually been a review of the history of Western international politics. With the exception of our discussion of the Taiwan Straits crisis of 1958, all of our analogies and analyses thus far have assumed that conclusions and lessons drawn from Western experience can appropriately be applied to Eastern and particularly East Asian realities. However, this assumption that Western generalizations are also universal generalizations is now largely discredited in almost every other field of political analysis, be it the study of comparative politics (e.g., democratization and nation-building), political theory (liberal individualism and bureaucratic rationality), and international law (state sovereignty and universal human rights). Why should the field of international politics be any different? Is it possible, indeed likely, that there are distinct and different non-Western conceptions of international politics, or rather (since the very term "international" assumes relations between entities that are national states) world order or regional order? Indeed, this is the premise of both Samuel Huntington, in his famous The Clash of Civilizations, and Henry Kissinger, in his recent World Order.[6]

Since we are examining confrontations between China and America and their potential for issuing in a great war, it obviously becomes essential to examine the distinct and different ways that the Chinese themselves—both traditionally and today—have thought about what we in the West call international politics, but what the Chinese see as China's place in East Asia and in the world. Perhaps when we look at the Sino-American confrontations through a Chinese prism, rather than through a Western one, we may glimpse a way off the road to war. This requires us to engage in a sort of intellectual Copernican revolution, i.e., instead of putting Western conceptions at the center of our understanding of world order, we will have to suspend, for heuristic purposes, these Western notions and put quite different Chinese conceptions at the center of our understanding.[7]

The Chinese Conception of Space:
The Central State and the World Order

As is well known, China's traditional conception of itself (and one that largely corresponded to reality for two thousand years from the 210s B.C.E. to the 1700s C.E.) was as the "Middle Kingdom" or Central State. China was by far the largest country, the most powerful state, and the most advanced civilization in the world that was seen by the Chinese (even if that world was largely the region of East Asia and South East Asia). Surrounding the Central State was a series of much smaller countries or "tributary states," several of which were also smaller versions of the political and cultural model provided by China; these were Korea, Liuqui (the Ryukyu Islands, including Okinawa), and Annam

(Vietnam). Together these tributary states composed a sort of "string of pearls" around the Central State.[8]

At the center of this Central State and Chinese world order was the capital city of Beijing ("Northern Capital"), at the center of Beijing was the imperial palace compound (the "Forbidden City"), and at the center of the imperial palace was the Emperor. The Emperor radiated authority and power, right and might, out of the imperial palace through the "Gate of Heavenly Peace" to Beijing, to the rest of China, and to the rest of the world beyond.

However, although Beijing was normally the imperial capital and center of China and the Chinese world order, the original capital and center was at Xi'an, some 600 miles to the southwest of Beijing. Xi'an was established as the capital by Qin Shohuang, the original Qin (or Ch'in) Emperor, from whom China took its name. If one draws a great circle with Xi'an at its center, it does nicely include all the lands which the Chinese traditionally saw to be included in their world order—and for the most part, only those lands.

The Chinese Conception of Time: Historical Cycles and China's Destiny

The Western conception of Western history (at least the conception since the Enlightenment and the "doctrine of progress") has largely been linear. Western history begins in a primitive state and a "Dark Age" and then advances steadily upward, admittedly with occasional setbacks (such as the Thirty Years' War or the two World Wars), through successive stages of higher technological, economic, and political development. The Western conception of Chinese history has been something similar: Chinese history begins admittedly with an impressive level of culture, but also with an authoritarian political system, one characterized by extensive cruelties, frequent turmoil, and periodic civil wars. The early Chinese encounters with the West issue in a long period of especially acute turmoil and war for China, but in the end—especially when America became the undisputed leading Western power—Western ideas and practices have at last put China on an upward path, similar to that which the West itself has taken before.

In contrast, the traditional Chinese conception of Chinese history has largely been cyclical (as in the theory of the "dynastic cycle"). Chinese history begins at an already-civilized level and, after a period of political turmoil and Warring States (475-221 B.C.E.), the Qin Emperor united China into one great Central State (221 B.C.E.). Forever after, China's destiny is to remain one great state and one great civilization. Particular dynasties will come and go, rise and fall, according to the dynastic cycle, and there will be periods of schism ("splitting") and disunion. But, in the end, the unity of China's state and of China's central place in the world will be restored.

These two conceptions of history—the Western and the Chinese—have several elements in common, but, in essence, they are different and even contradictory. They can be combined, however, into a new one, which might be described as the Chinese historical conception with Western characteristics, and the contemporary Chinese leadership has done so. In this combined conception, there has indeed been a long series of dynastic cycles, but successive cycles have, in large part, played out at successively higher levels of development. At its height (the 18th century), the Qing (Ch'ing) dynasty reached a stage even higher than that reached by its predecessor, the Ming (the 15th century). The subsequent decline of the Qing was so deep, and the ensuing time of troubles was so grave that it could accurately be called "the 100 Years of Humiliation." However, in 1949, China under the leadership of the Communist Party, began a new period of unity and advancement, and this period is taking China to the highest level of development in its entire history of two-and-a-half millennia. The culmination of China's dynasties and the fulfillment of China's destiny means that the China of the 21st century will not only become more like the China of the 18th century and before. It will mean that China will become even more Chinese than it was before, because the essence of China will be realizing its potential more fully. Moreover, it will be doing so not only at an even higher level (incorporating all the benefits of Western science and technology), but on an even wider scale (extending the Chinese definition of the world order from East Asia to the world beyond, a world order which ultimately will include, in some still-indistinct sense, the West itself).

The Chinese Conception of Military Power and Strategy: Power Projection over Land

In the traditional Chinese conception of military power, a strong and effective military force was indeed at the core of the Central State and of imperial power.[9] However, the idea was that the military should rarely be used in addressing a strategic problem, and never as the first resort. Rather it was best held in reserve and used as a last resort. Again however, it would be best if other rulers and potential adversaries knew that this reserve of military power actually existed and could be deployed when the Chinese rulers deemed it necessary. In the meantime, it would also be best if the actual realities of unequal power were clothed with a symbolic veil of reciprocal respect and cooperation. The imperial military was a sort of "cannon behind the curtain," which every party knew was there, but which was discreetly covered. In the fullest realization of this conception, military power was a center of gravity, a solid and weighty mass which radiated outward gravitational lines of force which gently but firmly and steadily bent the will of other rulers—and of potential adversaries—so that they would more and more be inclined and conformed to Chinese designs and priorities.

In the long course of China's history, this concept of military power was, for the most part, only applied to the use of armies, i.e., the gravitational force lines were only projected across land. However, there had been a few rare exceptions when that power was also projected across the sea. The most important of these cases was Taiwan. (There were also two abortive invasions of Japan, undertaken by the Yuan or Mongol dynasty, and the epic but temporary voyages of Admiral Zheng He, undertaken during the Ming dynasty).

The Chinese Conception of Military Operations and Tactics: Encirclement and the Sudden Blow

These ideas about the center of gravity, the last resort, and the cannon behind the curtain were elements of the traditional Chinese conception of strategy. But the Chinese also have had a traditional conception of what might be seen as operations and tactics. Here, the focus has been on the steady and persistent accumulation of positions of strength, of peripheral bases of gravity in addition to the above-mentioned core center of gravity.[10] Over time, these accumulated bases add up and amount to an encirclement of the diminishing positions of strength of a potential adversary or target. Finally, there comes a time when the Chinese positions or bases are so strong vis-à-vis those of the opponent that everyone, including the opponent, can draw the obvious and sensible conclusion that the opponent should accept the realities and conform to the Chinese design, i.e., to accept his appropriate place within the Chinese world order. This acceptance of military realities is also clothed with the appearance that the opponent is doing so willingly, because he sees this to be the course that is most reasonable and in conformity with the world order, an order that is best for all.

Of course, there will also be occasions when the opponent does not draw and act upon these obvious military realities. In such cases, the Chinese tactic has been to await an auspicious moment, one in which the opponent is especially weak and vulnerable, and then to strike a sudden blow, one that is both dramatic and effective. This in itself creates a new reality so that everyone, including of course the opponent, can draw the same obvious and sensible conclusion that the opponent could and should have accepted before. The realities have now been demonstrated with a clarity and a starkness that could leave the opponent humiliated, but the Chinese tactic will often include some element (such as the quick withdrawal of the victorious Chinese military force to nearby positions) which will allow the opponent to retain some degree of respect (i.e., "face").

The Chinese Conception of Economic Power and Strategy: Exchange of Goods Through Trade

The traditional Chinese conception of economic power was analogous. A healthy and productive economic base was also at the core of the Central State and of imperial power. But here, the idea was that the economy should frequently be used in addressing a strategic problem, and often as a first resort. It would be best if other rulers and potential adversaries were well aware of the advantages to them of peaceful economic relations with China, particularly the exchange of goods through trade. However, the foreign rulers, with their small economies and inferior cultures, would need Chinese goods far more than the Chinese rulers would need theirs. Therefore, it would also be best if the actual realities of unequal attractiveness were balanced with foreign rulers also giving the Chinese signs and symbols of deference to the Chinese conception of the world order, with the Chinese Emperor at its center. This was important to the Chinese notion of imperial legitimacy. Thus, the famous "kowtow" ritual at the imperial court in Beijing. In the fullest realization of this conception, economic power was also a center of gravity, a solid and weighty mass which radiated outward gravitational lines of force which gently but firmly and steadily shaped the will of other rulers—and of potential adversaries—so that they would more and more be inclined and conformed to Chinese designs and priorities.

In the long course of imperial history, this Chinese conception of economic power was, for the most part, only applied to the exchange of goods, i.e., the gravitational force lines were only projected through trade. However, there had been occasional exceptions, when that power was also projected through China's supply of precious metals, i.e., through finance.

Our review of traditional Chinese conceptions of China's geography, history, and destiny can be useful in interpreting contemporary perspectives and objectives in the minds of Chinese leaders and, indeed, of some of the wider Chinese population. And our similar review of traditional Chinese conceptions of the strategy, operations, and tactics needed to achieve Chinese objectives can be particularly useful in explaining recent actions of the Chinese government and anticipating its future moves. We will put a special focus on actions and moves in two arenas: (1) The naval arena of China's three littoral seas—the Yellow Sea, the East China Sea, and the South China Sea—and (2) the financial arena of China's massive holdings of U.S. currency and debt, and the resulting status of being the world's leading creditor state. These are the very arenas which many scholars think have no real precedents in China's history. Rather, naval and financial arenas are supposed to be arenas of Western history, and now universal or global reality. However, the contemporary Chinese leadership looks upon these arenas through their own distinct Chinese prism.

The Three China Seas and Chinese Naval Power

China has not been a dominant naval presence in its three littoral seas—the Yellow Sea, the East China Sea, and the South China Sea—for 180 years, i.e., ever since the arrival of the British navy in force during the First Opium War. Instead, a succession of foreign navies has dominated these seas, first the British, then the Japanese, then, ever since Second World War, the American. Moreover, even before the arrival of foreign navies, China itself for centuries had not operated much of a navy there. It has been natural, therefore, for historians of Chinese strategy and its military to not only think that China is a land power, but that it is *only* a land power. And this view has been largely accurate—up until now.

However, there is an alternative interpretation of the place of these three littoral seas in the Chinese mind. The reason that China for centuries did not deploy a significant navy in them was that in those times there was no significant foreign navy which posed a threat there. A Chinese naval presence was therefore unnecessary. Then, when the British navy arrived, it immediately overwhelmed Chinese forces and established a dominant presence. This dominance by foreign navies continued in an unbroken chain down until contemporary times. A Chinese naval presence was therefore impossible.

However, the three littoral seas have never been excluded from the Chinese conception of the Central State and the world order. (For example, they are included within the great circle's delineation of China's proper realm.) The Chinese have always assumed that these three seas should be understood to be "Chinese lakes," as much dominated and secured by Chinese power as is Chinese land. Of course, Taiwan—the large island which connects two of these seas, the East China Sea and the South China Sea—must be Chinese because it is both Chinese land and central to the Chinese lakes.

And so it is natural for the contemporary Chinese leadership to think that the proper destiny of these three seas—the seas between the Chinese mainland and what the Chinese call the "First Island

Chain"—will only be fulfilled when they are dominated by Chinese military power. (The First Island Chain consists of Japan, the Ryukus, Taiwan, and the Philippines.) This will include not only naval power narrowly defined, but also land-based aircraft and missiles which can project power and denial capability over these seas. It is therefore only a matter of time—a time that could arrive with an auspicious moment and strategic opportunity—until China's destiny in these seas will be realized.

In the meantime, China will steadily and persistently seek to accumulate positions of strength in these seas, and some of these positions will add up to a kind of encirclement of sections within them. These positions will include islands—even very tiny ones—which are scattered around the seas. Such islands might appear trivial from a practical perspective (although some are in or adjacent to deep-sea oil fields, such as the Senkaku Islands in the East China Sea and the Spratly Islands in the South China Sea). However, from a strategic perspective, they are important symbols and can become markers or even bases for encirclement of the seas. This is particularly the case, given the vigorous Chinese use of the international law concept of the Exclusive Economic Zone (EEZ), which extends 200 miles out from recognized land territory.

This is one way to interpret the series of recent Chinese naval and diplomatic actions over such islands in each of the three seas. Beginning in the Spring of 2009 (and at the time when the global economic crisis had put the United States into substantial disarray), China created a succession of naval and diplomatic incidents, and these have continued down to the present time. These incidents have occurred over (1) U.S. naval maneuvers in support of South Korea in the Yellow Sea; (2) the Senkaku (Daioyu) Islands claimed by Japan in the East China Sea; and (3) the Paracel (Xisha) Islands claimed by Vietnam in the South China Sea, and (4) the Spratly (Nansha) Islands claimed by the Philippines, also in the South China Sea.

Each of these encounters has directly challenged some state which also claims jurisdiction over the island or surrounding section of the sea. By now, the list of these challenged states adds up to (from north to south) South Korea, Japan, Taiwan, Vietnam, and the Philippines, i.e., every state which borders on the vast maritime realm stretching from the southern part of the Yellow Sea through the East China Sea, to the northern part of the South China Sea. However, we can also see that each of these encounters has indirectly challenged the United States as a formal ally of most of these states (South Korea, Japan, the Philippines) or as a potential protector of the others (Taiwan and Vietnam). One of the Chinese purposes has been to test the U.S. resolve to protect the interests of the challenged states—particularly those interests which could be seen to be as trivial as the islands themselves—and perhaps to demonstrate to everyone—particularly to the challenged state—that, given the new strategic realities of the current period, the U.S. is not really a reliable ally and protector after all.

By now, after several years of such incidents, challenges, and testings, China has not definitively achieved its purposes. The islands and the waters around them remain disputed and contested, and, because of its generally firm statements and consistent support, the United States remains a plausible ally or protector. It seems that the current period has not been an especially auspicious moment for China. However, the traditional Chinese response to such developments (or lack of them) is to simply return to being patient while awaiting the arrival—eventual and inevitable—of the next auspicious moment.

In the meantime, China is building other kinds of positions of strength. This is with a massive build-up of advanced weapons systems which can project power over and deny access to the three littoral seas.[11] These include, most dramatically, procurement and deployment of a large fleet of surface vessels, including China's first aircraft carrier. However, although this surface fleet has a good deal of symbolic meaning, it does not have much substantive importance. China's surface fleet by itself will not pose a significant threat to the U.S. Navy for many years— if ever. Instead, the real, substantive threat to the U.S. Navy comes first from China's large number of advanced attack submarines and second, and even more ominous, from the thousands of surface-to-sea missiles which the Chinese are deploying. The most threatening of these is the rapid development by the Chinese of an anti-ship ballistic missile (ASBM). The U.S. surface fleet—including its magnificent and splendid aircraft carriers—now has no effective defense against an ASBM threat, and there is no such defense in the now-foreseeable future.

Holdings of U.S. Currency and Debt and
Chinese Financial Power

China now has the largest foreign exchange reserves, and particularly the largest holdings of U.S. currency and debt, in the world, making it the world's leading creditor state. Yet, historically, China did not see itself as a financial power, and it did not have a large and powerful financial sector within it. In this respect, it differed from a number of Western great powers, whose power included being a leading creditor state and major financial power. These have been, successively, the Netherlands, Britain, and the United States. On occasion France has also been a major financial power (as well as, briefly in the 1980s, Japan). An important question, therefore, is how one might expect China to convert its financial power into strategic power and thereby advance its regional and global ambitions, since it has had very little experience in doing so. And here, it is once again useful to look at traditional Chinese conceptions of strategy, operations, and tactics.

First, it is natural for the Chinese to extend their historical practices in the arena of trade to the arena of finance. China's financial strength can be used in addressing a strategic problem and often as a first resort, so long as this does not contradict other strategic objectives. For example, China's setting of the exchange rate between the yuan (RMB) and the dollar steers a course between the two objectives of (1) advancing Chinese industry through promoting exports and (2) avoiding social discontent by managing the inflation rate. In the fullest realization of this strategic conception, China's enormous financial reserves become a center of gravity, a solid and weighty mass which radiates outward gravitational lines of force which gently but firmly and steadily shape the will of debtor nations and potential adversaries so that they will more and more be inclined and conformed to, or at least accepting of, Chinese designs and priorities.

The most important of these potential adversaries and the most important of China's debtor nations is, of course, the United States. One would expect that China will not readily resort to the "financial nuclear option," i.e., quickly dumping large amounts of dollars on the global foreign-exchange markets; that would also inflict severe economic damage upon the Chinese. Rather, the most likely course is for China to use the less dramatic but still discernible option of not renewing its purchases of U.S. government debt. And these moments of non-renewal—a non-event which can have as much as an impact and influence as an event—could coincide with those moments when China is engaged in a dispute with the U.S. government on some issue in a completely different strategic arena, e.g., in one of the three China seas.

In the meantime, China will steadily and persistently seek to accumulate positions of strength in the financial arena, and some of these positions will add up to a kind of encirclement of the American financial position. In particular, one can expect the Chinese to draw the developing economies and neighboring states of Southeast Asia into a dense network of debt dependency. The debt network could even extend beyond, to other regions where historically the United States has been the major creditor state. Indeed, this is already beginning to happen in Africa and Latin America, and given the current great financial instability and vulnerability of countries in Southern Europe, it is even beginning to happen there.

China has now combined its great financial strengths with its parallel great strengths in the construction of large infrastructure projects into a grand strategy of financial and infrastructure diplomacy. Its main vehicles are the Chinese-led Asian Infrastructure Investment Bank, which has been operating since 2016, and the broader and bigger Belt and Road Initiative, which was announced in 2013 and has been operating since 2016. In turn, the Belt and Road Initiative is composed of two major parts, the Silk Road Economic Belt and the 21st Century Maritime Silk Road.

The Prospects for a Great War from the Perspective of Chinese History

Our earlier review of the history of Western international politics, and particularly of the two perennial themes of the dynamics of hegemonic transitions and the dynamics of alliance systems, had led us to the most disturbing of conclusions: There is a high probability that, sometime in the relevant future, there will be a great war between the rising power of China and the status-quo power of the United States and its alliance system in the Western Pacific. We have now reviewed a very different history, that of the Chinese regional order. Does this alternative history give us reason to hope that a great war between China and the United States can be avoided? Here, we will find that, while the components of the answer are complex, the sum of the answer is rather clear and direct.

It is obvious that China sees its three littoral seas—the three China Seas—to be a natural and intrinsic part of its territory, of its great-circle realm, and that it sees itself to be less than whole and complete until it has established full dominion and effective control over these seas, as well as over Taiwan, which lies between two of them. More broadly, this is the maritime realm that lies between the Chinese mainland and the "First Island Chain." The Chinese will be persistent and relentless in pressing for dominion over this realm. At the same time, however, they will also be patient and flexible in their ways and timing in achieving this great goal.

China's patience is enhanced by its economic strength and strategy. As we have noted, the Chinese have traditionally seen military action as a last resort, while using economic resources is a first resort. The Chinese have been practicing this approach toward many of the countries in the First Island Chain. As long as their economic strategy seems to be gradually drawing these countries into a network of economic dependency, they will usually see no need to resort to much more risky military action to achieve their objectives.

This combination of patience in tactics and persistence in objectives will issue in a distinctive method of moving forward. The Chinese may allow a particular disputed area to be calm for a period of time, even for a long time. However, they will always be looking for some emergent opportunity, an auspicious moment, when they can quickly or even forcefully move forward and accomplish some kind of fait accompli. This means that we can expect a pattern of periods of calm punctuated by abrupt and sharp crises. Indeed, there will be a series of succeeding crises, moving back and forth through the three China seas and up and down between the Chinese coast and that First Island Chain. It is as if China itself is like one of those great rivers of China—the Yellow River or the Yangtze—flowing into the seas of China—always persistent and continuing, always adjusting its flow around a local obstacle for now, while always pressing against this obstacle to wear it down, and to wash it away in the very long run.

Because of the patience and flexibility of the Chinese, it is quite likely that, as any particular crisis develops, it can be somehow managed by Chinese and American leaders, so that it does not escalate into an actual war. Indeed, the probability that any one crisis will erupt into a war may be quite low. However, because of the persistence and relentlessness of the Chinese, it is almost inevitable that this one crisis will be followed by another, and then by another and then by .... While the probability of any one crisis issuing in a war is quite low, the probability of a continuing series of crises eventually issuing in a war is quite high.

This dynamic is accentuated by other factors that are likely to be operating. In the aftermath of a particular crisis being successfully managed and temporarily resolved, it would be altogether reasonable for U.S. policymakers to draw the conclusion that they needed to strengthen the U.S. security commitment to one or more allies. By enhancing deterrence, the U.S. might deter a future crisis. But while deterrence might be increased, flexibility would be reduced, and this could have grave consequences when the next crisis develops.

Moreover, domestic politics, and in particular leadership politics, will always be operating. China and the United States each will have their own distinct variations on this theme. With respect to China, political scientists often assert that contemporary Chinese leaders are especially reliant upon Chinese nationalism as a central source of their legitimacy with the general population. At the same time as the Chinese military, especially the Chinese navy, gains in military strength vis-à-vis the United States, it also gains in political strength vis-à-vis civilian figures within the Chinese leadership. Both of these factors will make it more difficult for Chinese leaders to give concessions, or perhaps to even be flexible, in the midst of a foreign crisis which involves nationalist values and military forces. This will especially be the case if the foreign crisis should occur at the same time that the leadership is facing an ongoing domestic crisis or serious challenges to its authority.[12]

In the United States, domestic politics operates in a different way, but it points in the same ominous direction. For the most part, the

U.S. political leadership no longer uses nationalism as a source of its legitimacy. Rather, it is now more likely to draw upon some kind of globalist or universalist ideology (e.g., democratization, globalization, or universal human rights). This does not appeal much to the general American population, but it does appeal to the major donors to each of the two political parties, the Democrats and the Republicans. But just like nationalism increases the Chinese leadership's drive to obtain dominion over the three China Seas, so too does the globalist and universalist ideology increase the U.S. leadership's determination to retain the U.S. alliance system in the same region. Thus, it is the political representatives of the largest American economic sectors, with their global economic interests, which are now the major and potential proponents of U.S. military action. Consequently, in both China and the United States, the effect of domestic politics is to reduce the chances for compromise over the three China Seas and to increase the probability of war.

Conclusion: The Immovable Object versus the Irresistible Force

In summary, when we look at the ongoing and unfolding Sino-American confrontations in East Asia through the prism of Western history, we see that the probability of a great war between China and America in the relevant future is quite high. However, when we look at these confrontations through the prism of Eastern history, we see that, while the probability of war remains high enough to be a cause for concern and attention, there can be some hope that a war can be averted. This is principally because of the Chinese qualities of patience and flexibility. But there is an obvious asymmetry between the two prisms and the two powers. The Western prism should provide the best predictions of the behavior of a Western nation, i.e., the United States, and this predicts U.S. reactiveness and inflexibility, qualities which tend toward war. The Eastern perspective should provide the best prediction of the behavior of an Eastern nation, i.e., China, and this predicts Chinese patience and flexibility, qualities which tend away from war.

Simply put, from a Western perspective, the United States has the character of an immovable object, while China is assuming the character of an irresistible force. If these two realities collide, the result will be an explosion. However, an Eastern perspective permits a subtler description and a different vista. The immovable object, the U.S. alliance system in the Western Pacific, is like a great dyke which was erected many years ago to hold back a flood. The irresistible force, the Chinese drive to achieve dominion over the three China seas, is like a great river which has flowed for many centuries, at times flooding and at times ebbing. The dyke has held back a flood from the river for a long time. But in the truly long run, in the fullness of time, the river will steadily erode, and then finally wash away, the dyke.

PART III

INSURGENCY

CHAPTER ELEVEN

GLOBALIZATION, EMPIRE, AND ISLAMIST TERRORISM

THE DECADE OF THE 1990s was clearly the era of globalization. The period between the fall of the Berlin Wall on November 9, 1989 (11/9) and the fall of the Twin Towers on September 9, 2001 (9/11) comprised a "long decade" in which globalization, as promoted by the United States, seemed to be rational, desirable, and inevitable. There appeared to be so many winners from globalization—e.g., the United States, Europe, East Asia, and even India—that all the losers together—e.g., Russia, the Muslim world, Africa, and perhaps Latin America—seemed to be, in the grand or global scheme of things, merely weak or marginalized.

This of course was not the first era when the spread of capitalism around the world had seemed to be rational, desirable, and inevitable. Much the same mentality characterized the period 1896-1914, the two decades or "Belle Epoque" before the First World War. This earlier era of globalization was also promoted by the leading world power of the day, the British Empire.[1] But underlying and backing up the supposed economic rationality of Belle-Epoque globalization was the military force of the British Army and the Royal Navy. When the losers (or dissatisfied winners) of globalization welled up in resentment and rose up in resistance, it was the military forces of the British Empire (and of junior and friendly empires such as the French, the Dutch, and the Belgian) that put them down. Whatever the conceits of that time that economic rationality by itself would spread global capitalism, any serious historian in our own time knows that some kind of empire was a necessary condition for the globalization of a century ago.

Contemporary Globalization and the American Empire

It should not be surprising, then, that near the end of the first decade of contemporary globalization, analysts of world affairs began to think about the need for an American empire. Resentment and resistance to globalization, particularly to its American version, developed in the late 1990s in Russia, the Muslim world, and, after the Asian financial crisis of 1997-1998, even in East and Southeast Asia. And there were also those "rogue states" which had always rejected American foreign policies root and branch—particularly North Korea, Iran, and Iraq. The spread of resistance to globalization naturally concentrated the minds of U.S. policymakers upon the potential need to employ U.S. military force at a variety of points around the globe.

The Kosovo War of 1999 can be interpreted as the first war of the global era. The Clinton administration went to war against one of the lesser (and least threatening to Americans) rogue states—the Serbia of Slobodan Milosevic. Its objectives were not only to end the human rights abuses in Kosovo but to expand NATO's responsibilities "out-of-area" in the direction of the Middle East and to establish a precedent for quick and effective military operations there.[2] The methods used (extended use of precision bombing, no use of U.S. ground forces, and not a single U.S. combat fatality) were seen as a demonstration of what the United States could do to other rogue states and more serious adversaries if it chose to do so, particularly Iraq, Syria, and Iran. The U.S. victory in the Kosovo War consequently made it much more likely that the United States would soon seek a similar victory over the most troublesome of these rogue states, the Iraq of Saddam Hussein.

Most of the persons that the George W. Bush administration would appoint to high positions in the Defense Department had already by

2000 set their sights upon the regime of Saddam Hussein ("regime change") and were determined to go to war with Iraq at the first convenient opportunity. (Of course, they said virtually nothing about their project during the 2000 presidential election campaign itself.) Indeed, given the growing focus upon the Saddam Hussein regime even within the Democratic Party by 2000, it seems wholly plausible that an Al Gore administration might have also sought to go to war against Iraq at a convenient opportunity. However, given the practice of the Clinton administration, it probably would only have done so after it had received the approval of either the United Nations or NATO.

In any event, three developments of the 1990s—the pervasive spread of globalization, the growing resistance to it, and the growing awareness of the potential need to use military force—logically culminated and combined by early 2001 into the idea that the time had come for some new kind of American ordering of the globe. Writers on world affairs began to apply a new term (actually an extremely old term) to America's role in the world: empire. A stream of books and articles announced the coming of the American empire.[3]

The Coming of the American Empire

This American empire was the logical culmination of America's supreme position on four dimensions of world affairs. In addition to being (1) the largest and most advanced economy within the global economy and the driving force promoting globalization, the United States was also (2) the sole superpower and even a hyperpower; (3) the only high-tech military power and the leader in the "revolution in military affairs;" and (4) the exemplar of "soft power" and the disseminator of popular culture throughout the globe.

America's rise to its supreme position on each of these four dimensions was already underway in the 1980s, but at that time its ascendancy was obscured by the formidable military challenge from the Soviet Union and by the formidable economic challenge from Japan. The collapse of the Soviet Union in 1991 and the stagnation of the Japanese economy since 1991, combined with the military and economic ascent of the United States in the 1990s, made the supreme position of the United

States clear to all, and this supreme position became the most central and important reality of international politics. Indeed, it contributed greatly to a reinvention of international politics into global politics.

With the coming of the 2000s—and the coming of a new century and a new millennium—it seemed that we were witnessing the coming of a new empire as well. Of course, this empire was not the first global empire; the Spanish empire of the 16th-18th centuries and the British empire of the 19th-20th centuries also had been empires with a global scope. However, the Spanish and British empires had always had to contend with challenges from other extensive empires or great powers. In contrast, the United States was now not only the sole superpower or hyperpower, it was the sole empire. For something approximating a sole empire, one had to go back to the Roman empire, but that empire was not on a global scale.

In short, the United States was something that had never before existed in history: a sole empire which was global in scope, and indeed which sought to reinvent the nations of the globe in its image. For, in the minds of the American political and economic elites, the American ideas are universal ideas. They are, in the words of the Declaration of Independence, the "self-evident truths" of the rights to "life, liberty, and the pursuit of happiness," or in a 2002 reformulation by Michael Mandelbaum, they are "peace, democracy, and free markets," which are "the ideas which conquered the world."[4]

The American Empire as the Cause of Islamist Terrorism

At the very time of its proclamation, however, the American empire was suddenly shocked by an unprecedented threat to the very heart of America itself, manifested in the terrorist attacks on the World Trade Center and the Pentagon on September 11, 2001, and the fear of new terrorist attacks upon the United States. The simultaneous occurrence of the coming of the global American empire and the coming of the global Islamist terrorist threat was not just an awful, indeed terrible, coincidence or irony, however. It appeared that there was a dialectical or symbiotic causal connection between the imperial and the terrorist trajectories. But in which direction did the causal connection go?

Immediately after the attacks of September 11, a great question went up: "Why do they hate us?" One of the answers, principally given by the anti-globalization movement, was that they (particularly Muslims) hate us (particularly Americans) because of the overwhelming American power which is intruding into their societies, i.e., because of the oppressive expansion of globalization and of the American empire which imposes it. Although oversimplified, this is one useful notion of the causal connection between the American empire and Islamic terrorism.

The advocates of globalization often describe it as a process: steadily progressing over time, pervasively spreading over space, and clearly inevitable in its development. In this conception, the economics of globalization are all-important; the politics of globalization are practically non-existent. But globalization can also be seen as a revolution, one of the most profound revolutions the world has ever known. (It is certainly more of a world revolution than communism ever was.)

Like all revolutions, the globalization revolution has produced both winners and losers. The winners from globalization are the business, professional, and even working classes which are competitive in the global market. These winners are largely found in the United States, Europe, and Northeast Asia, where they comprise the dominant groups within the population. By 2001, these beneficiaries of globalization were led by the United States and were organized into the American empire. Similar classes which benefit from globalization are found in China and India, where they comprise a rapidly growing part of the population. In other regions of the globe, however—Russia, the Muslim world, Latin America, and Africa—the winners in the globalization revolution probably comprise only a small elite, one which is deeply resented by the rest of the population.

Revolutions normally produce reactions, however. At first, the losers from the revolution have no theory or ideology with which to comprehend and critique the revolution, and relatedly they have no leaders or organizations with which to combat it. They are capable only of resentment. But if an ideology, leaders, and organizations should emerge, the losers can move to resistance. And if these elements should come together into a comprehensive movement, the losers become capable of a full-scale reaction to the revolution.

During the 1990s, there was no longer any obvious ideology available to the losers from globalization since the once-robust contender, Marxism, was now largely discredited and abandoned. There were also no obvious leaders of the losers. The national states which had resisted global capitalism in the past were now either too weak to do so (e.g., Russia and the rogue states) or were now winners themselves (China and India). And, given the absence of ideology and leadership, there was also no organization of the losers.

The Muslim world was the region which had one of the highest proportions of losers within its population, but it also was the region which was symbiotically interconnected with the winners in the greatest number of important ways (e.g., the global oil market, U.S. military bases in the region, U.S. support of Israel against the Palestinians, Muslim immigrants in Europe). It was natural, therefore, that it was the Muslim world which developed the most pronounced grievances against globalization and against the United States. Consequently, it was the Muslim world which provided an anti-globalization ideology—Islamism—which could fill the void left by the discrediting of the prior anti-globalization ideology, Marxism.[5] Islamism is not the same as Islam; it is more ideological and less theological. Like the secular ideologies developed within the modern West, Islamism is explicitly methodical and political, not customary and spiritual. But Islamism is also not the same as Marxism; it is more communal and less universal. Like Islam, it can appeal only to Muslims around the globe, not to the workers of the world. In any event, for the Muslim losers from globalization—and for the dissatisfied Muslim winners who claim to represent these losers—Islamism is the ideology that fits, the system of ideas whose time has come, the hope for the wretched of the earth of our own time. As they say, and say with conviction, "Islam is the answer."

Thus, by 2001, the ideological element for resistance to globalization and the United States by the Muslim world was widespread and well-developed. It could be observed by anyone who had eyes to see. The leadership and organization for the resistance were less evident, however; instead of these elements, there still appeared to be only a void. Of course, with the terrorist attacks of 9/11, this void suddenly seemed to be filled by Osama bin Laden and Al Qaeda, and more generally by transnational networks of Islamist terrorists with global reach.

Islamist Terrorism as the Cause of the American Empire

The Bush administration therefore formulated a different notion—indeed a reverse notion—of the causal connection between the coming of the American empire and the coming of Islamist terrorism. One year after the attacks, on September 17, 2002, the administration presented its new "National Security Strategy of the United States of America."[6] This important document declared that the United States and the world confronted a new and unprecedented reality: the simultaneous existence of both terrorist networks with global reach and rogue states with weapons of mass destruction (WMD). This meant that very soon these terrorists might acquire these weapons from these states and then use them against the United States and its allies, with destruction that would be truly massive and terrible. Obviously such a disaster had to be prevented; also obviously, according to this document, this unprecedented threat had to be met with unprecedented methods.

The strategy of unilateral pre-emption. The unprecedented method announced by the Bush administration for the new global era—the era of both global American power and global Islamist terrorism—was pre-emptive military attacks (or, more accurately, preventive war) by the United States upon any emerging threat that terrorist groups might receive weapons of mass destruction from rogue states. If possible, a U.S. pre-emptive attack would be undertaken in a multilateral way, in the sense that other nations (e.g., the United Nations or the NATO allies) would approve it; if necessary, however, the U.S. action would be unilateral, i.e., the United States would go it alone.[7] The new U.S. strategy of pre-emption and unilateralism was supposed to govern the global era; it would replace the old U.S. strategy of containment and deterrence which governed the Cold War era, but which seemed to be incapable of dealing with terrorist groups. The "Bush Doctrine" of 2002 would be comparable in importance, therefore, to the Truman Doctrine of 1947, which formulated the policy of containment, and to the national security document of 1950, NSC-68, which formulated the strategy of nuclear deterrence.

Iraq as the central rogue state in the new American strategy. At the time of the announcement of the new National Security Strategy, the rogue states that seemed to be developing WMD were Iraq, Iran, and North Korea. But it was also plausible that Islamist terrorist groups might receive WMD, including nuclear weapons, from rogue elements within the military of America's putative ally, Pakistan. The new strategy of unilateral pre-emption might reasonably have been applied to any one of these rogue threats.

However, the Bush administration focused upon the threat from Iraq.[8] This suggested, even in 2002, that the true origin of the new strategy of unilateral pre-emption was not 9/11, nor the threat that rogue states might provide WMD to terrorist groups. Of course, when the U.S. military invaded and occupied that country in 2003, it was discovered that Iraq did not have WMD. Conversely, during 2003-2004 it became clear that North Korea and Iran were far along in developing nuclear weapons and that Pakistan's rogue elements had already sold nuclear technology through the global underground economy. Some other explanation is needed to fully understand the focus upon Iraq.

Iraq as the model dominion in the new American empire. The Bush administration wanted to do more to rogue states than to just disarm their weapons of mass destruction with a pre-emptive military attack. It also intended to implement "regime change," i.e., to overthrow an existing government and to replace it with one that would become an American ally. It also intended to dismantle the existing political and economic system and to replace it with one that would be characterized by liberal democracy, free markets, and an open society. In short, the Bush administration envisioned that a pre-emptive military attack would initiate a process that would culminate in a new extension of "the ideas that conquered the world." It would also be a new extension of the American empire. The state targeted to become the first new dominion of the empire was Iraq.

In the minds of the anti-globalization movement, and in the rhetoric and perhaps the minds of Islamist terrorists themselves, the growth of the American empire had been the cause for the growth of Islamist terrorism. But in the minds of the American political and economic elites, and in the rhetoric and perhaps the minds of officials of the Bush administration, the growth of Islamist terrorism had become the cause for the growth of the American empire. As it happened, both causal theories were in some sense correct. There was a dialectical and symbiotic connection, even an escalating and vicious cycle, between the two global forces, and the world seemed to be witnessing a titanic and explosive struggle between them.

Four Perspectives on American Foreign Policy

The coming of the American empire was not just an inevitable and automatic consequence of America's supremacy on the four dimensions of economic globalization, relative power, military strength, and cultural diffusion. As with much of American foreign policy, the global imperial project was the outcome of a domestic political struggle. In particular, it was a product of changes in the relative power of four different groups within the United States, each with its own distinct perspective on America's role in the world and particularly in the establishment of an American empire on a global scale. We can identify these groups as (1) traditional liberals; (2) traditional conservatives; (3) neo-liberals; and (4) neo-conservatives.

These four contemporary groups have some similarities and continuities with what Walter Russell Mead has called the four historical traditions of American foreign policy.[9] Mead names each tradition after a particular American historical figure, resulting in (1) the Jeffersonian; (2) the Jacksonian; (3) the Wilsonian; and (4) the Hamiltonian traditions. But the contemporary groups differ from the historical traditions in some important ways, particularly because of the new conditions and perspectives created by globalization.

The national perspectives: traditional liberals and traditional conservatives. For much of the 20th century, American politics was dominated by the agenda of the traditional liberals. The central concern of this group has been the American domestic economy, enhanced by domestic social reform. Consequently, the central purpose of American foreign policy should be to protect and promote this domestic economy; it is certainly not to engage in foreign interventions and undertakings which would disrupt economic prosperity and social progress (and which clearly was a consequence of the Vietnam War). Among the more recent presidencies, the traditional liberal perspective was best represented by the Carter administration. And among the four historical approaches identified by Mead, the traditional liberal perspective has been virtually the same as the Jeffersonian tradition.

The central concern of traditional conservatives has been American national security, enhanced by national unity. Consequently, the central purpose of American foreign policy should be to protect and promote this security; it is certainly not to engage in foreign interventions and undertakings which are remote from American vital interests and which would drain America's strength or multiply its foreign enemies (which, for some traditional conservatives, was a consequence of the Vietnam War). Among the more recent presidencies, the traditional conservative perspective was probably best represented by the administration of George H.W. Bush, although his idea of a "New World Order" was remote from traditional conservative concerns. And among the four historical approaches of Mead, the traditional conservative perspective has been similar to the Jacksonian tradition in regard to its objectives, i.e., the security of the American people, although perhaps it has been more like the Hamiltonian tradition in regard to its means, i.e., a regard for the discerning and prudent ("realistic") use of force.

Whatever their differences on a variety of liberal-conservative dimensions, the two traditional groups share a national perspective, i.e., they view the United States as a national state within a world of national states which engage in the conduct of international relations. American foreign policy toward these other national states should be governed by the principle of the national interest, i.e., the protection and promotion of the interests of Americans.

The global perspectives: neo-liberals and neo-conservatives. Conversely, the two "neo" groups share a global perspective, i.e., they view the United States as a unique power within a global arena. This arena is filled with many different kinds of powers, but all of them have much less power and influence than the United States.

The central concern of the neo-liberals has been the American role in the global economy and in global society. They want the United States, with its great and unique power and influence, to be the leader in the grand project of globalization, which is progressively eliminating borders and opening nations. The great goal is to establish a global order characterized by liberal democracies, free markets, open societies, and the "democratic peace." Among the more recent presidencies, the neo-liberal perspective was represented by the Clinton administration and the Obama administration, and among Mead's four historical approaches, it has been very similar to the Wilsonian tradition.

The central concern of the neo-conservatives has been the American role in global security. They want the United States with its great and unique power and influence, to be the leader in a grand project to eliminate military or terrorist threats to the security of America and its allies. These allies include one which finds itself in one of the least secure environments on the globe, i.e., Israel. This grand project entails the progressive reduction or elimination of such threats as rogue states and terrorist organizations, above all those with potential access to weapons of mass destruction. Among the more recent presidencies, the neo-conservative perspective was present to a degree in the first Reagan administration, particularly in regard to its tough military policy directed at the Soviet Union and in regard to the "Reagan Doctrine," which promoted anti-communist guerrilla movements against Marxist regimes. However, it was under George W. Bush that the neo-conservative perspective reached its greatest strength. This was particularly so in regard to the administration's foreign policy toward the Middle East, including its support of Israel and its war against Iraq, and in regard to the "Bush Doctrine." As we have seen, this new doctrine advocated pre-emptive military action by the United States against states which pose a threat because of their weapons of mass destruction; if necessary, such action can be taken unilaterally. Among Mead's four historical approaches, the neo-conservative perspective has been similar to the Hamiltonian tradition in regard to objectives, i.e., defining American security interests in expansive, even global terms, but similar to the Jacksonian tradition in regard to means, i.e., the intensive and decisive use of force.

From national perspectives to global perspectives. When the largest American business enterprises looked mostly to the American or national market, there was a strong economic and political base for the traditional (i.e., national) conservative perspective. Similarly, when the largest American organizations that promoted social reform were industrial labor unions, there was a strong economic and political base for the traditional (i.e., national) liberal perspective. These two solid bases for national perspectives existed in America for much of the twentieth century.

Beginning in the 1960s, however, there came the great leap outward of American business, the transformation of national corporations first into multinational ones and then into global ones. Also beginning in the 1960s, there came the great advance upward of American business, the transformation of an industrial economy first into a post-industrial one and then into an information one. Both of these great transformations, from a national to a global economy and from an industrial to an information economy, greatly enlarged the scope of the perspective of business enterprises. They also greatly undermined the industrial labor unions and brought about a sharp decline in their membership and political strength. By the late 1980s, the economic and political bases for traditional or national perspectives had largely collapsed. Then, when the Soviet Union—that giant monument to statist and protectionist industry—also collapsed and the Cold War came to an end, the American multinational corporations and post-industrial enterprises had not just the Free World, but whole world—the great globe itself— as their arena of operations. This quickly gave rise to the rhetoric of the "New World Order" and to the reality of the grand project of globalization. The now-global corporations and information enterprises quickly became the strong and solid economic and political base for the neo-liberal perspective. They were joined by a myriad of new non-governmental organizations (NGOs) and internet groups which promoted universal human rights and which operated on a global scale. These all came together to form a grand coalition in the Clinton administration and largely shaped its foreign policies.[10]

Finally, in the George W. Bush administration, the neo-conservatives and a good part of the neo-liberals came together to form an even grander coalition. The neo-conservative perspective was well-repre-sented by top civilian officials in the Defense Department, e.g., Deputy Secretary of Defense Paul Wolfowitz, Under Secretary of Defense for Policy Douglas Feith, and at least a dozen of their immediate subordi-nates.[11] (In contrast, however, the top military officers largely continued to hold a traditional-conservative perspective). In regard to the Mid-dle East, the neo-conservatives had a special interest in the security of Israel. Since Israel saw Iraq, Syria, and Iran to be the major threats to its security, the neo-conservatives did also, and this led them to advo-cate "regime change" for these "rogue states." Moreover, because of its peculiar and vulnerable military position in the Middle East geography, Israel since 1948 had almost always adhered to a strategy of pre-emp-tion. This led the neo-conservatives to favor pre-emption too, not only as a strategy for Israel, but for any realistic state, particularly the United States. Finally, because of its peculiar and isolated diplomatic position in international organizations and in international law, Israel since 1967 had almost always adhered to a policy of unilateralism. This led the neo-conservatives to favor unilateralism too, not only as a policy for Israel, but for any realistic state, particularly the United States.

The neo-conservatives were thus enthusiastic supporters of the Bush strategy of unilateral pre-emption. Indeed, Paul Wolfowitz was a prominent architect of it. From the Israel-centric perspective of the neo-conservatives, what was good for Israel was good for the United States, and what was true for Israel was true for the United States. Indeed, in its relationship to the rest of the world, the United States appeared to be more or less just a big Israel.

Conversely, the neo-liberal perspective was well-represented in the Bush administration by the Treasury Department and the State Depart-ment (but not by Secretary of State—and former army general—Colin Powell, who largely tried to hold onto a traditional-conservative per-spective). In regard to the Middle East, the neo-liberals had a special interest in increasing U.S. influence over the global oil market, as well as promoting liberal-democratic reforms in the region. As the most com-mitted and consistent promoters of American-style globalization, they knew full well the central importance of both controlling the lifeblood of the global economy and creating more regimes open to globalization.

Both the neo-conservatives and the neo-liberals saw the overthrow of Saddam Hussein's rogue regime—which ruled an Iraq that might achieve weapons of mass destruction and was also rich in oil reserves—to be a fulfillment of its own central interests in the Middle East. Historically, pro-Israeli groups and the oil industry have often opposed each other in regard to U.S. policies toward that region. The fact that these two groups came together in the Bush administration around a policy of regime change in Iraq gave a new and extraordinary energy—a sort of fusion power—to that project. The drive toward war with Iraq and toward the new and expanded empire that was expected to follow in its wake was thus already underway before September 11, 2001. The terrorist attacks on that date, although they had no known connection with Saddam Hussein and his regime, provided the Bush administration with still more explosive energy which it used to drive the United States down its predetermined path toward war and empire.

Four Acts in the Imperial Drama

In the course of its history, the United States has experienced a number of military disasters which were seen at the time as being due to a surprise or provocative attack. These attacks sparked American wars which turned out to have tremendous consequences, particularly for the expansion of American power and the extension of an American empire.

The attack on Fort Sumter by Confederate forces on April 12, 1861, ignited the American Civil War. At the beginning, the objective of the United States was merely to reabsorb the Southern states into the Union. As the war developed, however, its actual consequences for the United States went beyond this, to the establishment of a strong and unified national state that stretched to the shores of the Pacific. This became an American empire which promoted liberal democracy and free markets on a continental scale. Indeed, this energized expansionist impulse then went beyond the North American continent and looked toward the Caribbean, particularly toward Cuba. As it happened, this country would become the locale of the next incident and the next ensuing war.

The blowing up of the battleship U.S.S. Maine in Havana harbor on February 15, 1898 was not really an attack (it now appears to have resulted from an internal explosion), but at the time Americans saw it as a surprise attack by Spanish forces, and it ignited the Spanish-American War. At the beginning, the objective of the United States was merely to liberate Cuba and Puerto Rico from Spanish rule. Again, however, the actual consequences of the war went beyond this, to the establishment of an American sphere of influence over the Caribbean basin and Central America. This became an effort to extend the American empire of liberal democracy and free markets to a hemispheric scale. In its relations with countries in the Caribbean and in Central America, the United States after 1898 engaged in unilateral pre-emption on many occasions, with the objective of regime change and with the use of military force. In many other aspects as well, the American sphere of influence in Latin America served as a sort of prototype for the American empire in other parts of the world. Indeed, this energized expansionist impulse of 1898 immediately went beyond the Western hemisphere and crossed the Pacific Ocean with the annexation of Hawaii and even the Philippines. As it happened, these territories would become, four decades later, the locale of a true surprise attack and an ensuing great war.

The attack on Pearl Harbor by Japanese forces on December 7, 1941, propelled America into the Second World War. At the beginning, the objective of the United States was merely to defeat Japan and, after Hitler declared war on the United States a few days later on December 11, to defeat Germany. However, the actual consequences of the war went beyond this, to the establishment of American spheres of influence over Western Europe and over Northeast Asia. This became an American empire of liberal democracy and free markets on a truly half-world or "Free-World" scale. Indeed, this energized expansionist impulse then went beyond the two end regions of the Eurasian land-mass and extended into the crucial region that lay between them. This was the Middle East, whose oil was essential for the well-being of the American allies in Western Europe and Northeast Asia. As it happened, however, the American presence in the Middle East would become, five decades later, the cause of another surprise attack and at least two ensuing wars, i.e., the war against Afghanistan and the war against Iraq.

The attacks on the World Trade Center and the Pentagon by Islamic terrorists on September 11, 2001, propelled America into its first war of the 21st century. At first this seemed to be a new kind of war, a war upon transnational terrorist networks with global reach rather than one upon national states. But the declaration of war upon terrorist networks also included as the enemy the states which harbored them, such as the Taliban regime in Afghanistan, and so the first phase of the new war against terrorist networks was the not-so-new war against Afghanistan. In January 2002, however, the Bush administration expanded the definition of prospective enemies to include "the axis of evil," i.e., rogue states which were on the path of acquiring weapons of mass destruction, in particular Iraq, Iran, and North Korea. Thus, the second phase of the new war became the not-so-new war against Iraq.

One of the justifications that the administration gave for the war against Iraq was that it would result in the spread of liberal democracy and free markets, not only to that country but also to its neighbors, particularly Iran and Syria, and perhaps to other countries in the Middle East as well. The vision was of another great leap forward in the American empire of liberal democracy and free markets, this time to much of the whole world, to virtually the entire globe.

The Effect of the Iraq War on the American Empire

Alas, within less than a year after the U.S. invasion, the unfolding failure in Iraq had already had a major impact upon the great expectations about the American empire. On the eve of the Iraq War and during its first months, there was a good deal of earnest discussion about the future development of the empire. But the steady growth of the Iraqi insurgency brought about a rapid decline in these expectations. Books about the American empire, which had been begun in 2001-2003, were brought to completion and published in 2004, but by that time, the agonies of the U.S. war in Iraq had already made proclamations of empire incongruous and obsolete. As it turned out, the golden age of speculations about the American empire was very brief.

Of course, there continued to be U.S. wars in the Middle East and in the broader Muslim world—the notorious "forever wars"—but there was not really much of an empire there. And proposals for new real wars were constrained by the effects of the Iraq War upon the U.S. Army and the U.S. Marines. The post-Vietnam military was a volunteer military, and underlying and ensuring a steady and sufficient stream of volunteers was the classical American way of war. At some level, the recruits to the U.S. military assumed that they would be defending the vital national interests of the United States, or at least that they would be sent into war according to some sort of reasonable principles (like those articulated by the Weinberger-Powell Doctrine). The Iraq War violated these assumptions, and the consequence was a decline in Army and Marine recruitment and retention, a decline that made it exceedingly difficult to launch a new war in some other country. This military reality was evident for all to see, including the enemies of the United States, and this greatly diminished the U.S. ability to deter its enemies with the threat to invade and occupy their country with U.S. ground forces. But since all empires must be able to credibly threaten invasions and occupations, this greatly diminished the U.S. ability to extend its empire, particularly into the Middle East or the broader Muslim world.

The American imperial project was greatly energized by 9/11 and the specter of Islamist terrorism. The course of the Iraq War aborted this new expansion of the American empire, but the threat from transnational networks of Islamist terrorists remained; indeed, that threat was probably greater after the war than it was before, and it remained directed both at globalization and at the United States which promotes it.

The actions of the U.S. military in Iraq angered many people throughout the Muslim world, and the failures of the U.S. counterinsurgency in Iraq emboldened many Islamist militants. The insurgency against U.S. forces in Iraq became a model for Islamist insurgents against U.S. forces elsewhere, and the Iraqi insurgency was copied in its tactics by the Taliban insurgents in Afghanistan. Moreover, the Iraqi insurgency became a recruiting station for Islamist terrorists who sought to directly attack the homelands of the United States and other Western nations.

Globalization was a world revolution, one whose chief promoter and defender was the United States. Although in the 1990s, the spread of this world revolution to the very limits of the globe seemed inevitable, a world reaction to it was already beginning to develop, or at least a reaction within the Muslim world. Islamism also represented a kind of globalization, and so did Islamist terrorists with global reach. The terrorist attacks of 9/11 were a quantum leap in the reach of Islamist terrorists, and the Iraqi insurgency provided a compelling model for military actions by Islamist movements. Together, they demonstrated the power of the new, Islamist version of globalization against the old, American one. Like the 1990s, the 2000s-2010s have been defined by globalization. But this time the decades have been defined by a grueling and bloody struggle between two warring globalizations, that of America and that of Islamism.

CHAPTER TWELVE

THE IRAQ WAR:

GLOBAL IDEOLOGY VERSUS LOCAL REALITIES

THE IRAQ WAR WAS the most consequential event for American foreign policy during the decade of the 2000s. As we have seen in Chapter 11, its origins lay in the hubris of the American globalization project of the 1990s, particularly as it expanded into the American imperial illusions of the early 2000s. The actual course of the war certainly did much to dampen the optimism of globalization, and it certainly went far in extinguishing the fantasy of empire.

But the consequences of the Iraq War reached even further than this. The war raised anew—really for the first time since the 1970s and the aftermath of the debacle of the Vietnam War—widespread discussion of the way the U.S. military fights its wars, i.e., the recurring question of "the American way of war." And the war also raised anew—really for the first time since the 1960s and the *détente* era when the United States accommodated itself to many communist regimes—widespread discussion of the way the U.S. government promotes democracy abroad, i.e., the recurring question of "idealism versus realism" in American foreign policy. Moreover, these new discussions are occurring within a new context, one in which, because of its dismal performance in the Iraq

War, the position of the United States in the world is much diminished from what it was before the war began.

The U.S. Military in Iraq: The Rumsfeld Transformation Project

On its way toward the war against Iraq which would lay the groundwork for the new American empire in the Middle East, the Bush administration confronted a major obstacle, and that was the very same U.S. military that was supposed to win the war and secure the empire. As Secretary of Defense Donald Rumsfeld well knew, the new American empire did not fit well with the traditional American military. As we discussed in Chapter 7, what military strategists and historians have called "the American way of war" was deeply imbued with a <u>national</u> perspective, i.e., the U.S. military, especially the U.S. Army, defended the vital national interests of the United States, and it did so by fighting the regular militaries of other national states. This conception was embodied in the Weinberger-Powell Doctrine. For the United States to use its military for the new <u>global</u> and <u>imperial</u> purposes, a new—and very different—American way of war would have to be invented and the Weinberger-Powell Doctrine overturned, and this was the conception that underlaid Rumsfeld's "project of military transformation."

The U.S. Army, under its Chief of Staff, General Eric Shinseki, was already engaged in its own transformation project, one which it had designed to take into account both the promise of new technologies but also the realities of Army organization and doctrine. The Army did not welcome Rumsfeld's version of transformation, with its focus upon high-tech solutions to virtually every military problem, including those tasks which traditionally only ground forces, "boots-on-the-ground," could do, and it put up some resistance. Moreover, Rumsfeld's notion of a small and light Army violated the Weinberger-Powell Doctrine's insistence on overwhelming force. However, Rumsfeld was characteristically arrogant and ruthless in imposing his will, and on the eve of the Iraq War the Army and the other military services had already been greatly shaped by the Rumsfeld "transformation."

When it invaded Iraq in March 2003, this new U.S. military was spectacularly successful against the military of Saddam Hussein.

(Of course, the old, American-way-of-war military had been similarly successful against Saddam Hussein's military back in 1991.) The "shock-and-awe" tactics of the U.S. Air Force and the fluid and flexible tactics of the unusually light and highly mobile U.S. Army and Marines quickly won the conventional war, so that President Bush on May 1, 2003 famously (and as it turned out, fatuously) declared "mission accomplished" and the end of "major combat operations." But it soon became clear that the real war, the counterinsurgency war, had just begun.

The U.S. Army had actually anticipated that its real challenge in Iraq would come *after* its defeat of Saddam Hussein's conventional forces. The Army had conducted a series of studies of previous U.S. military occupations, and these had produced some sophisticated conclusions.[1] But one simple ground rule for occupations was that, in order to establish security and deter insurgency, it was necessary to have a ratio of about 20 soldiers for every 1000 civilians within the occupied population. This was an application of the Weinberger-Powell Doctrine tenet of overwhelming force to the specific problem of a post-war military occupation. These soldiers could include collaborating units drawn from the occupied country, but of course the core forces had to be provided by the U.S. military. Given that Iraq had a population of about 25 million, the number of occupation troops would have to be about 500,000. This is why the Army Chief of Staff, General Shinseki, had stated on the eve of the war that the forces required for establishing the peace would have to consist of "several hundred thousand" soldiers for several years. For this he was publicly rebuked and ridiculed by both Rumsfeld and Deputy Defense Secretary Paul Wolfowitz as being "wildly off the mark."[2] The conclusions of the Army studies and the statement of Shinseki did not conform to Rumsfeld's notion of a light and lean U.S. Army.

The United States invaded Iraq with about 140,000 troops (not all of them combat personnel), and allied units—especially British forces—added another 40,000. These numbers were enough to defeat Iraq's conventional forces, but they were obviously not enough to establish security and deter insurgency. For that, other military forces—either allied or Iraqi—were needed. It was here, however, that the principles and practice of the Bush administration, particularly its emphasis on unilateralism, issued in fatal consequences. Because of its doctrinal fixation on unilateralism, the administration had insulted (e.g., Rumsfeld's remark about "Old Europe") and marginalized many traditional U.S. allies during the run-up to the war, and therefore it could not assemble troops from most of these allies to participate in the occupation. (This was in contrast to what the Clinton administration had done in Kosovo and even to what the Bush administration had done in Afghanistan.) Further, and as we will elaborate below, because of its ideological fixation on liberal democracy, the Bush administration immediately abolished the Iraqi army and other security forces, since they had been instruments of the Saddam Hussein regime, and therefore it could not draw upon Iraqi security units to collaborate in the occupation. In essence, the U.S. military, along with the British military, were left alone to provide law and order, and their forces were far too few to do so.

Now began the damaging consequences of Rumsfeld's violation of the Weinberger-Powell Doctrine's tenet of overwhelming force. An interregnum, or rather an anarchy, of looting, sabotage, kidnappings, and murders immediately ensued. This in turn provided the conditions for the beginning and growth of a vigorous and organized insurgency. Moreover, since the U.S. military had too few forces to secure or destroy the vast stores of arms and ammunition which the old regime had distributed around Iraq, the insurgents had easy access to all the weapons that they needed.[3]

The Iraqi Insurgency and the U.S. Military Dilemma

The overwhelming majority of the insurgents were drawn from the Sunni population, who had been the beneficiaries of Saddam's regime. The insurgents quickly moved to confirm the isolation of U.S. occupation forces by attacking the few allies that they had. Using an array of classical insurgent tactics—bombings, ambushes, kidnappings, and beheadings—they repeatedly attacked the military units, civilian organizations, and simple individuals from every nation which was providing support to the occupation. In most cases, the governments of these nations had provided their support without mobilizing their own publics behind it, and in some cases they had done so despite the clear opposition of public opinion (e.g., Spain and Italy). The insurgents' attacks upon exposed allied personnel also exposed the gap which existed between the allied governments and their publics, which had hardly been a robust example of democracy in action. Of even more fundamental and fatal importance were the insurgents' attacks upon Iraqis who were working with the occupation. A particularly crucial target was the U.S. effort to recruit and organize new Iraqi security forces (e.g., repeated insurgent bombings of police stations).

The U.S. military soon found that it had no obvious good options for putting down the insurgency. If the U.S. ground forces engaged in direct assaults upon urban areas sheltering the insurgents (e.g., Fallujah and other cities in the "Sunni Triangle," composed of central and western Iraq), the resulting fatalities among U.S. forces would arouse the opposition of American public opinion, while the fatalities among local civilians would arouse the opposition of the Iraqi and allied publics. Similarly, U.S. air strikes upon these urban areas would inflame Iraqi and allied public opinion. Finally, if the U.S. military simply tried to maintain a defensible position in Iraq, it would suffer a slow but steady stream of fatalities, which would eventually arouse the opposition of the American public (the specter of the Vietnam War). More fundamentally, neither the classical American way of war nor the new American way of war, which Rumsfeld sought to establish with his transformation project, had any effective answer to the challenge posed by the insurgency in Iraq.

Some Americans thought that the Iraqi insurgency represented a new kind of war. Unlike the Vietnam War, it was more urban than rural. But the U.S. military had already had an experience with urban guerrilla warfare in Mogadishu, Somalia in 1993 (depicted in the film, "Blackhawk Down"), hardly an encouraging example. And the French military had a far more serious and prolonged experience with urban guerrilla warfare in Algeria in 1954-1962 (depicted in the film, "The Battle of Algiers"). In any event, the Iraqi insurgency was not really that new in kind; indeed, it was merely a new example of another classical way of war, which was the guerrilla ("little war") or insurgent way of war. And as in most insurgent wars, the ultimate solution in Iraq would have to be grounded not in the military operations, but in the political process. The fundamental problem to be solved in Iraq, therefore, involved the U.S. political project for Iraq. The Bush administration made loud and repeated proclamations that it was bringing a liberal democracy, market economy, and open society to that country. But it soon became evident that there was very little connection between these proclamations and either the actual realities of Iraq or the actual policies of the administration.

The U.S. Government in Iraq: The Bush Democratization Project

The Bush administration claimed that it would convert Iraq into a liberal democracy, market economy, and open society. Iraq, in turn, would be a model for similar changes which would soon ensue in other countries of the Middle East (particularly Syria, Iran, and Saudi Arabia). For its vision of the future, the administration projected a sort of democratic domino theory, with the end result being an "empire of liberty" (in Thomas Jefferson's phrase) in the Middle East and beyond.

Reaching for models from the past to legitimate this vision of the future, the administration repeatedly cited the successful U.S. occupations and democratizations of West Germany and Japan after the Second World War. These nations had become solid allies of the United States within the great system of alliances (an empire of liberty of a sort) with which American fought and won the Cold War.

However, the Bush administration never mentioned the many other U.S. efforts in the course of the 20th century to use military force to democratize countries, particularly within the Caribbean Basin and Central America during the 1900s-1930s (Cuba, the Dominican Republic, Haiti, and Nicaragua) and again during the 1960s-1990s (the Dominican Republic and Haiti again and also Grenada and Panama). Most of these efforts at democratization ended not only in failure, but in the establishment of brutal dictatorial regimes (including Trujillo in the Dominican Republic and Somoza in the Dominican Republic). And of course the administration never mentioned the epic U.S. failure in South Vietnam. Together, these failed U.S. efforts at democratization add up to about a dozen cases. If any honest discussion about the prospects for U.S. democratization in Iraq and other countries of the Middle East had included any analysis of a few of these cases, the discussion would have ended with a general consensus that the prospects were bleak.

Then there were the cases of the very recent efforts to democratize the multiethnic republics of the former Yugoslavia and the multiethnic republics of the former Soviet Union. These efforts had usually been accompanied by violent and even genocidal conflicts between the ethnic groups. But be the process peaceful or violent, the democratization of multiethnic societies had almost always issued in secession or partition. Given these results of democratization in the multiethnic countries of the communist world in the 1990s—especially the violent results in the Caucasus and the Balkans which are so proximate to Iraq both geographically and historically—it is almost incredible that anyone could seriously argue that the most relevant comparisons to Iraq were the homogeneous nations of West Germany and Japan in the 1940s. Only a globalist mentality and ideology would so blithely ignore such important local and historical particularities. Consequently, the Bush political democratization project, like the Rumsfeld military transformation project, soon ran aground in the local realities of Iraq.

As soon as the U.S. military defeated the Iraqi Army and toppled the Saddam Hussein regime, the Bush administration's ideology caused it to immediately abolish that Army and other security forces which had functioned under that regime. The abolition of these forces and the anarchy which resulted was an important contributor to the insurgency which followed. Moreover, just because the United States destroyed the old authority, this did not mean that it really sought to establish a new democracy, as that term is normally defined. It did not do so because a real democracy would have contradicted the primary interests of the two globalist groups—the neo-liberals and the neo-conservatives—who had produced the war in the first place and who were now designing the occupation. In order to understand what a real democracy would have meant in the real circumstances of Iraq, it is important to consider each of the three ethnic communities there—the Shi'ites, the Sunnis, and the Kurds, and we will be dealing with each in the course of this chapter. We will begin with the Shi'ites.

The Numerical Majority of the Iraqi Shi'ites

By the normal definition of democracy, one would have expected an electoral system based upon one person/one vote and majority rule. However, the Shi'ites comprised about 65 percent of the Iraqi population, and in such a system they could easily achieve a great preponderance of power and control of the Iraqi state. The Shi'ites took very seriously their version of Islam and Islamic law; this made them repugnant to the neo-liberals, with their ideological fixation on such secular values as the free market, the open society, and Western conceptions of human rights. The Shi'ites of Iraq also had many close connections with the Shi'ites of Iran; this made them repugnant to the neo-conservatives, with their primary interest in the security of Israel and the stability of U.S. allies in the Persian Gulf.

The Bush administration therefore was determined that, whatever kind of democracy might be established in Iraq, it could not issue in Shi'ite rule. Consequently, the administration would not allow a system of majority rule, i.e., a simple democracy. Rather, the system would have to be some kind of <u>limited</u> democracy, be it a liberal, federal, or elite one, or some combination thereof. This explains why in the period May 2003-June 2004 the U.S. occupation (the Coalition Provisional Authority, headed by the imperious but ineffective L. Paul Bremer III) persistently tried to marginalize Shi'ite religious leaders (e.g., the Grand Ayatollah Sistani) and political parties (e.g., the Supreme Council for the Islamic Revolution in Iraq). It also explains why it persistently tried to inflate political groupings of secularized Shi'ites (e.g., Ahmed Chalabi and his Iraqi National Congress), which had few followers among the vast Shi'ite population. This strategy had manifestly failed by June 2004, when the Coalition Provisional Authority was succeeded by the collaborating Iraqi government headed by Ayad Allawi, a secularized Shi'ite, who also had little following among the Iraqi population.[4] Allawi understood that he would have to work with Sistani and the

Islamic Shi'ites, and so the U.S. authorities in Iraq soon came to understand this also. However, Sistani and the Shi'ite Islamic parties, which were much better organized than the Shi'ite secular groups, naturally wanted an Iraqi constitution which would institute majority rule. This demand put them on a collision course with the other two major ethnic communities of Iraq, the Sunnis and the Kurds.

The Sunni and Kurdish minorities in Iraq of course opposed Shi'ite rule and therefore majority rule. The Sunnis, who were the source of most of the insurgency, really wanted minority rule of Iraq by themselves; that is, they wanted an authoritarian system like that which had served their interests under every regime since Iraq was created by the British in 1920.[5] The Kurds really wanted an independent Kurdish state or at most a loose kind of federal system for Iraq. Neither the Sunnis nor the Kurds wanted an Iraq which was democratic, while the Shi'ites wanted an Iraq which was (from the U.S. perspective) too democratic. The United States was unable to find a stable democratic solution to this three-part political problem. And since there was no stable political solution, there could be no stable foundation for the military operations against the insurgency.

The Radical Socio-Economic Project

The disconnection between the notions of the U.S. promoters of the Iraq War and the realities within Iraq itself went even further than the U.S. military transformation and political democratization projects. The neo-liberals also insisted upon a radical transformation of the Iraqi economy and Iraqi society. Bremer promulgated a series of decrees and measures designed to dismantle the state-controlled Iraqi economy and to bring about privatization and openness to American investment. (These measures were illegal under international law, since established international conventions forbid an occupying power from changing the economic structure of an occupied country.) Bremer also promoted programs to greatly increase the power of women in Iraqi society. The neo-conservatives supported these neo-liberal objectives for their own reasons. They wanted to ensure that Iraq could not again become a strong state which controlled an organized society based upon an Arab or Muslim collectivist identity. However, these radical U.S. economic and social measures were largely abortive because their institutionalization was made impossible by the growing and widespread insurgency. Indeed, because they were so offensive to the traditional Iraqi way of life, they helped to generate support for that insurgency.

The neo-conservative civilians in the Defense Department sometimes demonstrated how little they cared about any real democratization in Iraq. Defense officials allowed a series of acts of commission and omission which assaulted Iraqi public opinion and which therefore undermined the legitimacy of any U.S. promises about democratization. These included the initial period of anarchy (dismissed by Rumsfeld as "stuff happens"); the perverted and illegal interrogation methods at Abu Ghraib prison, which would inevitably become common knowledge among the Iraqi public; and the failure to spend already-appropriated funds to provide such basic physical necessities as electricity and sewers. For some neo-conservatives it was not really necessary that Iraq be democratic, merely that it be weak.

In short, because of the primary interests and insistent demands of both the neo-liberals and the neo-conservatives the proclamations of the Bush administration soon lost whatever credibility they had had in the first weeks of the U.S. occupation. Iraqis saw the U.S. objective of liberal democracy to be phony, its objective of free markets to be self-serving, and its objective of an open society to be offensive, and all three objectives to be illegitimate. The global perspectives, indeed, the universal conceits and imperial arrogance of the two U.S. neo-groups utterly ignored the local, intractable realities within Iraq itself and thereby ensured that the whole set of U.S. political, economic, and social projects would end as a failure.

Furthermore, because the United States could not produce a political solution which had legitimacy, it could not establish the sound political basis necessary for a military solution to the insurgency. This meant that the U.S. counterinsurgency effort and the Rumsfeld transformation project would also end as a failure. Indeed, it soon seemed that the combination of political, economic, social, and military failures would make the entire Iraq War a failure, one on an epic scale.

The Fatal History of the Iraqi Sunnis

At the core of the Iraqi political problem, and therefore of all the other problems that the United States has faced in Iraq, is Iraq's Sunni community. Any U.S. strategy toward Iraq should comprehend the real nature of the Sunnis, and that nature is deeper and darker than most Americans have understood.

The Sunni Arabs long dominated and abused other ethnic communities in Iraq, particularly the Shi'ite Arabs and the Kurds, but they have always comprised a minority of Iraq's population (now about 15-20 percent). Because of their long history of oppression and because of their support for any Islamist insurgencies—insurgencies that certainly have included Shi'ites and Kurds among their targets—the Sunni Arabs have much to answer for, and they laid the groundwork for a terrible civil war in Iraq.

Whatever the public pronouncements of their leaders might be, the Sunni Arabs always want minority rule of Iraq by themselves. They want a Sunni authoritarian system like every regime which ruled Iraq after it was created by the British in 1920 until it was invaded by the Americans in 2003, and, even before that, which ruled Mesopotamia under the Ottoman Empire. Since the Sunni Arab minority was in fact a rather small one, any regime composed by the Sunnis was especially authoritarian; the Sunni regime compensated for its especially small social base by employing unusually brutal methods against the Shi'ite and Kurdish communities. As Iraqi society underwent progressive modernization in the course of the 20th century, the Shi'ites and the Kurds steadily acquired more of the economic and educational resources that enabled their political mobilization and organization. This largely explains why successive Sunni regimes had to become steadily more severe, leading to the brutal rule of the Baath Party and culminating in the genocidal regime of Saddam Hussein. Only by increasing pressure from above could the regime keep down the pressure from below, coming from the increasingly mobilized Shi'ites and Kurds.

Saddam's regime was often compared to the Soviet regime or the Nazi one. The outer organizational forms often followed a Soviet model, while the inner ideological spirit had much in common with a

Nazi mentality. In the latter comparison, Saddam Hussein was said to play the role of Hitler, the Baath Party that of the Nazi Party, and the Iraqi people that of the German people. A more accurate comparison, however, would have been between the Baath party and the elite Nazi party unit, the S.S., and between the Sunni Arab community and the Nazi Party as a whole, which with its auxiliary organizations (e.g., the Hitler Youth) eventually comprised as much as 15 percent of the population of Nazi Germany.

By the late 1990s, the Sunnis were not merely the only beneficiaries of their authoritarian regime, they could not even imagine an acceptable political alternative—and certainly not any kind of democracy. They also knew that if their regime were to be overthrown and its elaborate security apparatus dismantled, total anarchy—indeed a Hobbesian state of war—very likely would ensue, and the long-suppressed Shi'ites and Kurds very likely would take their revenge.

From the Sunni perspective, it was bad enough when the United States destroyed Saddam Hussein's regime in April 2003. Yet they still had a measure of protection left in what remained of the Iraqi army and the Baath Party. But then in May 2003, the head of the U.S. occupation authority, Paul Bremer, decreed the abolition of both the army and the party, and he also authorized a deep purge of Baath Party members from all Iraqi institutions, including the health services and the public utilities. Bremer's orders meant that several hundred thousand Sunnis were immediately thrown out of work.

The Sunnis were thus suddenly plunged into an economic condition equivalent to the Great Depression. Much worse, they saw themselves with the prospect of a massacre similar to others that have occurred in the Middle East, for example, the Armenian genocide of 1915-18, the Lebanese civil war of 1975-90, and of course the all-too-relevant Kurdish genocide implemented by Saddam Hussein in 1987-89. It should have been no surprise that the Sunnis would become desperate, even desperadoes, and that they would flee into any form of organized resistance to the U.S. occupation that they could find.

Bremer's measures certainly cannot be explained by lessons drawn from previous U.S. occupations. The Bush administration always cited the successful U.S. occupations in Germany and Japan, but in those countries the occupation authorities, while removing the top military and political levels, initially worked with and relied upon local military and security units to maintain order. They also left the civil institutions largely intact so that they could continue to perform their essential functions. The administration ignored these German and Japanese (as well as Austrian and Italian) precedents. It also ignored the advice of many U.S. civilian officials and military officers who had had recent experience with occupation tasks, particularly in Bosnia and Kosovo.[6]

One explanation for Bremer's measures is that the leaders of both the Shi'ites and the Kurds insisted upon them: they would not support the U.S. occupation if it simply meant a new—even if reformed and restrained—Baath regime. But as the four U.S. occupations after the Second World War demonstrate, one can abolish a regime, an organized and integrated entity, while still running a country with the aid of former adherents of the regime, who are now merely disaggregated individuals or units. This was the path not taken. The reason it was not taken is because the Chalabi and the secular Shi'ites wanted to not just rule over Iraq, but they also wanted to control and fill all of the attractive institutional positions which the Baath party members had held, i.e., a classic case of patronage politics. Since Chalabi and the secular Shi'ites were the only Iraqis with which the neo-conservatives in and around the Defense Department felt comfortable in the crucial Spring of 2003, what they wanted, they got.

However, despite the Bremer policies and unlike their Nazi counterparts in Germany in 1945, the Sunni Arabs in Iraq 2003 had not been totally defeated, devastated, dismembered, and demoralized. Consequently, they were soon able to initiate and support a vigorous and vicious insurgency composed of the underground elements that remained from the Baath security apparatus and the insurgent units that quickly grew out of Sunni Islamist organizations. It was not long before there was a fully-developed insurgency in the notorious Sunni Triangle. And it was also not long before the Sunni insurgents began extensive and persistent attacks upon the Shi'ite population, which they had long despised and they now feared. As for the Sunni leaders, they repeatedly demonstrated their total lack of statesmanship or indeed of any sense of justice due to the Shi'ites and the Kurds. For example, after the insurgent bombing of the major Shi'ite shrine in Samarra in February 2006, the Sunnis themselves could have apprehended the perpetrators and turned them over for justice, but they did not do so. Thus began a new and continuing quantum leap in the revenge cycle of Sunni-Shi'ite violence.

For many reasons—some based upon American democratic ideals but much more those based upon strategic calculations and economic interests involving the Sunni regimes of the Persian Gulf oil producers—the Bush administration chose not to crush the Sunni Arab community of Iraq like the Truman administration had crushed the Nazi Party and its supporters in Germany. Instead, it tried to co-opt or even appease the Sunnis leaders. The result for several grim and grueling years from 2003 to 2006 was a total failure to subdue the Sunni insurgents in Iraq, including Al Qaeda.

Kurdish Autonomy

In contrast to both the Shi'ites and the Sunnis, the Kurds really wanted an independent Kurdish state, or at most a very loose kind of federal system for Iraq. For them, Iraq at best was a geographical expression, and more commonly it was a genocidal repression.

The United States had excellent relations with the Kurds, having protected their territory with a no-fly zone since the Gulf War and having provided them with substantial economic aid. In return, the Kurds had constructed in their protected territory or mini-state not only a prosperous economy but a vibrant democracy. The Kurdish mini-state seemed to provide an excellent model for the rest of Iraq.

There was a problem, however. The Kurds feared and loathed the rest of Iraq and did not think of themselves as Iraqis. Conversely, the rest of Iraq despised and resented the Kurds and did not think of them as Iraqis either. Thus the Kurds consistently opposed any Iraqi constitution which would institute either a centralized political system or majority rule. They also insisted upon retaining their own well-organized and effective Kurdish militia (really an army). These demands put the Kurds on a collision course with the other two major ethnic communities of Iraq.

In summary, the Shi'ites wanted majority rule of Iraq by themselves. The Sunnis wanted minority rule of Iraq by themselves. The Kurds wanted majority rule of Kurdistan by themselves. In a sense, the Shi'ites and the Kurds each wanted a democracy, but their conceptions of democracy were contradictory. Conversely, the Shi'ites and the Sunnis each wanted an Iraq, but their conceptions of Iraq were antithetical. Finally, neither the Sunnis nor the Kurds wanted an Iraq which was democratic. For this three-body political problem, there was no stable democratic solution and that is why the United States has never been able to find one.

The Delusion of American Iraqis

In its public pronouncements, the Bush administration rarely acknowledged the existence of the three ethnic communities and their strong identities. The administration persisted in describing Iraqis as if they were simply individuals defined by their economic interest in a free market, their social interest in an open society, and their political interest in a liberal democracy. In short, the administration described Iraqis as if they were Americans. In this, it was delusional.

In 1917, Woodrow Wilson, the original author of the U.S. democratization project, described six U.S. senators who were trying to prevent America's entry into the first World War "to make the world safe for democracy" as "a little group of willful men." By 1920, with the debacle of the Versailles Treaty and the shambles of democratization in war-torn and revolutionary Europe, many Americans had come to think of Wilson as rather willful, too. Almost ninety years later, George W. Bush, the most recent in a long parade of Wilsonian presidents, along with a little group of willful men in his administration, propelled America's entry into the Iraq War "to make the Muslim world safe for democracy." It is now evident that this contemporary little group of men was not only willful, but ignorant and arrogant, too.

From Imperial Fantasies to Counterinsurgency Realities

And so it was that the United States found itself once again deeply immersed in a counterinsurgency war. All the careful efforts by the

U.S. Army after Vietnam to prevent civilian policymakers from putting it once again into a counterinsurgency war—efforts which were exemplified by the Weinberger-Powell Doctrine—had come to naught. The grimy and grinding realities of the war in Iraq steadily pushed the whole repugnant topic of how to fight insurgents back on the agenda of the U.S. Army—and of the U.S. government more generally—after an absence of three decades. Out of necessity, American policy analysts and military strategists began to turn their attention to past experiences with counterinsurgency wars and to what lessons they might provide for the present ones, both in Iraq and in Afghanistan. But it would not be until 2006 that the U.S. Army would be able to apply these lessons. It would do so by attending to the local realities of Iraq—not the global ideology of the Bush administration—and in particular by understanding and explaining divisions among the Sunnis themselves. It turned out that the Sunnis could be as ruthless toward each other as they had been toward the Shi'ites and the Kurds.

How to Fight Counterinsurgency Wars: The Historical Record

During the past century or so, there have been many (about two dozen) major efforts by foreign or imperial powers to subdue an insurgency within some particular locality. Some of these counterinsurgency campaigns have been successful, most notably those undertaken by the United States in the Philippines in the 1900s and again in the 1950s; by the U.S. in Nicaragua, Haiti, and the Dominican Republic in the 1910s-1920s and in El Salvador in the 1980s; and by Britain in Iraq in the 1920s, in Malaya in the 1940s-1950s, and in Kenya in the 1950s. Other counterinsurgencies have been unsuccessful, most notably those undertaken by France in Indochina in the late 1940s-1950s and in Algeria in the 1950s-1960s; by the United States in Indochina in the 1960s-1970s; and by the Soviet Union in Afghanistan in the 1980s. And of course, the U.S. counterinsurgency efforts in Afghanistan, after 18 years, have not achieved convincing success.

Military analysts have offered a variety of factors and conditions to explain why some counterinsurgencies have been successful and others have not. However, one factor—notably absent or feeble in Iraq from

2003 to 2006 and still the case in Afghanistan—has been essential in every successful case, and that is the active and effective cooperation of local military or at least militia forces with the military forces of the foreign power. These local forces know the local people and their language, customs, and nuances. They can provide the equivalent of what in domestic U.S. law enforcement is known as community policing, and only they—and not foreign troops—can do so.

There is another feature of local military forces which makes them essential for a successful counterinsurgency. Because they are local (and native and indigenous), everyone in the locality knows that they and the communities from which they come are not only on the scene now, but they have been so in the past and will be so in the future. Their survival depends upon making the counterinsurgency successful, because they have no obvious place to escape to if it fails. In contrast, everyone in the locality (and in the foreign power) knows that the foreign military forces can always go home. Moreover, if the foreign power is a democratic one (especially one in our contemporary, post-modern era, with its high aversion to military casualties in a long war of attrition, which all counterinsurgencies are), everyone will know that eventually this foreign power will indeed bring its troops home. The insurgent forces will have many good reasons to believe that they will be able to outwait the foreign ones. A war of attrition (and therefore a counterinsurgency war) is a war of wills, and in a war of wills the side that must stay and fight will have more staying willpower than the side that can choose between staying put and going away. A counterinsurgency war, in other words, is an arena in which Albert Hirschman's famous analysis of "exit" versus "voice" fully applies.[7]

Consequently, in every successful counterinsurgency war, the foreign power has had to carry out a policy of localization. In the Vietnam War, the Nixon administration understood this, and "Vietnamization" was a centerpiece of its military strategy. In the Iraq war, the Bush administration kept talking about how "when the Iraqi troops stand up, our troops can stand down," but the hoped-for Iraqi military forces never came close to the efficacy which was obtained in that other grueling counterinsurgency war by the military forces of South Vietnam. (It is perhaps indicative of the great difficulty of the challenge in Iraq that the Bush administration almost never used the term "Iraqification" or anything like it.) As bad as conditions were in South Vietnam, there were at least a large number of soldiers there who identified with something called South Vietnam. In contrast, in Iraq the bulk of the local soldiers identified most not with something called Iraq, but instead with their religious or ethnic community, i.e., Shi'ites, Sunnis, or Kurds.

The Ultimate Insurgent Weapon: The Suicide Bomber

The challenges posed by a classical insurgency are bad enough, but they have been amplified by a new development. Since the 1980s, Islamist insurgents have deployed a new and formidable weapon: the suicide bomber. This tactic was not invented by Islamist insurgents (the Japanese kamikaze pilots were famous predecessors, and the Tamil Liberation Front in Sri Lanka made extensive use of it), but suicide bombing is now especially prevalent among Islamist terrorist groups. (In the 1980s, these groups were primarily Shi'ite and backed by Iran; in the 2000s-2010s, they primarily have been Sunni and have been parts of a widespread, transnational, even internet, network.)

An especially cogent analysis of the causes and conditions which give rise to suicide bombing has been given by Robert Pape, a political scientist and military strategist at the University of Chicago.[8] Pape sees suicide bombing to be the product of two conditions: (1) a foreign power is occupying a particular country with its military forces (or those foreign military forces are so nearby the country that they constitute a continuous and pervasive threat of occupation). Prominent examples have been Israel in the West Bank and Gaza; India in Kashmir; and the United States in Lebanon (1982-1984), in Saudi Arabia (1990-2003), and of course in Iraq and Afghanistan. (2) The foreign occupying power is a democratic political system. This makes its public opinion important, and suicide terrorism can have a large and visible impact upon this public opinion. We might add that this feature is especially true in a post-modern, highly individualist, and self-centered liberal democracy such as those in much of the West today. The contrast with a pre-modern, highly communalist, honor-centered Muslim culture could not be greater. All suicide bombers come from very intense and dense communities; only these communities can create the very special incentives necessary for suicide bombing.

Pape's analysis clearly enhances the argument that under contemporary conditions a foreign military force engaged in counterinsurgency operations will find itself in a very unstable and even counterproductive situation. It therefore also enhances the argument that a foreign power (especially one that is a liberal democracy) will have to rely not only upon strong local military forces, but also upon a strong local political authority (and in some situations, even authoritarianism), which will essentially occupy its own country.

If the local military force and political authority are from the same community as that of the insurgent organization, then they are very likely to be able to acquire the intelligence information which is necessary to root out the insurgent's supporters within that community. This is especially relevant in regard to suicide bombing because this tactic requires a substantial amount of community support. Conversely, if the local military force and political authority are from a different community than that of the insurgent organization, they may not have the intelligence, but they very likely will have the will to root out (i.e., to ruthlessly devastate) that community and the insurgent's supporters within that community, which is both alien and a threat to them. This extreme version of the traditional imperial formulas of indirect rule and divide and rule was used by the British in most of their successful counterinsurgencies, e.g., enabling the Sunnis to repress the Shi'ites in Iraq in the 1920s; the Malays to repress the rural Chinese in Malaya in the 1950s; and several smaller tribes to repress the rural Kikuyu in Kenya in the 1950s.

And so a review of the history of counterinsurgency wars and also of the dynamics of suicide bombing demonstrates the central and fundamental importance of the local realities, and particularly the importance of local military and political allies. It was when the U.S. Army in Iraq was driven to understand and to exploit these local realities that the dismal and downward course of the Iraq War underwent an apparent and impressive turnaround in 2006-2008.

Competing Levels of Local Realities

Given the fact that virtually all of the insurgents in Iraq emanated from and were supported by the Sunni community, the most obvious way that the U.S. Army could have exploited the local realities would have been to ally with the Shi'ite and Kurdish communities, who, as we have seen, had every good reason to crush both the Sunni insurgents and the wider Sunni community which sustained them. This would have meant allying with the Shi'ite and Kurdish militias to the point of empowering them to perform much of the actual counterinsurgency operations, in a manner similar to the employment of local military forces in the past successful counterinsurgency wars which we have discussed above.

However, as we have also noted, the Bush administration was determined that the Shi'ites could not dominate the new Iraq. The administration greatly feared Iran, and it greatly feared that a Shi'ite Iraq would become an ally, even a puppet state, of Shi'ite Iran. This fear of Iran and of its expansion was especially pronounced among the administration's neo-conservatives who feared Iran's growing threat to Israel, and also among administration figures with close business ties with the oil industry and therefore with close personal ties with the Sunni monarchs of the Persian Gulf oil producers. This included not only Vice President Dick Cheney, but President Bush himself. The Bush administration thus vetoed any attempts by the U.S Army to work out an alliance with the Shi'ites.

As for the Kurdish community, the Kurdish militias were quite effective in putting down Sunni insurgents in the Kurdish regions in northern Iraq. But, for the most part, they were uninterested in operating in other areas where the population was largely Arab (either Sunni or Shi'ite), i.e., the central and southern regions of Iraq. Allying with the Kurds would not by itself be sufficient to solve the insurgency problem.

Consequently, the Army had to find its local allies someplace within the Sunni community itself. Although it took awhile to do so, in 2006 the Army succeeded in this by going down beneath the social level of the ethnic community to the social level of the tribe. For it turned out that Iraq, like most Arab societies, was full of a wide variety of tribes which had long competed and conflicted with each other. The obvious and natural strategy was to play them off against each other, to employ the ancient imperial formula of divide and rule. It was when the Army dropped down to the tribal level within the Sunni community that it was at last able to produce an apparent turnaround in the counterinsurgency war.

The Apparent Turnaround in the Iraq War

From the beginning of the Iraqi insurgency in Summer 2003 to the U.S. Congressional elections in November 2006, there was little or no evidence that the United States was winning the war in Iraq. Virtually all independent military and political strategists agreed that the only question was how the United States would lose and what would be the consequences of that loss (e.g., would they be as bad as Vietnam or would they be worse?).

Then something happened. Indeed, enough had happened by early 2008 that some critics of the war began to ask the question of "What if we win?" The best way to answer this new question was to examine what happened to make it possible to raise it. This was because the nature of any "win" would have been determined by the new conditions that brought it about. Here we have at least two plausible—and quite different—answers, or a tale of two tales.

The Bush Administration's Tale: The U.S. Surge

The Bush administration and its supporters pointed to "the surge." The increase in 2007 in the numbers of U.S. troops in Iraq (actually only an addition of about 25,000) had at last tipped the balance and provided the margin of victory against the Sunni insurgents. And along with the U.S. military surge had come a U.S. political surge. The administration's persistent pressure on the national government of Iraq (such as it was) had at last paid dividends and caused that government to open itself to moderate Sunni leaders, so that the Sunni population on the whole had withdrawn their support from the insurgents.

The U.S. Military's Tale: The Military's Turn to Local Realities

There is however, a second tale of the U.S. winning in Iraq. The people who were actually doing the winning, the U.S. military itself, pointed to something more than the surge in U.S. troops and political pressure. This was the surge in Sunni allies at the local level, such as the Awakening Councils. Often composed of Sunni insurgents who had turned against Al Qaeda in Mesopotamia, this surge began largely independent of U.S. initiatives. Al Qaeda had engaged in actions highly offensive to the local Sunni tribes, such as marginalizing or even assassinating their sheiks and forcing their women into marriages with Al Qaeda members. The result by early 2006 was a growing civil war within the Sunni insurgency itself, particularly within Anbar, that province where the insurgency had been most successful.

However, this development in the Sunni tribes nicely complemented the new approach being developed by the U.S. Army and particularly by the man who would become the new U.S. military commander in Iraq, General David Petraeus. Petraeus had no special expertise in such local conditions as Iraqi tribal organization, Sunni identity, or Arab culture. But he was the leading and most sophisticated Army expert on counterinsurgency (indeed, he literally wrote the book—the new U.S. Field Manual—on the topic), and he put knowledge of local realities and cooperation with local forces at the center of his counterinsurgency doctrine. He was perfectly predisposed to see and take advantage of the Sunni tribal developments. This has included paying members (i.e., active males) of the Awakening Councils about $300 a month (a substantial sum in the conditions of Iraq). By early 2008, there were more than 70,000 members of these councils, and the plan was to increase that number up to 100,000.

The Sunnis: The Fish and the Sea

It was this Sunni civil war—and specifically the Sunni local tribes and Awakening Councils—that really accounted for the winning against the Al Qaeda insurgents (a winning by local groups against a transnational network). The U.S. military under General Petraeus supported and enabled the Sunni Awakening, and it even advised and guided it. But we should not delude ourselves that the U.S. military ever commanded it.

The Sunni Awakening did much to dry up the Sunni sea in which the Al Qaeda insurgents swam. Or rather, there had been three different insurgent fish swimming in this sea—the transnational Al Qaeda, the Baath resistance, and the local tribes, all cooperating in savagely attacking the hapless whale that was the U.S. military. Now however, one fish—the tribes—had turned upon another—Al Qaeda. The sea—the Sunni population—would support and sustain the Sunni fish which was most likely to win and to protect them from their worst, long-term, enemies. And these, unfortunately, were the Shi'ites.

The Sunnis, the Shi'ites, and the Surge

The Sunnis thus were putting themselves in a position to secure their own interests in a post-U.S. Iraq. They sought to regain the military organization and experience which they lost with the overthrow of Saddam's regime and the abolition of the Baath-dominated Iraqi army and security forces. Moreover, the Awakening Councils pressed to have their members admitted into the new Iraqi army and police (such as they were), which were now dominated by Shi'ites. The Shi'ites had every good reason to keep the Sunnis out of these forces (or at least to keep them as marginalized as the Shi'ites were once kept by the Sunnis). The Sunni Awakening Councils were thus embarked upon a collision course with the Shi'ite ("Iraqi") security forces.

The U.S. success against the Sunni insurgents thus was not really explained by the surge in U.S. troops. Indeed, the majority of the surge military operations were directed against Shi'ite militias and were either in Shi'ite areas or to protect Sunni ones. The surge was also complemented by the wall, the extensive system of barriers which were constructed to separate districts of Baghdad. However, it was by containing the Shi'ite militias that the surge established the political conditions that allowed the national central government and some Sunni politicians to make an appearance of compromise on some political issues. But these political conditions were quite fragile and temporary. The leaders of the Shi'ite militias, most importantly Moqta-da-al-Sadr, asked their men to avoid combat with U.S. soldiers and to lay low, at least until the surge was over, and the U.S. troops had ebbed home. Then, the real war from their perspective—the one against the Sunnis—would once again begin.

The Nature of the U.S. Win

We can now see the real nature of the U.S. win in Iraq in 2007-2008. The necessary condition for the U.S. win over the Sunni insurgents had been the empowering of the Sunni tribes. Because these tribes were largely local and found in areas which were largely Sunni, they were the Sunnis who were least threatening to the Shi'ites. Indeed, if these tribes were to control their own locales (but no more), they would actually help to further the Shi'ite objective of an Iraq composed of ethnical-ly-separate and largely autonomous regions (all the more so since the Sunni tribes are usually found where the oil fields are not). However, when these Sunni tribes or the Awakening Councils pressed to re-es-tablish Sunni control of national Iraqi institutions, the Shi'ites and the Shi'ite militias resisted. The more the Sunni allies of the U.S. tried to achieve their national goals, the more the Shi'ites fought to prevent this. And when the Obama administration began to remove U.S. mil-itary forces from Iraq in 2010, this is what the Shi'ites, including the national government now dominated by the Shi'ites, did. By 2012, the Shi'ites had achieved their goal of marginalizing the Sunnis so much that they even ruled the Sunni regions of central and western Iraq like they were occupied provinces. Not surprisingly, the Sunnis now launched a new insurgency, this time one that took the grotesque form of the Islamic State.

The myth of a unified Iraq national state has always been a delu-sion—or even a lie—ever since its invention by British imperialists in the 1920s, and the myth of a unified and democratic Iraq has also always been a delusion—or even a lie—ever since its invention by American Wilsonians in the 2000s. Ideas have consequences, and the ideas of an Iraqi nation and an Iraqi democracy have had terrible conse-quences indeed—the killing of thousands of American soldiers and also tens of thousands of innocent civilians of all communities within Iraq. Perhaps, therefore, these ideas themselves also deserve to die.

An American Rendezvous with Mesopotamian History

The course of the Iraq War not only revealed delusions about Iraq itself. It also revealed as delusions ideas of constructing an American-style empire in the Middle East or spreading American-style globalization to the Muslim world. In the aftermath of the Iraq War, the United States was still the greatest of the great powers, and it was still the largest of the large economies. But the greatness of its power was not so great that it could hold sway over the Muslim world, or that it could confidently undertake counterinsurgency warfare, or that it was still widely acknowledged as the "superpower." And the largeness of its economy was not so large that its own particular model of globalization was the only practical one and the one which other countries had to follow. This became even more the case in the aftermath of the U.S.-initiated global finance crisis of 2008 and the ensuing Great Recession.

Since the beginning of recorded history, Mesopotamia—a term which means "the land between the two rivers" of the Tigris and the Euphrates, and the land which we know today as Iraq—has seen a long succession, a great parade, of imperial powers come and go. So too, the imperial power of our own time has come to Iraq. Just how the United States will eventually leave Iraq is still unknown. However, one thing is virtually certain, and that is, one way or another, the American empire will be gone.

CHAPTER THIRTEEN

THE NEO-CONSERVATIVES AND THE IRAQ WAR

AT THE TIME OF the Iraq War, there was a great deal of attention given to the role of the neo-conservative movement in American's foreign policy and especially in the war itself. That role was very controversial at the time, and it remains so more than fifteen years after the war began. But the term "neo-conservative" has largely disappeared from public discourse. This is largely because the neo-conservatives, with their reputation sullied by their role in the Iraq War, have largely wanted this to be so.

To properly understand the real role of the neo-conservatives in the Iraq War, and particularly in its origins, it will be best to go back to the origins of the neo-conservatives themselves. This was in the late 1960s, at the time of that earlier failed war, the Vietnam War. As it happened, this rather peculiar intellectual and political movement represented a rather creative response to the failures of both traditional liberalism and traditional conservatism as they had manifested themselves by the late 1960s.

Liberals and Conservatives

For much of the past century, Americans considered their politics to be defined by the opposition between two tendencies, liberal and conservative, which largely corresponded to the opposition between the two parties, respectively Democrats and Republicans. In this regard, the American experience in the 20th century more or less followed the British prototype of the 19th century.[1]

Of course, for roughly half a century, from 1932 to 1980, the liberal tendency was the dominant one in American politics, and as is usually the case with dominant political tendencies, the liberals themselves had been divided into several distinct variations. In the 1900s-1910s, there was a strong progressive movement composed of people who were generally more intellectual, more professional, more elite, and more radical than ordinary liberals, they advocated a strong state in which professional civil servants (i.e., people like the progressives themselves) would implement innovative social reforms. Later, in the 1930s, there was a strong Marxist movement with goals similar to but more radical than those of the progressives; it too was composed of people who thought of themselves as more intellectual, more elite (indeed as a "vanguard"), and more radical than ordinary liberals. Finally, in the 1980s, there was a New Left (the Marxists of the 1930s having become the Old Left); instead of advocating a strong state, they were very much concerned with individual free expression, but they also advocated innovative social reforms and even a sort of cultural revolution. Composed as they were of elitist intellectuals, these successive radical variations on a liberal theme rarely elected representatives to public office, but they did supply many of the ideas which, in later years, would become the public policies of the Democratic, or liberal, Party when it controlled the government.

Throughout the half century from 1932 to 1980 the Republican Party and the conservative tendency were in a minority position in American politics. Consequently, whatever differences existed between conservatives seemed of little importance or interest in the big political picture. These differences were made even less interesting because, unlike the case with liberals, very few conservatives were intellectuals. However, the social and cultural turmoil of the 1960s produced a new tendency among conservatives, which would eventually become very important and interesting (and also intellectual) indeed.

The Debacle of the Liberal Projects

In the 1960s, the long-standing hegemony of liberal ideas and the Democratic Party was confounded with the debacle of major liberal projects in both the domestic and the international arenas. With regard to domestic affairs, both of the two great liberal projects of the early 1960s, the Civil Rights movement and the Great Society programs, had something go very wrong by the late 1960s. The Civil Rights movement mutated into the Black Power movement, with a good deal of animus directed at Jewish civil servants and municipal employees, particularly teachers.[2] The Great Society programs seemed to make social conditions, especially among African-Americans, worse rather than better.

Conservatives could interpret these two failures as simply confirming their earlier opinions about liberal projects. Liberals, of course, had to come up with a different approach; most sought to deny the debacles or even to accept them as welcome developments and advances of fundamental liberal values, especially those of free expression and cultural liberation.

What was most interesting, however, was the response of those (rather few) liberals who had the honesty to see both the failures of the liberal projects and the need to explain them within some intellectually coherent framework. There were "liberals who been mugged by reality" in the phrase of one of them, Irving Kristol. They came to recognize that political reforms would always be constrained by social and cultural realities, and that these realities could only be changed by careful and patient efforts if they could be changed at all. Having been mugged by social and cultural realities, these former liberals began to publish a series of astute and discerning analyses of social and cultural constraints, particularly in their new journal, The Public Interest. No longer traditional liberals, but also not merely traditional conservatives, they eventually assumed the name (given by Irving Kristol again) of "neo-conservatives."

With regard to foreign affairs, the great liberal debacle was of course the Vietnam War. It had been liberals, particularly the Democratic administrations of John Kennedy and Lyndon Johnson that had taken the United States into the war in the first place, but after 1968 liberals abandoned not only the war but an activist U.S. foreign policy more generally. In a version of denial, they blamed the war not on its originators (liberals like themselves), but on the conservative party, i.e., the Republicans, and on conservative institutions, especially the U.S. military.

As for conservatives, they continued to support a strong U.S. position and an active U.S. role in the world, but they now strongly emphasized the necessity for discernment, prudence, and realism in foreign policy. This became the "realist" approach of Richard Nixon and, most famously, Henry Kissinger. When applied to the Soviet Union, it became the policy of "détente." It soon generated intense opposition from the group that was becoming the neo-conservatives.

The Neo-Conservative Perspective on Foreign Policy

The neo-conservatives taking ideas very seriously, naturally took the ideas, the ideology, of communism very seriously too, and given their backgrounds within a variety of Marxist movements, they understood this ideology very well. They became the most intellectual, the most ideological, of anti-communists. Translated into power politics and foreign policy, this meant that they became the most anti-Soviet as well, thoroughly focused upon the threat posed to the United States and its allies, especially Israel, by the massive power of the Soviet Union. Their concentrated and uncompromising focus upon communist ideology and the Soviet threat made the neo-conservatives very different from the traditional conservatives or realists. There thus opened up a great divide among conservatives in regard to U.S. foreign policy, which has now persisted for more than forty years—through successive eras of Cold-War, rogue-state, and Islamist threats—down to the present day.

Because the neo-conservatives were so focused upon Soviet power and the strong Soviet state, they clearly saw the need for a counterpart strong American state to contain and to ultimately defeat the Soviet threat, and, more generally, to promote U.S. leadership within the international arena. However, as observed above, with regard to the domestic arena, the neo-conservatives were very critical or skeptical about the efficacy and value of social reforms implemented by a strong state. This opened up a great contradiction within the neo-conserva-tive ideology itself between its foreign-policy and its domestic-policy elements, which also has now persisted for more than forty years. This contradiction reached its highest and most absurd point with the Iraq War, when the neo-conservatives urged that a strong U.S. state, an American hegemony, could and should impose not only regime change but fundamental political, economic, and social reforms on another society, one which was totally different from America.

In the 1970s, during the Nixon and Ford administration (and with respect to foreign policy, really the Kissinger administration), there was obviously no place within the Executive Branch for neo-conserva-tives. Instead, they found their political perch and protection under the wings of a few members of Congress. The most prominent and most supportive of these was Senator Henry Jackson, a Cold-War Democrat and defense hawk from the state of Washington (or, as some of his critics alleged, the senator from Boeing). Richard Perle, in particular, began his abrasive and controversial policy career as Jackson's chief for-eign-policy advisor.

The Neo-Conservatives in the Reagan Administration

By 1980, the ideas of traditional liberals were old and tired. Even worse, these ideas had demonstrably failed in both the domestic-policy and the foreign-policy arenas, especially during the then-current Carter admin-istration. But traditional conservatives were in a condition that was not much better. Although their policy failures, as during the recent Ford administration, were less obvious than those of the liberals, their ideas, insofar as they had any ideas at all, were not only old but also seemed to be irrelevant.

This great void of policy ideas, the joint product of both traditional liberals and traditional conservatives, provided a unique opportunity for the promotion of the competing ideas of the neo-conservatives, and the election of Ronald Reagan seemed to provide the vehicle for their implementation.

As it turned out, however, the <u>domestic</u> policy proposals of the neo-conservatives did not have much operational impact during the

Reagan years. Indeed, the social and cultural deformities, which the neo-conservatives had decried during the 1970s, were probably worse at the end of the Reagan administration than they had been at its beginning, and they would continue to get worse during the succeeding administration of George H.W. Bush.

It was a completely different story with respect to the <u>foreign</u> policy proposals of the neo-conservatives, however. Here, their impact was immense. Neo-conservatives claim that their ideas won the Cold War, and a good case can be made that they are at least partly right (that is, their ideas were one crucial part of the total ensemble of several causes which brought about first the unraveling of the Soviet bloc, and then the collapse of the Soviet Union itself).

The Neo-Conservatives in the 1990s

But now that the neo-conservatives had won the Cold War (at least in their own estimation), what would be their next project? As it happened, the question concerning a new mission arose at the same time as the beginning of a new decade—the 1990s—and the advent of a new generation—the second—of neo-conservatives.

It was natural that the neo-conservatives, like other groups or institutions which had fought the Soviet Union, such as the U.S. military, would look around and see what was left on the planet which bore a resemblance to the lost Soviet threat. The most obvious counterpart was Communist China, but there were also a series of "rogue states." Even in 1990, the most threatening of these seemed to be Iraq, Iran, and North Korea (the same three states which, a dozen years later, President George W. Bush would deem "the axis of evil"). Being in the very center of the Middle East, the first two of these states, Iraq and Iran, posed a manifest threat to both U.S. economic interests in the oil of the Persian Gulf and U.S. political interests in the security of Israel.

For many foreign-policy analysts, Iraq's invasion of Kuwait in 1990 and the Gulf War in 1991 confirmed both that rogue states could be a threat to U.S. interests and that the best way to deal with them was with military power. For neo-conservatives, however, the U.S. experience with Iraq taught an additional lesson. To them, the outcome of the Gulf War, in which Saddam Hussein was defeated but not deposed, demonstrated that while military victory was necessary, it was not sufficient, and that a military victory had to continue until it achieved a regime change. The sudden collapse of the Soviet Union and its allied communist regimes in Eastern Europe seemed to prove that regime change was possible and indeed that it was possible at a fundamental level and on a large scale.

But hadn't the earlier neo-conservative insistence upon the intractability of social and cultural realities made for skepticism and caution in regard to social reforms? Moreover, this skepticism and caution had been grounded in a solid professionalism. The original neo-conservatives were not only public intellectuals, but most were also professional social scientists, with very extensive professional education and experience on social and cultural matters. However, their professional specialties had dealt almost exclusively with American or <u>domestic</u> conditions. They definitely were not professionals in the fields of comparative politics, comparative sociology, or comparative anthropology. With rare exceptions (e.g., Richard Pipes at Harvard, who was a distinguished historian of Russia, and Bernard Lewis of Princeton, who was a distinguished historian of the Middle East), neo-conservatives knew very little about the actual realities within foreign societies. Further, most neo-conservatives definitely were not professionals in the fields of international politics, foreign policy, and military strategy, either. With rare exceptions (e.g., Albert Wohlstetter of Chicago and his protégé, Paul Wolfowitz), neo-conservatives knew very little about the actual realities of diplomatic negotiations or military operations. Consequently, when in the 1990s, the neo-conservatives began to promote regime change in a wide variety of countries, ranging from Iraq and Iran to North Korea and China, they were doing so from a position which was actually a great intellectual void.

None of this inhibited the neo-conservatives from charging forward into the new, post-Cold-War era. The collapse of the Soviet Union therefore moved new threats to the United States and to its allies, especially Israel, to the top of the neo-conservative agenda. At the same time, it also opened up new opportunities for the exercise of U.S. power—indeed U.S. hegemony—since there was now no counterpart superpower to check and contain the United States, and these new opportunities moved to the center of the neo-conservative worldview.

The special interest of the neo-conservatives in the security of Israel helped to shape their developing conceptions about international politics, foreign policy, and military strategy in the new era. Since Israel saw Iraq, Iran, and Syria as the major threats to its security, the neo-conservatives did also, and this led them to advocate regime change for these rogue states. Moreover, because of its peculiar and vulnerable military position in the Middle East geography, Israel since 1948 had almost always adhered to a strategy of pre-emption. This led the neo-conservatives to favor pre-emption too, not only as a strategy for Israel, but for any realistic state, particularly the United States. Finally because of its peculiar and isolated diplomatic position in international organizations and in international law, Israel since 1967 had almost always adhered to a policy of unilateralism. This led the neo-conservatives to favor unilateralism too, not only as a policy for Israel, but for any realistic state, particularly the United States. More particularly, since the United Nations and European countries, including the European Union, often took positions critical of Israel, the neo-conservatives began to take positions which were critical of the U.N. and the E.U., and many specific European countries as well. By the late 1990s, the neo-conservatives had developed an animus toward Europe which was probably more intense than that of any other major political group within the United States.

The Neo-Conservatives and Their Allies in the Bush Administration

As we have described the neo-conservatives thus far, it would seem unlikely that, by themselves, they could effect a major change in U.S. foreign policy, especially to bring about an actual war. After all, they were merely committed intellectuals rather than experienced executives. And even as intellectuals they had not, for the most part, held distinguished professorships at major universities (as had such major foreign-policy decision-makers in earlier administrations as McGeorge Bundy, Walt Rostow, Henry Kissinger, and Zbigniew Brzezinski). Rather, they were resident scholars at Washington think tanks and essayists in elite opinion journals.

Any major U.S. foreign policy, particularly one involving a substantial amount of American lives and money, of blood and treasure, will be the product of a grand coalition of substantial interests (a sort of domestic coalition of the willing), and not the achievement of any one interest by itself. These interests also need to be represented among the top foreign-policy decision-makers within an administration. Normally, these decision-makers include the President himself, his National Security Advisor, the Secretary of State, and the Secretary of Defense.

In the particular case of the administration of George W. Bush, the top decision-makers also included, obviously although oddly, the Vice President, Dick Cheney. And in the particular case of the Iraq War, they also included, again obviously although oddly, the Deputy Secretary of Defense, Paul Wolfowitz.

Of all of these top six foreign-policy decision-makers in the Bush administration, only one—Paul Wolfowitz—was ever identified as an actual neo-conservative. However, two of the others had long-held views which overlapped with those of neo-conservatives and therefore they could form an alliance of mutual interest, a coalition of the willing, with them.[3]

An obvious principal in Iraq decision-making was Secretary of Defense Ronald Rumsfeld. His view of the world can be described as a sort of super-nationalism, a belief in the forceful use—if necessary, unilaterally and pre-emptively—of U.S. military power, particularly that based upon America's overwhelming advantage in high-tech weaponry.

Clearly, this perspective shared much in common with that of the neo-conservatives, and so there was a natural basis for an alliance by Rumsfeld with them. During the 1990s, Rumsfeld cooperated with prominent neo-conservatives, including Paul Wolfowitz, on a number of panels dealing with defense-policy issues, particularly what to do about Iraq. It is not surprising, therefore, that Rumsfeld would be very comfortable in appointing Wolfowitz as his Deputy in the Defense Department. (Wolfowitz, in turn, appointed other neo-conservatives to be his own principal subordinates.)

In addition, however, Rumsfeld's perspective shared much in common with very substantial American corporate interests. His worldview largely corresponds with that of the defense industry, and it can be fairly said that he, for the most part, has represented their interests within the Bush administration.

Another obvious principal in Iraq decision-making was Vice President Dick Cheney. His view of the world was almost identical to that of Rumsfeld with respect to the features mentioned above, and so he too had much in common with the neo-conservatives and could readily make an alliance with them. In the 1990s, Cheney also cooperated with prominent neo-conservatives on a number of panels dealing with defense-policy issues, especially what to do about Iraq. In addition, Cheney had a focused appreciation for the central role of global oil production and distribution within the overall global economy. In particular, he had long focused upon the roles played in global oil by Iraq, Iran, and Saudi Arabia. Cheney's worldview largely corresponded with that of the oil industry, and it can be fairly said that he, for the most part, represented their interests within the Bush administration.

As for two of the other top decision-makers, National Secretary Advisor Condoleezza Rice and Secretary of State Colin Powell, it appears that neither of them was a principal promoter of war against Iraq. Rice largely saw herself as the articulate voice of the President, one who converted his policy preferences into coherent and rational form. Similarly, Powell largely saw himself as the "good soldier" of the President, one who implemented his policy preferences in the best possible way.

Finally, and most importantly, there was President Bush himself. His approach toward Iraq appears to have undergone a major transformation after 9/11. Before then, Bush's general views on U.S. foreign policy seem to have had more in common with those of traditional conservatives, especially "realists" (such as his father and his father's principal foreign-policy advisors, Brent Scowcroft and James Baker), than with those of neo-conservatives especially internationalists who sought "regime change."

However, 9/11 presented the President with a terrible problem and an awesome responsibility. How could terrorist attacks by non-state actors and transnational networks like Al Qaeda be prevented in the future? As the President, with the ultimate responsibility for American security, Bush had to come up with a convincing answer (or at least one convincing to himself). The problem of terrorist attacks was accentuated by the now almost-forgotten anthrax scare of October 2001, which briefly but directly raised the specter of biological weapons (one kind of weapon of mass destruction).

The conventional answers of traditional conservatives or realists to foreign threats had always been a combination of containment and deterrence. This formula had worked very well with adversaries which were states, even if they were superpowers with weapons of mass destruction, because these had specific resources of territory and people which they wanted to preserve and which the United States could creditably threaten. But the formula of containment and deterrence provided no convincing solution to the problem posed by non-state, transnational actors who had no territory or people which they wanted to defend. A state could be deterred, but a non-state actor had to be destroyed. With the new problem conceived in this way, it then seemed only logical that the United States would have to not only pursue particular terrorists but root out the very sources of terrorism, i.e., to "drain the swamp."

The traditional conservatives or realists did have an answer of sorts to this new problem. This was for the United States to work closely with allied states, and especially with their intelligence and security agencies, to root out terrorist networks. For Colin Powell, the top realist in the administration, this answer was satisfactory enough.

Unfortunately, there were a significant number of states where this kind of cooperation was not feasible (especially those notorious rogue states). In order to achieve ultimate U.S. security (and as President, this is what Bush was responsible to achieve), these rogue states themselves would have to be destroyed, i.e., there would have to be regime change. It was this last step that the realists or traditional conservatives were unwilling to take, which meant that they could not provide Bush with a convincing answer to his terrible dilemma.

In contrast, the neo-conservatives already had articulated and available this very answer to the President's problem, along with a legitimating theory and rhetoric about democratization.[4] Given the desperate mentality in the autumn of 2001, it is not surprising that he adopted it. Of course, it was the top neo-conservative in the administration, Paul Wolfowitz, who was most articulate in presenting the regime-change solution and the democratization legitimation. If any-one can be deemed the architect of the Iraq War, it was he, and his own appointees and subordinates in DOD had a big role in implementing (and enforcing) this war policy. However, Donald Rumsfeld and Dick Cheney each had his own reasons—more super-nationalist than literally neo-conservative and based upon their particular corporate experiences—for promoting regime change in Iraq, and perhaps in other rogue states in the Middle East as well.

In summary, Rumsfeld, Wolfowitz, and Cheney can be seen as the principal figures who caused the Iraq War. Rumsfeld and Wolfowitz were each, in his own way, a necessary cause and perhaps Cheney as well, but no one of them by himself was a sufficient cause. The combination of the three, however, comes close to being a sufficient cause, and when President Bush embracing their views is added, the decision-making ensemble is complete and indeed sufficient.

As for the neo-conservatives beyond Wolfowitz, what can be said about their responsibility for the war? First, there were the neo-conservative *officials*. The most prominent of these were associates of Wolfowitz working in or with DOD, e.g., Douglas Feith and Richard Perle. Zealous promoters and implementors of the war policy, they certainly contributed to it, although they were not important enough to have caused it.

Second, and more familiar publicly, there were the neo-conservative intellectuals. The most prominent of these were editors and writers in neo-conservative journals, such as Commentary, The Weekly Standard, and National Review, e.g. Norman Podhoretz, William Kristol, Robert Kagan, and Charles Krauthammer. Also zealous promoters of the war (but not in positions to implement it), they were often arrogant and ruthless in attacking and belittling its critics. They contributed in their own way to the war policy, although they were not important enough to have caused it.

Ideas Have Consequences

Still, neo-conservative intellectuals have always claimed that ideas have consequences. This is one of the reasons that they have been so energetic and ruthless (and, on occasion, vicious) in attacking the ideas (and, on occasion, the persons) of their opponents. This means, however, that the neo-conservatives' own ideas have consequences too. Following their own logic, it must be said that the neo-conservatives' ideas about the necessity and desirability of a war against Iraq did indeed have the consequences of the war against Iraq. As such, the neo-conservative intellectuals, especially those named above, are responsible for these consequences.

The Iraq War Had Consequences Too

The Iraq War, which the neo-conservatives so enthusiastically helped to bring about, has had consequences of its own. Appropriately and justly, this includes consequences for the neo-conservatives themselves.

Each of the three central neo-conservative concepts about U.S. foreign policy and national strategy was invalidated and discredited by the actual course of the Iraq War. First, the strategy of pre-emption required a high degree of accurate intelligence about the actual extent and physical location of a presumed threat to U.S. security. The clear debacle of U.S. intelligence about Saddam Hussein's presumed weapons of mass destruction did much to discredit any U.S. claims about similar threats for years thereafter.

Second, the strategy of unilateralism required a high capacity to achieve U.S. objectives with U.S. military forces alone. The manifestly insufficient number of U.S. troops in Iraq (and even in Afghanistan) for containing and defeating the insurgencies in these countries, and the desperate attempts of the Bush administration to persuade other governments to keep their own troops there, demonstrated the hubris and folly of unilateralism with respect to most U.S. military operations.

Third, the strategy of democratization required that a U.S. project of regime change result in at least the public appearance of steady progress toward a stable democracy in the target country. The clear reality of sectarian conflict—verging upon civil war—in Iraq demonstrated the superficiality and unreality of a U.S. democratization project with respect to most countries with long-standing religious and ethnic cleavages.

The Consequences for the Neo-Conservatives

The climax, the apotheosis, of the neo-conservative vision was probably President George W. Bush's Second Inaugural Address in January 2005. Flushed with his electoral triumph of two months before, he did not recognize that his democratization fantasy had already been fatally wounded by his foolish war in Iraq. From that moment on, it was all downhill for the reputation of the neo-conservatives. Soon, there was hardly a neo-conservative who wanted to be identified as such. It had become an ideological position that dared not speak its name. In that sense, the dénouement of the neo-conservatives of the 1990s, who were principally of a second generation, has a lot in common with the dénouement of the American communists of the 1930s, who also were principally of a second generation. Arrogant and ruthless when a brief political conjuncture (the capitalist crisis of the 1930s; the American unipolar movement of the 1990s) made it appear that the time of their ascendancy had at last arrived, each of these two ideological sects later quietly tried to hide their past errors when their ideas were revealed to be delusions and the political conjuncture had changed.

The neo-conservatives were also busy trying to put the blame for the Iraq debacle on someone else. Their favorite argument was that the goals of the war (i.e., their own goals) were sound, but the execution (i.e., that done by Secretary of Defense Rumsfeld and by the U.S. military commanders) had been incompetent. With respect to Rumsfeld, their accusations were certainly correct, but with respect to the military commanders, their accusations were misleading and dishonest.

The neo-conservatives have lingered on, mostly in their think tanks and in their opinion journals and largely because of institutional inertia. But the world, including the world of ideas and the world of foreign policy making, instead moved on to policies and ideas which were more informed by other ideologies, such as the progressive globalism of the Obama administration. Left behind in the debacle of the Iraq War—and in the dust and the blood—was not only the reputation of the neo-conservatives. There were also the thousands of American soldiers killed and the tens of thousands of American soldiers maimed or wounded. These were the Americans for whom the neo-conservatives' ideas truly had consequences, and for whose dreadful fate the neo-conservatives are also responsible.

Chapter Fourteen

Empire and Immigration

The 1990s-2010s, like the 1890s-1900s, have been an age of empire. A hundred years before, however, there were many empires. They included both the overseas empires of the national states of Western Europe—particularly those of Britain, France, and the Netherlands—and the overland empires of the multinational states of Eastern Europe—those ruled by the Habsburg, Romanoff, and Ottoman dynasties. After the Cold War, there was only one empire—the global empire of the United States, a state which was neither national nor multinational in the traditional meaning, but which instead was more accurately described as multicultural and transnational. This new and strange American empire was the context and the arena in which all the great and global events of the time were taking place.

The decades after the Cold War, like those of a hundred years before, have also been an age of immigration. In the earlier era, however, large numbers of people were leaving the national states and imperial metropoles of Western Europe to emigrate to their colonies or to the United States. At the same time, many people were leaving the rural hinterlands of the multinational states of Eastern Europe to migrate to their metropolitan centers or, again, to the United States. In our era, the direction of imperial migration has largely been the reverse of the Western pattern, while reminiscent of the former Eastern one. Large numbers of people have left the former colonies of the Western European empires to emigrate to their once-imperial metropoles. At the same time, many people have left the dominions of the American empire to emigrate to the United States. In the earlier era, the United States was receiving many immigrants from Europe, but not from its recently-acquired empire in the Caribbean and the Philippines. In our era, the United States has been receiving many immigrants from its long-established empire in Latin America and East Asia, but not from Europe.

The Double Dynamic

The former age of empire reinvented the national states of Western Europe into imperial states, but the imperial metropole remained a national state in the classical meaning. It still made sense to talk of the national interest of Britain, France, or the Netherlands, and it still made sense to talk of international politics. Our own age of empire reinvented the United States into an imperial state. Because of the impact of imperial immigration, however, the United States is no longer a national state in the classical sense, or even in the traditional American sense as understood during much of the 20th century. The conjunction of American empire—America expanding into the world—and American immigration—the world coming into America—has made the very idea of the American national interest problematic. There seems to be a causal connection between empire and immigration, so that the two have come together as a dynamic duo to utterly transform our world. Empire and immigration have reinvented and perhaps even displaced the traditional ideas of national interest and international politics with the new ideas of transnational interests and global politics.

Empire and immigration could be interesting enough topics for professional analysts of American foreign policy and international (or global) politics, but to others they could seem to be matters that are rather theoretical and abstract. However, these two features of the early 21st century soon intersected with a third, which was the first war of the 21st century. This was the war between the United States and Islamist terrorists. It has often been observed that Al Qaeda, ISIS, and transnational networks of Islamist terrorists with global reach are another version, the dark side, of the globalization which the United States has so vigorously promoted and which has been a central feature of the American empire. And, of course, central components in these transnational terrorist networks are some of the Muslim immigrants who are residing within Europe and the United States. The World Trade Center and the Pentagon were the most pronounced symbols of, respectively, the economic power and the military power of the American empire. The attacks upon them were planned and prepared by Muslim immigrants within Europe and the United States. The continuing threat of new terrorist attacks emanating from Muslim immigrants has pushed the issue of immigration to the top of the agenda of what was once called "national security" but what now may be more accurately seen as imperial security.

European and American Versions of Empire

At first glance, it would seem that the European experience with empire and immigration has little relevance to Americans. For one thing, the Europeans explicitly and officially referred to their imperial systems with the term "empire," and they referred to subordinate territories with terms such as "colonies" and "dependencies." In contrast, Americans have rarely used these terms when they have referred to their own imperial relationships. The closest American counterparts to European-style colonies and dependencies were the territories that the United States acquired after its victory in the Spanish-American War, particularly the Philippines and Puerto Rico. However, each of these countries was soon designated to be a "commonwealth," and there was a common understanding that each would eventually become independent if and when it wished to do so. At any rate, these and several smaller formal dependencies of the United States (e.g., American Samoa, Guam, the U.S. Virgin Islands, and the Panama Canal Zone), when taken all together, never amounted to anything as important to America as the formal dependencies of the European empires were to the metropolitan nations in Europe itself.

A narrow focus upon explicit and official dependencies alone would be misleading, however. Some European empires included vast areas in which the imperial rule was informal or indirect. Local leaders could even be given the title of king, prince, sultan, or sheik, and retain some of the elements of sovereignty. This was the case with much of the British empire (e.g., the Indian princely states, the Federated Malay States, and the sheikdoms of the Persian Gulf) and even the French empire (e.g., Morocco, Tunisia, Laos, Cambodia, and Annam). These forms of imperial rule were not that much different from the kind of hegemony that the United States exercised at the same time over the countries of the Caribbean and Central America (backed up in the 1910s-1920s by ongoing U.S. military occupations in the Dominican Republic, Haiti, and Nicaragua, and thereafter by the clear potential for further U.S. military intervention).

Beginning in the 1920s, the European nations themselves started to replace the term "empire" with words which connoted more equality between the various territories in the imperial system. This development was partly due to the example and influence of the United States after the First World War. It was also accentuated by the rhetoric of freedom and democracy which the Western Allies used so frequently during the Second World War. In the immediate aftermath of that war, Europeans could reasonably think that there was not that much difference between the three great imperial systems of Britain, France, and the United States—by then officially designated as the British Commonwealth, the French Union, and the Inter-American System.

Of course, each of the European overseas empires soon went through a painful and sometimes violent period of decolonization. The British fought and more or less won wars in Malaya and Kenya, the French fought and lost wars in Indochina and Algeria, and the Dutch did much the same in Indonesia. Surely, it might be said, the United States never experienced anything like this violent decolonization, which might seem to be proof that it never really had colonies to begin with. From a European perspective, however, the long series of abortive Marxist governments or movements in the Caribbean and Central America (Guatemala 1944-54, Dominican Republic 1965, Nicaragua 1978-1990, Grenada 1978-1983, and El Salvador 1980-1992) represented attempts of local populations to achieve decolonization. These efforts failed because American power (and military intervention) was still overwhelming, whereas European power had been drastically weakened during the Second World War. Furthermore, the Castro revolution in Cuba represented a successful (if eventually pyrrhic) effort at decolonization.

The American experience with empire in the 20th century, thus, did have much in common with the European one. Americans today, however, will argue that their global role—and rule—in the 21st century is something new and unique. They say if there is now any American empire, it is one defined by the "soft power" of information networks and popular culture rather than by the hard power of economic exploitation and military force. It is an empire representative of the information age, rather than the industrial age. Whatever they may think about their empire, however, Americans should not be surprised if Europeans and almost all other peoples around the world persist in perceiving an American empire to be very similar to the earlier empires in their own historical experience.

The contemporary American experience with immigration also has much in common with the European one. For both the United States and for several European states, the vast immigration of the last several decades has been closely connected with the nature of their empires.

Post-Imperial Immigration into Europe

Decolonization was not the last chapter in the long narrative of the European empires. A new chapter has been written since the 1960s by the massive migration of formerly-colonial peoples into the European metropoles. Thus, Britain has received immigrants especially from India, Pakistan, and what had been the British West Indies; France especially from Algeria, Morocco, Tunisia, and what had been French West Africa; the Netherlands from Indonesia and Suriname; and Belgium from what had been the Belgian Congo. For the most part, large-scale immigration from the colonies into the metropole commenced about the same time that decolonization was occurring or not long after. It has continued until the present day; post-imperial immigration thus has been underway for more than five decades.

What explains this massive and prolonged immigration from the successor states of the European empires into the European metropoles? Why has it occurred after the empires came to an end rather than at some earlier time? The answers to these questions seem to lie principally within the metropoles themselves.

Some historians of Europe have seen the period 1914-1945 to be another Thirty Years' War. It certainly was a period of successive great catastrophes—the First World War, the Communist revolutions in Russia and in parts of Central Europe, the Great Depression, the Nazi and Fascist dictatorships, the Second World War, the Holocaust, and the omnipresence of class conflict throughout the period. After 1945, it was natural that creative and constructive political leaders were determined to remove the causes of these catastrophes so that they would never happen again.

Fifty years later, we can see that these political leaders succeeded. To remove the causes of the two world wars, the Nazi and Fascist dictatorships, and the Holocaust, they promoted supra-national and European institutions and also post-nationalist and post-racist ideologies. The most recent and most pronounced versions of these ideologies are multiculturalism and universal human rights. To remove the causes of the Great Depression, they promoted the managed economy and European economic integration. To remove the causes of class conflict and communist revolutions, they promoted the welfare state and the rise of the working class into a middle-class lifestyle. Together, these great and successful projects to remove the causes of the great catastrophes of the first half of the 20th century represent the finest achievements of European civilization in the second half of that century.

Who Will Do the Dirty Work?

The last of these great achievements of European nations—that all their citizens were entitled to a middle-class lifestyle—had embedded within it an intrinsic flaw: there would no longer be anyone to do the decidedly non-middle-class work that has been necessary in any modern economy—the dirty (and sometimes dangerous or degrading) jobs in the farms, the factories, the streets, the hospitals, and even the middle-class homes and gardens. The dirty little secret of the modern European (and not only European) nations is that none of their citizens want to do the dirty work.

Thus, as soon as the welfare state and middle-class expectations were fully established for the citizens of the European nations (by the early 1960s in many of them), there developed a need for workers who were not citizens, i.e., immigrants or "guest workers" (the term invented at the time). One obvious place where European nations could find these immigrant workers was in the countries to their south—e.g., Algeria for France and Turkey for West Germany. (At the same time, Mexico and Puerto Rico were performing a similar role for the United States.) More generally, however, the obvious place to find immigrant workers was among the colonies or other dependent territories of the nation's empire. The colonial peoples had already been doing a good deal of the dirty work of the empire for several generations—in the plantations, factories, streets, homes, and gardens of the colonies. This included working to maintain the European civil officials, military officers, and other emigrants to the colonies in a comfortable middle-class lifestyle. It was natural, then, that as the working-class citizens of European nations ascended into some version of middle-class life (or at least middle-class pretensions) that their necessary and essential working-class functions were filled by working-class immigrants from the colonies. Colonial workers not only knew how to work, they also were more likely than non-colonial peoples to know the distinctive national language, codes, and rules of the citizens within the metropole.

Who Will Be the Europeans?

The sociological phenomenon of the ascending working class was reinforced by the demographic phenomenon of the descending birth rate. The 1960s saw the end of the post-war baby boom and its replacement with a baby dearth, which has continued to the present day. Demographers observe that, in order for a particular population to sustain its numbers at its current level, it should have an average reproduction rate of 2.1 births per woman. The reproduction rate for every European nation has fallen below 1.5 during the last couple of decades. When one projects these demographic statistics forward, it would appear inevitable that, in half a century, most European nations (or, more precisely, European-descended peoples) will have less than two-thirds the population they have today. Furthermore, a much larger percentage of that population will be old and no longer able to work than is the case today. The only peoples in Europe whose birth rates are high enough to sustain or increase their populations are the communities composed of immigrants from the former imperial territories.

As it happens, the largest of these immigrant communities are Muslim. These Muslim communities already form 5-10 percent of the population of some European countries, and that percentage is steadily increasing. They now perform functions essential to the economic system, and they are poised to make a significant impact on the political system as well, becoming a force in democratic elections, multiparty politics, and coalition governments.

One might have expected that the European nations might have developed a strong resistance to admitting immigrants—particularly Muslim immigrants—whose culture was obviously very different from their own traditional national or European ones. However, this potential resistance was aborted by one of the other achievements of the European political leadership in its successful efforts to remove the causes of the great catastrophes of the twentieth century—the development of post-nationalist, post-racist, and multicultural ideologies. In doing so, however, they may have prepared the conditions for a different kind of great conflict in the 21st century.

Muslim Immigrants in Europe and America

The specter of Islamic terrorism which now haunts the West has focused attention upon Muslim immigrants into Western countries. These immigrants form communities which have long been hostile to the culture—be it seen as either Christian or as secular—of the host countries, and they now pose serious problems for domestic security. Muslim immigrants thus have an anomalous position in both Europe and America. The particular nature of the anomaly is different, however, in the two regions of the West.

For Muslim countries have not been long-established parts of the American empire, in contrast to Europe. Even such putative allies as Saudi Arabia and Jordan have often engaged in independent, unfriendly, and distinctly un-colonial behavior toward the United States. Accordingly, Muslim immigrant communities comprise only a small part (about one percent) of the population of the United States. Consequently, American political leaders do not have to take Muslim political demands into account, although some progressive ones will do so for ideological reasons.

The Two Nations of Europe

The most important division created by Muslim immigrants, however, will not be between Europe and America, but within the European states themselves. In the next couple of decades, the prospects are for several European states, particularly the once-imperial ones, to become two nations. The first will be the European nation, descended from the European and imperial peoples; it will be secular, rich, old, and feeble. The second will be the anti-European nation, descended from the non-European and colonial peoples; it will be Islamic, poor, young, and virile. It will be a kind of overseas colony of a foreign nation (an obviously familiar occurrence in European history, but this time the foreign nation will be the *umma* of Islam, and the colonized country will be Europe itself), and it will form the beginnings of a kind of settler state. The two nations will regard each other with mutual contempt, but in the new anti-European nation there will be a growing rage, and in the old European nation there will be a growing fear. They will provide the perfect conditions for endemic Islamic terrorism, or at least for a terrified once-imperial people.

At the same time that some European states are becoming two nations, they are becoming subordinate states within the European Union, conforming to economic policies which are made by the European Commission in Brussels and to monetary policies which are made by the European Central Bank in Frankfurt. They have also become subordinate dominions within the American empire (or perhaps within an American commonwealth of nations), conforming to military policies which are implemented through NATO in Brussels but which are actually made in Washington. In short, post-imperial immigration has resulted in European states which are becoming bi-national, while quasi-imperial subordination has resulted in European states which are becoming post-national or even sub-national. It is a long way from where European nations and national consciousness were two centuries ago, in the immediate aftermath of the French Revolution and at the beginning of the Industrial Revolution.

The European metropoles began their imperial narratives as nation states. The creators and exemplars of the nation state were Britain and France, and the creators and exemplars of the overseas empires of the industrial age were the British Empire and the French Empire. In the first half of the twentieth century and at the high point of the modern and industrial age, these were respectively the largest and second-largest overseas empires in the world.

At the beginning of the 21st century, however, the long imperial narratives of Britain and France have reached the point that, in many ways, they are no longer nations at all. For about a century (i.e., from about the 1830s to the 1940s) the imperial narrative seemed to provide the latest chapters, indeed the fulfillment, of the much longer national narrative, and for both Britain and France this was a narrative that reached back more than a thousand years. The British Empire and the French Empire, each in their own way, seemed to be the consummation of the longest and grandest historical dramas since that of the Roman Empire. Now, however, a half-century after the end of these two empires, it seems that empire, in particular immigration from the empire into its metropole and heartland, may have actually brought about the end of the British and the French national narratives.

This melancholy tale of empire, immigration, and national disintegration may not merely be a history that is relevant only to Europe. Perhaps it provides a warning, or a prophesy, for America as well.

Pre-Imperial Immigration into America

The American immigration of our time does seem to have some similarities with the massive immigration of the 1890s-1910s. In particular, some observers see Latin-American immigrants replicating the earlier path of Italian immigrants and Asian immigrants replicating the earlier path of East European Jews. In the early 20th century, there was widespread concern that immigrants from Southern and Eastern Europe could not be assimilated into the American way of life. By the 1960s, however, these groups were largely integrated into American society. By analogy, one might expect Latin American and Asian immigrants to be largely integrated within a few decades.

However, it is also useful to recall important differences between the circumstances of immigration a century ago and those today. First, the United States was then a self-conscious and self-confident national state. The American political class and the federal and state governments promulgated what was known as "the American Creed," and they vigorously promoted what was known as the Americanization program, i.e., assimilation of immigrants into "the melting pot." Second, the growing industrial economy of the time enabled immigrants to gain a step on the ladder of upward social mobility (and also outward geographical mobility and dispersion). Third, the restrictive Immigration Act of 1924 sharply curtailed immigration for a period of four decades until the very different and unrestrictive Immigration Act of 1965. This converted immigrant communities from the turbulent streams of the 1890s-1910s into the settled masses of the 1920s-1950s, upon which the Americanization program could steadily and relentlessly work its way. Fourth, almost none of the immigrants came from areas which were in the American empire of the time (i.e., from Latin America or the Philippines). This meant that they did not bring with them the resentments and grievances of colonized populations. On the contrary, many immigrants were fleeing the foreign empires of Eastern Europe.

Even with these four factors favorable to assimilation, however, some immigrants brought with them particular ideologies prevalent in the lands that they had left behind (e.g., Anarchism among some Italians, Marxism among some Jews). For a few immigrants, these ideologies legitimated their sense of separation from and opposition to the dominant American culture of liberal democracy, the free market, and competitive individualism. This produced a few obstacles on the road to assimilation (e.g., the "Red Scare" of 1919-1920 and the deportation of some Anarchists and Marxists; the activities of the Communist Party in the 1930s-1940s; McCarthyism in the 1950s).

These four factors favorable to assimilation have been largely absent during the contemporary era of American immigration. In particular, the reigning ideology of multiculturalism has placed far greater obstacles on the road to assimilation than Anarchism and Marxism ever did.

Imperial Immigration into America

The contemporary era of immigration into America began with the Immigration Act of 1965, which radically eliminated previous restrictions on immigration from non-European regions (and in effect also radically increased restrictions on immigration from Europe). We have been living under this new and very different immigration regime for more than five decades.

In contrast to the earlier American experience with immigration, in the contemporary era most immigrants to the United States have come from the various regions of the American empire. By far the largest number have come from the oldest domains of the empire, i.e., those countries that fell under the hegemony of the United States as a result of its wars with Mexico (1846-1848) and with Spain (1898): Mexico, Puerto Rico, the Dominican Republic, Haiti, Central America, and the Philippines. In addition, many immigrants have come from countries within the empire which America established in the Western Pacific after the Second World War or, more exactly, after the Korean War, particularly from South Korea and Taiwan and also from the abortive domain of Indochina.

With respect to immigration coming principally from the territories of one's own empire, the contemporary American experience has been similar to the contemporary European one. However, whereas in Europe the great surge in immigration has come in the post-imperial era, in the United States it has come in the high-imperial era, at a time when the American empire has been in its ascendancy. In the past five decades or so, there have been powerful factors common to both Europe and America which have generated the need for immigrants.

As it happens, the United States has been characterized by its own version of the sociological, demographic, and ideological factors which we have described for Europe: the ascent of working-class American citizens into a middle-class lifestyle or at least into middle-class pretensions; the decline in the reproduction rate of the European-descended majority; and the establishment of a post-national, multicultural ideology. This has resulted in the same kind of structural demand for immigrant workers in the United States as in Europe. Once the structure of demand has been established in the imperial center, the imperial territories become the most practical source of supply for reasons that are similar in both Europe and America.

There were also some distinctive aspects about the U.S. relationship with its domains in the Western Pacific which shaped U.S. immigration policy. In the early 1960s, South Korea and Taiwan were on the front lines of the Cold War, and they were also suffering from poor and distressed economic conditions. They pushed hard for the abolition of U.S. restrictions on their immigrants, and given their central importance in the Cold-War conflict, U.S. policymakers had to comply. This was one major fact in bringing about the new openness embodied in the Immigration Act of 1965.

However, the largest immigrant communities in the United States are Latin American in their origin. Latino-Americans now compose the largest minority in the United States, having recently surpassed African-Americans in numbers. Latino immigrants obviously already perform functions essential to the American economic system, and Latino-Americans are steadily acquiring political power, including a kind of veto power on many issues where they have a concern.

Two Nations or Amerexico?

Is it possible that imperial immigration might cause the United States to become two nations, as is now the prospect for some European countries? The first nation could be the Anglo nation, descended from European peoples; as in Europe, much of this nation would be secular, rich, old, and feeble. The second nation could be a Latino nation, descended from Latin-American peoples; much of it would be religious, particularly Christian (evangelical and Pentecostal Protestant, as well as Roman Catholic), poor, young, and robust. These two nations would regard each other with mutual suspicion and, in a few aspects, with contempt. It is probably too much to predict that in the Anglo nation there will be a widespread fear of some kind of Latino terrorism, although young Latinos in the United States may learn something from their Islamic counterparts in Europe. However, it is certainly likely that there will be a widespread perception and therefore fear of Latino crime. The gated communities of Anglos, which are already widespread in the southwestern United States, are likely to become an even more central part of the Anglo way of life, the distinctive architectural style and urban design of the Anglo nation.

Still, Latino-American culture is probably closer to Anglo-American culture than Muslim culture is to European culture, if only because the two American cultures share a common origin in the Christian religion. This may retard the development of the two distinct nations within the United States. More likely, perhaps already happening, is the development in the Southwest of something that is a blend of American and Mexican features, a sort of "Amerexico."[1] This is a society whose upper or capital-owning class is Anglo-American, whose professional and middle classes are largely Anglo-American but partly Mexican-American, and whose working and lower classes—those that do the dirty work—are Mexican-American. It is characterized by a racial division of labor, a rough correlation between class and color. As such, it has important similarities to the colonial societies of the European empires, which were also characterized by a racial or ethnic division of labor. Indeed, as the ratio of Mexican-Americans to Anglo-Americans increases, Amerexico will more and more resemble something like Northern Ireland in the United Kingdom, or perhaps even all of Ireland as it was in the British Empire. If so, the United States would have become not only an empire abroad, but also one at home.

Empire and Emigration

Essential to every empire is an imperial class—the civil officials, military officers, and business managers who go forth from the empire's metropole to its dominions and colonies and who carry out its policies and practices. In other words, it is inherent in an empire that there be people who will be imperial emigrants. Imperial emigrants are even more necessary to an empire than are the imperial immigrants that have been the focus of our attention.

Who will comprise the imperial emigrants, the imperial class, of the American empire? Here it is useful to distinguish between the three different components—civil, military, and business—of an imperial class.

The military services of the United States have had more than 70 years of experience of peacetime service overseas, especially in Germany, Japan, and South Korea but also elsewhere. More than any other American institutions, the military services know how and why to serve. They are the true heirs to the legendary civil officials, and not just the dedicated military officers, of the British Empire. Moreover, America does not seem to lack business entrepreneurs, managers, and professionals who are willing to go overseas, especially to those countries which are long-established (and more predictable) realms of the American empire, particularly Latin America, Western and now Eastern Europe, and East Asia. These American businesspeople are the counterparts to the merchants, managers, and engineers of the British Empire.

The problem, perhaps the void, in the American imperial class lies in the civil officials. There is no obvious equivalent of the Indian Civil Service or the Colonial Civil Service of the British Empire, that distinguished cadre of graduates from Oxford and Cambridge who went out to serve for long and hard years as district officers in the remote regions of the empire. The graduates of the best American universities are "organization kids," who are intent upon having a successful career within America itself.[2] In any event, the U.S. State Department (and even the Central Intelligence Agency) can hardly be compared to the civil services of the British Empire, either in regard to effectiveness or to morale.

The real civil servants of the American empire are not American in their physical origin.

They are, however, American in their intellectual apparatus. They are the foreign students who come to American universities and who learn American principles and practices. In particular, they are the economics majors and business-school students who come to believe in the free market, and the political-science majors and law-school students who come to believe in liberal democracy and the rule of law. When (and if) they return to their home countries, they will know both the culture and customs of their own society and the principles and practices of American society. These foreign students are both imperial immigrants—when they arrive in America for their studies—and imperial emigrants—when they return home for their careers.

From the perspective of the American empire, these imperial immigrants-emigrants—local in their outer appearance, American in their inner attitudes—are the perfect candidates for political and economic leadership in the empire's domains. And, indeed, a significant number of current officials in Latin America, Western and Eastern Europe, and East Asia are graduates of American universities, and an even larger cadre of graduates is now entering into official careers. The ability of the American empire to govern its domains will depend upon its success in producing this distinct kind of immigrant-emigrant to serve as its distinct kind of imperial civil official. In the empires of the past, the metropole served as the mind, and the colonies served as the body. The American empire is attempting to solve the imperial mind-body problem in a new way. In a sense, it seeks to perform a series of brain-transplants, to put an imperial mind into a colonial body.

The earlier European empires—the empires of the industrial age—also made some effort to educate and enculturate the best and the brightest from the colonies in the principles and practices of the empire. These efforts were successful in important ways (for example, they resulted in some exceptionally creative works of literature), but in the end they could not prevent—indeed they helped to cause—the rise of colonial nationalism and the demise of the empire. The American empire—the empire of the information age—is based even more upon ideas than the empires of the past. They are, in the formulation of Michael Mandelbaum "the ideas that conquered the world—peace, democracy, and free markets."[3] In essence, these are the same ideals that Thomas Jefferson wrote into the birth certificate of the United States, the Declaration of Independence—"life, liberty, and the pursuit of happiness." As long as the American empire appears to be providing some semblance of life, liberty, and the pursuit of happiness to the peoples of its vast realm, it has a good chance of thriving.

If, however, the American empire fails to prevent a series of wars, or a new round of dictatorships, or a global economic depression, then its ideas clearly would no longer be in control of the world, and its particular and peculiar imperial civil service would no longer be in control of the empire's domains. The empire would then come to an end, like all the European empires before it. But there would still be one massive legacy left from the imperial age. That would be the vast population of imperial immigrants within the once-imperial and now-diminished metropole, the territory of the United States, itself.

PART IV

POLITICAL ECONOMY

CHAPTER FIFTEEN

BETWEEN AMERICA AND THE WORLD:
THE NEW YORK FOREIGN POLICY ELITE

A CENTRAL FEATURE OF the contemporary global era has been the rise of "global cities." Now about two dozen in number and forming a great archipelago around the Northern Hemisphere, these great megalopolises are the dynamic drivers of the global economy. Of these two dozen global cities, two in particular stand out: one, London, is the megalopolis of what was the first global empire, the British, and the other, New York, is the megalopolis of what has been the second, the American. Together, these two great global cities have been the two great superpowers of the global system and the global era. But of these two super-global cities, one has been the very capital of the global system and era; this has been New York.

New York as the Capital of the American Century

This predominance of New York in the world and in an era is, of course, not something new. In the early 1990s, New York was sometimes described as being "the capital of the American Century," just as that century reached its apotheosis with America's victory in the Cold War.[1]

This description echoed the great cultural historian, Walter Benjamin, who had famously described Paris as having been "the capital of the 19th century." The American Century had begun in the 1940s. Henry Luce proclaimed its coming in 1941, but the actual birthdate of the American Century was in 1945, on the occasion of America's victory in the Second World War. And as we shall see in this chapter, the actual birthplace of the American Century was New York.

The attending physicians at this birth were from what was long known as the "New York foreign policy elite." It was this elite which in the 1940s brought forth such men as Averell Harriman, Robert Lovett, Dean Acheson, John McCloy, and George Kennan, who were "present at the creation" of the liberal international order and who were the founding fathers of the American Century. But there has actually been a New York foreign policy elite ever since the founding of the United States itself, at the end of the 18th century. This role of this elite has waxed and waned in the course of U.S. history, according to a pattern that we shall discuss. But its time of greatest consequence was the first six decades of the American Century, i.e., the period from the end of the Second World War to the end of the Cold War, and that is the period that we will mainly focus upon in this chapter.

The best perspective from which to view the waxing and waning fortunes of the New York foreign policy elite is to view the shifting relations between New York's and America's interests in the rest of the world. In geographic terms, these American interests can be conceived of as the four major regions or sections of the United States, i.e., New York and its hinterland, the Midwest, the South, and the West. In economic terms, these American interests can be conceived of as the four, and more recently the five major sectors of the American economy. Historically, these sectors were finance, industry, and agriculture; after the Second World War these three were joined by defense, or what President Eisenhower termed the "military-industrial complex," and after the Cold War, these four were joined by information technology, or what is often termed "Silicon Valley."

Each of these geographic sections and economic sectors has had its own interests in regard to the rest of the world, its own foreign policy. When the interests of New York (and in particular of finance) have been compatible with those of the other sections and sectors, the New York foreign policy elite has ascended and assumed leadership of the foreign policy of the nation. But when the interests of New York (and of finance) have diverged from those of other sections and sectors, the New York foreign policy elite has lost that leadership.

The Origins of the New York Foreign Policy Elite:
New York as the Broker between America and Europe

For more than three centuries, New York has been a place lying somewhat between Europe and America. The New York foreign policy elite originated in the role that New York played as the broker between these two worlds.

New York versus America. For the first century of the United States, New York was viewed by most of the rest of the country as, well, un-American. During the American Revolution, New York was the most pro-British city in the colonies. During the Civil War, New York was the most anti-war city in the Union. (At the very moment, July 1863, of the great Union victories of Gettysburg in the East and Vicksburg in the West, the largest anti-draft riots in American history erupted in New York.) During the populist era, New York was seen as the ally of British finance. And at the end of the 19th century, New York had the largest concentration of foreign-born (and foreign-language) inhabitants in the nation. For many Americans, New York was part of the foreign problem, not part of the American solution.

New York vis-à-vis Europe. Indeed, by the turn of the century, the most distinguished New Yorkers (i.e., the new financial elite, exemplified by J.P. Morgan) thought of New York as almost part of Europe. They formed an urban and urbane patriciate, whose standards of excellence and elegance were set in Europe and especially in England. The material foundation of this patriciate was the close ties between the new financial elite of New York and the older one of the City of London, the former being a sort of junior partner of the latter. But around this financial connection there developed English-like social and cultural institutions and a transatlantic worldview. This worldview was memorialized in the architecture of the day, and it can still be seen in the New York townhouses, the Hudson River country estates (such as Franklin Roosevelt's Hyde Park), and the neo-gothic Episcopal churches of the region, which are all variations on an English theme. But the most consequential embodiment of the transatlantic worldview was probably the preparatory schools (whose exemplar was Groton), where the New York patriciate educated its young and which were modeled on the English public schools. It was here, from about 1890 to 1914, that the future foreign policy elite of the 1940s was formed.[2] Thus, the architects of the American Century were molded within the most English of American institutions.

Free trade versus protectionism. Although many Americans considered New York to be part of the foreign problem rather than part of the American solution, there had always been exceptions. In particular, the commercial and financial elites of New York provided crucial services to the agricultural elites of the South in support of Southern trade with England, both before and after the Civil War. This economic coalition between New York finance and Southern agriculture provided a continuing base for the Democratic Party and its policy of free trade. It was opposed, of course, by another great economic combine, the industry of New England, Pennsylvania, and the Midwest, which provided the base for the Republican Party and its policy of protectionism.

From the First World War to the Great Depression: New York, Internationalism, and Isolationism

This contest between the free trade and the protectionist coalitions was accentuated by the First World War. The United States became a creditor nation in 1914, and New York banks loaned vast sums to the allies, especially Britain, during the war. When the war was over, the only way the allies could pay their debts to the New York banks was to export their industrial goods to American markets. This put European industry and American banks in direct conflict with American industry. The New York free-traders and internationalists lost the first round of this conflict, the fight over ratifications by the U.S. Senate of the Versailles Treaty and the League of Nations. The Senate rejected the Treaty and the League in March 1920.

New York and the Council on Foreign Relations. In response to this defeat and in order to organize better for future battles against isolationism and protectionism, New York internationalists founded the Council on Foreign Relations in 1921. The origins of the Council lay in the many meetings which had been held between the staffs of the American and the British delegations at the Paris peace conference in 1919. Having discovered that they shared many conceptions and goals about the post-war world, these American and British foreign affairs experts decided to establish permanent organizations within their respective countries, which would be composed of men who were either leaders in international finance and commerce or in the professional study of international affairs. These organizations would continue the mutual communication and cooperation which had developed between the Americans and the British in regard to international issues. In Britain, this became the Royal Institute of International Affairs. In America, it became the Council on Foreign Relations. The necessity for such an American organization became especially clear to New York international businessmen after the defeat of the Treaty and the League in the U.S. Senate and the defeat of the Democrats and free trade in the U.S. presidential election of 1920.[3]

The new Council of Foreign Relations was composed of bankers (e.g., Russell Leffingwell, Norman Davis, and Paul Warburg) and lawyers (e.g., Paul Cravath) in New York, as well as distinguished academics from universities stretched out along the Eastern seaboard, from Harvard (Archibald Cary Coolidge) to Johns Hopkins (Isaiah Bowman). The Council's first president was John W. Davis, a Wall Street lawyer and the Democratic candidate for President of the United States in 1924. But the Council also sought the support of Elihu Root, another Wall Street lawyer who had been Theodore Roosevelt's Secretary of State and was now a Republican elder statesman. It arranged for the new Woodrow Wilson Foundation to give Root a $25,000 award for his contributions to international cooperation, which he in turn would give to the Council to fund its new journal, Foreign Affairs.[4] Thus, from its beginning, the Council sought to construct a bipartisan coalition in support of free trade and internationalism.

New York also provided two of the Republican Secretaries of State in the 1920s, Charles Evans Hughes and Henry L. Stimson; both had been Wall Street lawyers. However, they and the other New York internationalists within the Republican Party could not overcome the heavy weight of protectionist industry, which continued to dominate the party throughout the decade.

Finance versus industry. Although the foreign policy disputes of the 1920s have often been characterized as being between internationalists and isolationists, this is not wholly accurate. The "isolationists" were often ready to support U.S. military interventions in Central America and the Caribbean, as well a more modest gunboat presence in China. They were really only isolationist in regard to Europe.

The pattern of foreign policy differences conformed to the pattern of economic sectors. New York banks were in the business of lending money. Although they were willing to lend to anyone with a good credit rating, it was natural that the most numerous and the biggest borrowers would be found in the most advanced economies of the day, i.e., in Europe (and prospectively Japan); thus the focus of the New York foreign policy elite on Europe. But for the borrowers to be able to repay these loans, they would have to export their goods to the United States; thus the focus of the New York foreign policy elite on free trade.

The perspective of American industrialists was quite different. They were in the business of selling goods. Although they were willing to sell to anyone willing and able to buy, it was natural that the best customers would be found in economies which did not produce these goods themselves. These were the less advanced economies of the day, especially those not bottled up in some European colonial empire, i.e., Latin America and China; thus the willingness of the American industrial elite to support intervention in these countries. As for Europe, however, it represented only hostile competitors in markets which Americans might otherwise have to themselves; thus the focus of the industrial elite on protectionism.

The privatized foreign policy of New York finance. Although the protectionists within the Republican Party made sure that the U.S. government in the 1920s did not engage in internationalist foreign policy toward Europe, this did not prevent New York banks from carrying out such a policy on their own, a sort of privatized foreign policy, which was composed of large-scale American bank loans to European countries, especially to Germany. The New York banks were the creators of the Dawes Plan (1924) and the Young Plan (1929), the most important elements of American relations with Europe in the 1920s. These Plans provided for a grand recycling of funds composed of (1) American bank loans to the German government; (2) German war reparation payments to the British and French governments; and (3) British and French repayments of war debts to American banks.[5]

These loans were a fundamental pillar of the political stability of the Weimar Republic and of the economic stability of Europe in the 1920s. As such, they were in some ways a prototype of the Marshall Plan a generation later. But although the New York bank loans were part of the solution for the European economy, they were part of the problem for American industry.

The consensus foreign policy of finance and industry. There was, however, one part of the world where American finance and industry could agree on an internationalist and interventionist foreign policy by the U.S. government, and that was Latin America. Although the biggest borrowers were found in Europe, New York banks had been engaged in loans to Latin America since the turn of the century, and they saw every reason to continue. On its part, industry saw Latin America as a natural market and not as a competitor. Thus, finance and industry could form a consensus on the Latin American policy of the U.S. government. As such, this was in some ways a prototype of the consensus and bipartisan foreign policy toward both Europe and Latin America a generation later.

Thus the New York foreign policy elite experienced successes as well as failures in its efforts in the 1920s. The Council on Foreign Relations soon became a solid and established organization. In 1929, the Council bought a new building at 45 East 65th Street to house its expanding operations. (It happened to be next door to the New York townhouse of Franklin Roosevelt.)[6]

The world economy between Britain and America. The international economic order of the 1920s, however, was an unstable equilibrium. Charles Kindleberger, a leading economic historian, has famously argued that the decade was a period in which there was no longer an economic hegemon, i.e., one great economic power which brings order to the world economy.[7] In Kindleberger's conception, a stable world economy requires an economic hegemon which performs three functions and therefore assumes three burdens. The hegemon must provide for other countries (1) a large and open market for their exports; (2) long-term loans for their economic development; and (3) short-term loans or support for the currencies of countries that undergo foreign-exchange crises that can detonate a banking crisis.

Before the First World War, Britain (in particular the City of London) performed these functions and assumed these burdens, and the world economy consequently operated smoothly and grew substantially. The war, however, greatly diminished Britain's economic assets and power. After the war, Britain still had the will, but it no longer had the ability to carry out the functions of an economic hegemon.

Conversely, the First World War greatly increased the economic assets and power of the United States. After the war, the U.S. had the ability, but it did not yet have the will to carry out all of the functions of an economic hegemon. The New York banks, as we have seen, did perform one of these functions to a degree, i.e., long-term lending (such as in the Dawes Plan). But the New York banks had not been able to overcome the opposition of American industry to a second function, opening the American market to foreign industrial goods. And they were not willing to strengthen the Federal Reserve System to the point that it could perform the third function: providing foreign-exchange support in a severe currency and banking crisis.

The world economy of the 1920s thus was suspended between a dying world, that of British hegemony, and a world not yet born, that of American hegemony. The shared conceptions of British and American international elites, of the Royal Institute of International Affairs and the Council on Foreign Relations, could cover over the structural gap between the declining hegemon and the ascending one in a time of economic prosperity. But this cover would be blown away in the gale of a severe economic crisis, and one came with the New York stock market crash of 1929.

New York and the Great Depression. With the stock market crash, a vast amount of American capital suddenly disappeared and was no longer available to provide long-term loans. There was now no one able to perform this hegemonic function. This resulted in the collapse of the great recycling project as (1) American bank loans to Germany dried up; (2) Germany defaulted on its reparation payments to Britain and France; and (3) Britain and France defaulted on their loan payments to American banks. Loans to Latin America also disappeared, and Latin Americans countries also defaulted on their loan payments.

The disappearance of American capital also led to the decrease in domestic demand for American goods, and the disappearance of American loans led foreign nations to maintain their needed foreign exchange by increasing their exports to the United States. American industry was thus faced both with the rapid shrinking of the U.S. market and with foreign producers dumping their goods on that market. This double whammy drove industry to organize and achieve even greater political power than before and to push Congress into enacting the famous Smoot-Hawley tariff of 1930, the most protectionist trade law in U.S. history. The United States was now even less willing to perform a second hegemonic function than before, and other countries joined the U.S. in closing their markets to international trade.

The rapid shrinkage of foreign markets generated a series of foreign-exchange and banking crises, which occurred first in smaller, export-oriented countries but which then spread throughout the world in a chain that reached from Austria in 1931 through Germany, France, and Britain to America in early 1933. But the U.S. Federal Reserve System was not able, and the New York banks were not willing to perform the third hegemonic function, i.e., to provide short-term loans to other banks at the early and still-manageable stage of the crisis.

Together, the stock market crash, loan defaults, and banking crises of 1929-1933 greatly diminished the financial assets and economic power of the New York financial elite; this in turn undermined the political power of the financial elite and of the New York foreign policy elite within it. At the same time, their traditional adversary, American industry, in organizing to enact the Smoot-Hawley Tariff, had enhanced its own political power. By 1932, the New York foreign policy elite was at the nadir of its political fortunes.

New York and the New Deal. With the election of Franklin Roosevelt as President in 1932, however, the old democratic free trade coalition of New York finance and Southern export agriculture returned to power. Roosevelt appointed as his Secretary of State Cordell Hull, a Congressman from Memphis, Tennessee, who had long been active in encouraging cotton exports. Hull's major project became the construction of Reciprocal Trade Agreements. More generally, the program of the New York internationalists began to be adopted as U.S. foreign economic policy. But as long as the Great Depression continued, American industry demanded protection, and progress toward free trade and internationalism was slow and fitful.[8]

Still, New York during the New Deal continued to embody the transatlantic worldview, and in an even more cosmopolitan form than before. New Deal New York was personified in Franklin Roosevelt as President, Herbert Lehman as Governor, and Fiorello LaGuardia as Mayor. These three respectively represented, in ethnic terms, the New York WASP elite, the New York Jewish elite, and the New York ethnic populations.[9] They typified the New York foreign policy elite, the New York financial elite, and the New York labor unions. Presiding over and integrating them all, of course, was "Dr. New Deal," Franklin Roosevelt himself.

At the very end of the Great Depression (and at the very beginning of the Second World War), the cosmopolitan worldview of New Deal New York was celebrated in one of the most splendid public spectacles ever seen in the United States—the New York World's Fair of 1939-1940. The Fair showed what New York offered to America and what, therefore, the New World could offer to the Old. Here could be seen, in an alabaster city gleaming, the New Deal promise of enlightened political leadership, progressive capitalist corporations, and public-spirited labor unions, all united in looking confidently and acting generously toward the rest of the world. It was at the New York World's Fair that one could first actually gaze upon what the (not-yet-named) American Century was supposed to look like, and what the United States would offer to Europe in the Marshall Plan and the liberal international order a decade later. But, of course, before that could occur, everyone at the World's Fair had to pass through the next World War.

From the Second World War to the Cold War: New York, the Grand Coalition, and the American Century

It was the Second World War that at last brought about a grand coalition of the three great sectors of the American economy—finance, industry, and agriculture—and the respective three great sections of American geography—the Northeast (led by New York), the Midwest, and the South. It was a coalition personified in Henry Stimson (the Republican lawyer and statesman from New York) as Secretary of War, Frank Knox (a Republican newspaper publisher from Chicago) as Secretary of the Navy, and Cordell Hull (the Democratic congressman from Memphis) as Secretary of State. Reaching out and integrating them all, of course, was "Dr. Win-the-War," Franklin Roosevelt.

New York and the Second World War. Even during the war, however, there was an echo of the pre-war disputes. This was in the debate over which military theater should receive the focus of the U.S. war effort, i.e., "Europe-first" or "Pacific-first." The former generally was supported by the Democratic Party and also by the New York financial and foreign policy elites. The latter generally was supported by the Republican Party and also by the Midwestern and Western regional elites. Not surprisingly, the actual result during the first two years of the war was to split the war effort into two roughly equal parts: half going to Europe and half to the Pacific. With this, the grand coalition at home was maintained.[10]

Franklin Roosevelt was also the perfect person to maintain another grand alliance, the one with Britain. There was no political leader in America whose personal background had more in common with the British upper class and therefore with the British foreign policy elite than the American President, who was also a New York patrician and "the squire of Hyde Park." And as it happened, Winston Churchill was also the perfect person to maintain the grand alliance with America. There was no political leader in Britain whose personal background had more in common with the American foreign policy elite than the British

Prime Minister, who was not only an architect of the Anglo-American alliance but the child of one (his father was English, and his mother was an American, indeed a New Yorker).

The Council on Foreign Relations immediately recognized that the new world war created both the necessity and the opportunity to correct the errors that the United States had made after the first one. In December 1939, the Council set up its War and Peace Studies project, an ensemble of four working groups to discuss and determine the goals that the United States should seek for the post-war world. The Council groups met frequently and steadily with the staffs of the U.S. Departments of State, War, and the Treasury during the war.

The War and Peace Studies project addressed the problem of post-war international security by recommending the resurrection of Woodrow Wilson's conception of the League of Nations. The project also addressed the problem of the post-war international economy, in particular, the interwar experience of the absence or collapse of the three hegemonic functions of international trade, long-term development loans, and short-term currency support. The Council saw the solution to these three crucial economic needs to be the establishment of three respective international economic organizations that would be under the leadership of the United States and would negotiate agreements, enforce rules, and provide funds to bring about an open, liberal, international economic order.[11]

The extent to which the Council proposals directly influenced U.S. policymakers is a matter of dispute; it is clear, however, that the actual policies which these policymakers pursued and achieved in regard to international security and the international economy were very similar to those proposed by the Council. By 1944, policymakers expected international security to be organized within the United Nations, and the international economy to be organized within the International Trade Organization (ITO) (eventually realized as the General Agreement on Tariffs and Trade, GATT), the International Bank for Reconstruction and Development (the World Bank), and the International Monetary Fund (the IMF).

The War and Peace Studies project brought a great expansion in the staff and the activities of the Council on Foreign Relations, and the pre-eminent role of the United States in the post-war world promised to do the same. Once again, the Council acquired a new building to house its expanding operations, this time at 58 East 68th Street (just off Park Avenue and known as the Harold Pratt House), which it moved into in 1945 and which has remained its New York headquarters until the present day.

New York and the Cold War. It was Europe's physical destruction in the Second World War (far more extensive than in the first one) which actually provided the base for continuing the grand coalition of finance, industry, and agriculture into the post-war, or Cold War, era. After the First World War, European industry had posed an immediate threat to the American markets of American industry. After the Second World War, however, now-shattered European industry itself provided an immediate market for American industry. New York finance and Southern agriculture continued to benefit from a secure and prosperous Europe but now were joined for the first time in this objective by their ancient adversary, Midwestern industry.

The 1940s were the heroic age of the New York foreign policy elite. It was they who created the great institutions that reorganized the post-war chaos into a new liberal world order.[12] This reorganization extended over three arenas.

First, there was the arena of international security. This was addressed first by the creation in 1945 of the United Nations and then, after the U.N. became stalemated by the Soviet-American conflict, by the creation of the Marshall Plan in 1947 and the North Atlantic Treaty Organization (NATO) in 1949. The principal architects of the Marshall Plan and NATO were Dean Acheson and John J. McCloy (lawyers) and Averell Harriman and Robert Lovett (investment bankers).

Second, there was the arena of the international economy. This was addressed by the creation in 1944-1948 of three institutions, one for each of the three crucial economic, and hegemonic, functions— international trade, development loans, and foreign-exchange support. These became respectively the GATT, the World Bank, and the IMF. Together, these comprised the Bretton Woods system, named after the conference which was held between American and British economic experts at Bretton Woods, New Hampshire, in the autumn of 1944 and which laid the foundation for these institutions. The principal architects were Henry Morgenthau, Jr. and again Dean Acheson and John McCloy.

The new international security and economic order, however, had to be supported by a hegemonic power. This led to the third arena, that of the U.S. national government. The New York foreign policy elite institutions which reorganized the U.S. government in 1947 into a national security state that could sustain the new liberal world order—the National Security Council, the Department of Defense, and the Central Intelligence Agency. Here the principal architects were James Forrestal, Ferdinand Eberstadt, and Robert Lovett (investment bankers).

Finally, giving policy direction and moral meaning to all of these new institutions were the new foreign policy of containment and the new strategic concepts to back it up—nuclear deterrence, commitment, and credibility. Here the principal authors were Averell Harriman, George Kennan (a foreign service officer), and Paul Nitze (an investment banker). Apart from Kennan, every one of these architects of the postwar world order was a New Yorker.

New York leadership and regional divisions. These creative innovations abroad and at home, in foreign policy and defense policy, were supported by the grand coalition of New York finance, Midwestern industry, and Southern agriculture. The coalition was personified within the Truman administration by the New Yorkers mentioned above, by President Harry Truman himself (a former senator from Missouri), and by Assistant Secretary of State Will Clayton (a cotton exporter from Mississippi, who continued the Cordell Hull tradition). It was joined by Arthur Vandenberg, who was a Republican Senator from Michigan and who was Chairman of the Senate Foreign Relations Committee in the 80th Congress (1947-1948) On all the creative innovations of the time, the Midwestern and Southern members of the coalition deferred to the leadership of the New York foreign policy elite. This was the great era of "bipartisanship" and "consensus" in foreign policy. This era was to last through the administration of Dwight Eisenhower, who perfectly combined European orientation, New York experience (as former President of Columbia University), and Republican support.

However, just as the "isolationism" of the 1920s-1930s really only applied to Europe, so did the "bipartisanship" and "consensus" of the 1940s-1950s also really only apply to Europe, Latin America, and to that most westernized part of Asia, Japan. It did not apply to the rest of East Asia, particularly China. There, the old division between the New York foreign policy elite and the Midwestern regional elite continued throughout the 1940s and the 1950s. Not surprisingly, the latter bitterly attacked the former for "losing" or even "selling out" China. It was the Midwestern elite who revered that most Asian and Republican of American generals, Douglas MacArthur. And it was the same Midwestern elite, and not some formless and mindless "populist" and "paranoid" mass, which provided that least civil and least progressive of Wisconsin Senators, Joseph McCarthy, with crucial support.[13]

Within the New York foreign policy elite itself, there were particular differences about how to carry out the policy of containment. The figures that we have mentioned all agreed upon the necessity for the United States to protect Europe and Japan (and their prospective hinterlands of the Middle East and South Korea) from the expansion of the Soviet Union and its allies, and they agreed that this protection should be achieved with a combination of nuclear deterrence and conventional forces. But other members of the foreign policy elite sometimes departed from this consensus position.

The author of the containment policy itself, George Kennan, thought that containment should largely be carried out with political and economic means rather than with military ones; he was not in favor, for example, of the creation of NATO. But Kennan was not really a member of the New York elite in the literal sense; he did not have a career in banking or in law but rather was a career foreign service officer. Dean Acheson dismissed Kennan as being woolly-minded, "vague," and "mystical."[14]

Conversely, John Foster Dulles, who was a leading Republican member of the New York elite and was Eisenhower's Secretary of State, thought that containment should be extended beyond Europe and Japan (and the Middle East and South Korea) to protect an arc of countries between them. These included Taiwan, Indochina, and Thailand (e.g., the Republic of China Treaty and the SEATO Treaty). Dulles also thought that containment could be achieved principally with nuclear deterrence (the threat of "massive retaliation") and that conventional forces could be de-emphasized and reduced. But Dulles was really trying to construct a compromise with the Midwestern elites of the Republican Party. As we have seen, these had always been interested in establishing an American position in Asia. But as fiscally-conservative businessmen, they did not want to spend what would be required to maintain large conventional forces abroad year after year. From their perspective, it was much more practical to rely upon nuclear deterrence or "more bang for the buck," as Charles Wilson, Eisenhower's Secretary of Defense and a former chairman of General Motors, put it.

The rise of the West and of Washington. Seen from the perspective of economic sectors and geographic sections, it was only a matter of time until the great achievements of the New York foreign policy elite—the liberal world order and the national security state—would bring into being forces that would undermine the leadership of that elite and the political consensus which it had constructed.

The liberal world order established the conditions for the revival of European and Japanese industry, the expansion of international trade, and therefore the emergence of foreign threats to American industry. This potential materialized in 1961, when the dollar shortage which Europe had experienced in the 1940s and 1950s was replaced with a dollar surplus by the 1960s. Those American industries which had invested in Europe (e.g., automobiles, computers) would remain in the internationalist coalition, but those industries which kept their production in the United States (e.g., textiles in the South, steel in the Midwest) abandoned internationalism and turned toward protectionism. They provided part of the base for Barry Goldwater and the opposition to Nelson Rockefeller in 1964.

The national security state brought about the creation of a fourth great economic center, the aerospace industry and the defense industry more generally, which was largely located in the West. The West, too, would defer to the New York foreign policy elite so long as that elite supported the Cold War. But if détente should become the preferred policy of New York, the West would also look elsewhere for its foreign policy leadership.

The national security state also established the conditions for a great expansion of the importance of Washington. It was natural that around the Defense Department, the State Department, and the Central Intelligence Agency there would be offices of military contractors and centers of foreign policy experts. In the long run, these centers would challenge the leadership of New York's Council on Foreign Relations.

From the Heroic Age to the Academic Age of American Foreign Policy

We have seen that the architects of the American Century were drawn largely from New York itself, particularly from the financial and legal communities of Wall Street or what might be seen as the first and second estates of the New York foreign policy elite. In the heroic age of American foreign policy, the heroes were the rather unlikely figures of bankers and lawyers.

A tale of two cities: New York and Cambridge. With the transition from the 1950s to the 1960s and from the Eisenhower administration to the Kennedy administration, a new era in the history of the American empire and of the New York elite began. Now, for the first time, major foreign policy makers were selected from the third estate of the New York foreign policy elite, the universities (in particular Harvard, MIT, and Columbia). The elevation of the professors coincided with the elevation of the President's National Security Advisor, from being largely a committee rapporteur under Truman and Eisenhower to being a co-equal with the Secretaries of State and Defense and the Director of the CIA under Kennedy and later Presidents. The National Security Advisor was now one of "the awesome foursome" as these four foreign policy officials were called in the 1960s. And he was also one of "the best and the brightest," as the academics appointed to foreign policy positions called themselves in the 1960s.[15]

The first of the professorial and powerful National Security Advisors was McGeorge Bundy (Harvard), followed by Walt Rostow (MIT), Henry Kissinger (Harvard), and Zbigniew Brzezinski (Columbia). Together, they added up to a twenty-year reign (1961-1981) for the professorial regime.

The heroic age of American foreign policy was thus succeeded by its academic age. And given the contrast between the accomplishments of the 1940s-1950s and those of the 1960s-1970s (e.g., the Marshall Plan versus the Alliance for Progress, the Atlantic Alliance versus "flexible response," the Bretton Woods system versus the Great Stagflation, and of course the Korean War versus the Vietnam War) it appears that the golden age of American foreign policy was succeeded by its silver or bronze one. "The brightest," it turned out, were not the best.

The apprenticeship of the academics: Dr. Faustus as a student prince. Although the foreign policy makers of the 1940s-1950s were authentic or at least economic members of the New York foreign policy elite while the National Security Advisors of the 1960s-1970s, were only academic members, three of the latter had undergone an apprentice relationship with an authentic member. These professors, each of whom had a reputation for monumental arrogance with their academic colleagues and their own students, had also each been the dutiful and pliant tutee of someone of great distinction or at least great wealth. McGeorge Bundy had served as the memoir-writer for Henry Stimson; Henry Kissinger as a speechwriter and report-writer for Nelson Rockefeller; and Zbigniew Brzezinski as a research-organizer and report-writer for David Rockefeller. It was as the protégés of lawyers and bankers that these professors reached high office.[16]

The twenty-year regime of the academics, which more or less corresponded to a twenty-year crisis in American foreign policy stretching from the Vietnam War to the Iranian hostage crisis, was finally brought to an end by Ronald Reagan. He was the first President since Warren Harding who appeared to have little connection to or interest in New York at all.

From the Vietnam War to the Great Diffusion:
New York versus the New Foreign Policy Centers

We noted in an earlier section that the very achievements of the New York foreign policy elite in the 1940s, the liberal world order and the national security state, had created the conditions for the foreign policy consensus to be eventually replaced by foreign policy cleavages. As it happened, the growing U.S. military involvement in the Vietnam War at first arrested the emergence of these cleavages.

New York and the Vietnam War. In the early 1960s, the political and economic elites of each of the four great regions supported the Vietnam War, each for their own reasons perhaps, but all believing in the grand concepts formulated by the New York foreign policy elite— containment, deterrence, commitment, and credibility. In July 1965, the most distinguished members of the New York elite, now known as "the wise men," advised Lyndon Johnson to deploy several hundred thousand U.S. combat troops to Vietnam. The leaders in this advice were Lovett, Acheson, and McCloy. In turn, the regional elites gave this Vietnam policy strong support.[17]

The Vietnam War, of course, set in train forces which would break apart the consensus era in American foreign policy and the grand coalition upon which it had been based. For our purposes, a crucial factor was the economic turmoil that soon developed—inflation and balance of payment deficits culminating in early 1968 with runs on the dollar. The war had become a crisis for New York financial institutions. The reasons why the New York foreign policy elite changed its position on the war are many. They include a concern that the war was driving apart the United States and its European allies; that it was producing divisions within the liberal political base of the elite, particularly in the media and in the universities; and that it was diverting the flow of government spending from where it was now needed, i.e., for social programs to put out the fires of urban riots. But the decisive and most urgent reason, the one that "wonderfully concentrated the mind" of the New York elite and the only one that had fully developed by early 1968, was the crisis of the dollar. In March 1968, at a famous meeting with Johnson, the same distinguished "wise men" turned against the war as decisively as they had supported it in July 1965.[18]

It is not surprising that Lyndon Johnson and the regional elites felt betrayed. These other elites each still had good reasons to support the war and indeed to prosecute it with even greater use of American air power. It was the "liberal Eastern Establishment," the same people who had led the way into the war who now stood in the way of winning it. Once again, they seemed to have sold out Asian countries in order to advance their European interests. Never again would the New York foreign policy elite receive the deference that it had received (and earned) from 1940 to 1965.

The new foreign policy centers. As it happened, at this same time (the late 1960s) new centers of foreign policy expertise and influence were being established outside of New York and its Council on Foreign Relations. The first of these, a great expansion of the foreign policy and defense policy staffs of the Brookings Institution in Washington, did not seem very threatening at the time. Nor did a similar expansion of the Carnegie Endowment for International Peace. The ideas and positions of the Brookings Institution and the Carnegie Endowment were virtually identical to those of the Council on Foreign Relations. However, they were in Washington rather than in New York, and they provided the models for other institutions with the same geography as Brookings and Carnegie but with a different ideology.

The expansion of the Brookings Institution and the Carnegie Endowment was followed in the 1970s by a similar expansion of the American Enterprise Institute (AEI) and the Georgetown University Center for Strategic and International Studies (CSIS), both also in Washington. AEI tended to propound views congenial to American industry generally and CSIS views congenial to the defense industry more particularly. Now, in effect both the Midwest and the West had their own centers of foreign policy expertise and influence, and they were in Washington where that influence counted most. Why should the elites of these regions follow the lead of anyone in New York, or indeed pay them any attention at all?

Thus, the Vietnam War dramatized the failure of the New York foreign policy elite, and the new Washington centers (and others, such as the Hoover Institution at Stanford) institutionalized the diffusion of foreign policy expertise.

From Détente to the Second Cold War:
New York versus America Again

The consequences of the Vietnam War and the diffusion of foreign policy expertise were confirmed by the continuing differences between New

York finance and other American economic interests. In each of the great foreign policy issues from the early 1970s to the mid-1980s, the New York foreign policy elite opposed the interests of some regional elite.

The Soviet Union and arms control. The New York international banks were the first major American economic interest to support détente in the early 1970s and the first to support a new détente in the mid-1980s. In the early 1970s the New York banks anticipated that they would benefit from lending to the Soviet Union and its East European allies. At the time, it appeared that the Soviet Union and Eastern Europe would be the area of the next great European boom, comparable to that in Western Europe in the 1950s and 1960s, which had been so profitable to New York international banks and to the multinational corporations which they serviced. In addition, arms control agreements with the Soviet Union (such as SALT I in 1972) would permit a reduction in U.S. defense spending and therefore an easing of the problems of the dollar.

In the case of the second détente, that of the mid-1980s, the importance of these factors was reversed. Few now anticipated that the Soviet bloc would be the site of a great economic boom, but the economic reforms of the Gorbachev era did promise new opportunities for profitable loans and investments for New York banks and corporations, especially for those with subsidiaries in Western Europe. By the mid-1980s, however, the more important consideration was the great concern of New York banks over the U.S. budget deficit. This drove them once again to seek cuts in U.S. defense spending and therefore arms control agreements with the Soviet Union.

The Council on Foreign Relations provided support for these two openings to the Soviet Union. In the early 1970s, it set up the "1980s Project," its largest single policy-research undertaking since the War and Peace Studies project of the early 1940s. Again in the mid-1980s, the Council organized membership meetings and research workshops, and published books and policy analyses on Soviet-American relations and security issues. In both the early 1970s and the mid-1980s, these Council projects made the case for greater cooperation and less confrontation with the Soviets, for arms control agreements, and for a U.S. focus on North-South rather than East-West issues.[19]

In supporting détente with the Soviet Union and a corresponding reduction in defense spending, the New York foreign policy elite of course opposed the interests of the defense industry and of a good part of the elites of the West and the South. These regional elites, in turn, provided the economic support for the new Cold War, which lasted roughly from 1979 to 1985, i.e., the last half of the Carter administration and the first Reagan administration. These Western and Southern elites now took their foreign policy guidance not from the Council on Foreign Relations, but from organizations such as the Georgetown Center for Strategic and International Studies, the Heritage Foundation, and the Hoover Institution.

The Middle East and the Arab-Israeli conflict. New York international banks, along with the major multinational oil companies, were the first major American economic interest to collaborate with OPEC in the early 1970s and to accept Arab positions in the Arab-Israeli conflict. In regard to OPEC, they opposed the interests of energy-intensive heavy industry and a good part of the elites of the Midwest. On the Arab-Israeli conflict, they opposed the interests of many in the Jewish community who had previously accepted their leadership on a variety of issues.

The conflict between the international banks and the multinational oil companies, on the one hand, and the Jewish community, on the other, inflicted a grave wound upon the New York foreign policy elite, for it brought about a schism within that elite itself. The schism was reflected in the enhanced role in foreign policy debates of the journal Commentary, which, although published in New York, took positions directly opposed to those of Foreign Affairs. It was also reflected in the enhanced role of the American-Israel Public Affairs Committee (AIPAC), which was located in Washington.

The collapse of oil prices in the 1980s brought about a decline of Arab economic power and a corresponding decline in the interest of New York international banks in supporting Arab political positions. By now, however, the Jewish community could turn to foreign policy centers and journals that supported their interests much better than the Council on Foreign Relations and Foreign Affairs.

The world market and free trade. As we have seen, the New York international banks and multinational corporations have consistently supported free trade. By the mid-1970s, however, much of the industry located within the United States could no longer compete in the world market. This was the case with the textile industry (principally located in the South) and with the steel and automobile industries (principally located in the Midwest). These industries thus came into conflict with the New York banks and corporations and with the New York foreign policy elite. Some firms in these industries (particularly General Motors and Ford) were themselves multinational corporations, and the interest of their management in free trade did not diverge much from that of New York. But the New York foreign policy elite was now in opposition to the interests, expressed in protectionism, of management in the textile and steel industries and of industrial labor in general. Labor had previously accepted the leadership of the New York elite on many foreign policy issues.

Unlike the defense industry and the Jewish community, protectionist industry and labor never developed their own strong centers and journals to represent their foreign policy positions. This in part explains why they achieved some protectionist measures from Congress, but not a fundamental change in U.S. foreign economic policy, as implemented by any president and his administration.

The creation of the Trilateral Commission. In the early 1970s, the Chairman of the Council on Foreign Relations, David Rockefeller, initiated a two-part change in that organization. The Council, as organizations are wont to do, had gradually expanded its membership over the years; by the early 1970s, with some 1500 members, it was hardly limited to an elite. Given the spirit of the time, the Council was under pressure to admit even more members from a variety of diverse groups, including women and minorities.[20]

The solution to this double bind was simple, but also double. On the one hand, Rockefeller created the Trilateral Commission in 1973, composed only of truly elite figures drawn from the United States, Europe, and Japan. As it happened, the new Trilateral Commission had about the same number of American members (less than 100) as the Council on Foreign Relations had when it was founded as a truly elite organization sixty years before. On the other hand, Rockefeller opened the membership of the Council itself even wider, expanding the number of members to about 2200. In addition, the Council began to engage in public education programs. As such, it began to look and act rather like its long-time, more-public, and less-elite ally, the Foreign Policy Association. It is often the case with organizations, however, that the more numerous are their members, the less weighty is their influence. For this reason alone, the Council on Foreign Relations would have lost a good deal of influence on foreign policy in the 1970s. In any event, it was no longer a very good place to look for a New York foreign policy elite. One could find the elite there, it is true, but it was rather like finding a diamond in the rough.

Nor, as it turned out, could one find a New York foreign policy elite in the Trilateral Commission. Here, one could certainly find a foreign policy elite, but even the American members were drawn as much from the rest of the country as they were from New York. Given the diversity, indeed the conflict, of interests among its American, Western European, and Japanese members and among its American members themselves, the Trilateral Commission was never able to compose the coherent and implementable policies that characterized the New York foreign policy elite from the 1920s to the 1960s.

Finally, in the 1980s, there came changes within the New York financial elite itself, the very core of the New York foreign policy elite. The deregulation policies of the Reagan administration greatly changed the world of New York finance. With all the new innovations and opportunities on Wall Street, the new generation of New York financiers and lawyers was largely uninterested and uninvolved in foreign affairs. As John McCloy remarked in 1982, "they're all too busy making money."[21]

Conclusion: From the New York Foreign Policy Elite to a National/Global Foreign Policy Elite

In brief, the New York foreign policy elite lost first the allegiance of the regional elites of the South and the Midwest in the 1960s, and then that of the regional elite of the West in the 1970s. As a result, it lost the foreign policy leadership of the country. Then, also in the 1970s, the New York foreign policy elite lost the allegiance of the Jewish elite.

But the Jewish elite was important within the politics of New York itself. Thus, the New York foreign policy elite lost the foreign policy leadership of the city. Finally, the New York foreign policy elite lost the allegiance of the younger Wall Street bankers and lawyers in the 1980s. Thus, the New York foreign policy elite lost the leadership of its core constituency.

Yet, by the late 1980s, the foreign policy of the Reagan administration was characterized by cooperation with the Soviet Union, cooperation with Arab governments, and vigorous support of free trade, the same positions which had long been advocated by the New York foreign policy elite. At the very moment that this elite was disappearing, its policies were embraced by that most Californian of administrations. These policies were continued by the George H.W. Bush administration, which was something of a blend of regions (rather like Bush himself, who was from both Connecticut and Texas). It was with these policies that Bush presided over the end of the Cold War, the collapse of the Soviet Union, the proclamation of a "New World Order," and a great leap forward into the new era of globalization.

The explanation for the existence of New York kinds of foreign policies, even with the decline of the New York foreign policy elite, lies in the spread of financial interests and institutions during the 1980s from New York to other regions of America, particularly to Chicago, Atlanta, Miami, and the cities of the West Coast. The financial elite of the United States was no longer identifiable with New York alone, but had become national or at least multi-regional in its location. This provided a new national foundation for a new consensus foreign policy. But with the end of the Cold War, this new foreign policy coalesced around the promotion of globalization. At the very moment that the foundation of U.S. foreign policy became national, its objectives and scope became global. But the most natural locus and focus for influence and expertise directed at that new global foreign policy was, and remains, the national capital, Washington.

Thus, when the elites of the different regions now coalesce around the same foreign policies, they do not do so in New York. Rather, they coalesce in Washington. Indeed, they most probably will convene for drinks and dinner at 1777 F Street, NW, two blocks from the White

House and one block from the Old Executive Office Building. For there, at the center of a circle whose one-mile radius encompasses the Brookings Institution, the Carnegie Endowment, the American Enterprise Institute, and the Center for Strategic and International Studies, can be found the Washington offices of the Council on Foreign Relations.

CHAPTER SIXTEEN

THE FOREIGN POLICY OF PLUTOCRACIES:

A TALE OF TWO COUNTRIES— AND TWO KINDS OF WEALTH

THE UNITED STATES AND indeed the entire Western world have recently been in the midst of their greatest economic crisis in many decades. The Great Recession of the 21st Century was comparable in depth and gravity to the Great Stagflation of the 1970s, and in some ways it was similar even to the Great Depression of the 1930s or to the earlier deep economic crisis of the 1890s, which at its time was also called "The Great Depression." It seems that these really great global economic crises come along about every forty years.[1]

The Contemporary Crisis and a Prior Concept

Given the length and depth of our contemporary crisis, it is not surprising that certain ideas and even terms from those earlier eras should now be making a reappearance in analyses and discussions about public affairs. One of these terms is plutocracy. The concept was originally invented during the great wealth boom, or first Gilded Age, of the 1880s, which culminated in the Great Depression of the 1890s, and it was then reinvented in the next great wealth boom, or second Gilded Age, of the 1920s, which culminated in the next Great Depression of the 1930s. Plutocracy described and depicted the sharp increase in inequality and the massive concentration of wealth and income which had occurred in the United States during those eras. The 1990s-2000s became a third era of such inequality and wealth concentration, and, as it turned out, it culminated in the Great Recession of the 2010s. It is not surprising, then, that the idea of plutocracy has made a comeback.

There has been extensive analysis of both the causes and the consequences of plutocracy, with a particular focus on the consequences for the economy and for democracy. These economic and political consequences are important; they affect us every day in such crucial matters as interest rates, employment opportunities, stock values, and the prospects for meaningful public policies to bring an end to our economic disorders and to restore our economic well-being. However, there has not yet been much discussion of how plutocracy might affect U.S. foreign policy and America's place in world affairs. Such matters may not affect us day-to-day or in the short run, but they will certainly make for big consequences which we may feel in the next few years or in the long run.

It is clear enough that the contemporary global economic crisis has seriously diminished U.S. leadership in the world and that it has weakened the projection of U.S. military power. And of particular importance, China appears to have drawn the conclusion that the economic crisis of America and its allies may be producing a tipping point in the distribution of power and leadership in world affairs.[2] As the Chinese see it, the U.S. economic debacle has clearly discredited the economic model that was the "Washington Consensus." It has also produced extraordinary partisan polarization and policy paralysis in the U.S political system, casting doubts on the American democratic model, and it caused substantial reductions in U.S. defense spending, casting doubt on American military capabilities and credibility. This is at the same time that China itself is expanding and modernizing its military, particularly its navy, and is now steadily pressing its claims of sovereignty—and exclusive and excluding authority—over its three littoral seas—the Yellow Sea, the East China Sea, and the South China Sea.

If plutocracy has had consequences for the U.S. economy and American democracy, is it possible that it also has had consequences for U.S. foreign policy and something to do with the decline of American power and leadership in the world? In this chapter, we will argue that plutocracy has indeed had such consequences, i.e., a plutocratic system has produced a different foreign policy and world role than would have been the case with a more genuinely democratic system. However, it is not plutocracy itself which is the most important factor in determining these outcomes, but rather the particular sectors of the economy which produce the great wealth which is the basis for the plutocracy. As it turns out, it makes a big difference if that wealth is based upon industrial sectors or upon a financial one.[3]

The First American Plutocratic Era (1880s-1890s): The Rising Great Power

The first Gilded Age of the 1870s-1880s certainly produced a plutocracy, and that plutocracy had a good deal to do with producing the Great Depression of the 1890s. However, the 1890s were also the very decade when the United States dramatically and decisively ascended into the status of a great power. The annexation of Hawaii (1893-1898), the successful deterring of Britain in the Venezuelan Crisis (1895), the victory in the Spanish-American War (1898), and the subsequent annexation of the Philippines and dominion over the Caribbean provided impressive evidence for that rise. Thereafter, the United States was taken very seriously by the other great powers of the time—particularly by the greatest power, Great Britain, which then acquiesced to the U.S. having primacy in the Western Hemisphere. If plutocracy is so bad for America, how could it have presided over this extraordinary rise in American power and influence?

The American plutocracy of the 1890s resulted from the recent and rapid development of a massive American industrial structure. This structure in turn was dominated by such industrial sectors as coal, steel, railroads, and oil. These new industries generated great wealth, and by the 1880s they had been organized into great cartels and trusts, which then generated even greater wealth for the men—be they called captains of industry or robber barons—who organized and directed them. A substantial banking or financial sector existed alongside these large industrial ones, but its role was to facilitate the organization of the industrial sectors, rather than to be the dominant sector itself.

The industrial sectors each had their own preferred domestic public policies which suited their particular sectors' needs. Together, they also had their own preferred version of democracy, i.e., a political system in which there were vivid democratic symbols and lively partisan elections, but whose legislation and administration normally allowed the industries to organize and operate as they wished, and allowed the plutocracy which was at the top of these industries to continue to accumulate and concentrate great wealth. In this system—democratic in form and plutocratic in content—the industrial sectors and their plutocracy controlled virtually all of the Republican Party and much of the Democratic Party as well.

As for a more truly democratic system, this was first advocated by the minority Populist Party and then, in 1896 and for a time thereafter, by the populist elements within the Democratic Party (famously represented by William Jennings Bryan). These populist or democratic forces could certainly make a lot of noise and get a lot of attention. However, the plutocratic forces had the advantage not only of great wealth with which they could readily buy politicians and policies, but also of great concentration, so that they could readily negotiate decisions amongst themselves and then persist in their direction and determination in carrying them out. Consequently, the plutocratic forces again and again prevailed over the democratic ones with respect to their preferred public policies in domestic affairs.

Since the industrial sectors and the plutocrats who dominated them had their preferred domestic policies and usually got their way, it would not be surprising if they also had their preferred foreign policies and that here too they would get their way. This was most obvious with the most economic of foreign policies, those with respect to foreign trade. On the one hand, American industries faced formidable competition from their counterparts in Europe, especially in Britain and Germany. In this case, the industries wanted a policy of trade barriers, of protectionism. On the other hand, the same industries perceived market opportunities in those underdeveloped countries where the United States might develop a preponderant political influence. These were the countries of Latin America, especially the Caribbean Basin and Central America, and in the Western Pacific, especially the emerging market of China. In this case, the industries wanted a policy of free trade (or even better, trade which would give preference to American products); this stance was often described as the "Open Door Policy." Given the other great powers who were also interested in these Latin American and Pacific markets, the United States would also need a strong navy to promote and protect its access to these markets. Of course, a big navy would itself provide a big market for the coal and steel industries. And on occasion, the continuation of this secure access might require actual intervention with U.S. military forces within some countries, usually with a combination of the Navy and the Marines.

These were the foreign and military policies which were promoted by the plutocratic forces, and they were opposed by the democratic ones. The democratic forces specifically contested protectionist trade policies, the construction of a big navy, and military interventions overseas. Had these forces gotten their way, they would have prevented, or at least delayed, much of the expansion and projection of U.S. military power into foreign countries. But as in domestic policies, so too in foreign and military policies, the plutocratic forces prevailed. And so it might be concluded that the industrial plutocracy of the 1890s was necessary for the dramatic and decisive rise of the United States to the status of a great power.

The Second American Plutocratic Era (1920s-1930s): The Divided Great Power

The next era of plutocracy was in the 1920s. Like the earlier era of the 1880s-1890s, this plutocracy was largely based upon the now vast and diverse American industrial structure, but by now there was a substantial American financial sector. This also provided members for the new plutocracy, and these had their own distinct economic interests and policy preferences. The American financial sector had been greatly expanded with the profits from the First World War and with the rise of the United States to the status of a creditor country. Nevertheless, the character and direction of the American plutocracy was set by industry rather than by finance.

Despite the great transformation in the U.S. economy since the 1890s, the foreign policy preferences of the industrial plutocracy remained much the same—a protectionist trade policy toward Europe and a free trade or open door policy toward Latin America and East Asia. Industry, for the most part, also continued to support a large navy to protect and promote its interests in these regions. The major U.S. diplomatic achievement of the 1920s was the Washington Naval Treaty with Britain and Japan, along with a parallel treaty between all the major powers regarding their interests in China. Together, these produced the "Washington System," which established U.S. leadership in the Pacific Ocean. This system for the Pacific and China suited the interests and preferences of much of American industry, and its creation was greatly facilitated by the cohesive plutocracy which supported it. Similarly, the plutocracy supported an active U.S. policy of military intervention in the Caribbean Basin and Central America in order to maintain stability and predictability in that region. With respect to Latin America and East Asia, there was no U.S. policy of isolationism during the 1920s, the second Gilded Age.

With respect to Europe, however, the plutocracy was divided. Industry wanted protectionism from imports from European competitors. In contrast, finance wanted European borrowers to be able to pay off their loans from American banks, and this required that European countries earn money from their exports to the United States. This contradiction between industry and finance, and the corresponding division within the plutocracy, meant that U.S. policy toward Europe often lacked coherence and consistency in the 1920s. Since industry dominated the plutocracy and since industry preferred protectionism, the U.S. policy toward Europe indeed seemed to be rather isolationist.

The onset of the Great Depression in the 1930s greatly weakened the American plutocracy and significantly pushed U.S. foreign policy to be even more isolationist. First, the contraction of markets worldwide made American industry even more insistent upon protecting what market it had left within the United States. Second, the stock market crash and the ensuing Depression destroyed a great deal of the paper assets of the plutocracy; this loss was confirmed by New Deal legislation, which imposed significant limitations upon great fortunes. Third, the destruction of paper assets naturally resulted in even greater losses for the financial component of the plutocracy than for the industrial one. This meant that what was left of the now-diminished plutocracy was even more dominated by industry than before.

Even American policies toward Latin America and East Asia became less active and interventionist. It was not that the United States adopted a policy of isolationism toward these regions. Rather, it simply became less willing to provide the economic and military resources necessary to sustain the previous active and interventionist policies. The populist and democratic forces in U.S. politics had rarely supported such policies as much as the plutocratic forces had, and indeed they often had opposed them. Now, with the plutocracy weakened and divided, the democratic forces could at last get their way.

What might have happened if somehow the plutocratic forces had remained strong and united into the 1930s and the Great Depression? (This might have been the case if Al Smith and the Democrats had won the election of 1928 rather than Herbert Hoover and the Republicans. Consequently, it would have been the Democratic Party and the democratic forces, rather than the Republican party and the plutocratic ones, which would have been discredited by the Depression, and the latter would likely have returned to power in the elections of 1930 and 1932.)

If some of the plutocratic foreign and military policies of the 1920s had persisted into this counterfactual 1930s, they probably would have produced outcomes similar to those which actually did occur, particularly the policies toward Latin America (where the outcomes were benign) and toward Europe (where the outcomes were malign). The big difference between the actual policies and the counterfactual ones would have been with respect to the Pacific and China. A plutocratic foreign and military policy would have been much more vigorous and consistent protecting U.S. interests in China, in building a strong U.S. Navy, and in restraining Japan. In the end, the history of the European war within the Second World War might have been much the same, but the history of the Pacific war would have been very different.

The British Plutocratic Era (1880s-1910s): The Good Times

During the same half-century (1880s-1930s) that the rising power of the United States was experiencing its two eras of plutocracy, the established power of Great Britain was experiencing its own variations on a plutocratic theme. But in Britain the plutocracy had a very different character from the American one, and it had very different consequences for foreign policy and for the place of the country in world affairs. The wealth of the British plutocracy, like that of the American one, had originated in the industrial revolution. But the British plutocracy itself was not really based upon industrial sectors; it was instead based upon the financial one.

The term plutocracy was little used in Britain during this half-century. Instead, public discussion talked about the aristocracy. That term had originated long before and had long applied to the owners of great landed estates. It was this same landed aristocracy that plantation owners in the American South—the "plantocracy"—had modeled themselves after during the decades before the Civil War. Indeed, it might be said that this Southern plantocracy, while imagining themselves as a sort of aristocracy, was actually the first version of a plutocracy in America, in this case one based upon a robust agricultural sector.

By the late Victorian era, the British aristocracy still affected the styles and symbols of a great landed upper class. However, the actual source of much of its wealth was no longer their landed estates. These were ceasing to be profitable, especially since the repeal of the Corn Laws (1846), which had provided them protection from imports of cheap foreign grain. During the industrial revolution, some estates had done well by exploiting coal deposits which by good fortune happened to be on their lands. However, much of the wealth of the British aristocracy was now derived from the growing financial sector. Of this, a major portion comprised investments abroad, most obviously in the dominions and colonies of the British Empire, but also in the emerging economies in independent nations of the time. The most important of these independent, emerging economies was the United States, but also significant was Germany. And so, by the late 19th century, the British elite were dominated by what was an aristocracy in form but what was becoming a plutocracy in fact.

The industrial revolution had begun in Britain, and by the middle of the 19th century Britain had become the "workshop of the world." The epic—and epoch-making—achievements of British industry were celebrated in the first World's Fair, the famous Crystal Palace Exposition of 1851. The great industries of this period were textiles, coal, steel, railroads, and shipbuilding. As we have seen, several of these industries would also be at the core of the massive industrial structure which developed in the United States by the late 19th century.

The great industrialists of Britain were not drawn from the old aristocracy, but rather from a middling class of "tradesmen" and "tinkerers," the most successful of whom rose to create a new capitalist class. British politics and policy were soon defined by the struggle between the old landed aristocracy and the new industrial capitalists, respectively represented by the Conservative Party and the Liberal Party. As long as British wealth was divided into these two economic sectors and these two political parties, no unified and cohesive plutocracy could develop. However, as we have seen, by the late 19th century much of the aristocracy based upon land had transformed itself to become an aristocracy based upon investments, i.e., upon finance. Moreover, by the early 20th century, much of capitalist class based upon industry had also transformed itself to become a capitalist class based upon finance. The earlier conflict between agricultural and industrial interests was transcended by a new convergence around shared financial interests. And so the earlier partisan conflict between the Conservative Party and the Liberal Party was transcended by a new bipartisan consensus on many issues of public policy. The convergence of economic interests and the consensus on policy issues allowed the creation of a cohesive and effective plutocracy, but in this case, one based upon an immense financial sector. Whereas in America, the industrial sectors dominated the economy and produced the plutocracy, with the financial sector playing a supporting role, in Britain by the late 19th century, the financial sector dominated the economy and produced the plutocracy, with the industrial sectors playing a supporting role.

Among these industrial sectors, shipbuilding deserves special attention. The British shipbuilding industry—centered upon Glasgow in Scotland and Belfast in Ireland—was for decades the greatest shipbuilding industry in the world. The workshop of the world also became the shipbuilder of the world. The industry provided the vast number of merchant ships which linked the dominions and colonies of the British Empire—and their agricultural products and raw materials—with the political metropole and industrial center of the empire, Great Britain itself. It also provided the vast armada of naval ships—the formidable Royal Navy—which protected and promoted the Empire and all the dense network of transportation and communication links between its far-flung parts—and not just the links of the Empire, but also the ocean trading links of much of the entire globe. The Empire was the world's greatest economic unit; it was even global in its scope. But the Empire was also the hegemonic economy within the still greater global economy. Not surprisingly, the ideology of the British Empire was in effect an ideology of globalization.

The imperial and global economies provided raw materials for Britain's industries and agricultural products for its workers. And they also provided markets for these industries. All of this vast imperial and global economic activity produced vast profits, which flooded into Britain, and particularly into the rapidly expanding banking center, the City of London. Now, in addition to being the workshop of the world and the shipbuilder of the world, Britain also became the banker of the world.

The bankers of the City of London of course sought high returns on their activities. These could be found with investments in the Empire, but they could also be found with similar investments in the emerging economies of independent nations. Given the availability of British capital and given the influence provided by British naval power, these emerging economies and independent countries had good reasons to provide a friendly environment for British investment. For several decades, therefore, such investments not only provided high returns, but they also seemed to provide low risk.

However, a problem arose when certain emerging economies began to build their own industries and their own supporting transportation infrastructures—such as railroads and seaports—with the aid of British capital. This occurred first in Belgium, then in western Germany, and then in the United States. Soon, these new foreign industries began to compete effectively with the original British ones. Britain ceased to be the only workshop of the world with respect to such industries as textiles, coal, steel, railroads, and even shipbuilding.

When the First World War broke out, it dramatically revealed the weakened state of British industry, particularly in contrast with that of Germany and the United States. Unable to produce what it needed for the war by its own industry or even with the resources of the British Empire as a whole, Britain had to make vast purchases of manufactured products, including armaments from the United States. In wartime, the British leadership in finance proved to be no substitute for British weakness in industry. The economic costs of the war soon transformed Britain from a creditor country into a debtor one (and conversely, the United States from a debtor country into a creditor one). It turned out that strong industrial sectors provided a nation with great resiliency when it faced challenges to its existence, but that a strong financial sector could disappear quickly.

What If? The Paths Not Taken

Was there an alternative path that Britain could have taken in the first decade of the 20th century, one which would have provided a more robust economy and a stronger military, and which would have better preserved Britain's power and leadership in world affairs? This question is rarely asked by Americans, since it was the United States, after all, which eventually would succeed Britain in that power and leadership (and which in large measure benefitted from Britain's decline). It is, however, a question that many British scholars asked in the second half of the 20th century, and they gave a variety of answers. Given the categories of our own analysis, this question becomes: was there a path which would have preserved and promoted the British industrial structure, including continually advancing it into new industrial sectors based upon the new technological innovations, i.e., in a way similar to that in the United States and in Germany? And, corresponding to this, was there a path which would have constrained and confined the British financial sector, so that it would have facilitated the movement of capital into new British industries (i.e., more like the United States) but it would not have advanced into the heights of being the dominant sector, with its dominance solidified by the politically cohesive aristocracy (i.e., plutocracy) at its top?

We will consider two such alternative paths, each of which was actively promoted in Britain at the beginning of the 20th century. One could be described as industrial transformation; the other was then entitled Imperial Federation. As it happens, these two paths could have been complementary and not contradictory to each other, and so together they could constitute one path.

A Path Not Taken: Industrial Transformation

One obvious response to the new competing industrial powers of the early 20th century would have been for Britain to develop new industries to succeed its old ones. In the 1870s-1880s, technological innovations in chemistry, electricity, and engineering provided the basis for whole new industrial sectors, i.e., chemicals, electric lights and machinery, and automobiles. And to a degree, Britain did develop these industries. By the 1900s, however, leadership in these new industries had passed either to Germany (chemicals), or to the United States (automobiles), or to both (electrical products). Instead, much of British financial capital continued to flow out of Britain into the Empire or into foreign economies, and it even continued to build up foreign industries so that these were better able to compete with the industries in Britain itself. This was because finance generally preferred to invest in old industries in new countries, rather than in new industries in the old country.

The movement of British financial capital out of British industry was paralleled by the movement of British human capital. For several generations, the talented young had gone into business enterprises and engineering projects. Now, they went instead into financial services and the civil service. By the eve of the First World War, this diversion of financial and human capital out of British industry meant that British industrial expansion and innovation had slowed to a rate much lower than that of those now-booming industrial economies—and rising great powers—of Germany and the United States.

Another Path Not Taken: Imperial Federation

At the beginning of the 20th century, it was well understood in Britain that Britain itself would be too small to provide the requisite market for the industries of the future. In particular, the automobile industry would thrive only with mass consumption and mass production (e.g., the United States), and an electrical machinery industry would thrive only with large factories and utilities serving large territories (e.g., both Germany and the United States). The United States had the advantage of having a large continental market within its own territory. Germany had a similar advantage with a large continental market within Mitteleuropa (Germany itself plus the Austro-Hungarian Empire). For Britain to compete effectively in the future, it would have to have its own continental-sized market. This, obviously, would have to be within the British Empire. In particular, its major dominions—Canada, Australia, New Zealand, and South Africa—were dominated by populations which were British in origins and in culture. Together, Britain and these four dominions could comprise an economy and a market comparable to the continental ones which were available to the United States and Germany.

Thus it was that some British thinkers and leaders put forward proposals for a "Greater Britain" or an "Imperial Federation." As these proposals matured, the idea was that there would be an imperial parliament and cabinet in London, composed of representatives from the dominions as well as from Britain itself. This imperial government would implement policies common to all the members of the imperial federation, particularly in the crucial arenas of defense, trade, and finance. Most other policy matters would be left to the member dominions themselves (as they were once left to the member states of the American federation).

Of course, it would have been very difficult to compose a common defense policy for such widely-separated dominions facing very different military threats. And, by the early 20th century, Canada in particular wanted to develop its own substantial industrial structure, and therefore to protect it with its own independent trade policy. But Britain could probably have satisfied these concerns and cautions on the part of the dominions by granting certain commitments and concessions in the course of imperial negotiations. The real obstacle to moving forward with Imperial Federation, and therefore to moving forward into the 20th century, came from within Britain itself. The British financial sector, the City of London, considered Imperial Federation to be merely a second-best choice, and one which would be an obstacle to its first choice, which was, in effect, globalization. With its worldwide power and leadership in financial matters, this sector wanted to operate freely on the widest possible scale, i.e., the global one, and not merely in the more constricted confines of the British Empire. Particular commitments and concessions to the dominions would have meant particular constraints on the global ambitions that the financial sector held at the time. And in the future, if there was an Imperial Federation, there would surely come a time when the global interests of the City of London would be contradicted by the local and parochial interests of some remote dominion. Thus it was that, after a major political struggle, industry's project of Imperial Federation was defeated by finance's project of globalization.

As it happened, three decades later and when British finance itself was much weaker vis-à-vis its foreign competitors, particularly American finance, it was quite willing to embrace a pallid substitute for imperial federation, in the form of "imperial preference." This policy abandoned free trade in the global economy and tried to substitute for it with protected trade within the British Empire. However, this now came along with granting greater independence to the dominions. By 1932, it was no longer possible to construct a true and robust Imperial Federation. Its time had once come, but that time was now long ago and far away.

The British Plutocratic Era (1920s-1930s): The Hard Times

After the First World War, Britain tried to restore its financial sector's central role in the global economy. The financial leaders thought that the best way to do this was to restore the British pound to the same value it had had before the war, and this was done in 1925 by Winston Churchill, who was then Chancellor of the Exchequer and who generally adhered to the views of the City of London. A strong, high-value pound was good for British finance. However, it was bad for British industry, since it made its products even less competitive with foreign industries than before (particularly those, once again, of the United States and Germany). This very quickly produced a serious recession in Britain, which would continue into the 1930s, when it deepened into the Great Depression. Thus, British industry was afflicted with a recession or depression for a decade-and-a-half.

The onset of the Great Depression soon produced a global financial crisis in 1931. Now it was the turn of the British financial sector itself to suffer. The financial panic produced a run on the pound, which then served as the primary global reserve currency. This forced the British government into desperate and unprecedented responses. At the Ottawa conference of 1932, free trade was abandoned and replaced by imperial preference within the Empire. At the Westminster Conference of the same year, the authority of Britain within the Empire was reduced, and the dominions were given more power in what was now called the British Commonwealth.

As radical as these changes were, the most important consequences of the financial crisis of 1931—and of the now-demonstrated fragility of the pound—was for British military spending. British leaders knew that any significant deficit spending might trigger a new run on the pound. Consequently, they had to put a cap on government spending, and this included military spending. It now seemed evident that Britain could no longer afford a "Continental commitment" and the military capability required to be an effective ally for other European states, particularly for France. This economic constraint was the underlying basis of what would soon become the Appeasement Policy. Appeasement was so widely accepted among British financial and political elites in the 1930s because they thought that it was the only policy that they could afford.

Instead, British military policy focused upon the one area where financial elites still thought that they could receive good returns, i.e., the

Empire. "Imperial policing" became the military counterpart to imperial preference, particularly with respect to some of the most profitable parts of the Empire, e.g., the oil-producing countries of the Middle East. Of course, a military force designed around imperial policing will be very different from one designed around a Continental commitment. The former will develop capabilities for counterinsurgency warfare, punitive expeditions, and "small wars." As important as these capabilities might be, they will be inadequate for engaging in conventional warfare, armored invasions, and big wars against great powers.

By the end of the 1930s, Britain faced military challenges from three great powers—Germany, Italy, and Japan—and during the Second World War, each of these powers put the British military to the test. Against Germany, a truly great power with a formidable conventional military supplied by a massive industrial sector, it is reasonable to conclude that much of the British military failed. Britain and the entire British Empire could never have defeated Germany on their own. It took the massive industrial sectors, and consequent military power, of the United States and the Soviet Union to bring the Germans down and to rescue Britain in Europe. Against Japan, also a truly great power, the performance of the British military was again unimpressive and inconsequential. Britain and the entire British Empire could not have defeated Japan on their own. It took the United States to defeat the Japanese and to rescue the British Empire in Asia. It was only against Italy, always problematic as a great power, that the British military seemed effective, as in its campaigns against the Italian military in North Africa and the Mediterranean. Of course, the Mediterranean had always been at the center of British imperial strategy, since it provided the crucial route to the Empire in the Middle East and in India and the Far East beyond.

In conclusion, the American experience in the first half of the 20th century suggests that a strong industrial sector will have a tendency to think in terms of big wars against great powers, since it has the capacity (and the interests) to produce the weapons to deter or fight such wars. Conversely, the British experience in the same era suggests that a strong financial sector will have a tendency to think in terms of small wars and imperial policing, since it calculates that only these wars will provide an acceptable mix of costs and benefits. In itself, it has no capacity to produce weapons, and it has no particular interests in investing in such capacity. Its most attractive investment prospects will usually be in other economic activities and in other countries, indeed in countries all over the globe.

The Origins of the Third American Plutocracy: The Grand Alliance

The American plutocracy of our time is based upon the financial sector and not upon industrial ones. As such, it has far more in common with the British plutocracy of the early 20th century than with the two previous American ones. Like the earlier plutocracies, the contemporary American plutocracy has been able to buy public policies, and for much the same reasons. The plutocratic forces are far more concentrated and cohesive and therefore more coherent and consistent than are the democratic forces. However, the high cost of electoral campaigns means that large campaign contributions can achieve much the same result as direct bribery. Moreover, the great complexity of much contemporary legislation and regulation means that well-funded business associations, i.e., lobbies, can in effect shape many public policies. These include not only the obvious arena of financial policy, but also the arenas which are our focus in this essay, i.e., foreign and military policies.

The power of the financial sector with respect to financial policy certainly was demonstrated in the course of the Great Recession. Almost all sectors of the U.S. economy and almost all parts of the American population were hurt by the effects of the Great Recession, but there is clear evidence that the financial sector—which actually produced the economic crisis—was hurt the least, along with the wealthy, the plutocracy at its top.[4] Indeed, many of the public policies implemented during this Recession preserved the health and wealth of the financial sector by subsidizing it at the expense of large segments of the population (especially ordinary taxpayers and small savers). It is clear enough that the financial plutocracy has been able to shape financial policy in its own interests and its own image. But what about its effect upon foreign and military policies and upon America's power and leadership in the world? For this we need to look into the origins of this third American plutocratic era.

We get some intimation of these foreign and military effects by looking again at the earlier eras of American plutocracy, when finance was only one part of a plutocracy which was dominated by industry. Even then, finance had its own foreign interests and therefore foreign policy. One particular focus was to have the U.S. State Department be a consistent force pressing foreign governments to repay the loans they had received from American banks. This was the case in the first decades of the 20th century in those new U.S. spheres of economic interest—Latin America, especially the Caribbean Basin and Central America, and East Asia, especially China. This policy of "dollar diplomacy" was backed up on occasion by military intervention, i.e., by "gunboat diplomacy." Since some industrial sectors, particularly those wishing to undertake direct investments in extractive industries in these countries, had interests similar to and compatible with the financial ones, the American plutocracy was largely united on such foreign and military policies, and it largely got its way. However, as we have seen, in the new economic conditions after the First World War, finance and industry were divided with respect to Europe and to free trade. In this case, it was industry that largely got its way with its preferred trade policy of protectionism and foreign policy of non-involvement.

After the Second World War however, economic conditions had once again dramatically changed. The financial sector was now even larger than before and continued to advance its vision of an open global economy, i.e., "liberal internationalism." But several industrial sectors now joined finance in this project. Whereas after the First World War, European industry had largely remained intact and could quickly again field competitors to their American counterparts, after the Second World War, much of European industry had been destroyed in the war and much of what remained was obsolete. As long as European industry was still rebuilding or modernizing (in the late 1940s-1950s), American industry still had valuable markets in Europe, and therefore it could join finance in supporting free trade. And by the time European industry was rebuilt and modernized (the 1960s), several American industrial sectors—particularly the automobile industry—had discovered the cost advantages of direct investment in European countries in order to produce their products there. Thus began the era of the "multinational corporation," which has continued to expand in both size and scope down to the present day.

This movement of American industrial production into foreign countries was facilitated by the American banks which provided all sorts of useful financial services to the multinational corporations. And soon, the banks became multinational too. There was now a grand alliance between the biggest and most important corporations in American industry and the biggest and most important banks in American finance, an alliance which agreed not only on free trade but also on free investment, and indeed on the openness of the entire international economy. This grand alliance provided the solid base for what soon became the dominant ideology shaping U.S. foreign policy and America's place in world affairs—liberal internationalism, which became liberal multinationalism in the 1970s, and which culminated in liberal globalization in the 1990s. However, although there was a grand alliance between finance and industry around an open global economy, there was not yet a full plutocracy. That would only come into being in the 1990s.

Industrial Sectors and Foreign Investments

The migration of American industries to foreign countries is, of course, an old and familiar story. Industrial history has always been characterized by the successive waves of new industrial sectors, in a grand parade stretching from textiles and shoes at the beginning of the Industrial Revolution; to iron and steel, railroads, and shipbuilding in the mid-19th century; to chemicals and electrical production in the late 19th century; to automobiles, aviation, and consumer electronics in the early 20th century; and most recently to computers and telecommunications in the late 20th century. As each industry came along in the grand parade, its own particular history was characterized by a sort of life cycle (sometimes termed "the product cycle"), which consisted of the successive stages of (1) innovation and rapid growth in the home market; (2) export of the product to foreign markets; (3) direct investment and production of the product in those foreign markets, first in ones whose economic development was most similar to the home market (i.e., comparable production skills, but lower labor costs) and then to other ones as they developed to a level where they also had similar markets and production capabilities; and finally, (4) export of this foreign production back into the original innovating country and its home market.[5] Thus, it is in the nature of industrial sectors that they are really pilgrims, born in one country, residing there as they grow up and mature, and then migrating from one country to the next for generations thereafter.

When American industrial corporations move production overseas, this obviously has consequences for the industrial portion of the U.S. gross domestic product (GDP). Economists often argue that such foreign direct investment also directly aids the U.S. economy by increasing the profits of American corporations, which then increases the dividends of American investors and even increases jobs for American workers if they provide services for this foreign production. However, the portion of the American economy actually producing these industrial products within the United States will of course decline.

At the micro or local level, when a mature industry leaves home, it obviously causes all sorts of disruptions to the workers, the families, and the communities it leaves behind. Sometimes the abandoned region is left bereft of any new industries and it never recovers; it remains a sort of ghost economy, depressed and depressing. Familiar American examples are parts of New England, much of upstate New York, and many cities in the Midwest (e.g., Cleveland, Detroit, and St. Louis). At the same time, however, other regions in the United States have developed their own new industries, and these have been large enough and dynamic enough to raise the economic level of the nation overall. As long as the grand parade of successive new industries has continued to move further, the American economy has continued to rise higher.

Foreign Investment versus Military Security

Although the consequences of overseas investment for American economic prosperity are complex and debatable, the consequences for

American military security are quite clear and definite. When the U.S. military has to procure certain crucial weapons components from overseas sources, this obviously poses the problem that vital supplies might be disrupted in wartime. And even if a kind of shrunken, rump production base remains in the United States, its costs will be higher because its scale, and the efficiencies that come with scale, will be smaller. However, not all industries have been equal when it comes to military security. Although soldiers certainly need uniforms and boots, it was not a cause for alarm when the American textile and shoe industries migrated overseas. Somehow, it seemed that these simple products would always be available from somewhere. But with some of the other industries, the military consequences were different. The problem for the military was first posed (in the 1960s) in a serious way with the shipbuilding industry. It was then posed a generation later (1980s) with the electronics industry. Recently, yet another generation later (2000s), it was posed again by the computer and software industry.

The migration of much of these industries overseas (especially to East Asia or South Asia) has created challenges and uncertainties for each of the U.S. military services. The biggest impact, however, has been on the U.S. Navy, which relies heavily on the products of all three of these industries. These three holes in the Navy's industrial base make for a more insecure and expensive—and smaller and weaker—U.S. Navy than would otherwise be the case. To compound the challenge (and to enhance the historical irony), these three industries are now principally located in East Asia, especially within China. And of course, it is China which is rapidly developing its own navy (the oddly named People's Liberation Army's Navy or PLAN), so that it will soon pose very serious challenges to the U.S. Navy in China's three littoral seas.

The shipbuilding case is of particular interest (as it was with Britain). The United States has not had a strong commercial shipbuilding industry for more than half a century, and one consequence is that it has an enormously, and now prohibitively, expensive naval shipbuilding industry. The U.S. Navy now has only about 250 ships (less than at any time since the 1930s). Of course, this is the same Navy that will have to protect the flow of vital weapons components to the U.S. across the broad and vulnerable expanse of the Pacific Ocean.

The Third American Plutocratic Era (1990s-2000s):
The Good Times

It is obvious that the 1990s were a decisive decade in shaping the future course of the United States in world affairs. It was then that the U.S. chose and embarked upon a particular path, one which by now has brought it to its current condition of increasing economic crisis, increasing political paralysis, increasing military weakness, and declining power and leadership in the world. The choice of that path was not inevitable—although the spokesmen for the grand alliance of finance and industry often said so at the time. However, once chosen, the consequences of that path do seem to have been inevitable.

Several developments came together in the 1990s. First and most obviously, the end of the Cold War and the collapse of the Soviet Union left the United States as "the sole superpower," even as "the American empire." In this liberating, even exuberant, time, it seemed that the U.S. could do whatever it wished in the rest of the world. Second, the consensus ideology of liberal internationalism—now ripened into liberal globalization—was an ideology which perfectly suited America's supreme power around the globe. Third, the American financial sector greatly expanded in wealth and power, both in absolute terms and in relation to the industrial sectors. Finance now became the dominant sector in the American economy, and also in American politics.[6] This is clearly evidenced by the success in finance of obtaining congressional legislation and executive decisions which almost completely deregulated the financial sector and liberated it from the regulatory regime which had been established by the Roosevelt administration and its New Deal, as its response to the Great Depression. Finally, the great increase in wealth and income inequality in the United States at last culminated in the creation of a new plutocracy. And, having been created by public policies with respect to deregulation and taxation, this plutocracy was an even more cohesive and consistent force in bringing about new versions of these policies, which in turn made the financial sector and the plutocracy on top of it even more wealthy and powerful. From the perspective of the American plutocracy, it was the beneficiary of a virtuous cycle; but from the perspective of the American democracy, it was the victim of a vicious cycle.

The first decade of the third American plutocratic era, thus, was characterized by those dramatic changes which we have enumerated. However, it was also characterized by a continuity with respect to the grand parade of successive industrial sectors. As is well known, the 1990s were the time of a spectacular development (and speculative boom) in the computer and telecommunications industry, one centered upon the Internet and the extraordinary opportunities and services which it made available When the speculative boom in high-tech ("dot.com") stocks burst in 2000, it caused the usual distress to investors (similar to what had happened many times before with speculative booms arising from new industries), but its effects should have been short-lived and sectorally limited. In any event, the boom had left behind a vast network of real assets that contributed directly and greatly to the productive capacity of the American economy. And, following the pattern of the past, after a decent interval of sobering up after the bust, American capital would have shifted into the next new industries coming down the road in the grand parade. The most promising candidates would have been biotechnology and renewable energy.

A Path Not Taken: Industrial Transformation

The second decade of the third American plutocratic era was very different. By now that plutocracy very much guided investment decisions, and by now that plutocracy was very much composed by finance. There is a natural tendency for finance to prefer investments in old technologies in new regions, rather than investments in new technologies in old regions. Finance's conception of risk management makes it most comfortable with incremental changes within established investment fields ("portfolio diversification"); with short-term profit horizons (quarterly or yearly balance sheets); and (something that developed in the 1990s) with the apparent predictive accuracy of complex computer models ("financial engineering"), which were based upon data drawn from a historically brief time (10-20 years). Investing in new industrial sectors such as biotechnology and clean energy did not conform to any of these conceptions of good risk management. What did conform, and conformed perfectly, was real estate. Beginning in the early 2000s, the financial sector thus directed the great majority of its new investments into real estate within what seemed to be areas of rapidly growing demand. This was a perfect case of preferring an old (very old) industry in new regions (or in old regions that appeared to be new in some way). Moreover, real estate was largely a consumption sector; it did not contribute to new production or productivity in any significant way.

There had been real estate booms and bubbles in the past, and these almost always had been followed by busts and bursts. But these real estate dramas had been located in particular regions, not impacting upon the national economy as a whole. And they had been only an accessory part of larger booms and busts in industrial sectors. This time, however, the dominance of finance within the economy, and the dominance of plutocracy within finance, made the boom and bust of the 2000s a pure, archetypical case of one made in finance's own interests and in its own image. It was now national, and not just local, in scope; and it was now just financial, and not also industrial, in substance.

When the financial crisis hit the U.S. economy in the Fall of 2008, the financial sector was powerful enough to make sure that it received first priority in the government's response, i.e., bailouts, on an unprecedented scale, of major financial institutions. These were all deemed "too big to fail." These bailouts included more than $150 billion to each of four financial corporations: AIG, Citigroup, Fannie Mae, and Freddie Mac. Together, these four bailouts alone amounted to more than the entire annual defense budget of the United States. Alternatively, each individual $150 billion corporate bailout was sufficient to purchase for the Air Force either all of the F-22s or all of the FA-35s that it has asked for, or to purchase for the Navy either all of the new aircraft carriers or all of the new attack submarines which it says it needs.

Another Path Not Taken: Financial Reconstruction

An alternative course would have been for the U.S. government to liquidate or break up several major financial institutions (including the big, bad four). This course would have followed successful precedents from the savings-and-loan crisis of the late 1980s and from the paradigmatic banking crisis of the 1930s. This would have had not only the advantage of minimizing the financial burdens placed upon the federal budget and the American taxpayer, but it also would have reduced the overall financial sector to a size where it would return to being a facilitator of the real, e.g., industrial, economy, and not being the dominant, and distorting, economic and political power. And within that reduced financial sector, this course would have reduced the size of the individual financial institutions, so that none of them would be too big to fail, and all of them could be better supervised by the regulatory authorities.

Of course, this alternative option of liquidation of particular financial corporations and of reform and reconstruction of the financial sector as a whole was not taken. Unlike the earlier eras of financial reform and reconstruction—the 1980s and the 1930s—by the 2000s the financial sector had grown to be the largest sector in the American economy; of even weightier consequence, it was now organized into a cohesive political force by the plutocracy at its top. And so, instead of the financial crisis—which was produced by the largest financial institutions—reducing the power of these institutions and this plutocracy, it ended up by increasing their power.

The Third American Plutocratic Era (2010s): The Hard Times

And so the United States entered the 2010s with the financial sector and its plutocracy fully in power. There is now little sign that this regime will be replaced by domestic forces within the U.S itself. The industrial sectors are now either too similar (e.g., multinational corporations) or too subordinated (debt-heavy firms) in their interests to financial interests to be an effective counterweight to the financial sector. And the democratic forces are now too disorganized (the populists) or too quiescent (the labor unions) to mount an effective opposition to the plutocratic forces. The domestic power of the contemporary American financial plutocracy bears similarities to that of the British financial plutocracy of the 1930s. And the hard times of this era also bear similarities to the hard times of that one.

But it would not be surprising if other similarities between the American condition of the 2010s and the British condition of the 1930s were to become manifest in other arenas, particularly with respect to the growth of foreign threats to the financial plutocracy and to the nation which it dominates, especially threats from rising industrial economies and rising great powers. We can already see that some kind of challenge will likely come from China.

In the 1930s, the established but weakened British financial sector confronted a large American one, distinguished by great financial resources and a strong creditor position. Similarly, today the established but weakened American financial sector confronts a rising Chinese one, one also distinguished by great financial resources and a strong creditor position. Historically, periods which have been characterized by both a declining global financial power and a rising one have issued in much financial instability and even prolonged global recession or depression.[7] The 1930s were one such period, and the 2010s were another. Also in the 1930s, the established but weakening British naval power confronted the rising Japanese naval power in the Western Pacific. Similarly today, the established but weakening U.S. naval power confronts the rising Chinese naval power in the same region, particularly in China's three littoral seas.[8]

We have already seen that a financial plutocracy is ill-suited for effective leadership in the global competition between great powers. Its neglect or even disdain for a healthy domestic industrial structure is one factor. Its attachment to a global reserve currency—despite the vulnerability and consequent sensitivity to government deficits which this brings—is another. Its preference for small wars or imperial policing, rather than for preparing the nation and its military for the deterring of great powers and large wars, is a third.

It is very likely, therefore, that we are steadily approaching the day when the United States and China will engage in some kind of confrontation over the seas that border China. These are seas that the U.S. considers to be part of the Western Pacific, which the U.S. Navy has dominated and secured since the end of the Second World War or for more than 70 years, but that China considers to be part of its territorial integrity and historical patrimony, which one day it will redeem, with the Chinese Navy playing a central role.

When the rising industrial and naval power of Japan confronted the British Empire and the Royal Navy in the Western Pacific, it was so strong that it could easily get its way. It was only because Japan also had to confront the formidable industrial and naval power of the United States that it was defeated, and then only in a long and terrible war. That industrial and naval power has dominated the Western Pacific ever since.

When the new rising industrial and naval power of China confronts the United States and the U.S. Navy in the Western Pacific, who then will get its way? One can still imagine that the old financial power, with its small-war military (and diminished navy) will do so, and will do so without having to fight a long and terrible war. But to imagine this, one has to believe—as a financial sector so often does—that "this time is different."[9] This is because a financial power achieving this kind of outcome for itself and for the nation that it dominates, against this kind of challenge from an industrial power, has never before happened in history.

CHAPTER SEVENTEEN

CREATING A SECOND
AMERICAN CENTURY

THE 20TH CENTURY WAS famously called the "American Century." The phrase itself was actually not used until 1941, by which time 40 percent of the 20th century had already passed. Moreover, 1941 was a year in which the superiority of America and of the American way of life was decidedly problematic. It had only been the previous year that the United States had finally exited the decade of the Great Depression. Nazi Germany's armies occupied most of Europe, stretching from the Atlantic coast of France to the heartland of the Soviet Union. At the same time, Imperial Japan's armies occupied most of East Asia, stretching from Manchuria through much of China to Indochina. Nevertheless, Henry Luce, who proclaimed the American century in a special issue of his Life magazine, was truly prescient. By the end of the 20th century it was widely acknowledged that it had indeed been the American one. Certainly, no other power and way of life could claim that title.

Moreover, as the 20th century passed into the 21st one, it seemed, in the circumstances of that moment, reasonable and even self-evident to say that the 21st century could be an American century too. Indeed, in the first couple of years of the 21st century, there was a little boom in the publication of books and articles which even went so far as to proclaim an American empire. Then, in an amazingly short time, a relentless series—almost a staccato burst—of events perforated and punctured this centennial and imperial dream—9/11, the Iraq War, the Afghan War, and the American-originated global economic crisis and ensuing Great Recession of 2008-2017. The political frustrations in Iraq and Afghanistan have largely discredited the long-standing U.S. democratization project, and the global economic crisis has largely discredited the long-standing U.S. globalization project. More generally, they have raised questions about the applicability abroad of such fundamental American values as liberal democracy and free markets, of "the Washington consensus" and "the American way."

At the same time that confident visions of a second American century and a new American empire have disappeared, another great power, one with its own distinctive culture and even way of life, has been steadily rising. Since 2001, China's ascent has neatly paralleled America's descent. And so no one is now making a convincing case that the 21st century could still become an American one. Conversely, there is already thoughtful commentary to the effect that this century is more likely to become a Chinese one.

This chapter will argue a contrary thesis, i.e., that the United States can still be the most prominent—although not dominant—of the great powers and that it can still offer the most attractive—although not dominant—of the ways of life. But to do this, America will have to become more American than it has been in recent years. This means that it will have to renovate or reinvent certain features or pillars which raised the United States to such global power and widespread prosperity in the second half of the 20th century, and which remain the only solid and enduring supports for a prominent American role in the 21st century.

The Pillars of the First American Century

The obvious way to begin our examination of the potential for American prominence in the 21st century is by looking at the sources or pillars of American prominence in the 20th. At first glance, however, this will result in a rather discouraging picture, since many of them no longer exist. Rather, they have been squandered or abandoned by successive generations of Americans—and particularly the American political and economic elites—during the very decades (roughly the 1980s-2000s) which comprise much of the golden age of the American century. But it turns out that each of these pillars can be reinvented and reconstructed to fit the new realities of the 21st century and to support the real potential for America's prominent role within it.

What was it about America in the 20th century that made it so dominant in the world, that raised the United States to the level of being the leading superpower and the American way of life to the level of being the standard aspired to by dozens of nations around the world? When discussing power, many international-affairs analysts reasonably focus upon military power ("hard power"), in this case America's large-scale and high-tech military forces. The United States first achieved supremacy in vast conventional forces (the Second World War), then in nuclear weapons (most of the Cold War), and most recently in information-age warfare (roughly since the 1980s, as in "the Revolution in Military Affairs," "C⁴"—command, control, communications, and computers, and "network-centric" and "cyber" warfare). And when discussing the attractiveness of the American way of life, many analysts focus upon particular American ideas and ideals, or ideological power ("soft power"), in this case liberal democracy, free markets, and the open society. These ideas and ideals characteristically were grouped together and advanced under some slogan, successively "the Free World," "The Alliance for Progress," "universal human rights," "the Washington Consensus," and "the Freedom Agenda."

There is no doubt that military power and ideological power—hard power and soft power—were central pillars of the first American century. However, we believe that the essential base for these—and for all power in international affairs—was and is economic power. (This may sound like economic reductionism or even Marxism. However, we are not arguing that economic power is <u>sufficient</u> to bring about an overall supremacy in world affairs, only that it is <u>necessary</u>). Economic power, in turn entails strength in three component dimensions: industrial, financial, and technological (or manufacturing, banking, and innovation). During the first American century (which spanned from the high industrial era to the early information era), the United States obviously led the world in each of these three dimensions.

Industrial superiority. Throughout the last century, the United States was the largest industrial or manufacturing economy in the world. Further, its industrial products were often competitive in world markets, i.e., they were readily exported, with the U.S. earning substantial foreign exchange. Further still, although the U.S. lost its competitive advantage successively in older industrial sectors (e.g., steel, automobiles, consumer electronics), it demonstrated an extraordinary capacity to innovate whole new industrial sectors (no other nation has ever matched the U.S. in this ability to continually reinvent its industrial economy), each of which then provided the U.S. with a new competitive edge in world markets, one which lasted for several decades (e.g., aerospace, computers, telecommunications).

Of course, many economists argue that, as an economy advances in its development and sophistication, it can leave behind its manufacturing component and simply move upward into a variety of service sectors (of which finance is one), and this argument is partly correct. However, although an economy may cease to produce industrial goods, it will continue to consume them (just as it earlier may have ceased to produce agricultural goods, but it obviously had to continue to consume them). Indeed, as an economy becomes more developed and richer, it may consume even more industrial products than it did before (e.g., the contemporary United States). These products have to come from somewhere, i.e., they have to be imported, with these imports paid for with exports, which would now have to come in the form of services. But only some services are exportable (i.e., "internationally-tradable"), of which finance is the most important. Indeed, advanced service economies are even leaving some of their service sectors behind and now importing these services (e.g., the outsourcing and offshoring of data processing and telephone call centers from the United States to India).

The real issue in economic development is not the simple move from manufacturing to services, but rather the more complex move from older, static sectors which are no longer capable of generating export earnings to newer, dynamic sectors which are capable of generating these earnings, and large amounts of them, sufficient to cover the costs of all those industrial products now being imported. This requires an economy to be continually re-creating itself by innovating new sectors which are capable of producing internationally-tradable goods or services. Some of these new sectors might have industrial features (e.g., new products of the renewable-energy and biotechnology sectors); some might have service features (e.g., new processes in the medical field).

Financial superiority. During much of the 20th century, the foreign-exchange earnings from its competitive exports obviously contributed to the financial strength of the United States; it became a creditor nation early in the 20th century and maintained this status until the 1970s. However, its political stability (and therefore its political predictability) also contributed to making the U.S. dollar the principal international reserve currency from the late 1930s down to the present time. With its own vast amounts of capital and with foreign investors having great confidence in both the stability of the U.S. dollar and the stability of U.S. banks, the United States was overwhelmingly the world's leading financial power during most of the 20th century.

Technological superiority. The reason why the United States could continually create new industrial sectors was that for most of the 20th century, it was also the leader in developing new technologies, both for new products and for new processes to make those products. As late as the 1930s, scientists and engineers in other nations (especially in Britain and Germany) might lead in some new invention, but then Americans would take the lead in expanding this invention into a new innovation, and then expanding this innovation into a new industry. And with the Second World War, Americans also assumed the lead in new inventions, a lead which has largely continued down to the present.

American technological superiority has been grounded in several unique or unusual features of the United States. Most obviously, the U.S. has long had the largest—and since the Second World War also the best—university system in the world. This has provided a vast pool of scientists and engineers to develop new inventions and innovations. Second, the U.S. free market system has allowed a large number of entrepreneurs to convert these new inventions and innovations into new industries. Indeed, the combination of advanced universities and energetic entrepreneurs (often located in the same places, such as around Boston and in the San Francisco Bay Area and Silicon Valley) has been the source of virtually all the new industrial sectors created in the United States since the Second World War. Third, the U.S. general population long achieved the highest average educational level in the world. Although this advantage has disappeared in the past three decades, it largely obtained during most of the 20th century. This educated general population of Americans provided numerous efficient and productive workers for the new industrial sectors.

From Economic Superiority to Military Superiority.

It was the great strength of the American economy that enabled the United States to possess great military power as well. The immense U.S. industrial capacity that existed in 1941, even after a decade of Great Depression, soon overwhelmed Nazi Germany and Imperial Japan with hitherto unimaginable quantities of tanks and artillery, warships and transports, and bomber and fighter aircraft. Military historians generally acknowledge that the German Army and the Japanese Army were both superb at the level of military operations or "operational art." But the U.S. military trumped this particular advantage of its enemies with its own great advantage in materiel and logistics. (The U.S. military was also often superior at the level of military strategy, but on this point there is more controversy among the historians.)

Military historians have also often discussed what they see as a distinctive "American Way of War." They agree that two of the central features of this way of war are (1) overwhelming mass, in both men and materiel, and (2) wide-ranging mobility, the projection and sustained support of that overwhelming mass across great distances. These features achieved their apotheosis in the Second World War.

Then, at the end of the Second World War the combination of heavy industry and high technology enabled the United States to become the first, and to remain the most advanced, nuclear power. Finally, at the end of the Cold War, the combination of high technology and new industries enabled the United States to decisively become the leader in the weapons and warfare of "the Revolution in Military Affairs" and of the more recent stages in the militarization of the information age. For most of the 20th century, no other great power could match America's military power, and the main reason that they could not do so was that they could not match America's economic power—power which was manifested in all three of the dimensions of industry, finance, and technology.

At the very moment of its apotheosis in 1945, the classical American way of war—defined by overwhelming mass and wide-ranging mobility—had been confronted with what might seem to be an intractable problem. In the past, the United States had normally been able to field larger armies (and larger mass) than its opponents. Now, with the Soviet Union, it faced an opponent which possessed even larger, more massive armies than its own. The U.S. responded to this challenge by drawing upon a third military feature—high technology—in which it had recently (in the course of the Second World War) acquired a substantial advantage. The United States first trumped the large Soviet armies with nuclear technology and weaponry and then, when the Soviets developed their own nuclear weapons, with the computer and telecommunication technologies and weapons of the information age. These U.S. military innovations amounted to new versions of the American way of war.

Beginning with the Vietnam War and then again with the recent Iraq War and the current Afghan War, however, the United States has again been confronted with what might seem to be an intractable problem. Neither its advantages in massive industrial-age armies or in nuclear weapons or even in high-tech information-age weapons have been very effective in putting down a determined and sustained insurgency (a sort of pre-industrial adversary).

The State of the Pillars Today: America versus China

As we complete our review of the pillars of the first American century, it is obvious that today two of the economic ones are greatly diminished. These are the industrial and the financial pillars; by themselves, they will certainly be insufficient to support a second American century.

In particular, America's industrial superiority is long gone. China is now the largest manufacturing economy in the world. China of course is the largest producer, and often the most competitive one, in such basic sectors as steel, shipbuilding, and consumer goods, and it is rapidly expanding and upgrading its automobile, chemical, and electrical sectors as well. These have been the basic sectors of any robust industrial economy, and they usually have been the generators of large export earnings. (They—along with aircraft production—were also the sectors which enabled the United States to win the Second World War and which long served as the basis for the American way of war.)

China's industrial superiority, and the export earnings it brings, has of course also been translated into financial strength. China's reserves of foreign currencies ($2 trillion)—especially the U.S. dollar—now exceed that of any other country; the Chinese government has often used this financial position to pressure the U.S. Treasury Department (China now holds $1 trillion in Treasury securities) and the Federal Reserve with respect to their policies affecting the value of the dollar. Even more importantly, it also used its financial strength to implement the most successful of any government's economic stimulus program to address the global economic crisis; after 2008, the most effective practitioners of Keynesianism and fiscal policy in the world were the Chinese.

Government Responses to Economic Crisis: America Then and China Now Versus America Now

Indeed, the Chinese government's response to the global economic crisis was remarkably similar to President Franklin Roosevelt's response to the Great Depression of the 1930s. Like FDR and the New Deal, the Chinese have put a heavy emphasis on large-scale spending on big infrastructure projects (in both America in the 1930s and in China today, these have been highways, railroads, bridges, dams, rural electrification, and public buildings). These infrastructure projects not only provide steady markets and continuing employment for such basic industries as steel, cement, heavy machinery, and construction; they also bring long-term productivity gains to the national economy. In contrast to both the Roosevelt administration in the 1930s and the

Chinese government in the 2010s, the Obama administration spent a little for new infrastructure, but most of its stimulus program was directed at simply maintaining existing employment in selected service sectors (and big Democratic Party constituencies), particularly state and local governments and public education.

The similarities between the U.S. response to the Great Depression of the 1930s and the Chinese response to the global economic crisis of the 2010s are not accidental. Both the U.S. then and China today possessed a vast industrial structure, which was suddenly suffering underutilization and excess capacity because of the economic crisis. With so much of the economy devoted to industry, and with industry thus having so much political influence, it is natural that governments will emphasize the revival of industry and manufacturing. An industry-centered (and industry-influenced) economic-recovery program will normally emphasize government spending and fiscal policy (i.e., some kind of Keynesianism).

However, in the United States of recent decades, industry has been a much smaller part of the economy than it was in the 1930s. Rather, finance became the largest single economic sector, as well as the most profitable and prestigious one; it is not surprising that finance became the most politically-influential economic sector as well. This meant that the U.S. response to the economic crisis (first that of the Bush administration in 2008 and then that of the Obama administration in 2009) was finance-centered (and finance-influenced), that is, it emphasized bailouts of "systemically-important" financial institutions, manipulation of interest rates, and monetary policy (i.e., some kind of Friedmanism).

The real (and ominous) 1930s analogue to the U.S. economy and economic policies after 2008, therefore, is not the United States of the 1930s, but rather the United Kingdom at that time. By then, Britain's decades of being "the workshop of the world" were long past, and the British economy and the economic policies of British governments were finance-centered and finance-designed; the City (and Lombard Street) was even more authoritative there than Wall Street has been here. The result was that in Britain during the Great Depression there never was anything approaching a New Deal, deficit spending, and fiscal policy (i.e., never anything like Keynesianism in Keynes' own country). Instead, Britain just experienced one long decade, a "lost decade," of dreary stagnation. Similarly, the United States experienced a generally stagnant economy for almost a decade after 2008.

In short, China's economic policies enabled it to exit from the global economic crisis with its economy even more developed and diverse than it was when the crisis began. Conversely, America's economic policies caused it to exit from the crisis with its economy even more distorted and debilitated than it was before.

It was only in 1941, when the United States had at last exited the Great Depression (with its economic recovery being the result of military rearmament as much as the product of the New Deal), that Henry Luce could creditably proclaim the American century. But it was also because the economic policies of the Roosevelt administration—both the New Deal and military spending, both civilian Keynesianism and military Keynesianism—had resulted in a vast and varied industrial structure that was not just the workshop, but also the wonder of the world (as exemplified in the New York World's Fair of 1939). This industrial structure was fully in place in 1941, and it would prove to be the most basic foundation of the American century.

A Remaining American Pillar: Technological Superiority

Amidst this dismal prospect, however, there still remains one strong American pillar, perhaps a lighthouse that can guide us through the gloom. The United States still retains its long-standing technological superiority. It is true that China is investing a great deal to achieve its own technological strength. This includes rapid expansion and upgrading of universities and research institutes. It also includes continued expansion and upgrading of rigorous education of the general population, which has been effective in steadily increasing its economic productivity. Historically, however, it has taken many years for an economy to translate industrial and financial superiority into technological superiority. (For example, the United States reached industrial superiority in the 1890s and financial superiority in the 1910s, but its universities did not clearly surpass the top British and German ones until the Second

World War.) The central and strategic question about who will achieve the technological superiority of the future will turn upon who achieves leadership in the new economic sectors of the future.

Today, the most obvious candidates for these sectors are (1) new sustainable or "green" energy sources and uses; (2) new biotechnology-based products and processes; (3) new medical and health treatments; and (4) new processes using artificial intelligence (AI). These economic sectors are clearly of vital importance to vast numbers of people around the world. Moreover, those countries with advanced or advancing economies would be able and willing to spend vast amounts of money to import the new products and processes of these sectors. If the United States can achieve leadership in them—like it earlier achieved leadership in such central economic sectors as aerospace, computers, and telecommunications—this will provide a robust pillar indeed for even broader American leadership in the world in the 21st century. The Chinese are not oblivious, however, to the promise of at least two of these new sectors, renewable energy and artificial intelligence, and they now call them strategic industries. And as part of their own economic stimulus program, they constructed large wind power farms and solar power plants and developed promising battery-powered automobiles.

It should be a prime objective of the U.S. government to maintain and even enhance America's technological superiority, particularly with respect to developing new economic sectors that will be leaders in global markets. This entails encouraging and enabling the traditional bases for U.S. technological superiority—the university system, with its numerous scientists and engineers; the free market system, with its numerous innovators and entrepreneurs; and, obviously in great need of improvement—the education system for the general population. Some economists have argued that only the quality of scientists and engineers is important for economic productivity and international competitiveness, and that the education level of the general population is not. However, the inventions of these scientists and engineers have to be transformed and expanded into entire economic sectors, i.e., they must be supported by a large base of technical, clerical, and industrial workers who are intelligent, skilled, and diligent, a base which must continually be reproduced and upgraded by the education system.

In any event, the United States is unlikely to remain a productive and competitive economy if it has to continue to support the large and growing number of its people who are so poorly educated that they are capable of doing no useful work at all and are therefore permanently unemployed and underemployed. In order to improve general education, it is high time to return to the traditional American value of competition. Numerous attempts to reform the monopolistic public schools (more accurately, government schools) have failed; the solution will come by enabling a large variety of private (i.e., non-government) schools to freely compete with the government ones. All good schools could receive public assistance; none should receive a public monopoly. (Unfortunately, since one of the Democratic Party's main constituencies is the public-school teachers' associations, the education policies of Democratic administrations will likely only make things worse).

The Military Pillar: An American Way of Counterinsurgency Warfare?

Any new American century will have to be supported by a strong military pillar, along with strong economic ones. This raises the question of the challenges which are posed by insurgent movements, such as recently in Iraq and currently in Afghanistan. Will a second American century have to incorporate a new American way of war: an American way of counterinsurgency warfare?

On the one hand, the dreary (but still debated) U.S. experience with counterinsurgency in Vietnam—which was at the height of the first American century—convinced the U.S. military for more than a generation thereafter that counterinsurgency warfare was incompatible with <u>any</u> version of the American way of war. On the other hand, the partial success in Iraq of the new (actually renewed) counterinsurgency doctrine of the U.S. military offers some hope. However, even General David Petraeus, who should be given a great deal of credit for developing the new doctrine and applying it to Iraq, accurately warned that the Taliban insurgency in Afghanistan posed a very different—and more difficult—challenge.

The clue to this conundrum lies in looking even more closely at the features of the American way of war as they have actually been demonstrated in U.S. military history. We have already mentioned the well-known features of overwhelming mass and wide-ranging mobility, along with the later addition of high technology. But when the United States fought its wars in the 20th century, it added yet another, largely unacknowledged feature, and that was a heavy reliance upon the ground forces of its allies. In the First World War, these were the French and the British armies; in the Second World War, the British and the Soviet armies; in the Korean War, the South Korean army; and in the Vietnam War, the South Vietnamese army. Even in the Gulf War of 1991, the U.S. military operated with substantial ground units provided by other members of its "coalition of the willing" (e.g., those of Britain, France, and Saudi Arabia). In short, the "overwhelming mass" of U.S. ground forces has always been something of an illusion; the ground forces of the U.S. allies were often more numerous (although less efficient and effective) than the ground forces of the U.S. itself, and these allied forces usually did much of the grubby, labor-intensive military tasks. The dirty little secret of the American way of war has been that it was America's allies who did much of the dirty work.

It was this secret that the U.S. Army and Marine Corps rediscovered and reapplied in Iraq in 2006-2007. They realized that the key to successful counterinsurgency was to ally with local forces—in this case the Sunni tribes or "Anbar Awakening"—who had their own, local reasons for joining the fight against the Al Qaeda insurgents. The U.S. military then tried to apply a similar strategy in Afghanistan by seeking to split various Pashtun tribes from the Taliban insurgents. However, one of the reasons that the Sunni tribes allied with the U.S. military in Iraq was that they feared the majority Shi'ite government, as well as the Al Qaeda insurgents. The Pashtun tribes in Afghanistan do not have a comparable fear—and therefore a comparable incentive—to cause them to ally with U.S. forces.

The general lesson to be learned about the potential for any American war of counterinsurgency warfare is that the United States will always have to rely upon local forces—be they local militaries or merely local militias—who have their own capabilities for effective counterinsurgency. The U.S. military may be able to add certain essential ingredients or necessary conditions (e.g., effective weapons, professional training, or simply ample pay), but it can never successfully do the grueling job and dirty work of counterinsurgency just by itself. This means that the United States should not undertake a counterinsurgency campaign in a particular country until it has developed a thorough knowledge and clear view of the local forces and potential allies there. In practice, this will also mean the U.S. normally should seek to solve its problems in that country without resorting to counterinsurgency operations by the regular U.S. military at all.

Rather, the primary focus of the U.S. military should be upon deterring and, if war comes, defeating the military forces of other great powers. But the 21st century is also the information age, and so this will entail that the United States draw upon its technological superiority to maintain and enhance its initial superiority in information-age warfare. This is especially the case with cyberwarfare, which is clearly going to be a central battlefield in the wars of the future. (The Chinese have made many attacks upon U.S. military computer systems, demonstrating their capability and intent to disrupt them in event of war.)

The reinvention and renovation of its economic and military pillars of power would put the United States once again in a position to exercise leadership in the world. However, although the U.S. would have recreated its ability to be a world leader, it would also have to learn again how to act like one. This is because since the end of the Cold War, U.S. political leaders have often acted toward other nations—and particularly toward other great powers—in a way guaranteed to provoke their annoyance and disdain, and even anger and contempt. This requires us to give some attention to both the cultural style of American leadership and the power context in which it is exercised.

Popular Culture and American Idealism

With all the talk among American political commentators about "soft power" and the attractiveness of American popular culture to the rest of the world, it is usually forgotten that this popular culture is chiefly popular with the young—particularly for those young who are still irresponsible, rebellious, and feckless. It has little attractiveness for the mature, particularly for those who are mature enough to be the leaders of these families, their communities, or their countries and who are responsible for their security and prosperity. In short, American popular culture is a culture for adolescents, not for adults, and adults around the world know and act upon this truth. If American leaders want to lead the leaders of other countries, they will have to act in the style of mature adults, not in the style of popular culture.

Similarly, with all the talk among American political leaders and commentators about American "idealism" and the attractiveness of American ideas and values to the rest of the world, it is usually forgotten that most of the political leaders of other countries are very realistic men, who see themselves as making sensible calculations about their nation's (and their own particular) interests and that they expect the leaders of other countries—including the United States—to do the same. This is particularly true of the current leaders of China and Russia. Having learned all about the claims of ideology when they were growing up and having put ideology aside when they became adults, they cannot really believe that U.S. political leaders in turn really believe that American "ideals" should be promoted for their own sake, for their "universal validity," rather than just as a legitimation or cover for U.S. interests. If American leaders want to lead such leaders of other countries, they will have to act in the style of realists, and not in the style of "idealists."

Regional Spheres of Influence and World Leadership

Realism also requires us to specify the new, 21st-century context of great powers in which the United States would be exercising its leadership. Although the re-creation of its economic and military power pillars would make the U.S. the most prominent power in the world, it would no longer be a dominant one. There will be other great powers as well—some rising (e.g., China and India), some declining (e.g., the European Union and Japan), and some rising in some respects but declining or unstable in other ones (e.g., Russia and Iran). If the United States is going to be an effective and constructive leader in world affairs, it will have to be able to lead at least some of these powers on issues of world importance. These include threats from transnational terrorist networks; nuclear proliferation; the global economy; global epidemics; and global warming. In particular, it will have to deal in an effective and constructive way with China, India, and Russia, powers which have risen or re-risen to the point that they seek to be the pre-eminent or even dominant power in a particular region—i.e., to have something like a traditional sphere of influence there. For China, this is Southeast Asia; for India (not quite yet, but likely within a decade), this will be South Asia; and for Russia, this is Central Asia, the Caucasus, and the neighboring Slavic (and Orthodox) states of Belarus and Ukraine.

With respect to these great powers and to these regions, the United States will have to make a choice. It can try to lead the small countries in the region in some kind of opposition or even alliance against the aspiring regional power (as the U.S. has done with Georgia and Ukraine against Russia). Alternatively, it can allow the regional power to exercise leadership in its region while that power allows the United States to exercise leadership in the world and on issues of world importance.

Even when the United States was at its height in the role of being a superpower, the United States reluctantly but realistically allowed the Soviet Union to exercise a brutal and oppressive dominance over Eastern Europe. However, that kind of intrusive political and economic control went far beyond the traditional norms for a sphere of influence. For the most part, great powers which were dominant in their particular regions have been satisfied with having their security interests preserved, along with some economic presence, while allowing a large amount of political autonomy within the smaller states. In this regard, it was the Soviet relationship with Finland—rather than its relationship with those neighbors where it had imposed communist regimes—which fit the traditional norm. Indeed, the current Russian relationship with most of the former Soviet republics in Central Asia now largely fits this norm, suggesting that the traditional pattern (which the Bush and Obama administrations derided as so "19th century") can be reasonably updated to fit the conditions of the 21st century.

The 19th century was one with its own distinctive features. Some historians have redefined it to be the century between 1815 and

1914—between the Napoleonic Wars and the First World War—and the 19th century then becomes an era distinguished by no general wars and by rapid economic growth, an era of unusual peace and prosperity. And, if any one nation was identified with that peace and prosperity, it was Britain. By the end of the 19th century, it was widely acknowledged that it had indeed been a British one. Certainly, no other power and way of life could claim that title.

But although Britain was the most prominent of the great powers, it generally was not a dominant one. It certainly dominated the world's oceans with its Royal Navy; it was the leader in the world economy, first in industry and then in finance; and it was the pre-eminent power on many issues of world importance, such as the repression of the slave trade and piracy and the development of international law. But Britain was not a dominant power on any particular continent (except Australia) and in any particular region (except in South Asia and the Indian subcontinent). Rather, it generally was satisfied with a division of the continents into competing spheres of influence, which then might result in a continental balance of power (e.g., Europe, Africa, East Asia, and even South America). Britain was the leading world power because it largely allowed other great powers to be the leaders in their own immediate regions; it was the leader of the leaders.

The United States may never again be a dominant power like it was during the American century. But a century can still be shaped and defined—and can still be guided toward greater peace and prosperity—by a nation that is only the most prominent of the great powers. And a grateful posterity can later look back upon that century and honor that nation by bestowing upon the century that nation's very own name.

CONCLUSION

Now, SOME SEVENTY YEARS after its beginning in the late 1940s, the global U.S. alliance system—which in effect has been the American way of global empire—has come to an end. Moreover, some thirty years after the United States thoroughly defeated the Soviet Union during 1989-1991, its position as the sole superpower is also ending. And so, as this book comes to its own end, we will review and reflect upon the current realities of the once-great U.S. alliance system and the new conflictual multipolar system.

The United States in Latin America

The U.S. hegemonic system in Latin America was the first to be established and institutionalized, and it has been the first to have clearly collapsed. First, the feckless and failed efforts of the Trump administration in early 2019 to overthrow the Maduro regime in Venezuela revealed to all—and especially to Latin Americans—that the United States was no longer the hegemonic power in Latin America, and not even a great one. Conversely, the influence of Russia, and of its ally Cuba, in Latin America is now greater than any time since the 1960s. In effect, the recent U.S. debacle in Venezuela has been as bad or worse than the 1962 U.S. debacle in Cuba at the Bay of Pigs. Indeed, the United States now confronts three Marxist regimes and Russian allies in Latin America—Cuba, Venezuela, and Nicaragua.

Second, the efforts of the Trump administration to manage the mass immigration crisis on the U.S.-Mexican border have been rendered feckless and failures by the Democratic Party's relentless opposition, both through the U.S. Congress and through the Federal courts. The United States is clearly not only not hegemonic vis-à-vis Mexico, but it is not even hegemonic on its own territorial frontier.

Third, the source of the current immigration crisis is the "Northern Triangle" of Central America—the three countries of Honduras, El Salvador, and Guatemala. These three countries (they have never been real nations, and now they are not even real societies) have collapsed into an anarchy of corrupt or impotent officials and warring and coercive drug gangs. These problems have been long developing, but the feckless and failed policies of both Democratic and Republican U.S. administrations have done nothing constructive about it. For any self-respecting hegemonic leader, having such countries within one's hegemonic system would be a disgrace. But the United States in Latin America is no longer a self-respecting hegemon.

The United States in Western Europe

The U.S. hegemonic system in Western Europe was the most elaborate and institutionalized, and it was also the most manifestly successful and widely acclaimed. It has not clearly collapsed, but it is now clearly afflicted with great disarray or even disease. First, the leading European power in the system, Germany, now behaves not as a member of an alliance, but more as a non-aligned or neutral nation between two alien great powers, the United States and Russia. It does not spend enough on defense to even maintain military forces to defend itself, much less other members of NATO. As Europe's economic and financial great power, and working through the European Union and the European Central Bank, it has crippled and exploited the economies of the Southern European members of NATO and the European Union. Moreover, in 2015, Chancellor Angela Merkel, conforming to long-standing pressure from German industry for more immigrants to expand Germany's labor pool, decided to immediately admit more than a million immigrants from the Middle East and North Africa. This reckless policy soon polarized and destabilized politics both in Germany itself and in the European Union more generally. Finally, Germany has insisted and persisted in deepening its dependence upon Russia for the majority of its oil and natural-gas needs, especially through the infamous pipeline across the Baltic Sea, Nord Stream 2. One is tempted to say that, with allies like Germany, the United States doesn't need adversaries.

Second, the most loyal U.S. ally in the system, Britain, now exemplifies disarray and disease, and cannot even unite itself as a United Kingdom, much less unite with the United States on alliance matters. Here, virtually every segment of the economic and political elites has been feckless and failing in the ways that they have addressed the issue of Brexit, or leaving the European Union. Since the British electorate has divided into roughly two equal halves on Brexit, while the economic elites have overwhelmingly opposed it, these elites, working through their representatives in Parliament, have done everything they can to sabotage it. They have thus overridden the bare majority of the electorate that voted for Brexit, showing typical elite contempt for ordinary people in the process. Moreover, Britain is afflicted with a perennial secessionist challenge from Scotland. Thus, Britain, which was for decades the model liberal-democratic dominion within the American empire, is now the model for nothing and for no one.

Third, there are the three other major European powers in NATO, i.e., France, Italy, and Spain, each of whom has recently undergone a great transformation in its political system. In France, the two establishment parties, the Socialists and the Republicans, have largely collapsed. The nation has been governed since 2017 by a weak and unpopular president, Emmanuel Macron, who represents French economic and bureaucratic elites and European establishment institutions. In 2019, the French state has been besieged by weekly mass demonstrations composed of angry populists (the "yellow vests"), which have often degenerated into violence and vandalism inflicted by enraged anarchists. France is now undergoing its greatest civil violence since its mass student demonstrations in May 1968.

Italy is now governed by an unstable coalition of two populist parties who agree upon nothing except their opposition to the Italian establishment parties and the European establishment institutions, particularly the European Union and the European Central Bank. Although these populist parties do not oppose NATO, they do not support it either. Rather, Italy, like Germany, now behaves more as a non-aligned or neutral nation between two alien great powers, in this case the United States and China. Indeed, in early 2019 Italy agreed to become a major participant in China's great Belt and Road project, particularly by turning over Italy's two major ports, Trieste and Genoa, to management and operation by Chinese state-directed companies.

Spain, like Italy, is now governed by unstable coalition governments and is experiencing the rise of populist parties on both the Left and the Right. Moreover, Spain, like Britain, is afflicted with a perennial secessionist challenge, in its case, from Catalonia. And Spain, like most of the Western European nations which had been stable liberal-democratic dominions within the American empire, is now characterized by large segments of the population losing faith in the liberal-democratic ideology and institutions which had been the legitimating and unifying basis of that empire and the acceptance of American leadership.

The United States in East Asia

The U.S. hegemonic system in East Asia, because it was a hub-and-spokes system rather than a multilateral alliance, was always the least institutionalized of America's three hegemonic systems. Thus, there was less in the system to collapse, as has happened in Latin America, or to descend into disarray and disease, as has happened in Western Europe. Nevertheless, in recent years, the relationship of the United States to the East Asian system's three full members—Japan, South Korea, and the Philippines—has undergone so much change that it is no longer accurate to call it a hegemonic system.

First, beginning with the weakest of the three members, the Philippines, we see that since he assumed power in 2016, President Rodrigo Duterte has repositioned the Philippines so that it, rather like Germany and Italy, no longer behaves as a member of an alliance but more as a non-aligned or neutral nation between two alien great powers, in this case the United States and China. Since the Philippines is the only U.S. treaty ally bordering on the South China Sea, this has greatly complicated U.S. efforts to develop and deploy an effective strategy to contain the steady, relentless Chinese expansion and consolidation of positions of strength in that region. Not surprisingly, that expansion and consolidation have now reached the point that China has the military strength to deny the access of American ships to the South China Sea any time it chooses.

Second, South Korea has recently undertaken a similar repositioning since President Moon Jae-in assumed office in 2017. Since the Korean War, South Korea has been one of the most loyal of all U.S. allies because it was only the U.S. that stood in the way of a new North Korean effort to conquer or coerce the country. For six decades, massive U.S. military power, ultimately backed by nuclear power, has deterred any major North Korean assault. However, for the last three decades, the North Korean leadership has steadily, persistently, and methodically built up their own nuclear deterrent capability. While doing so, it deterred any U.S. preventive strike on its growing nuclear weapons program by threatening the vast Seoul urban region with tens of thousands of artillery pieces. In effect, North Korea used its massive conventional capability to deter a U.S. attack on its developing nuclear capability. Now that nuclear capability has reached the stage that North Korea can credibly threaten to attack the cities of the United States itself.

Thus, President Moon must resolve a momentous strategic dilemma. On the one hand, he does not want the U.S. to withdraw its deterrent protection from South Korea. On the other hand, he does not want the U.S. to do anything to provoke North Korea into launching an artillery barrage that would destroy Seoul. He has tried to resolve this dilemma by being cooperative and accommodating to both sides. Thus, in its own distinct way, South Korea, like Germany, Italy, and the Philippines, now behaves rather like a non-aligned or neutral nation between two powers, in this case, the United States and North Korea.

Third, Japan has also been one of the most loyal of U.S. allies, also since the time of the Korean War. But unlike South Korea, its island geography means that it does not have to worry about any conventional attack from North Korea, or probably even from China. Thus, Japan has not been driven to reposition itself among the powers. Rather, it still behaves very much like an alliance partner. Indeed, at the present time, it is probably the only major nation left in the global U.S. alliance system that still does so. If so, that once-vast multinational and multilateral system has now shrunk to being merely a bilateral alliance between two nations, the United States and Japan. And if so, the global American empire is ending up where it all began: in Tokyo and Tokyo Bay.

From Triple Alliance to Triple Adversaries

And so the grand triple alliance system of the United States, the American way of empire, now lies in ruins. It is the end of an era, the end of what has turned out to be the short American Century.

It may seem bad enough for most Americans that their empire has ended, but their contemporary reality is actually even worse. The collapse of the American empire does not just leave a vacuum, but there are now several revisionist powers pushing simultaneously to fill that vacuum. The greatest of these is China, now moving to be the next global superpower, even the pre-eminent superpower. The next greatest is Russia, now moving to return as the major power in Eastern Europe and also a power with an important role in other regions of the world. In addition, there is Iran, which is now moving to be the major power in the Middle East, one whose power is extended throughout the region by Shi'ite proxy groups and which will be entrenched if it acquires nuclear weapons. Moreover, China has that useful ally of a now-nuclear North Korea, which keeps the United States off-balance in Northeast Asia, and Russia has that useful ally of Cuba, which keeps the United States off-balance in the Caribbean basin.

It would be bad enough if the United States, now bereft of its protective alliance systems, had one major adversary to confront and contain. But with China, Russia, and Iran, it simultaneously has three. The last time that the United States had three major adversaries to confront was, of course, during the Second World War, when it was fighting Germany, Italy, and Japan.

How did the United States arrive at its current condition of three ruined alliance systems and three expansionist major powers? Historically, the leaders of a great power wisely try to follow the strategic principle of "the conservation of enemies," of having only one major adversary at a time. This maxim is just a variation on the more general strategic principle of divide and rule. To take the most obvious example, any strategic thinker, seeing that China was the obvious rising power for the 21st Century, would also see that Russia was the obvious power to contain China on the landmass of Eurasia. Just as Richard Nixon and Henry Kissinger dealt with China, the second communist power, to contain the Soviet Union, the greatest communist power, American leaders after the Cold War should have worked with Russia, the second revisionist power, to contain China, the greatest revisionist power.

However, after its great Cold-War victory, the globalist economic elites of the United States, working through the political elites of both the Democratic and Republican parties, recklessly violated these wise strategic principles, and, in doing so, they threw away the great legacy of America's Cold-War victory, and they threw their fellow Americans into their current dangerous condition. And these same globalist elites persist in their reckless multiplication of enemies even today.

One day, someplace in the ruins of the American empire, and perhaps in the ruins of the United States itself, there may be found, unlikely as it seems, a few historians who will look back upon our time, and they will try to determine the causes of our amazing rise and fall. They will surely conclude that the chief cause was the extraordinary ambition, pride, greed, and fantasies—indeed, *hubris*—of the American globalist economic and political elites. It was they who pushed the United States down the wrong path after the Cold War.

And there will be some historians who will conclude that it didn't have to end this way.

ACKNOWLEDGEMENTS

THE IDEAS AND ARGUMENTS in this book were largely developed during many years of teaching at Swarthmore College, particularly in my courses and seminars on American Foreign Policy, International Politics, and Defense Policy. They were greatly enriched and refined by the questions, contributions, and research of my students, who have always been a delight, and with many of whom I have long continued to have engaging discussions.

I have similarly benefited from many years of participation in the activities of the splendid Foreign Policy Research Institute (FPRI) in Philadelphia. The lectures, seminars, and conferences that FPRI has presented offer the very latest—and deepest—analyses of American foreign policy and international politics available anywhere. In large measure, this has been the result of the extraordinary leadership of its two recent presidents, the late Harvey Sicherman and now Alan Luxenberg. Alan, in particular, has been an amazingly innovative, effective, and gracious leader. Several of the chapters in this book were first presented in an FPRI setting.

Over the years, I of course have had many discussions about the topics of this book, with a wide array of professional friends and colleagues in the fields of foreign policy and international politics. One, in particular, stands out for the breadth of his knowledge, the acuity of his thinking, the rigor of his reasoning, and the invaluable contributions that he has made to my own thinking: Thomas Ferguson, Professor of Political Science at the University of Massachusetts, Boston, and Director of Research for the Institute for New Economic Thinking (INET).

Moreover, two of the chapters in this book were originally presented to conferences of INET, under the auspices of Tom.

Many of the chapters in this book were initially published as articles in The National Interest and The American Interest. I am exceedingly grateful to their extraordinary editors at the time, i.e., Owen Harries of The National Interest and Adam Garfinkle of The American Interest, who first conceived of what an essay could do, and then invited and encouraged me to write it.

Finally, I want to thank Laurence Jarvik, Editor of Washington Books, for persistently urging me to gather together some of my earlier works into the unified form that is this book. And I also especially want to thank Deborah Sloman, Administrative Assistant of the Political Science Department at Swarthmore, who typed every single word of the text, and often typed it several times, always doing so with her consistent efficiency, professionalism, and grace.

NOTE: Some of the ideas in this book have appeared in a different form, as follows :

Chapter 1: An earlier version was "Fracturing at the Core of the Global Order: The Death of the Seventy-Year American Empire," a paper presented to the Conference of the Institute for New Economic Thinking, Edinburgh, Scotland, October, 2017.

Chapter 2: An initial version was published as "The Protestant Deformation and American Foreign Policy," Orbis, Spring 1998, pp. 221-239. A revised version was "The Protestant Deformation," The American Interest, Winter 2005, pp. 4-16.

Chapter 3: An earlier version was published as "War, Peace, and the Ideologies of the Twentieth Century," Current History, January 1999, pp. 3-8.

Chapter 4: An earlier version was published as "America's Democratization Projects Abroad: The Successes versus the Failures," The American Spectator, October 2006, pp. 40-47. Reprinted in James Piereson, editor, The Pursuit of Liberty: Can the Ideals That Made America Great Provide a Model for the World? (New York: Encounter Books, 2008), pp. 17-34.

Chapter 5: An earlier version was published as "The Adolescent Empire: America and the Imperial Idea," The National Interest, Summer 1997, pp. 3-15.

Chapter 6: An earlier version was published as "America's Grand Strategy: A Pattern of History," The National Interest, Spring 1996, pp. 3-19.

Chapter 7: An initial version was published as "Global Trends and American Strategic Traditions," in Pelham G. Boyer and Robert S. Wood, editors, Strategic Transformation and Naval Power in the 21st Century (Newport, RI: Naval War College Press, 1998), pp. 7-31. A revised version was published as "American Strategy in the Global Era," Naval War College Review, Winter 2000, pp. 7-24.

Chapter 8: An earlier version was published as "The American Way of Victory," The National Interest, Summer 2000, pp. 5-16.

Chapter 9: An earlier version was published as "The Next NATO: Building an American Commonwealth of Nations," The National Interest, Fall 2001, pp. 5-16.

Chapter 10: An earlier version was "Two Paths to War: The Origins of the First World War versus the Dynamics of Contemporary Sino-American Confrontations," a paper presented to the Conference of the Institute for New Economic Thinking, Paris, France, April 2015. Parts were initially published in "Confronting a Powerful China with Western Characteristics," Orbis, Winter 2012, pp. 39-59.

Chapter 11: An earlier version was published as "Confronting the Unipolar Moment: The American Empire and Islamic Terrorism," Current History, December 2002, pp. 403-408.

Chapter 12: Not previously published.

Chapter 13: An earlier version was published as "The Neoconservatives Are History," <u>Orbis</u>, Fall 2006, pp. 756-769.

Chapter 14: An initial version was published as "Migration and the Dynamics of Empire," <u>The National Interest</u>, Spring 2003, pp. 5-16. Reprinted as "Who Will Do The Dirty Work?" in Andrew J. Bacevich, editor, <u>The Imperial Tense: Prospects and Problems of American Empire</u> (Chicago: Ivan R. Dee, 2003), pp. 245-260.

Chapter 15: An earlier version was published as "Between Europe and America: The New York Foreign Policy Elite," in Martin Shefter, editor, <u>Capital of the American Century: The National and International Influence of New York City</u> (New York: Russell Sage Foundation, 1993), pp. 71-94.

Chapter 16: an earlier version was published as "The Foreign Policy of Plutocracies," <u>The American Interest</u>, November/December 2011, pp. 5-17.

Chapter 17: An earlier version was published as "Pillars of the Next American Century," <u>The American Interest</u>, November/December 2009, pp. 4-13.

END NOTES

Chapter 2

1. An outstanding exception is Walter A. McDougall, who has discussed the issue directly and extensively in two books: Especially his The Tragedy of U.S. Foreign Policy: How America's Civil Religion Betrayed the National Interest (New Haven: Yale University Press, 2016); and also his Promised Land, Crusader State: The American Encounter with the World Since 1776 (Boston: Houghton Mifflin, 1997).
2. Samuel P. Huntington, The Clash of Civilizations and the Remaking of World Order (New York: Simon and Schuster, 1996).

Chapter 7

1. Peter Drucker, Landmarks of Tomorrow: A Report on the New "Post-Modern World" (New Brunswick, New Jersey: Transaction Publishers, 1996).
2. Raymond Vernon and Ethan B. Kapstein, editors, Defense and Dependence in a Global Economy (Washington, D.C. Congressional Quarterly Inc. 1992).
3. Martin von Creveld, The Transformation of War (New York: The Free Press, 1991); Edward N. Luttwak, "Where are the Great Powers?" Foreign Affairs, July/August 1994, pp. 23-30; and "Toward Post-Heroic Warfare," Foreign Affairs, May/June 1995, pp. 109-122.
4. James Kurth, "The Post-Modern State," The National Interest, 28, Summer 1992, pp. 26-33.

5. Arthur M. Schlesinger, Jr., The Disuniting of America: Reflections on a Multicultural Society (New York: Norton, 1993). I discussed this ideological transformation in my "NATO Expansion and the Idea of the West," Orbis, Fall 1997, pp. 563-567; and "The Real Clash," The National Interest, Fall 1994, pp. 3-15.

6. James Kurth, "First War of the Global Era: Kosovo and U.S. Grand Strategy," in Andrew J. Bacevich and Eliot A. Cohen, editors, War over Kosovo: Politics and Strategy in a Global Age (New York: Columbia University Press, 2001), pp. 63-96.

7. Samuel P. Huntington, The Clash of Civilizations and the Remaking of World Order (New York: Simon and Schuster, 1996).

8. I discussed the dilemma posed by the Baltic states in my "To Sing a Different Song: The Choices for the Baltic States," The National Interest, Summer 1999, pp. 81-87; and "The Baltics: Between Russia and the West," Current History, October 1999, pp. 334-339.

9. John K. Fairbank, editor, The Chinese World Order: Traditional China's Foreign Relations (Cambridge: Harvard University Press, 1968).

10. The classic exposition was Russell F. Weigley, The American Way of War: A History of United States Military Strategy and Policy (Bloomington, IN: Indiana University Press, 1973).

11. Harry G. Summers, Jr., On Strategy: A Critical Analysis of the Vietnam War (Novato, CA: The Presidio Press, 1982) and On Strategy II: A Critical Analysis of the Gulf War (New York: Dell Publishing, 1992).

12. Peter J. Boyer, "The New War Machine," The New Yorker, June 20, 2003, pp. 55-71.

Chapter 8

1. Karl Polanyi, The Great Transformation: The Political and Economic Origins of Our Time (Boston, Beacon Press, 1957), chapter I.

2. Realist theories of international relations focus on international security; liberal theories focus on the international economy. In the actual practice of foreign policy, however, successful strategies have combined both, e.g., the British strategy of the 19th century and the American strategy during the Cold War. At its best, the

Anglo-American tradition in international relations has been both realist and liberal. I discussed realist and liberal theories in my "Inside the Cave: The Banality of I.R. Studies," The National Interest (Fall 1998), pp. 29-40.

3. P.M.H. Bell, The Origins of the Second World War in Europe, second edition (New York: Longman, 1997), chapter 3.

4. Charles P. Kindleberger, The World in Depression 1929-1939 (Berkeley: University of California Press, 1973), chapter 14.

5. Akira Iriye, The Origins of the Second World War in Asia and the Pacific (New York: Longman, 1987), chapter 1.

Chapter 9

1. Thomas L. Friedman, The Lexus and the Olive Tree (New York: Anchor Books, 2000), chapters 6-7.

2. I proposed the Finnish model in my "To Sing a Different Song, The Choices for the Baltic States," The National Interest, Summer 1999, pg. 81-87.

3. James Kurth, "The Baltics: Between Russia and the West," Current History, October 1999, pg. 334-339.

Chapter 10

1. Graham T. Allison, Destined for War: Can America and China Escape Thucydides's Trap? (Boston: Houghton Mifflin, 2017).

2. Henry Kissinger, On China (New York: The Penguin Press, 2011); Henry Kissinger, World Order (New York: The Penguin Press, 2014).

3. Taylor Downing, 1983: Reagan, Andropov, and a World on the Brink (New York: Little, Brown, 2018); Marc Ambinder, The Brink: President Reagan and the War Scare of 1983 (New York: Simon and Schuster, 2018); Nate Jones, Able Archer 83: The Secret History of the NATO Exercise that Almost Triggered Nuclear War (New York: The New Press, 2016).

4. Robert D. Kaplan, Asia's Cauldron: The South China Sea and the End of a Stable Pacific (New York: Random House, 2014).

5. A systematic study of the interaction of alliance systems, arms races, and successive crises is provided by John A. Vasquez, The War Puzzle Revisited (New York: Cambridge University Press, 2009).

6. Samuel P. Huntington, The Clash of Civilizations and the Remaking of World Order (New York: Simon and Schuster, 1996); Kissinger, World Order.

7. The following discussion of Chinese conceptions is drawn from my article, "Confronting a Powerful China with Western Characteristics," Orbis, Winter 2012, pp. 39-59.

8. John King Fairbank, editor, The Chinese World Order: Traditional China's Foreign Relations (Cambridge, MA: Harvard University Press, 1968).

9. Alastair Iain Johnston, Cultural Realism: Strategic Culture and Grand Strategy in Chinese History (Princeton, NJ: Princeton University Press, 1995); Kissinger, On China, chapter 1. A comprehensive and excellent account of the strategic conceptions developed during the more recent Communist era is given by Avery Goldstein, Rising to the Challenge: China's Grand Strategy and International Security (Stanford, CA: Stanford University Press, 2005).

10. Kissinger, On China, chapter 1: David Lai, "Learning from the Stones: A Go Approach to Mastering China's Strategic Concept, Shi" (Carlisle, PA: U.S. Army War College Strategic Studies Institute, 2004). Kissinger and Lai both emphasize the mindset developed by the ancient Chinese game of strategy, wei qi (more commonly known by its Japanese name, go).

    Useful accounts of the Chinese military during the Communist era are given by John Wilson Lewis and Xue Litai, Imagined Enemies: China Prepares for Uncertain War (Stanford, CA: Stanford University Press, 2006); and Andrew Scobell, China's Use of Military Force: Beyond the Great Wall and the Long March (Cambridge, UK: Cambridge University Press, 2003).

11. An excellent history and analysis of the rise of Chinese naval power is given by Toshi Yoshihara and James R. Holmes, Red Star Over the Pacific: China's Rise and the Challenge to U.S. Maritime Strategy (Annapolis, MD: Naval Institute Press, 2010).

12. Susan L. Shirk, China: Fragile Superpower (New York: Oxford University Press, 2007).

Chapter 11

1. Niall Ferguson, Empire: The Rise and Demise of the British World Order and the Lessons for Global Power (New York: Basic Books, 2002); also his Colossus: The Price of America's Empire (New York: The Penguin Press, 2004).

2. James Kurth, "First War of the Global Era: Kosovo and U.S. Grand Strategy," in Andrew J. Bacevich and Eliot A. Cohen, editors, War Over Kosovo: Politics and Strategy in a Global Age (New York: Columbia University Press, 2001), pp. 63-96.

3. See, for example, Andrew J. Bacevich, The American Empire (Cambridge, MA: Harvard University Press, 2002); the five articles in the special issue on "An American Empire?" of The Wilson Quarterly, Summer 2002; and the diverse collection of articles gathered in Andrew J. Bacevich, editor, The Imperial Tense: Prospects and Problems of American Empire (Chicago: Ivan R. Dee, 2003).

4. Michael Mandelbaum, The Ideas That Conquered the World: Peace, Democracy, and Free Markets in the Twenty-First Century (New York: Public Affairs, 2002).

5. Samuel P. Huntington, The Clash of Civilizations and the Remaking of World Order (New York: Simon and Schuster, 1996); Roger Scruton, The West and The Rest: Globalization and the Terrorist Threat (Wilmington, DE: ISI Books, 2002).

6. The National Security Strategy of the United States of America (Washington, D.C.: The White House, 2002).

7. The strategy of unilateral pre-emption was not really unprecedented in the history of American foreign policy. It was a method used by the United States on several occasions in the 19th and early 20th centuries. See John Lewis Gaddis, Surprise, Security, and the American Experience (Cambridge, MA: Harvard University Press, 2004).

8. The development of the administration's focus upon Iraq was discussed in Bob Woodward, Plan of Attack (New York: Simon and Schuster, 2004); James Fallows, "Bush's Lost Year," The Atlantic Monthly, October 2004, pp. 68-84; and Chaim Kaufmann, "Threat Inflation and the Failure of the Marketplace of Ideas: The Selling of the Iraq War," International Security, Summer 2004, pp. 5-48.

9. Walter Russell Mead, <u>Special Providence: American Foreign Policy and How It Changed the World</u> (New York: Alfred A. Knopf, 2002).

10. A useful and detailed account of foreign policy making in the Clinton administration is given by David Halberstam, <u>War in a Time of Peace: Bush, Clinton, and the Generals</u> (New York: Scribner, 2001).

11. Stefan Halper and Jonathan Clarke, <u>America Alone: The Neo-Conservatives and the Global Order</u> (New York: Cambridge University Press, 2004).

Chapter 12

1. James Fallows, "Blind Into Baghdad," <u>The Atlantic Monthly</u>, January/February 2004, pp. 53-74.

2. <u>Ibid</u>, pp. 72-73.

3. The misconception and mistakes of the U.S. occupation authorities in Baghdad during 2003-2004 are extensively described by William Langewiesche, "Welcome to the Green Zone: The American Bubble in Baghdad," <u>The Atlantic Monthly</u>, November 2004, pp. 60-88.

4. Bremer gives his own account in his memoir: L. Paul Bremer III, with Malcolm McConnell, <u>My Year in Iraq: The Struggle to Build a Future of Hope</u> (New York: Simon and Schuster, 2006).

5. Toby Dodge, <u>Inventing Iraq: The Failure of Nation Building and a History Denied</u> (New York: Columbia University Press, 2003).

6. James Dobbins et al, <u>America's Role in Nation-Building: From Germany to Iraq</u> (Santa Monica, CA: Rand, 2003); James Fallows, "Blind into Baghdad," <u>The Atlantic Monthly</u>, January/February 2004, pp. 53-74.

7. Albert O. Hirschman, <u>Exit, Voice, and Loyalty: Responses to Decline in Firms, Organizations, and States</u> (Cambridge, MA: Harvard University Press, 1970).

8. Robert Pape, <u>Dying to Win: The Strategic Logic of Suicide Terrorism</u> (New York: Random House, 2005).

Chapter 13

1. William Anthony Hay, "What Is Democracy? Liberal Institutions and Stability in Changing Societies." <u>Orbis</u>, Winter 2006, pp. 133-151.

2. Jim Sleeper, The Closest of Strangers: Liberalism and the Politics of Race in New York (New York: Norton, 1990).
3. James Mann, The Rise of the Vulcans: The History of Bush's War Cabinet (New York: Penguin Books, 2004) provides a detailed description of Dick Cheney, Donald Rumsfeld, Paul Wolfowitz, Colin Powell, and Condoleezza Rice.
4. Bob Woodward, Plan of Attack (New York: Simon and Schuster, 2004).

Chapter 14

1. Peter Andreas, "The Making of Amerexico: (Mis)Handling Illegal Immigration," World Policy Journal, Summer 1994, pp. 45-56.
2. David Brooks, "The Organization Kid," The Atlantic Monthly, April 2001, pp. 40-54.
3. Michael Mandelbaum, The Ideas That Conquered The World: Peace, Democracy, and Free Markets in the Twenty-first Century (New York: Public Affairs, 2002).

Chapter 15

1. Martin Shefter, editor, Capital of the American Century: The National and International Influence of New York City (New York: Russell Sage Foundation, 1993). An initial version of this chapter was published in this book as "Between Europe and America: The New York Foreign Policy Elite," pp. 71-94.
2. Walter Isaacson and Evan Thomas, The Wise Men: Six Friends and the World They Made (New York: Simon and Schuster, 1986), chapter 1.
3. Robert D. Schulzinger, The Wise Men of Foreign Affairs: The History of the Council on Foreign Relations (New York: Columbia University Press, 1984), chapter 1; Leonard Silk and Mark Silk, The American Establishment (New York: Basic Books, 1980), chapter 6.
4. Schulzinger, The Wise Men of Foreign Affairs, p. 10
5. Derek H. Aldcroft, From Versailles to Wall Street, 1919-1929 (Berkeley: University of California Press, 1977).
6. Schulzinger, The Wise Men of Foreign Affairs, p. 30

7. Charles P. Kindleberger, The World in Depression, 1929-1939 (Berkeley: University of California Press, 1973), chapter 14.

8. Robert Dallek, Franklin D. Roosevelt and American Foreign Policy, 1932-1945 (New York: Oxford University Press, 1979), parts 1 and 2.

9. Roosevelt, of course, was of Dutch ancestry, and not Anglo-Saxon in the most literal sense; LaGuardia had an Italian father and a Jewish mother.

10. Dallek, Franklin D. Roosevelt and American Foreign Policy, part 4; Franz Schurmann, The Logic of World Power (New York: Pantheon Books, 1974), part 1.

11. Schulzinger, The Wise Men of Foreign Affairs, chapters 3-4.

12. Isaacson and Thomas, The Wise Men, chapters 11-14.

13. Michael Paul Rogin, The Intellectuals and McCarthy: The Radical Specter (Cambridge, Mass: MIT Press, 1967). Interpretations of McCarthyism that stress populism and paranoia are Richard Hofstadter, The Paranoid Style in American Politics and Other Essays (New York: Vintage books, 1967) and his The Age of Reform (New York: Knopf, 1956); Seymour Martin Lipset and Earl Raab, The Politics of Unreason (New York: Harper and Row, 1970).

14. Isaacson and Thomas, The Wise Men, pp. 474, 580.

15. David Halberstam, The Best and the Brightest (New York: Random House, 1972).

16. Henry Kissinger dedicates his memoirs to "the memory of Nelson Aldrich Rockefeller" and calls him "the single most influential person in my life" who "introduced me to high-level policymaking;" Kissinger adds that he was "intoxicated" by his "proximity to power—and I daresay wealth." Kissinger, White House Years (Boston: Little, Brown, 1979) p. 4. Also see Zbigniew Brzezinski, Power and Principle (New York: Farrar, Straus and Giroux, 1983).

17. Isaacson and Thomas, The Wise Men, pp. 649-657.

18. Ibid, pp. 698-706.

19. Schulzinger, The Wise Men of Foreign Affairs, chapter 8; Council on Foreign Relations, Annual report, July 1, 1986-June 30, 1987 (New York) (1987).

20. Schulzinger, The Wise Men of Foreign Affairs, pp. 213-214.

21. Quoted in Alan Brinkley, "Minister Without Portfolio—The Most Influential Private Citizen in America: The Life and times of John McCloy," Harper's (February 1983), p. 46.

Chapter 16

1. For comparisons of these economic crises, see Peter Gourevitch, Politics in Hard Times: Comparative Responses to International Economic Crises (Ithaca, NY: Cornell University Press, 1986); James Kurth, "A Tale of Four Crises: The Politics of Great Depressions and Recessions," Orbis, Summer 2011, pp. 500-523.

2. Michael Auslin, "Tipping Point in the Indo-Pacific," The American Interest, Spring (March/April) 2011, pp. 17-24.

3. Tyler Cowen, "The Inequality that Matters," The American Interest, Winter (January/February) 2011, pp. 29-38.

4. Don Peck, "Can the Middle Class Be Saved?" The Atlantic, September 2011, pp. 60-78.

5. James R. Kurth, "The Political Consequences of the Product Cycle: Industrial History and Political Outcomes," International Organization, Winter 1979, pp. 1-34. In the case of the automobile industry, the classic product cycle has even been extended into a fifth phase, with the product being manufactured by foreign corporations within the original home market (the United States).

6. Jeff Madrick, Age of Greed: The Triumph of Finance and the Decline of America, 1970 to the Present (New York: Alfred A. Knopf, 2011).

7. This was the classic thesis of Charles Kindleberger, The World in Depression, 1929-1939 (Berkeley, CA: University of California Press, 1973).

8. Contrasting views of the potential Chinese challenge are given in Auslin, "Tipping Point in the Indo-Pacific"; Henry Kissinger, On China (New York: The Penguin Press, 2011), chapter 18; and James R. Holmes and Toshi Yoshihara, Red Star over the Pacific: China's Rise and the Challenge to U.S. Maritime Strategy (Annapolis, MD: Naval Institute Press, 2010).

9. Carmen M. Reinhart and Kenneth S. Rogoff, This Time is Different: Eight Centuries of Financial Folly (Princeton, NJ: Princeton University Press, 2009).

BIBLIOGRAPHY

Acheson, Dean. Present at the Creation: My Years in the State Department (New York: W.W. Norton, 1969).

Bacevich, Andrew J. American Empire: The Reality and Consequences of U.S. Diplomacy (Cambridge, MA: Harvard University Press, 2002).

Bacevich, Andrew J., editor. The Imperial Tense: Prospects and Problems of the American Empire (Chicago: Ivan R. Dee, 2013).

Bacevich, Andrew J., editor. The Long War: A New History of U.S. National Security Policy Since World War II (New York: Columbia University Press, 2007).

Bacevich, Andrew J. Twilight of the American Century (Notre Dame, IN: Notre Dame Press, 2018).

Ferguson, Niall. Colossus: The Rise and Fall of the American Empire (New York: The Penguin Press, 2004).

Fonte, John. Sovereignty or Submission: Will Americans Rule Themselves or Be Ruled by Others? (New York: Encounter Books, 2011).

Fukuyama Francis. The Origins of Political Order: From Prehuman Times to the French Revolution (New York: Farrar, Straus and Giroux, 2011).

Fukuyama, Francis. Political Order and Political Decay: From the Industrial Revolution to the Globalization of Democracy (New York: Farrar, Straus and Giroux, 2014).

Gaddis, John Lewis. Strategies of Containment: A Critical Appraisal of American National Security Policy During the Cold War, revised and expanded edition (New York: Oxford University Press, 2005).

Gilpin, Robert. The Challenge of Global Capitalism: The World Economy in the 21st Century (Princeton, NJ: Princeton University Press, 2000).

Gilpin, Robert. Global Political Economy: Understanding the International Economic Order (Princeton, NJ: Princeton University Press, 2011).

Gilpin, Robert. U.S. Power and the Multinational Corporation: The Political Economy of Foreign Direct Investment (New York: Basic Books, 1975).

Hazony, Yoram. The Virtue of Nationalism (New York: Basic Books, 2018).

Hendrickson, David C. Republic in Peril: American Empire and the Liberal Tradition (New York: Oxford University Press, 2017).

Hopkins, A.G. American Empire: A Global History (Princeton, NJ: Princeton University Press, 2018).

Huntington, Samuel P. American Politics: The Promise of Disharmony (Cambridge, MA: The Belknap Press of Harvard University Press, 1981).

Huntington, Samuel P. The Clash of Civilizations and the Remaking of World Order (New York: Simon and Schuster, 1996).

Huntington, Samuel P. Who Are We? The Challenges to America's National Identity (New York: Simon and Schuster, 2004).

Ikenberry, G. John. After Victory: Institutions, Strategic Restraint, and the Rebuilding of Order after Major Wars (Princeton, NJ: Princeton University Press, 2000).

Ikenberry, G. John. Liberal Leviathan: The Origins, Crisis, and Transformation of the American World Order (Princeton, NJ: Princeton University Press, 2011).

Immerwahr, Daniel. How to Hide an Empire: A History of the Greater United States (New York: Farrar, Straus and Giroux, 2019).

Isaacson Walter and Evan Thomas. The Wise Men: Six Friends and the World They Made: Acheson, Bohlen, Harriman, Kennan, Lovett, McCloy (New York: Simon and Schuster, 1986).

Kennan, George F. American Diplomacy: Sixtieth-Anniversary Expanded Edition, with a new introduction by John J. Mearsheimer (Chicago: University of Chicago Press, 2012).

Kennan, George F. Memoirs 1925-1950 (Boston: Little, Brown, 1967).

Kissinger, Henry. Diplomacy (New York: Touchstone Book, Simon and Schuster, 1994).

Kissinger, Henry. On China (New York: The Penguin Press, 2011).

Kissinger, Henry. World Order (New York: The Penguin Press, 2014).

LaFeber, Walter. The American Age: United States Foreign Policy at Home and Abroad since 1750 (New York: W.W. Norton, 1989).

Mandelbaum, Michael. The Case for Goliath: How America Acts as the World's Government in the Twenty-First Century (New York: Public Affairs, 2006).

McCormick, Thomas J. America's Half-Century: United States Foreign Policy in the Cold War (Baltimore: The Johns Hopkins University Press, 1989).

McCoy, Alfred W. In the Shadows of the American Century: The Rise and Decline of U.S. Global Power (Chicago: Haymarket Books, 2017).

McDougall, Walter A. Promised Land, Crusader State: The American Encounter with the World Since 1776 (Boston: Houghton Mifflin, 1997).

McDougall, Walter A. The Tragedy of U.S. Foreign Policy: How America's Civil Religion Betrayed the National Interest (New Haven: Yale University Press, 2016).

Mead, Walter Russell. Special Providence: American Foreign Policy and How It Changed the World (New York: Alfred A. Knopf, 2002).

Mearsheimer, John J. The Great Delusion: Liberal Dreams and International Realities (New Haven: Yale University Press, 2018).

Mearsheimer, John J. The Tragedy of Great Power Politics, updated edition (New York: W.W. Norton, 2014).

Schurmann, Franz. The Logic of World Power (New York: Pantheon Books, 1974).

Shefter, Martin, editor. Capital of the American Century: The National and International Influence of New York City (New York: Russell Sage Foundation, 1993).

Tooze, Adam. Crashed: How a Decade of Financial Crises Changed the World (New York: Viking, 2018).

Walt, Stephen M. The Hell of Good Intentions: America's Foreign Policy Elite and the Decline of U.S. Primacy (New York: Farrar, Straus and Giroux, 2018).

Weigley, Russell F. The American Way of War: A History of United States Military Strategy and Policy (Bloomington, IN: Indiana University Press, 1973).

Williams, William Appleman. The Tragedy of American Diplomacy, new edition (New York: W.W. Norton, 1972).

INDEX

ABOUT THE AUTHOR

James Kurth has taught at Swarthmore, Harvard, UC San Diego, and the US Naval War College. He received his doctorate under Harvard's Samuel P. Huntington after graduation from Stanford, was a member of Princeton's Institute for Advanced Study, editor of *Orbis,* and advised the Chief of Naval Operations. A world traveler who has visited more than 50 countries, he is a member of the Council on Foreign Relations, Senior Fellow at the Foreign Policy Research Institute, and serves as an elder at Proclamation Presbyterian Church in Bryn Mawr, Pennsylvania.

CPSIA information can be obtained
at www.ICGtesting.com
Printed in the USA
FSHW012248050721
82942FS